Library of
Davidson College

FOURTEEN
YEARS
IN THE
SANDWICH
ISLANDS

Charles de Varigny
(Geneva, about 1869)

FOURTEEN YEARS IN THE SANDWICH ISLANDS 1855–1868

CHARLES DE VARIGNY

TRANSLATED AND WITH AN INTRODUCTION
BY ALFONS L. KORN

THE UNIVERSITY PRESS OF HAWAII
AND
THE HAWAIIAN HISTORICAL SOCIETY
HONOLULU

COPYRIGHT © 1981 BY THE UNIVERSITY PRESS OF HAWAII
ALL RIGHTS RESERVED
MANUFACTURED IN THE UNITED STATES OF AMERICA

THE ILLUSTRATIONS REPRODUCED
IN THE PHOTO SECTION OF THIS BOOK ARE TAKEN
FROM CHARLES DE VARIGNY'S *Voyage aux Iles Sandwich*
PUBLISHED IN 1873 BY HACHETTE AND COMPANY
IN THEIR TRAVEL MAGAZINE *Le Tour du Monde*.
THE CAPTIONS AND CREDIT LINES ARE DIRECT TRANSLATIONS
FROM THE FRENCH, WITH A FEW MINOR ALTERATIONS.

THE PHOTOGRAPHS OF VARIGNY AND OF HIS CHILDREN ARE FROM
THE HAWAI STATE ARCHIVES; THAT OF MME DE VARIGNY IN 1869,
FROM THE BISHOP MUSEUM COLLECTION. THE PHOTO OF MME DE
VARIGNY IN THE 1880S WAS PROVIDED BY NICOLE STEDMAN,
A GREAT GRANDDAUGHTER OF THE VARIGNYS.

Library of Congress Cataloging in Publication Data

Varigny, Charles Victor Crosnier De, 1829–1899.
Fourteen years in the Sandwich Islands.

Translation of Quatorze ans aux îles Sandwich.
Includes index.
1. Hawaii—Politics and government—To 1893.
2. Hawaii—Description and travel—To 1950.
3. Varigny, Charles Victor Crosnier de, 1829–1899.
4. Statesmen—Hawaii—Biography.   I. Title.
DU627.V3713   996.9'02   80-26141
ISBN 0-8248-0709-X

CONTENTS

Acknowledgments — vii

Translator's Introduction — ix

FOURTEEN YEARS IN THE SANDWICH ISLANDS

Preface: Paris, January 20, 1874 — xxvii

PART ONE: SECRETARY, THE FRENCH CONSULATE, HONOLULU, 1855–1863

1. My Arrival in the Islands, 1855 — 3
2. Kamehameha the Founder — 19
3. Missionaries and Other Agents of Change — 30
4. Birth of Constitutional Government — 44
5. The "New Era" of Kamehameha IV — 57
6. Excursion to the Island of Hawaii — 70
7. Perils of an Island Economy — 97
8. Idyll on Kauai — 107

PART TWO: CABINET MINISTER, THE HAWAIIAN KINGDOM, 1863–1870

9. Appointment as Minister of Finance — 127
10. The Governmental System of Kamehameha V — 142

11. *A Plan for Constitutional Reform* — 155
12. *The Royal Coup d'État* — 168
13. *Figures and Forecasts* — 183
14. *Appointment as Minister of Foreign Affairs* — 194
15. *Ministerial Forebodings* — 202
16. *Kilauea Erupts, 1868* — 209
17. *Scenes of Disaster* — 224
18. *More Scenes of Disaster* — 232
19. *My Leave of Absence, 1868–1870* — 242

Epilogue: Paris, January 20, 1874 — 248

APPENDIXES

A. *A Chronological Résumé* — 255
B. *Excerpts from the "Memoires" of Louise de Varigny* — 263

Index — 279

ACKNOWLEDGMENTS

My interest in Charles de Varigny dates back to a time, now more than fourteen years ago, when I was trying to assemble information about certain European and British associates of the last three monarchs of the Kamehameha dynastic line. As a possible starting point, I began to translate certain chapters and scattered passages in Varigny's *Quatorze Ans aux Iles Sandwich*. During ensuing years what had originated as an exploratory exercise was transformed into a perennial work in progress. In any event, over these years I have become deeply indebted to a number of persons.

A chance encounter at the State Archives in Honolulu in June of 1967 with a visitor from Palo Alto, Nicole Stedman, who like myself was looking into Varigny records, has proved inestimably useful in advancing an uncertain project. A fourth generation descendant of Charles and Louise de Varigny, Mrs. Stedman not only revealed to me the existence of the latter's private memoirs dealing with the fourteen years in the Hawaiian Kingdom, but also permitted me to examine earlier and later portions of the memoir. My indebtedness to Mrs. Stedman is by no means limited to such initial assistance. Her trust and good will have continued to be shown in more ways than I can enumerate.

Through Nicole, I have met other relatives, including her uncle M. Bernard Kiener, a direct descendant, and his wife, Françoise, who, in 1967 and again ten years later, visited the city where his grandfather Henry de Varigny was born. Then in 1977 I had the further pleasure of conversing with Mme Georges René Laederich, sister of Bernard Kiener, who as the eldest child of Laurence de Varigny and Jacques Kiener could well recall her grandfather. Because of the friendly and gracious interest of all these descendants and others unnamed, I have been able to flesh out the chronological résumé

(Appendix A) and to publish in translation excerpts (Appendix B) from a unique record of mid-nineteenth century Hawaii as seen through observant French eyes.

Among persons in Hawaii to be thanked here, the first is Agnes Conrad, state archivist, who in 1967 introduced me to Nicole Stedman and who has been of assistance in a variety of ways. I am indebted to Pauline King Joerger for useful biographical information concerning Varigny's relations with several of his unadmiring American contemporaries. To Mlle Renée Heyum, curator of the Pacific Collection at Hamilton Library, University of Hawaii at Manoa, I owe thanks for much bibliographical guidance and also for permitting me to consult her leather-bound copy of Charles de Varigny's *Voyage aux Iles Sandwich,* published in Hachette's famous travel magazine, *Le Tour du Monde,* in 1873. Thanks go also to George Kerr for bibliographical searches on my behalf in California and for much rewarding shop talk. My wife, Laura, solved several biographical puzzles in dating and also in the identification of individuals. She has been of the greatest assistance in the compilation of the various excerpts included in Appendix B.

I wish also to acknowledge the help of Janyce Blair, who originally launched my manuscript on its journey into print. Finally I am grateful to both Don Yoder for his acute and sensitive suggestions for improving the readability of the translation, and to Elizabeth Bushnell, who saw to it that the manuscript became a book.

As the printing and publication of this book has been made possible solely through the generous cooperation of the Hawaiian Historical Society, I here wish to express my deep appreciation to its officers and membership.

TRANSLATOR'S INTRODUCTION

Quatorze Ans aux Iles Sandwich was published by Hachette and Company, 79 Boulevard Saint-Germain, just a little over a century ago. To most people the name of the author, a certain C. de Varigny, was unknown. His best and indeed his only claim to biographical distinction and to the notice of France's expanding reading public was that he had lived for a number of years in the Hawaiian Kingdom and there, in Hawaii's capital city of Honolulu on the island of Oahu, had held high political office. In 1863 King Kamehameha V had appointed Varigny to be his minister of finance. Two years later the same king elevated him to the post of minister of foreign affairs, at that time a key executive office, whereby the young Frenchman automatically became head of the cabinet. Moreover, through an understanding with the Hawaiian government amounting to dual citizenship, very readily endorsed by the French foreign office in Paris, Varigny was able to accept both appointments without jeopardizing his or his family's rights and privileges as citizens of France.

During this same period, two honors in succession confirmed Varigny in his dual role as French patriot and servant of the Hawaiian crown. As early as 1864, after Kamehameha V had appointed him finance minister, he was named Chevalier of the Legion of Honor by Napoleon III. Three years later Kamehameha V commissioned him as Knight Commander of the Order of Kamehameha—an award named for the king's grandfather and founder of the dynasty. Thus by 1867 and at the notably early age of thirty-eight, Charles-Victor Crosnier de Varigny had reason to feel that he had achieved the summit of his political ambition in Hawaii.

Fourteen Years in the Sandwich Islands is, in essence, the story of that ambition. To understand his book more fully and follow it to the end the reader needs to know how and why he came to write it. One purpose of this introduction accordingly is to call attention to the special biographical interest of what were probably the most difficult years of Charles de Varigny's entire life. These were the six years between his return to France in 1868 on a long-promised leave of absence and the publication in 1874 of his Sandwich Islands memoir.

Urgent reasons had compelled him to request the leave. For one thing, as he explains in chapter nineteen, his health was deteriorating. He needed also to take care of certain unspecified "family matters." The king granted him his wish with the proviso that Varigny's ministerial leave should be combined with a special diplomatic mission, all other "important policy matters" having been settled.

> Only the revision of our commercial treaties required my attention. Kamehameha V told me of his wish to shift the scene of negotiations to Paris, and entrusted to me their direction. I should be leaving the kingdom in my capacity as minister of foreign affairs, charged with a special mission requiring me to consult with officials of several European governments. The length of my absence was limited to one year.

During this critical time between Varigny's arrival in France late in 1868 as Hawaii's minister plenipotentiary and the publication of his book by Hachette in 1874, Varigny underwent three disturbing experiences. In each of these his personal and family concerns became deeply involved with the turn of political events both in the Hawaiian Islands and in Europe. The first of these troubling experiences was the ignominious failure of the treaty negotiations he had undertaken to conduct with a number of European nations, including France, Great Britain, and the new North German Confederation. The second was the outbreak of the Franco-Prussian War of 1870–1871, ending in the defeat of Napoleon III's forces by Bismarck's armies, followed by the months of France's bloody civil war. The third reversal in Varigny's personal and official fortunes was the sudden death in November of 1872 of his patron, Kamehameha V, an event that ruled out any likelihood of Varigny's further employment in a diplomatic capacity by the Hawaiian government. The immediate and inward impact of this series of unfortunate circumstances upon Varigny's spirits cannot easily be documented in detail, but their shadow nevertheless can be said to hang over certain pages in Varigny's writing, especially in the somber and uncharacteristically self-deprecating sentences of his important preface.

> I do not know whether the history of a small kingdom of Oceania will attract the interest of a public so much concerned at this moment with so many and

such very difficult questions. I sometimes begin to doubt it. The more we feel depressed by the world around us, the more we resort to the charms of fiction; and fiction has been scrupulously banished from these pages. Writing them I have tried above all to tell the truth. I hope I have succeeded.

At the end of his year's leave of absence, Varigny in November 1869 submitted to Kamehameha V in Honolulu his resignation as foreign minister. However, the king deferred acting on the request until November 1870, after the defeat of Napoleon III's armies at Sedan and the fall of the Second Empire. Varigny's reasons for resigning were the same as those he had earlier cited in requesting the leave: "Family matters and concern for my health required a protracted European sojourn." In his memoir he refrains from stating that major trade treaties he had attempted to negotiate with France and Great Britain had brought no substantial advantages to any of the parties concerned. Neither does he fully disclose the fact that his fellow cabinet members in Honolulu were unanimously relieved to see him step aside: "My absence, as it became prolonged, imposed added burdens of work and responsibility upon my colleagues in Hawaii." The king informed him nevertheless that "he hoped I would decide to return to Hawaii, and assured me in most friendly terms of his desire that I might keep my ministerial portfolio."

It is Louise de Varigny in her own memoirs who explains that "family matters" as much as reasons of health (including young Henry's asthma) weighed heavily in the minds of herself and her husband in deciding to remain in France. Indeed, at the same time that Charles de Varigny was engaged in drafting his letter of resignation, the couple were seeking a permanent home base in the heart of Paris, after having lived a migratory existence for an entire year in France and Switzerland. Thus it was with a glad sense of relief that parents and children together, early in January of 1870, moved into a leased apartment on the Left Bank in Paris at 82 Boulevard Saint-Germain.

As it happened, the new address at number 82 proved to be but a few minutes distant from Hachette's recently expanded Paris headquarters, main editorial offices and handsome modern salesrooms, at number 79. But there is no solid evidence suggesting that as early as 1870 Varigny had definitely resolved to turn to full-time authorship and free-lance journalism as a means of support. Indeed, Mme de Varigny's journal explains that the overruling desire of the parents at this critical juncture in their situation was to make certain that each of the children would receive a suitable French education. Above all, the thought of the elders was to keep the family close together and intact, and for this purpose their location in the old university quarter promised to meet their combined as well as individual needs. Very probably the greatest single asset of their new address was that it was close to the *lycée* where Henry was enrolled, the Collège Saint Louis, and it was furthermore conveniently near the École de Médecine to which the boy had long aspired. Not the least advantage of the neighborhood, especially from Louise de Varigny's point of view, was that the cost of managing a household of five on the Left Bank would not exceed the family's precariously curtailed means.

For many months after July 19, 1870, during the course of the Franco-Prussian War and its aftermath in France's civil struggle, the apartment at 82 Boulevard Saint-Germain stood vacant. In early September, only a day or two after the fall of the Second Empire and the proclamation by the Provisional Government of the Third Republic, Charles de Varigny, as his wife records, hastened from Paris to Tours "to place himself at the disposal of the government." After the loss of Metz, he was among the entourage of Marshall Bazaine's retreat into Normandy. Shortly thereafter on his leave to Switzerland, where Louise de Varigny and the children had fled from Paris for safety, "Charles wrote his 'Notes on a Journey to Tours,' since then successfully published," but in which periodical or newspaper and on what date Mme de Varigny failed to record. Varigny's later wartime experiences as a participant-observer, while the French capital was at Bordeaux and Paris was held by the Commune, are never once alluded to in *Fourteen Years in the Sandwich Islands,* not even in its swiftly panoramic epilogue. Yet his intense awareness of contemporary France, quite as much as his memories of a bygone Hawaii, appears mysteriously to have turned him to the profession of writing as his true vocation and destiny.

While still in Hawaii, Varigny had contributed to the official government newspaper, the *Hawaiian Gazette,* several articles on his travels in the islands. The majority of these were unsigned, but others had been published under the assumed name of "Montaigne." Written in English, the articles and their essay style were markedly French, but nevertheless amateurish to a degree that evoked mocking comment in the columns of the opposition press. Now writing in France in his mother tongue, Varigny found the Parisian editorial response much more gratifying. Between 1871 and 1874 four manuscripts from the pen of Charles de Varigny were accepted and published under excellent imprints. These successful ventures, although entirely journalistic and ephemeral, were early signs of his more practiced craftsmanship, soon to be demonstrated in *Quatorze Ans aux Iles Sandwich.*

That twenty-chapter book (counting its epilogue) cannot be described accurately as a wholly independent or *sui generis* work, composed in conformity to a single predetermined plan. On the contrary, its genesis is best accounted for by the fact that scattered portions of its diverse contents owe their origin to casual writings published by Varigny on different earlier occasions of his career. His detailed report on the public school system in Hawaii, as he describes it in chapter thirteen, is unquestionably a revised version of his article on the same subject published in *Le Temps,* February 12, 1872, under the heading *"Variétés: L'Instruction Publique aux Iles Havai (Sandwich)."* A still more important example of Varigny's economical method of refurbishing and recycling previously published matter is the opening section of the first chapter of his book, "Voyage from San Francisco to Honolulu—First Impressions." Here the narrator's memories of his arrival in Hawaii in 1855 on the clipper-bark *Restless,* followed by his initial description of the picturesque people of the town, are straightforward adaptations of the opening portion of his earlier *Voyage aux Iles Sandwich (Iles Havai), 1855-1868,* published in Hachette's popular world-travel magazine, *Le Tour du Monde,* in 1873. Indeed, there is solid evidence that the antecedent success of Varigny's serial contributions to *Le Tour du Monde* persuaded Hachette to publish, only one year later and by way of sequel, *Quatorze Ans aux Iles Sandwich.* Thus what began in germinal form as a travelogue in *Le Tour du Monde* ended in becoming a far more diverse and mixed work of Parisian journalism, quite unlike any other nineteenth-century book about life in the Hawaiian Islands. A kind of generic oddity, *Fourteen Years in the Sandwich Islands* may be described as part travelogue, part Hawaiian history, part intellectual autobiography, forced by Varigny's overall and controlling first-person narrative point of view into the mold of a political memoir.

About every political memoir, a first question is: for whom is the author writing? Varigny in his preface supplies his own answer. The audience he had in mind in 1874 was his immediate French contemporaries, survivors of his country's defeat in the Franco-Prussian War, participants like himself in the civil war that followed, and now his fellow-witnesses of the difficult birth of the Third Republic. Varigny himself rightly felt no need in his preface to specify by name these all too vividly remembered events of France's recent years. But their effect upon the nation's morale is implied pervasively in the argument of his book as a whole concerning the possibility of human progress. Varigny thus in his preface confronts his French readership with a hard question. We have watched France fall, he is saying, but we want her to rise again: the overriding question is, in what guise?

Though the rhetorical style of the preface is adapted to the broadest type of political appeal, the book itself suggests that Varigny and his editors felt a need to interest a variety of readers with more specialized tastes. This meant, as a practical problem, writing in such a way as to satisfy the reader's wish for entertainment and "escape" as well as for knowledge—preferably new and useful knowledge. An underlying purpose of the book throughout thus became that of capturing, within the framework of an exotic narrative and setting, the reader's interest in geography and history, as illustrated in a Pacific archipelago and its people. Both the intellectual and imaginative appeal of the book rests in part on the way Varigny ingeniously utilized geography and chronology—"the eyes of history"—to tell his unusual story.

There is then the problem of Varigny's reliability. He himself poses that question when he claims in his preface that "it is enough to mention that the documents I have relied on are authentic," and that when such archival evidence (presumably either printed or written) was lacking, "I was able to draw upon personal testimony, Hawaiian family traditions, and particularly the old native chants." For Varigny's French contemporaries, including Hachette's editors, these reassurances apparently served to close the question of his veracity or at least to keep it professionally at bay. Varigny's readers today, however, need to be warned. In certain respects *Fourteen Years in the Sandwich Islands* is deficient, and in general the book needs to be handled with care.

In judging Varigny's trustworthiness as a historian it is necessary to differentiate one part of his writing from another. Varigny himself does exactly that when, at a kind of turning-point at the start of his fifth chapter, he draws a crucial distinction between the documentary basis of the first four retrospective chapters of his book and his autobiographical intention in those remaining, where he turns to the history of his own time.

> In preceding pages I was obliged sometimes to draw upon tradition and sometimes to examine incomplete archives. From this point forward I rely upon my own notes and memories. I have seen, I have known personally, the individuals and events I am about to describe.

Varigny's distinction here between his preliminary chapters of historical flashback and the later portion of his book deriving, partly at least, from his own first-hand experience should be kept in mind by readers today. In either instance, whether he is writing in retrospect or drawing upon his own more or less unmediated knowledge, the soundest test of his veracity remains the same. It requires a comparison of Varigny's version of a given set of events with corresponding historical data as provided in other extrinsic records. But obviously such a collation of Varigny's text with its sources or probable parallels is not easy to make, chiefly because he chose not to divulge the identity of whatever documents he used containing relevant data. Despite Varigny's lack of bibliographical guidance, it is nevertheless rewarding to compare his version of how history came to be made in Hawaii

—for example, his account of the origin and development of the Kamehameha dynasty—with alternative versions of the same events as set forth in other early histories of the Hawaiian Islands based on authentic data from primary sources. Such a broad comparison, if it is sufficiently analytical, can be illuminating even though it cannot identify minutely the possible documentary origins and accuracy of this or that portion of Varigny's narrative. Above all, it can contribute to a more clear understanding of the relationship of *Fourteen Years in the Sandwich Islands* to the earlier historiography of nineteenth-century Hawaii in general.

Two books of major importance in their field, constituting the earliest documentary histories of the kingdom up to the late 1840s, were available to Varigny from the time of his arrival in the islands in February of 1855. The first of these prior works was the Reverend Sheldon Dibble's *History of the Sandwich Islands,* published at Lahainaluna Seminary on the island of Maui in 1843. The second book, also first published in 1843, but very soon reissued and in 1847 extensively revised, won rapid and respectful notice by a special learned world. Published originally in both Boston and London, this was James Jackson Jarves' *The History of the Hawaiian or Sandwich Islands.* A valuable feature of Dibble's book is that it contains miscellaneous oral lore ("tradition") gathered from village elders by student converts while they were attending the mission school on Maui during the 1830s and 1840s. A distinction of Jarves' book is that he took care to acknowledge certain of his important printed sources, including writings of William Ellis, British missionary to the South Seas and traveler in Hawaii during the early 1820s. Jarves also drew information regarding the old way of Hawaiian life, but as filtered through the mind of a zealous convert, from David Malo's *Ka Moolelo Hawaii* (later known in translation as *Hawaiian Antiquities*).

It would require a monograph to do justice to the large question of Varigny's deployment of data he abstracted for his special purposes and French audience from a wide range of unacknowledged sources both in print and in manuscript. In addition to Dibble and Jarves, some of the books he undoubtedly "consulted" were by other later authors, including most notably Manley Hopkins' *Hawaii: The Past, Present, and Future of Its Island-Kingdom* (2nd ed.; London, 1866). Other portions of Varigny's text clearly derive from genuine archival records, such as copies of the minute books he had kept in his capacity as foreign minister and head of the cabinet.

Varigny was not, however, either a plagiarist or a historical pastiche maker. Instead, he abridged, simplified, assimilated, and as a journalistic practitioner of *haute vulgarisation* systematically popularized his specialized data in such a way as to hold the interest of his general audience and also serve his didactic purpose as announced in his preface. This does not mean that Varigny's debt to Dibble and Jarves, in the portion of his book concerning Hawaiian events down into the 1840s, was inconsequential. Indeed, a close reading of Varigny's account of the character and career of Kamehameha I indicates that it contains little substantial information which had not appeared earlier, but in more densely packed detail, in the documentary histories of Dibble and Jarves. Where Varigny's narrative departed radically from their precedent was in his latter-day revisionist perspective, permitting him to interpret and adapt, according to his French ideology and from his own individual point of view, the same events and circumstances already set forth in the writings of his two American predecessors.

The revisionist aspect of Varigny's book is readily apparent in his rhetorical vocabulary and more especially in his dependence on certain key concepts and terms. Indeed, the most striking disparities between the writings of Dibble, Jarves, and Varigny center around their differing conclusions about the nature of human progress. All refer to "progress" and "civilization" in describing major historical changes in the life of the islands, but each uses the terms in individual ways and in special contexts, implying important differences in their several conceptions of historical causality.

All three authors in the end have occasion to refer to the "providential" aspect of the most far-reaching and momentous changes that have characterized the history of Hawaii, especially during post-contact times. In Dibble's mission-inspired book, as should be expected, references to the direct intercession of divine providence in Hawaiian affairs are exceedingly numerous. Such allusions range from the providential geological origin of the archipelago to the advent of the first American missionaries in 1820. For Dibble, one of the most impressive instances of the immediate "interposition" of deity in the political life of mid-nineteenth-century Hawaii was the act of Rear Admiral Richard Thomas of the British Royal Navy when he restored Hawaiian sovereignty over the islands in 1842, after their "seizure" by his high-handed predecessor, Lord George Paulet, commander of the *Carysfort:*

> In the recent events the friends of the nation can find much ground for hope, and the friends of Christianity at these islands are admonished nevermore to distrust that Providence which, in addition to former instances of His care, has added this signal and manifest interposition.

Unlike Dibble's evangelically generated volume, Jarves' book is basically a work of straightforward documentary history. Nevertheless his closing word on the meaning of Hawaiian history is cast in a variant form of the familiar providential mold. This becomes most evident in Jarves' final chapter, where he reflects on the role of divine providence in determining the history of mankind. Thus he cites as a prevalent theory ("the views of many'') the notion that there are "races like individuals which have their time and purpose," and that when these conditioning factors have been fulfilled, such races then decline and perish. But while history shows this to have been true in the past, later history also demonstrates that certain peoples and nations which have accepted "revelation as their guide" have continued to flourish and prosper. Preeminent instances of such providential favor, according to Jarves, are England, France, and the United States. The bearing of the lesson on the demographic plight of the nineteenth-century Hawaiians is inescapable.

> So long as they maintain those principles derived from Christian revelation, and the nearer they approach to the intent of their author, so long are they sure of life and success. Thus will it be with the Hawaiians, if their physical and mental stock has enough vigor to bud anew and bear fruit.

Whether or not Jarves himself accepted so grim a reading of the workings of providence is questionable. In fact, elsewhere in his book he took disarming pains to declare that he regarded it as part of his duty as historian to present the beliefs of persons with whom he did not necessarily agree. But Charles de Varigny, writing a full quarter of a century later than Jarves, is never more forthright, optimistic, and invariably partisan than when asserting his own unswerving faith in the inevitability of human progress everywhere. That message finds its earliest formulation in Varigny's preface, signed and dated —Paris, January 20, 1874—when he was preparing the final draft of his manuscript for the press. There he refers to a "providential law," deistically ordained but operating thereafter in the manner of a benevolent law of nature.

> No, progress is not an empty word. It is the law of humanity, a providential law, laid down by God himself, which a whole people as well as individuals obey, sometimes without being aware of doing so. It has been my fortune, in a remote corner of the earth, in Oceania, to record the existence and power of that law, to follow its rapid pace, and to cooperate with it, even though in only a small degree. I can testify to its presence, and to the deep faith I derive from it in the future of the human race.

Readers of *Fourteen Years in the Sandwich Islands,* especially those interested in the fierce "extinctionist" controversy in nineteenth-century Hawaii, will discover in Varigny's book a succession of similar passages in which he reiterates his own trustful, rational, positivistic religion of progress, using much the same forensic vocabulary as he had employed in his preface.

All around me were people predicting the inevitable decline of the native race in the immediate future and the absorption of the country in the United States. I rebelled against the political and religious fatalism that condemned the people to death and oblivion, in order to add one more star to the union flag.

Neither in his brief preface nor elsewhere does Varigny define precisely what aspects of human progress he considered to be most vital to the immediate well-being of the French people in the 1870s. Instead, he trusted to the wits of his readers to supply their own prescriptive definitions, simply by pondering the broad message of his book. Charles de Varigny assumed that by drawing intelligent comparisons, but also by allowing for obvious differences, his contemporary audience would gain a profounder understanding of the meaning of civilization everywhere in the world. Such a knowledge would be achieved, according to the argument of his preface's promise, by examining stage by stage the historical development of a Polynesian people as they had sought to build a more enlightened, orderly, and just society in the Hawaiian Islands over the past one hundred or so years.

The fundamental notion underlying Varigny's approach to Hawaiian history is that civilization involves change. It is by means of movement through time that people potentially achieve improvement in their lives, provided that the conditions and processes involved in progressive change are methodically studied and, whenever possible, reviewed, criticized, readjusted, and controlled. As Varigny outlines for his French readership major phases of advancing civilization in the islands since the visits of Captain Cook in the late 1770s, the first great example he cites of such a leap into the future is, of course, the establishment by Kamehameha I of a unified Hawaiian kingdom, where heretofore on their scattered islands had existed only a hodgepodge *("un ramassis")* of warring tribes. Likewise, under the energizing military, political, and administrative leadership of the founder of the dynasty, came the inauguration during the 1790s of systematic diplomatic relations with a friendly foreign power, Great Britain, through its farseeing emissary, Captain George Vancouver. Then in 1819, shortly after the death of Kamehameha I, a radical politico-religious reform was swiftly carried out when a small circle of forceful high-born Hawaiians voluntarily abolished, though at the cost of incipient civil war, certain of their ancient and most burdensome and unjust taboos. Scarcely a year after this spontaneous court-centered coup d'état came the introduction in the islands of the "New Learning" of Christianity, as taught by successive bands of American Protestant missionaries.

A truly massive and epoch-making surge forward took place during the

1840s and 1850s. This occurred during the long rule of Kamehameha III, second son of the conqueror, when the king and his council of high chiefs, assisted by their new missionary mentors, now transformed what had previously been a dynastic chiefdom into a rudimentary quasi-Western monarchy, operating under a bill of rights and a constitution, and governing according to parliamentary principles. Finally, in Charles de Varigny's own time, during the reigns of Kamehameha IV and Kamehameha V, young grandsons of the founder, these two royal brothers together with their cabinet ministers, succeeded in setting in motion a coherent set of political, social, and economic programs. The object of these was to strengthen Hawaii's internal and external security and to generate among the Hawaiian people a fuller sense of their emergent national identity.

Meanwhile, as a permanent legacy of the advent of the missionaries back in the 1820s and 1830s, a system of free public schools was being steadily developed throughout all main islands of the Hawaiian chain. Its purpose was to ensure the existence of a competent and responsible Hawaiian citizenry. The curricular heart of the system, at both its elementary and more selective level, was its insistence on numeracy and literacy, either in Hawaiian or English but preferably (at least for the most capable) in both languages. Such a system of public instruction would be imperative, if the kingdom were to keep in step with the pace of progress in other advancing regions of the civilized globe. Thus the schools of Hawaii would serve the Hawaiian people as well-springs of modern knowledge and power. They would constitute a self-perpetuating factor in the institutional development of the islands, determining the life and vigor of the society as a dynamic whole.

A very marked stylistic feature of Varigny's account of the political development of Hawaii during the first three-quarters of the nineteenth century is that he rarely uses the kind of specialized terminology with which such a subject would be treated normally today. No doubt one of the merits of his writing, contributing greatly to its readability though by no means always to its logic, is its freedom from professional or technological argot. Let it be noted, however, that he does possess a pronounced liking for the word "plan," identical in both French and English in the sense of project or program, and as an ordered sequence of operations to achieve an end.

That he does not use a sophisticated vocabulary does not mean that Varigny was oblivious to the root references of various modern technical terms and concepts. Here a distinction can be drawn between a historian's fidelity to sources when principally concerned with reconstructing events of the past and his more speculative, even imaginative, capacity for perceiving issues and problems that emerge out of the past, reach into the indefinite present, and sometimes point forward to an ambiguous and uncertain future. A respectable case can be made for the originality and interest of Varigny's very much present- and future-minded book on the second grounds. It is as if he intuitively recognized certain political, social, and economic currents of change in his time as on-going historical phenomena, even while he lacked a satisfactory language or vocabulary for naming and describing such phenomena in fairly fixed clear terms. Thus he refers variously to the "American party," the "missionary party," the "annexationist party," as if the terms were synonymous. But at no point in his narrative does he pause to explain in what sense as interest groups their members conducted themselves in the manner or style of an organized political party.

Thus it is obvious to a reader today, if one pays close attention to their implication and context, that when Varigny employs such tired counter words as "progress" and "civilization," the actual events and operative processes he had in mind in the 1870s are conceptually akin to processes of modernization in the sense in which that term has become standard in the late twentieth century. In fact, if one were seeking an appropriate epigraph for Varigny's book, Robert L. Heilbroner's *The Great Ascent: The Struggle for Economic Development in Our Time* (New York: Harper & Row, 1963), provides in its first axiom such a quotation, where Heilbroner describes processes of modernization as these have functioned in various "developing societies" of both the nineteenth and twentieth centuries.

> Economic development is not primarily an economic but a political and social process. . . . In its initial stages it is the process by which such societies are created. Much of its early development is, accordingly, pre-economic. It is concerned with the shaping of attitudes and the creation, forcibly or otherwise, of workable institutional structures. All this requires far-reaching social change, and this social change, in turn, requires for its inception the mobilization of powerful political energies. [Page 16]

An important integral motif of *Fourteen Years in the Sandwich Islands,* introduced by Varigny here and there with a note of self-conscious dedication and rededication, is this same theme of heroic human energies and their powerful political mobilization under the modernizing rule of the five Kamehameha kings.

Was there actually in France, during the years immediately following the Franco-Prussian War, an audience ready to respond to Varigny's humanitarian faith in universal progress as voiced in his preface? The answer is yes. It is borne out by the fact that Hachette and Company in 1874 not only published *Fourteen Years in the Sandwich Islands* in the first place but that in the following year the book was republished in Milan in an Italian translation, accompanied by the same illustrations originally used in Varigny's successful travelogue issues in *Le Tour du Monde* in 1873. During the later nineteenth century, leading French encyclopedias at the end of their articles on the Hawaiian Islands listed Varigny's memoir among their brief bibliographical acknowledgments, rightly recognizing his work to be the earliest comprehensive account in French of life in the Hawaiian Kingdom written for general readers.

Exactly how long Hachette's Paris edition remained in print is uncertain. However, it was long enough to launch Charles de Varigny safely on his subsequent career as a prolific author of books and articles relating by no means solely to Oceania. During the 1890s, his series of articles in *Le Temps* entitled *"La Vie d'Outremer"* make it clear that his journalistic interests had come by that time to range the globe. Thus one of his chief purposes in his sixties was to direct the armchair traveler's attention overseas to wherever old world and new world governments and their variant nationalisms, competing sometimes for economic power but often largely for prestige and opportune diplomatic advantage, supplied his featured articles in *Le Temps* with endless newsworthy copy.

What about the reception of *Fourteen Years in the Sandwich Islands* by its earliest readers in Hawaii? The answer is disappointing, particularly for the 1870s. Owing to the absence of any record of who Varigny's readers in the kingdom may have been, it is as if neither the author nor his book had existed. Fortunately, the reasons can be documented why his memoir to all appearances aroused no interest in the islands until the mid-1880s. Over a period of four months, from July 1 to November 1, 1884, the *Pacific Commercial Advertiser* published an extended commentary on Varigny's work, including copious excerpts in good translation. Headed "Varigny's *Fourteen Years in the Sandwich Islands*," the opening article by an anonymous writer* pointed out two explanations why the book during the ten years following its publication had aroused so little attention in the country it was designed to celebrate. Not only was it written in French, but it was also intended primarily for a French audience. Furthermore, because of his outspoken views, especially in defense of the independence of the islands from foreign intervention, Charles de Varigny had offended powerful members of the American community.

> The contents of the book before us are full of interest for residents in these islands, and especially so for the large number who themselves remember the

---
*See last footnote in epilogue, on Godfrey Rhodes.

times of which they give a history. Nevertheless, it seems to be little known here, even by repute. This is probably because it has never been translated. . . . The little attention paid to it may in part also be because it would naturally be assumed by many that certain portions of it, which deal with the social and political condition of this country at the epoch when M. de Varigny took part in its affairs, were not likely to be palatable reading. The author had his own ideas about various matters and especially about "American influence" in these islands which he evidently thought it was his mission to counteract to the best of his ability. . . . As a matter of fact, however, there is in this volume a manifest attempt at impartiality—an endeavor to suit party and personal feeling and [yet] give every section of the community its due. . . . All the same it is creditable to M. de Varigny that he made an effort (which must be palpable to every unprejudiced reader) to deal fairly with friends and antagonists alike.

Who were these "many" individuals who, as the writer cautiously implies, had found the book so distasteful that their influence in the 1870s could succeed in consigning Varigny's book to near oblivion? In later issues of the anonymous reviewer's commentary he makes it clear enough that these persons could only have been prominent members of the so-called "missionary party," as repeatedly referred to by Varigny in his memoir. It was these folk who in Varigny's time had resisted certain policies inaugurated during the reign of Kamehameha V, policies systematically intended to strengthen the power of the crown. It was they likewise who had opposed the king and his ministers in 1864 when Kamehameha V by royal fiat handed down a new, more conservative constitution to replace the earlier "liberal" and missionary-inspired constitution of 1852.

The reviewer seems to be hinting that Varigny's old political opposition, possibly through its influence on the press as in the community at large, had somehow encouraged giving Varigny's book the silent treatment. Such a possibility is at best doubtful and in any event is difficult to prove today. What remains certain is that old charges brought against Varigny in the Hawaiian press during the 1860s, especially in the *Pacific Commercial Advertiser* (then under missionary-allied ownership and management), had cast grave aspersions on Varigny's character.

Among the severest allegations brought against Varigny by his opponents was that he remained a "foreigner," a Frenchman who during all his first eight years in Hawaii had failed to become sufficiently "identified with the country." Not many months after his appointment in 1863 as finance minister (when he was thirty-four), this accusation became the central thrust of an attack in the *Pacific Commercial Advertiser,* December 24, 1863: "Of Mon. de Varigny's personal characteristics no one can complain. He may be the shrewdest of financiers; he may be the most ingenious in devising ways of raising money . . . but he has not the least affinity to the people, and moreover has little, and as far as we know, no affinity with the great body of foreign residents doing business here." Indeed, because of the fact that the new cabinet of Kamehameha V had failed to be "representative" (i.e., to include certain Americans identified with the earlier period of mission-allied predominance), therefore that ministerial body "must go down to posterity as the first 'Copperhead Ministry' of Hawaii Nei."

The journalistic vehemence of 1863 was temperate, however, compared with what followed two years later, after Varigny's elevation to the post of foreign minister. Now the case for indictment included disloyalty to crown and nation.

> He is not Hawaiian in feeling, but in sentiment and sympathies is as completely a Frenchman as the day he left France. Besides this he is under the sacred oath or obligation of the famous French Legion of Honor, which enacts true allegiance to the French emperor before all other sovereigns. . . . If M. de Varigny desires to serve our King and people let him give up his allegiance to Napoleon, and resign all claim and title to the Legion of Honor, for the highest authority says, "Ye cannot serve two masters."

It must have been partly in response to such aspersions impugning the character of his chief minister that Kamehameha V countered the Napoleonic award by commissioning Varigny in 1867 as Knight Commander of the Order of Kamehameha. It is reasonable also to believe that the sharp memory of these journalistic attacks was one of the deeper psychological causes that prompted Charles de Varigny in the Paris of the early 1870s to defend his official probity and vindicate his French sense of personal honor by writing *Fourteen Years in the Sandwich Islands.*

FOURTEEN YEARS
IN THE SANDWICH ISLANDS

Pauline, Hélène,
and Henry de Varigny
(San Francisco, 1864)

Louise de Varigny
(Geneva, about 1869)

PREFACE

I do not know whether the history of a small kingdom of Oceania will attract the interest of a public so much concerned at this moment with so many and such very difficult questions. I sometimes begin to doubt it. The more we feel depressed by the world around us, the more we resort to the charms of fiction; and fiction has been scrupulously banished from these pages. Writing them I have tried above all to tell the truth. I hope I have succeeded.

Fourteen years of my life I spent in the Sandwich Islands. Thus the events I describe in the second part of this book I saw unfold before my own eyes, and in writing it I had only to consult my personal notes and memories.

In 1863 I was asked to accept a governmental appointment as minister of finance in the Sandwich Islands; then in 1865 I was summoned to serve as minister of foreign affairs and secretary of the army and navy. I had official archives at my disposal and with the help of these I have been able to trace the course of historical events down the years and reconstruct the Hawaiian past.

It is enough to mention that the documents I have relied upon are entirely authentic. When these were lacking, I was able to draw upon personal testimony, Hawaiian family traditions, and particularly the old native chants: a body of knowledge both inexhaustible and varied, though unfortunately now on the verge of extinction.

In less than a century the Hawaiian Islands have passed from extreme barbarism, from the most appalling pagan conditions, to a state of civilization remarkable indeed. All the problems that preoccupy Europe have been encountered in this small society and have there found a solution: sometimes good, sometimes modest, but on the whole satisfactory. Within this short span of time one can follow step by step the march of a civilization being born, observe the obstacles that confront it, and share sympathetically in the material and moral progress of a small nation among whose indigenous inhabitants today one will search in vain for a man or woman twenty years old who does not know how to read, write, and count.

No, progress is not an empty word. It is the law of humanity, a providential law, laid down by God himself, which a whole people as well as individuals obey, sometimes without being aware of doing so. It has been my fortune, in a remote corner of the earth, in Oceania, and in a country whose very name is scarcely recognized, to record the existence and power of that law, to follow its rapid pace, and to cooperate with it, even though in only a small degree. I can testify to its presence, and to the deep faith I derive from it in the future of the human race.

My purpose has been more than fulfilled if I can bring some of my readers to share with me this conviction.

Paris, January 20, 1874　　　　　　　　　　　　　　　　　　　　C. DE VARIGNY

PART ONE

SECRETARY, THE FRENCH CONSULATE, HONOLULU, 1855–1863

CHAPTER 1

MY ARRIVAL
IN THE ISLANDS, 1855

Voyage from San Francisco to Honolulu.—First impressions.—Discovery of the islands by Juan Gaetano in 1555.—Social, political, and religious conditions in the archipelago.—Cook's voyage.—A Hawaiian legend.

In January of 1855 the voyage from San Francisco to the Sandwich Islands was still by small sailing vessel, no more than 150 to 300 tons; departures were every two weeks. It would be hard to imagine anything more uncomfortable for a voyage of 700 leagues,* requiring at that time eighteen to thirty days at sea. Meals were atrocious, cabins were small and cramped, overrun by cockroaches; the ships, high-masted and without much outbound cargo, rolled and pitched dreadfully. I had booked passage on the American schooner *Restless*.

All crossings are pretty much the same. I refer especially to voyages out, up to the moment of arrival. Because an ocean passenger is always at the center of a circle at whose perimeter sky and sea blend, there is nothing to divert the traveler's attention—nothing but reading, conversation with one's companions, or a passing encounter (very rare then in those waters) with another vessel in full white sail swelling in the breeze. After the usual sequence of good and bad weather, calm and strong winds, and a total of twenty-eight days of most dreary navigation, we sighted on the horizon the high mountains of Oahu. Beyond them, at the foot of their sheltering screen, lay Honolulu, the capital of the Hawaiian Kingdom.†

---

*The league, a French measure of distance, was estimated in English-speaking countries at three miles. [A. L. K.] NOTE: The footnotes throughout the translation are identified by initials as either the author's (C. de V.) or the translator's (A. L. K.).

†The "Hawaiian Archipelago" and the "Sandwich Archipelago" are synonymous geographical terms, though the chain is most familiar to foreigners under the name of "Sandwich," bestowed upon them by Captain Cook in honor of the Englishman Lord Sandwich, First Lord of the Admiralty, in 1778. The proper designation is the Hawaiian Islands, named after the largest. The natives and the local government did not refer to them in other terms. [C. de V.]

Nothing is so welcome to eyes wearied by the sea's immensity and sunlight reflected on restless waves as that fixed and motionless point of land which an alert eye distinguishes from the clouds resembling it at the exact moment when the point breaks free. Ashore, for both the sailor and the land traveler, pleasures beckon on all sides. It is aboard ship that we curse the calm, the inactivity, the absence of all movement and change, twenty times a day. But it is precisely this same awareness of monotony—desperate monotony—that stimulates curiosity and arouses an expectation of surprise. This is a feeling that journeys by land but faintly approximate. The traveler from France to Italy leaves France little by little and little by little he finds himself in Italy. The shift is gradual, for even in our era of rapid locomotion neither departure nor arrival produces a strong sense of contrast—at Lyon we are still in Paris, at Marseille we sense the nearness of Italy. By ship, on the other hand, the transition from one country to another is abrupt. Between the day after departure and the day before arrival, nothing much has changed except perhaps the wind. Up to the instant we confront the new shore where we are about to disembark, mentally we remain but a few miles from the one left behind.

This is the difference, I think, that explains the sharpness of impression produced by certain places the traveler reaches by ship. Of all the localities I have visited in my many travels, I particularly recall those I first saw from the sea: my memory retraces their vivid outlines precisely; every detail is indelible and complete. I cannot say as much for the regions I approached by land, for my more confused recollections of these reflect a sense of contrast much less incisive, a transition far more piecemeal.

On Sunday, February 18, 1855, the *Restless* passed Diamond Head, a volcanic mountain prominently situated like a welcoming watchtower at the extreme eastern part of the island of Oahu. By daybreak we arrived at the entrance of the port of Honolulu. On the right stretched a sandy beach, lined with a thick grove of soaring coconut trees; on the left, in distant outline through the light haze, rose the summits of the Waianae Range; in front, a narrow channel between two sandbanks afforded passage to ships entering the harbor. Quite close appeared some worse than primitive quays; and beside them, extending their full length, were numerous whaling vessels flying flags of all nations, but the large majority under the ensign of the United States. Beyond these quays were some shops, shipyards, and low-roofed dwellings; and in the distance lofty rounded hillsides banked almost to their tops with luxuriant green vegetation. Above the center of the town rose several church steeples silhouetted against their mountainous background. A narrow, sandy peninsula, covered at high tide by the sea, projected for several cable lengths on the right. A small rowboat shoved off from our schooner and carried a piece of cable to this bit of strand, where it was harnessed to the yokes of some twenty oxen, who slowly and laboriously towed us into the harbor basin proper.

It was almost noon before we were able to drop anchor. Finally a number of canoes, loaded with tropical fruits, surrounded the *Restless*. Balanced by outrigger beams hewn from coconut palms, these were manned by natives whose paddles made their frail craft fly over the water. Several whaleboats followed behind them and brought us ashore. There could be nothing more primitive than the manner of disembarking practiced at that time. The handsome wharves that are now the pride of Honolulu, rivaling indeed those of San Francisco, did not exist as yet. The newcomer landed on the beach where the whaleboats were run aground, and seldom did he depart with dry feet.

At the waterfront, some of the copper-colored natives would usually stage an argument, in their barbarously incomprehensible English, over the privilege of carrying the traveler's trunk and escorting him to the town's hotels. How far away one felt in those days, not only from Europe but even from America! The contrast existed everywhere: in the inhabitants, in the climate, in nature itself. What struck one first of all was not simply the barbarism of it all. Far more it was the suggestion of a new civilization springing into life but still in a first rough stage. The half-European dress, a language displaying the same aspiration, under a tropical sky, all within a natural setting that owed less to grandeur than to mere charm, caused not only astonishment in the viewer but also a mixture of disappointment. There was just enough "local color" to whet curiosity, but not enough to satisfy it.

Several days of rest at the hotel, a rapid summarizing look at the town, brought succeeding impressions little different from those I have just sketched. Honolulu had to a notable degree the look of an overgrown village of the American Far West, a frontier settlement that had somehow strayed off to the tropics. The white cottages with green blinds, jostling the old native-style houses built on a bamboo framework with roofs of plaited pandanus leaves, had a certain air of pretentiousness amid their gardens of recent vintage and their newly planted trees. On the verandas of the cottages a few Europeans or Americans lounged about in Chinese rattan armchairs, nonchalantly puffing on their cheroots. At the doors of the grass huts, squatting in picturesque groups, natives passed to each other the classic pipe. In the streets some of the kanaka women, proudly straddling their horses, riding with their legs enswathed in long folds of gaudy material, swept past at a gallop as they greeted their friends and acquaintances with shouts of laughter before vanishing into the dust clouds kicked up by their steeds. A scene as strange as it was diverting: the atmosphere of openhearted friendliness breathed by the native riders, the erect and elegant carriage of the head, the childlike grace and animation—all cast a spell upon the watcher's gaze. One had a sense of being enveloped by crowds of carefree tropical girls, happy to exist, eager to enjoy to the full life's noisy babble and excitement.

Such, in fact, is the natural character of the people of the Hawaiian Kingdom, and later experience confirmed me in my early general impressions, although bringing out in sharper relief the faults of the Hawaiians along with their virtues.

Royal capital of the kingdom and seat of the government, Honolulu was at that time a small city of 10,000 inhabitants. A seacoast community, established in an arid plain, where the vegetation was limited to coconut palms and a few gardens whose recently planted saplings struggled with a dry climate and a shortage of irrigation, Honolulu owed its importance only to its harbor, the best in the island chain. Situated 700 marine leagues from San Francisco, the nearest port of call, and an almost equal distance from America and Japan, the town had been and still was at this period the rallying station for the entire whale fishing fleet, which from November to February came there each year for revictualing, repairing gear, and unloading the produce of the fisheries from one vessel to another. Two or three hundred whaling vessels, a great majority American, put into harbor there each winter. To these Honolulu owed its material prosperity. It was the whalers who brought fortunes to the merchants and grog shops and who, during each season, on departing, left behind them thousands of silver coins for the foreign population as a whole to live on during the remainder of the year.

Except for the whaling fleet, commerce during the 1850s had fallen off badly. The time had passed when the Californians, intoxicated by their Gold Rush and scornful of farming (which one day would make them rich), were forced to rely on Chile, Peru, the Atlantic states, and the Hawaiian Islands for flour and grain, potatoes, yams, and fruits—in short, the necessities for a market expanding in variety and scale each day. However, the sudden demand caused by the discovery of gold in 1848, and by the vast number of immigrants arriving in 1849–1852, was followed by a period of almost total economic stagnation. Numerous ships drawn from all parts of the world, over a period of several years and without slackening, had dumped on the market of San Francisco all nature's bounty. A serious depression finally befell this overstimulated import market; speculators desponded, while in the Sacramento and San Joaquin valleys farmers replaced the gold rushers, who then headed for the Sierra Nevada; and, by a strange reversal of events prophetic of California's future as a great agricultural state, flour and grain began to be exported from San Francisco to Chile itself, which five years earlier had been the storehouse from which these same products had been pouring in.

The encouragement given to Hawaiian agriculture by the California gold had consequently almost ceased. Except for certain products needed for the local and native markets, not much was demanded of the island soil. In the plains huge herds of prosperous cattle grazed freely on the always plentiful grass; in the shady valleys taro fields abounded *(Arum esculentum)*, the dietary staple of the Kanakas; in the uplands several cereal grains; then here and there a few small plantations of sugarcane or of coffee and arrowroot. These constituted the total yield of a rich and fertile land, destined (if only circumstances had been otherwise) for a considerable amount of agricultural production.

At that time Honolulu assumed above all the appearance of a port of transit. After the excessive activity for four months of the year resulting from the visit of the whaling fleet, there followed in March an almost absolute doldrum, lasting until October. The port became deserted; from time to time the arrival of some clipper ship en route for China, or one of the sailing vessels that linked the archipelago to California, provided a stir of movement along the waterfront, whose entire span lazily cradled only a few interisland schooners. The white population, busy during their four-month season, but sluggishly inactive for the rest of the year, were paying little attention to their own business, much to that of their neighbors, and chiefly concerned with finding shady nooks and pleasant relaxation outside Honolulu.

In 1855, Kamehameha, the third of that name, the ruler of the Hawaiian Islands, had just died. He was a direct descendant of Kamehameha I, called the Napoleon of the islands, and the founder of the reigning dynasty.

Let us now turn back three centuries. Imperial rule of the seas still belonged, not without contest, to the Spaniards. Their star was waning; that of England was ascending. The little-known Pacific Ocean offered to the eye of the navigator immense solitudes out of whose mysterious expanses there arose only a scattering of islands, and these had been carefully avoided rather than sought out. The rare ships that dared to face the tempests of Cape Horn continued slowly northward and sailed timorously the coasts of the two Americas; it took them two years for a journey from Europe to Chile or to Peru and then to complete the return. The lust for gold, the urgent needs of the Spanish treasury, brought only a few clumsily maneuvered ships into the ports of Panama, Acapulco, and Manzanillo. Loaded with gold and silver, they returned to Europe, avoiding frequented latitudes. Fearing storms less than they did hostile encounters, they sought a precarious safety in the seas off India, even though these were dreaded because of their typhoons. But they did not hesitate at times to risk themselves and their goods by groping their way across the Pacific, thus conquering the enormous area that separates America from Asia.

One of these daring navigators, Don Juan Gaetano, first discovered the Hawaiian Islands, an achievement wrongly attributed to Captain Cook. In 1865, when the Hawaiian king entrusted to me the post of minister of foreign affairs, it seemed to me to be highly desirable to examine the truth, the actual facts, concerning the geographical discovery and history of the islands. Merest chance led me to study a map antedating 1778, on which one found, apart from egregious errors, indication of a group of islands approximately situated in the same latitudes as the Hawaiian Archipelago. I thereupon wrote to the governor of the Philippines requesting of him that a search be made of the archives of his government. This investigation, authorized and expedited by the cabinet in Madrid, reached the conclusion I anticipated, and on November 17, 1865, I received a letter* from the governor-general containing proof that it was indeed Don Juan Gaetano who made the discovery.

By not claiming and advertising his deserts, Gaetano conformed to the professional traditions of the Spanish navigators. They were in general, in case of hostile pursuit, jealous of preserving the advantages of a haven of refuge, as well as a port for rest and recreation and for taking aboard needed supplies.

The Hawaiian Archipelago is situated between the 23rd and 18th degree of latitude north and between the 160th and 155th degree of longitude west of the meridian of Greenwich. In other words, the six central islands describe a curve running from the southeast to the northwest. Arriving from the southeast, one approaches first the large island of Hawaii, which gives its name to the entire group. Ages ago, Hawaii's high mountains, covered with perennial snow, cast their huge shadows far out over the sea. The craggy, broken summits were crowned by active volcanoes ejecting rivers of fiery lava that eventually vanished into the ocean, creating here and there menacing capes, shaping deep gulfs, and year after year altering the contours of the land. The island has thus grown in size, for in the long unceasing struggle between the ocean's waves and subterranean flames, the fire has won out, sometimes conquering only several feet, sometimes entire leagues.

In 1868 I saw the volcano, as the result of a terrible eruption, roll floods of lava down the mountainside and into the sea, a monstrous tide whose accumulated mass formed a promontory more than a league long and at least 500 feet high. Within two centuries this same lava, today black and sterile, when decomposed by the salutary action of the sunshine and rain, will be

---

*In Foreign Office and Executive Correspondence, Archives of Hawaii. [A. L. K.]

converted into fertile soil covered with a thick vegetation. It will require no more than willing human hands to reward mankind by the hundredfold.

In actuality, the island of Hawaii is made up of three mountains together with their surrounding sloping flanks, separated by high plateaus covered with handsome forests and luxuriant pastures. The southern area, with its ruggedly irregular but gracious coastline, is notable for its groves of orange trees, coconut palms, and pandanus. At the western end magnificent cliffs rise up, whose bosky woods reach up to their summits, where tumbling cascades descend for distances of 300 to 700 meters.* On the north and the east, the volcanoes have left traces of their recent destruction: great rivers of congealed lava, arid plains sprinkled with a deprived type of vegetation, rocks among which large herds of wild goats wander about today in primeval peace. The interior of the island, measuring thirty leagues in length and about the same in breadth, is eminently suited for pasture. In fact, the mountains provide forage for numerous herds of wild bullocks and boars running about free. These are the lineal but now feral descendants of the stock animals introduced by Vancouver in 1793.

Being fish-eaters essentially, the early people settled along the seacoasts, keeping a good distance away from the volcanoes on the flanks and summits of the inland mountains. Along the beaches the old Hawaiians found sheltering vegetation—coconut palms or the pandanus with its multiple roots reaching out like tentacles; the *hau* tree distinguished by its changing blossoms, white during morning, yellow at noon, red in the evening; and numerous orange trees,† ever loaded with flowers and fruit, under a sky always clear. All these shielded from the scorching sun the native grass houses, with roofs fashioned of suitable foliage, along with the shored canoes next to them, hewn from tree trunks by means of stone tools.

Separated from Hawaii by a narrow channel only ten leagues wide, Maui displays somewhat the same appearance as Hawaii, except that the volcano, extinct now for ages, no longer threatens the safety of the inhabitants. Hale-a-ka-la (House of the Sun), a mountain of 10,000 feet, reminds one, only because of its height and contour, of the colossal volcanoes of Hawaii. The island is smaller, the hills less high; the layers of vegetal humus indicate that the lava has been congealed for a very long time, and that nature has peacefully carried on the work of disintegration and transformation. Farther on,

---

*The meter amounts to 39.37 inches; hence the more spectacular waterfalls range roughly from about 1,000 to 2,300 feet in height. [A. L. K.]

†Varigny was mistaken if he believed that the ancient Hawaiians had orange trees. The same confusion appears in his version of the popular tradition of "the return of Lono," in which a priest at Kealakekua instructs the people to bring offerings of "bananas, oranges, and coconuts" for Captain Cook and there is mention of "orangewood branches." [A. L. K.]

about twenty leagues to the northwest, Gaetano and his men came upon the hills of Oahu. At that time the harbor of Honolulu was still unknown; only some fishing huts marked the situation of the future capital. The volcanic forces to which the islands owed their existence had evidently been less pronounced on Oahu. Craters were numerous but not so elevated; well covered with plants and vegetal matter, the hills were less towering, the cliffs not so sudden and steep.

Finally, to the west and out of sight behind the horizon, the bewitching, sirenlike island of Kauai rose from the sea. On Kauai delightful waterfalls performed capricious leaps and turns against a green background, and most of the traces of volcanic action had faded away. Everywhere, in this last but most ancient isle of all, nature had flung an idyllic cloak over the convulsions of past centuries.

Such was the appearance of the Hawaiian Archipelago in 1555 when Juan Gaetano, aboard his ponderous galleon bearing the ensign of imperial Spain, ranged slowly along the coasts and greeted each of the islands in succession. He named them as a group the Garden Isles: *Li Giardini*.

Did he go ashore? On this point the Spaniard's journal is silent. Native traditions only hint darkly at confused memories of floating islands glimpsed far off at sea, and of the awe awakened in the watchers by so inexplicable a vision. A gifted author, J. J. Jarves, has fashioned from these uncertain clues a romantic novel treating native life, *Kiana*,* a remarkable recreation which I believe to be quite in the spirit of the aboriginal customs and manners of that period.

History takes over from legend only with the arrival of Cook. The old Hawaiians had no written language and only the unlettered folk chants transmitted from generation to generation (or, to speak more exactly, from mother to daughter) served to perpetuate the remembrance of past events. In early times it was the practice in each chiefly family to choose a young girl, gifted with a good memory, who was instructed from childhood in the traditional poetry of the tribes and of her ancestors. Thus taught by her whole line of forebears, the woman then passed on to one of her daughters the sacred trust, while adding to it, in a kind of rhythmical singing style, an account of the events and experiences which she had witnessed in turn.

One can readily imagine wherein such oral archives prove defective. Un-

---

Kiana: A Tradition of Hawaii (Boston and Cambridge: James Munroe and Company; London: S. Low, Sons, and Company, 1857). The story was originally published in installments in the *Polynesian* in 1841. In *The Two Lives of James Jackson Jarves* (New Haven: Yale University Press, 1951), p. 157, Francis Steegmuller describes *Kiana* as "the feeblest of romances, and it is perhaps a tribute to the literary taste or discretion of Kamehameha IV . . . that in his letter of thanks he avoided all mention of its contents." [A. L. K.]

functional details abound, dates are missing, feats of arms and genealogical lists take up considerable time, while superstition assigns to each deed a supernatural origin. For all that, there emerges from the poetic totality a racy aroma, an accent of truth, an enchanting local color.

I still remember several evening sessions I spent upon an island shore, where the waves whispered to the sand, and where I listened to these unsophisticated imaginative promptings, these confused memories of the affairs of vanished generations. How far I felt at that time from Europe! How different was everything—everything except the passion, magnificence, and outrage of human nature, everywhere the same! It is from such chants, a number of which are still extant today, that I have drawn certain details in my account of Hawaii's history.

A sizable population, which Cook estimated at 400,000, lived in the archipelago. Speaking the same language, imbued with the same superstitious notions, the Kanakas—so named from the word *kanaka,* which in their language means "men," and by which they refer to themselves—the Kanakas, as I was about to say, were far from comprising a unified nation, ruled by the same laws, obeying, as today, a single monarch.

In each island reigned several chiefs, all separated from one another, not less by rival ambitions and family feuds than by the convolutions of the land and barriers to easy communication. Hawaiian tribes had little acquaintance with each other from isle to isle, and within the same island area mountains and precipices interposed themselves as so many obstacles, acting thus as territorial frontiers.

The chief was sacred, himself and his familial connections; over his subjects he exercised the power of life and death. No one was permitted to eat with him; it was a form of *lèse-majesté* merely to cast one's shadow upon his august person, also a crime merely to enter his grass house without his command. Absolute overlord of everyone about him, he was himself a slave all the while to racial custom and to tribal rank.

Below the chief, who represented brute force, and often side by side with him, sat intellectual power as personified in the priest. The latter was at one and the same time tribal soothsayer and sacrificial agent, and councillor to the chief as well. It was he who interpreted auguries good or bad, who prescribed the occasions of ceremonies of the *kapu* system, the tabu. Among these old Hawaiians religious superstition had been elevated, as among so many other races and nations, to the status of a political institution.

Wars among the chiefs were ordinary occurrences. Each coveted the territory of his neighbor and dreamed of increasing his own. On successful occasions, the trophies of the vanquished—lands, wives, canoes, slaves—were shared by the victorious high chief among his henchmen and warriors. Necessity alone tempered the chief's tyranny, not merely the heavy prerequisite that he surround himself with as many warriors as possible, but also that he make certain, above all, of their loyalty. In fact, abuses of power produced numerous malcontents, who sometimes expressed their disaffection by becoming deserters. The fugitive rebels were ever sure of being cordially welcomed by the next neighboring chief, exceedingly pleased to augment his own forces at the same time that he diminished those of his enemies.

Human life as such among the tribes was regarded as valueless and inspired no respect. Their religious superstitions further relieved the people of such notions. Murder committed by anyone other than a chief was punished, but with a modest penalty. Robbery, on the other hand, entailed the pangs of death. Hospitality was a supreme law, which no person could or would seek to evade. No one was permitted to refuse food or drink, even to his bitterest enemy. Hospitality was carried so far that the first foreigners to land in the islands were convinced for a time that the most extreme form of communism prevailed among members of the same tribe. It was nothing of the kind: theft was punished by horrible penalties. Someone who had stolen, no matter what, was seized and trussed up by hands and feet, then placed in a canoe to be delivered over to the mercy of the waves. The victim, destroyed eventually through the searing rays of the tropical sun, expired only after an excessively slow and harrowing death.

The various ranks and privileges of the chiefs were hereditary, but were transmitted through the female line. The womb ennobled. The widow succeeded the husband—at least the first wife did so, for polygamy was the regular practice. The women avenged themselves in their fashion; and it is enough to say that they had no notion of chastity. Nothing was more common than for a native to offer to lend his wife or daughter to his guest; he felt himself insulted if the latter refused, and the women considered this state of affairs as something quite simple and natural. A girl took pride in the number of her lovers, and a youth judged himself lucky when he married a woman whose beauty, appreciated by all his friends, hid from them no secrets.

During the times here described, paganism reached its apogee. Comparatively simple at the start, the religious rituals represented nothing more than a confused medley of bizarre or cruel practices, whose primitive significance was lost in the dark night of the past. Tyrannical and capricious gods governed without mercy a population without moral rule. Terror performed the role of faith. Bloody ceremonies, restrictions imposed by the chiefs and priests according to whim, resulted in a pattern of religious experience based not only on the blind superstition of the people but also on the no less blind despotism of their governors. The Kanakas believed in an afterlife, if to believe means only to dread: in other words, to attribute to the dead the power to inflict their malevolence upon the living.

A god was born of each of their terrors. Pele, the volcano goddess, swallowed up villages, devoured crops, sowed across her path seeds of sterility and of death. Behind her strode Kamohoalii, god of pestilential vapors; Keuakepo, god of fiery rainstorms; Kanokekili [Kanehekili] god of thunders; they dwelt in the volcanoes and had no other pleasure save that of destroying human beings. To appease them, it was necessary to deliver up offerings; not only offerings to the priests, but even to the very volcanoes into which were hurled the human victims designated for such sacrifice by their spiritual guardians. Always prone to attribute godhead to the object of their fears, the old Hawaiians populated the earth and the seas with cruel divinities; and to shark-gods they delivered up their women and their children.

One indeed turns up vague notions in their native traditions of the creation of the world, also of a flood, but these traditions display neither the simple and clear belief of the American Indians in the existence of a Great Spirit, sovereign of sky and earth, nor the pagan idea of a god, and overlord of gods, enthroned like Jupiter of antiquity on an Olympus subject to his laws. No more did any recognizable philosophical idea emerge out of the unorganized chaos of their superstitions.

Without being godlike in their daily conduct, the early Hawaiian chiefs nevertheless partook of the nature of divinity by reason of the terror they inspired. One of them, Lono, who vanished from the scene many long years ago, became the object of a special cult. People believed he was immortal and they awaited his return. The following translation of an ancient chant explains how and why, upon his arrival in the islands, the Kanakas addressed Captain Cook by the name Lono and why, as a result of an error which he tried in no way to dispel, Cook received from them honors they accorded only to gods.

> Lono, chief of the island of Hawaii, was living in olden times with his wife at Kealakekua. The name of this wife, who was exceedingly beautiful and also Lono's sole lover, was Kaikilani. The two had had a house built for them under an overhanging rock, a shady nook sheltered from the sun, providing a splendid view of the open sea. A young chief of the tribe fell in love with Kaikilani, but whenever he passed by she would turn her head away. One morning he climbed up the overhanging rock and leaning over the top he spoke to Kaikilani the following words: "Kaikilani, your lover greets thee! Love the one, leave the other, and he who is speaking will be forever thine." Lono, hearing these designing words, killed Kaikilani. Overwhelmed by remorse, he carried the lifeless form of his wife to a temple and shuddered and wept. Next he

went running about Hawaii everywhere, starting fights with everyone he met. The astonished people said, "Is Lono crazy?" He answered, "My great love has caused me to lose my wits." After arranging for the games and sacrifices in honor of Kaikilani, he embarked in a canoe with a triangular sail to journey to some of the unknown countries. Before taking leave he uttered a prophecy, saying, "Weep not. I shall return a long time from now, upon a floating island. You folk will see me no more, but your grandchildren's grandchildren will again one day gaze upon the face of Lono!"

The native chants mention the names of seventy-four chiefs preceding Kamehameha, who in the course of time unified the entire chain of islands under his laws. Born about 1760, he was only eighteen when, on January 19, 1778, Cook visited Kauai, the northernmost island of the group. Did the great navigator expect to encounter any islands in this latitude? That would seem quite probable, notwithstanding the silence of his journal on this point. Furthermore, Cook omits all mention of the oceanic discoveries of his predecessors and contemporaries. There is, moreover, another equally insistent fact: in 1748, thirty years before Cook's circumnavigation of the globe, a map published by Anson indicated the existence of a group of islands in the exact latitude containing the Hawaiian Archipelago, but misplacing the islands by an error of ten degrees longitude. Another island is likewise designated on the map as the island of San Francisco, with an error of only one degree, and this location corresponds precisely to that of the large island of Hawaii. It seems inadmissible that a navigator as experienced and also as well read as Cook should not have been familiar with the Anson map. Besides, he was not at all surprised, they say, when the sailors of the *Resolution,* who had been assigned to watch duty, cried out their signal, "Land on the port side!" The next day the *Resolution* and the *Discovery* dropped anchor in Waimea Bay, one of the ports of the island of Kauai.

Cook stopped at Waimea but a few days and then set sail for the northwest coast of America. Only one year later, on January 17, 1779, he touched again at the large island of Hawaii and found mooring in Kealakekua Bay, where he was to meet his death.

Ledyard has published an account of the voyages of Captain Cook and of his death, *Life of Captain Cook,* in which he provides a thorough and detailed narrative of the events that preceded the catastrophe at Kealakekua. But there is also another extant version of the same event, more original and direct and much less familiar, preserved among the native chants. The English version related the occurrences from the European point of view; the Hawaiian narrative from the native. The last seems to me the more authentic and deserves priority:

This is the *mele* (chant)* of Kupa, son of Kapupua, a member of the canoe fleet of Kalaimano, chief of Kealakekua. I was a child when the happenings I tell of took place, but I shall never forget them up to the day of my death, and my recollections are accurate.

My father lived near the *puʻuhonua* of Honaunau (city of refuge and residence of the chief). One night, a little before dawn, he rose and after waking me and seeing that my mother brought us our breakfast of poi (a paste of taro) and fish, he set off with me beside him for the seashore, to go crab catching. We were just then in the midst of the week when the tabu had been placed on the canoes, and nobody could put out to sea in one without risk of being offered as a sacrifice to Kailii,† god of war. Today times are changed indeed, when anybody can go fishing at any time and in any place he chooses. While we were on the beach, my father, who had excellent eyesight, particularly for seeing things at a distance, told me to take a look out to sea and tell him if I noticed anything; but it was still dark and I saw nothing. He watched a while longer and then set off for the house of the chief.

He returned shortly after with Kalaimano. Pointing a finger, he called Kalaimano's attention to something out at sea. As daylight was now increasing, I too sighted a pair of floating forests. The trees were stripped of their leaves. The floating forests (the *Resolution* and the *Discovery*) gradually rose higher on the surface of the water, but they neither came any closer to the land nor did they withdraw. The chief summoned the people and they all went down to the beach, uttering exclamations of astonishment and fear; for we had never seen anything like this before. Kalaimano spoke to the priest: "You never forewarned us of anything to match this. If it is the dwelling place of a god, what are we to do? And if it is an island, would it not be proper to place it under a tabu?"

The priest replied, "Send a few men to look over the island, but without setting foot on it. Then they will return and tell us what they have seen. But as we are now in the period when the canoes are tabu, send your very best swimmers instead."

The chief accordingly commanded my father and several other persons to perform this task, and I won my father's permission to accompany him. The distance was short and if I became tired I could hang onto him, swimming with my hand upon his shoulder. Warily we approached these isles which close by resembled huge houses floating on the water, but their leafless trees stood straight up in the air. Upon these islands we saw some gods who were very different indeed from ourselves. They were eating and drinking blood, and after eating of the flesh they tossed into the water a thick green skin (the ships came from Monterey and the sailors were probably on the deck eating watermelon); others breathed fire and smoke through their mouths and nostrils; all had faces

---

*Unless otherwise indicated, parenthetical explanations in text have been supplied by Varigny. [A. L. K.]

†A bad misspelling or a confused allusion to the wargod Kū-kā-ili-moku. [A. L. K.]

of dazzling whiteness and their eyes glittered; skins of various colors enveloped their bodies; they had holes on their thighs into which they thrust their hands; they put a great many things into these holes, which appeared to be stuffed with treasures.

We could not believe our eyes. They were examining us also, but without any signs of being afraid of us. While making our circuit around these islands, my father said to me, "Here is some iron (literally, 'hard stone') such as I found in the pieces of wood that the sea had cast ashore (it was a long while ago, and you were not yet born); now this iron is fastened to the floating island, but perhaps I can detach it from the wood and then place it on the altar of Mokualii, the canoe god, who will then be good to me." He tried indeed to rip off a piece of iron, but he scratched his fingers and despite his strength he was not able to break it.

As I watched him working, all at once I heard a sound similar to that of thunder or the rumblings of Pele and then I saw my father, as if knocked over by a stone or burned by the fire of some god, sink down in the water and in a moment or two return to the surface, weak and unable to speak. Frightened by this anger of a god, we fled. Several of his comrades helped bring Kapupua back upon the beach; but he stirred no more, the god having struck him down with his thunder. We reported to Kalaimano and to the priest what he had seen and heard, and the latter said to us: "Listen, men, women, and children of Hawaii! What you have assumed to be a floating island is the great war canoe of your god Lono, who left Hawaii a great while ago to explore the sea, and who now today returns to you. Ready yourselves accordingly to welcome him, and then do this. Let each one of you prepare a canoe for him. Lono himself will remove the tabu and by so doing absolve you of wrong. Load your canoes with bananas, oranges, and coconuts, and gather round his warships. Your submission and your offerings will appease his anger, and perhaps Lono when pacified will condescend to visit his people. But let none of you lay a hand on his sacred vessels. Respect them as you respect the altar of Kailii himself."

Kalaimano approved the speech of the priest, and all the canoes loaded with fruits surrounded the vessels of the god and presented their gifts to him, by means of ropes let up and down from the decks of Lono's ships. All this while, no one risked confronting his presence; and Lono, being satisfied, withheld his thunderings and allowed us to return in peace. At night all the men, women, and children abandoned their grass houses and came out to camp on the shore, for the priest had said: "Always keep yourselves on the alert to receive Lono, as no one can say whether he will be pleased to pay us a visit at night or during the day."

Lono did not come, but during the night we beheld some terrifying sights. Lono and his company hurled fiery arrows at the stars. These flew from their bows with a fearsome whistling sound, piercing the stars and causing them to rain down upon the sea in blazing fragments.* Flames of strange colors rose

---

*In Ledyard's account, he mentions guns being fired aboard ship to impress the superstitious minds of the natives. [C. de V.]

and descended the length of the tree trunks of the ships and then raced along the surface of the sea. Extraordinary noises and reverberations burst out at intervals, sometimes resembling the violent furies of Pele, sometimes imitating the calls and songs of birds. We spent the night in a state of utter fear, not knowing what Lono would decide and expecting at any moment to perish from his thunderclaps.

In the morning, however, Lono came toward us. By command of the chief, we offered him homage of the kind reserved for gods; but whether because of disdain Lono affected not to understand us, or whether his long absence had made him forget our language, he did not respond to any of our supplications and prayers. Whole days passed by in the same way. The ships of the god were tabu for us and none of us visited them.

One morning several of the lesser gods from Lono's retinue approached us and seized by force some of the sacred fish intended for Pele's altar. In order to prevent their committing this sacrilege, we had offered them the remainder of our regular fish supply. Kalaimano was present. He said nothing, although his face radiated his anger. Another day the lesser gods arrived and began to tear down the barrier around the *marai* (sacred place), constructed of *hau* and orangewood branches, and to drag the pieces toward the sea, either merely to dump them into the water or to load them aboard their vessels.* Lono did not accompany them. Our chief interposed and told them to stop these proceedings; they laughed and continued. While Kalaimano was speaking to them, Lono suddenly arrived. He vaulted over the wall of the enclosure and advanced toward the *marai*. Kalaimano placed himself in Lono's path and the latter rudely shoved Kalaimano aside. Our chief then seized Lono with his two arms in order to halt the god's advance and to carry him outside the enclosure, but Lono struggled so much that Kalaimano, locking him firmly in his fierce embrace, caused Lono to cry out in pain. "He screams. Obviously, he is not a god!" said the chief, and he straightway killed Lono. Those who had been demolishing the barrier then fled, but on the order of Kalaimano, our anger now reaching a climax, we threw ourselves on the fleeing creatures and, strange to say, those whom we struck fell to the ground and their blood flowed just the same as does ours. The foreign persons in the canoes held off, maintaining their distance from the range of our arrows and stones, but mounted against us a tremendous explosion of fire. This was followed by a noise resembling thunder. All of the Kanakas touched by that fire fell down and started bleeding, without anyone being able to see just what it was that had pierced their bodies. The men of Lono's party, those who had remained aboard the large canoes, heard the uproar and directed upon us other thunderclaps more deafening still, whose sounds positively stunned us.

Kalaimano remained on the beach, continuing to wield his powerful bow, but all of his arrows fell short of our enemies. His retainers stayed close to him.

---

*Mention of this is made in the English account. At the time of departure, the sailors had been ordered to gather some wood and they seized on that enclosing the *marai*, drier than other wood and already cut. [C. de V.]

One of these covered the chief's breast with a woven mat, and other comrades kept moistening it with water so as to prevent his being burned by the fire. But the anger of the gods is inexorable, and when the invisible fire at last penetrated the dampened mat and reached his body, Kalaimano fell to the earth as the blood came streaming from his mouth.

Many other dead bodies lay scattered about the beach, and even the trunks of the coconut trees were pitted by that fire which kills from afar. No prayer, no sacrifice, could propitiate the gods and save the life of our chief. The next day the sacred canoes vanished without anyone's being able to say where they had gone. Kalaimano was dead.

So it was, O sons of Kealakekua, that your forefathers, the Kanakas, witnessed on one and the same day the death of both their god and their chief.

CHAPTER 2

KAMEHAMEHA THE FOUNDER

Youth of Kamehameha I.—His wars.—An army annihilated by the volcano.—Two English sailors.—Visit of Vancouver.—Conquest of the islands of Maui and Oahu.—A daring plan.—Subjugation of the island of Kauai.—Visions of the future.—Death of Kamehameha I.

The murder of Captain Cook, news of which was reported throughout the whole world, had the result of confirming European navigators in their first notion of the barbarism and cruelty of the Sandwich Islanders, and the desirability of steering clear of the inhospitable Hawaiian shores. A number of years elapsed when no ship ventured to come near them.

In 1780 one of the principal chiefs of the island of Hawaii died. He was Kalaniopuu, chief of Kau, a miserably poor district frequently laid waste by volcanic eruptions, and his son Kiwalao succeeded him. Like his father, the son had long fixed his eyes on the neighboring district of Kona, part of the hereditary realm of Kamehameha. Sheltered from the trade winds by the high mountain of Mauna Loa, this district was one of the most fertile in the whole island, and famous above all for its fisheries. Under the pretext of paying his last respects to his father, Kiwalao assembled all his warriors and embarked with them on a flotilla of war vessels with the intention, he said, of landing at Kailua: the most important settlement of Kamehameha's district and also the place chosen by Kiwalao for the burial of his father. In fact, tradition had succeeded over the years in establishing Kailua as the consecrated burial ground for the high chiefs of Hawaii. Warned of his rival's plans, Kamehameha invited him to proceed as he wished to Kailua, but with a reduced escort. When Kiwalao refused to leave behind a single canoe or man, Kamehameha advanced in preparation for the encounter. At Keei took place a battle all the more savage, because the two chiefs were kinsmen, and upon the death of the one the other would succeed him by customary right. The forces were well matched. For several days the fighting, alternately suspended and revived, continued without notable advantage on either side. On the evening of the eighth day, Kiwalao was killed in the confusion of combat. His soldiers were scattered and Kamehameha was left in control of the field as the rightful ruler of Kona and Kau.

Meanwhile, he had to conquer one by one the fortified locations where the liege men and warriors of Kiwalao had found refuge. He himself barely escaped death near Hilo. Nevertheless, Kamehameha's persistence compensated for his uncertain military fortune. Despite the reinforcements of men and provisions which his enemies were receiving from Kahekili, chief of Maui and Oahu, who was allied with Kiwalao and jealous of the Kona chief's early successes, Kamehameha finally succeeded in circumventing Kahekili and thereby establishing the whole of the island of Hawaii under his own sole dominion.

Having completed this conquest, Kamehameha determined to clinch it. He turned his full forces against Kahekili on the latter's home ground. Taking advantage of the absence of Kahekili on a journey to Oahu, Kamehameha staged a raid upon the island of Maui, where Kahekili's son met him in battle at Wailuku with forces more numerous than the invaders. Despite his handicap, the tactics of Kamehameha, especially his coolheadedness and personal courage, assured him a brilliant victory. The bloodshed was appalling. A stream, the Iao, was so swollen with dead bodies that this human dam blocked and deflected the current. The battlefield was named Kepaniwai, Dike of Waters. It forms today part of one of the richest plantations of the island.

While Kamehameha was waging war profitably on Maui, a rebellion broke out on Hawaii, led by various conquered but unsubdued supporters of Kiwalao. Before setting forth on his expedition, Kamehameha appointed Kiana [Kaiana] as his representative, one of the warriors most loyal to his cause. The latter assembled the other local chiefs, together with their trustworthy supporting tribesmen, and confidently awaited the arrival of the rebels commanded by Keaoua [Keoua], one of Kiwalao's friends. After dividing his army into three parts, Keaoua proceeded from Hilo in the direction of Kau. The advance guard had barely reached the Kau district when they first heard the rumblings of a terrifying earthquake. The warriors staggered like drunken men. A rainstorm of cinders darkened the sky. To judge by the descriptions preserved in native chants, the volcanic activity almost equaled in violence that of the later eruption of April in 1868, the intensity of which I can personally swear to, and shall return to in a later chapter.

The rear guard was equally tested, but no more than the advance guard did they suffer any serious losses. As they pressed ahead, however, the men of the rear guard confronted a startling spectacle bound to fill them with superstitious terror. The center portion of Keaoua's forces had been transformed into an army of corpses. Completely asphyxiated by the sulphurous fumes, they had fallen to earth like so many men dropping off to sleep. A single dog was a survivor: his modest earthbound height had protected him from the flood of lethal gases that within a few moments had annihilated the middle corps of the army. One still discovers in the southeast region of the volcano the whitened ashy bones of the warriors of Keaoua.

Discouraged by this unexpected stroke of fate, the high chief Kiana gave orders to withdraw from the scene in retreat. During this time Kamehameha was returning by war canoe to defend his threatened realm. Without allowing his opponent time to strengthen his exhausted troops, Kamehameha joined battle with Keaoua, overcame him, and forced him to flee to the mountains. Deserted by the rest of his army and despairing of his fortunes, Keaoua for a time wandered about the desert wastelands of Kau, but finally decided to beg for mercy and surrender himself to the generosity of his enemy. Escorted by seven of his comrades-in-arms, the conquered chief left the caves where he had taken refuge and crossed the mountains which cut off Kau from Kona. During his journey, he was treated with special respect by all the natives, who admired him for his courage but who predicted that he was marching to his death. He was killed finally at the hands of Keeaumoku, one of the warrior chiefs under Kamehameha. The latter wept, so it is said, for the murder committed against his orders; but the honors which he later saw fit to heap upon his royal follower lead me to believe that if he did not actually command the execution of Keaoua, he still regarded the act of Keeaumoku as too useful to his own interests not to deserve reward.

The death of Keaoua ended the insurrection on Hawaii. Kamehameha remained sole ruler of the island, but his successes were offset by his reverses on Maui, where his chiefs after suffering defeat upon defeat were forced to abandon their offensive campaign and bring back to Hilo the remnants of their troops. Confident of his future, Kamehameha was able to await a more favorable opportunity.

Ever since the visit of Cook in 1778, Kamehameha had been aware of the enormous advantages possessed by foreigners as compared with his own people. He understood the benefits to be derived from having among his retinue some of the foreign sailors, workmen who were skilled in the uses of tools, particularly blacksmiths who could operate iron forges, and who were good navigators besides. In 1789 an American schooner commanded by a certain Captain Metcalfe was anchored along the coast of Maui. During the night some natives stole one of the ship's small boats. A skirmish occurred between the sailors and the Kanakas. The natives, routed by a few volleys of gunfire, left behind them more than a hundred of their number on the beach, while the schooner hastily set off at full sail in order to escape an attack of reprisal. As the foreigners made their departure, however, they abandoned on the beach a quartermaster, Isaac Davis, and a seaman, John Young, neither of whom had been able to climb aboard and escape.* Kamehameha rescued these two wretches from certain death, and thanks to kind treatment and attractive promises linked them through gratitude and self-interest to his own fortunes. Both Davis and Young achieved the rank of high chiefs, a status which they passed on to their children, whose history is closely intertwined with that of the Kamehameha dynasty.

The last descendant of John Young married in 1855 the late King Kamehameha IV; she was Queen Emma, who visited Europe in 1863–1864.† My frequent meetings with her over a period of fourteen years have enabled me to testify to her excellent qualities. Beloved and respected everywhere, she has dedicated her life since the death of her husband to charitable works. The natives always refer to her as "the good Queen Emma." Descendants of Davis are still living in the islands. One of them married a relative of the king, a chiefess who is governor of the island of Hawaii; the other, up to a few years ago, was a member of the supreme court.

On March 3, 1792, Vancouver, the most famous of English circumnavigators of recent times, arrived at the island of Hawaii. A lieutenant under Cook's command in 1778, he had witnessed Cook's tragic death. The visit of Vancouver has major importance as a historic turning point in an account of the Hawaiian Islands. It is a date which marks the beginning, indeed the germ, of civilization in Hawaii: the first religious stirrings. Up to that day European civilization had not been displayed to this barbarous folk except in violent and threatening forms; they had known only its force, without appreciating its virtues. Kamehameha alone had caught a confused glimpse of it: not so much the social benefits that western civilization might bring to his race as the advantages it could afford him in his struggle against his military and political enemies.

To Vancouver belongs the glory, a rare glory during this era, of proving himself a just and good man in his dealings with the Kanakas, who today still venerate his memory as their first benefactor.

Already, over a period of some years, contacts between foreigners and natives were becoming more and more frequent; for sandalwood, then growing plentifully in the islands, had become an object of commercial exchange. Various Americans and Europeans, attracted by the lure of gain and

---

*Varigny telescopes the misfortunes or fortunes (1789–1790) of the two beached foreigners, Young and Davis. Isaac Davis was the sole survivor of the schooner *Fair American,* whose crew had been killed in a skirmish with natives. John Young, boatswain of the *Eleanora,* was forcibly "retained" by strict order of Kamehameha as a means of preventing Captain Metcalf of the *Fair American* from seeking revenge. [A. L. K.]

†Emma visited England, France, and parts of the United States in 1865–1866. [A. L. K.]

the peacefulness of life in Hawaii, now that Kamehameha had become the sole ruler, sometimes took advantage of the opportunity to spend several weeks in the islands in order to trade with the Kanakas and purchase from them, for ridiculously small sums, the sandalwood that they would later sell at very dear rates in China. During his first visit, Vancouver obtained from Kamehameha a promise of protection for these foreigners while in port, and the Englishman on his part promised various useful presents on the occasion of his own next call at Honolulu. He returned, in fact, on February 14, 1793, bringing with him a bullock, five cows, some sheep, and several rams. The enormous flocks and herds which today graze the pastures of the archipelago have thus sprung from Vancouver's gift. To protect these animals and to permit them to breed, Kamehameha imposed on them a sacred tabu which was at last removed only after a number of years.

Kamehameha did not want to be outdone in generosity, and as testimony of his gratitude he dispatched across the water and alongside Vancouver's vessels a whole flotilla of canoes, heaped with fruits and gift offerings of every description. The canoes returned with agricultural implements, grain, tools, and iron, the major objects of native desire. Accompanied by his sub-chiefs and by Kaahumanu, his favorite wife, escorted also by his war canoes, and surrounded by all the savage pomp by which he liked to astonish the imagination of his subjects, Kamehameha himself came abroad the vessels of Vancouver. He visited them foot by foot; nothing escaped his scrutiny. It pleased his lively intelligence and curiosity to take full account of everything he saw, but his bland expressionless face revealed none of his impressions.

This official visit was followed by several others, during which etiquette was laid aside. Vancouver came to the reasonable conclusion that nothing less than the sovereignty and rule of a single chief could assure the welfare of the archipelago and put an end to the bloody intertribal warfare of high chiefs quarreling among themselves. Furthermore, no less a measure could provide relative security for foreign commerce. Far from diverting Kamehameha from his ambitious enterprises, Vancouver encouraged him in them and applied himself to assisting in their execution. He intuitively recognized Kamehameha's sharp intelligence, indeed the great spirit of this savage who knew how to shape a plan and pursue its accomplishment, and who combined a statesman's skill and wisdom with the coolheaded courage of a brilliant military leader.

On February 21, 1794, amid the same royal display as on his first visit, Kamehameha made a final appearance upon Vancouver's ship, scheduled to sail the following day. Many canoes loaded with provisions accompanied the Hawaiian chief, and there were tears in his eyes as he took leave of the English gentleman he called his friend. During this visit a conversation took place which was later to bring results of which neither Kamehameha nor Vancouver perhaps had any inkling at that time. Kamehameha requested Vancouver to send him some missionaries from England to teach his people. After receiving such a promise from Vancouver, Kamehameha in the presence of his fellow chiefs solemnly asked him to solicit in addition, in behalf of his people and himself, the goodwill and friendship of the king of England. Whether or not Vancouver and his officers rightly comprehended Kamehameha's language and intention, or whether at the particular moment the Englishman was somehow carried away by philanthropic impulse, Vancouver nevertheless understood, or affected to understand, that Kamehameha was placing his kingdom under the protection of England. In any event, Vancouver declared, though in rather ambiguous terms, that he accepted in the name of the king of England the offer Kamehameha had just proposed.

This misunderstanding, which in fact England never formally or officially took advantage of, continued over many years and did not cease until 1843, the year when the British cabinet, in a mutual agreement with France, recognized the absolute independence of the Hawaiian Kingdom. As for the promise by Vancouver to send missionaries, this too as it happened was never carried out. Wholly preoccupied with the large-scale military offensives of the French Republic and the First Empire, England was absorbed in more urgent political developments than the doings of a small kingdom in faraway Oceania. What England could not do at that time, and what she is attempting to do today—namely, to establish a Christian mission in the islands—the Americans would undertake to achieve only a few years later, with what results I shall describe in a subsequent chapter.

Meanwhile, Kamehameha did not forget to keep a watchful eye on events occurring on Maui. Though delayed on Hawaii by the need to reorganize his army and simultaneously show suitable deference to Vancouver, Kamehameha was nevertheless not distracted. The Maui chieftains had been impressed by Vancouver's presence and convinced by his friendly treatment of Kamehameha that Vancouver would give Kamehameha decisive support in case of war. However, Vancouver's departure now emboldened Kamehameha's enemies on Maui, with the result that Kahekili formed an alliance with Kaeo, king of Kauai. The two chieftains combined their war fleets at Oahu and then set sail for Hawaii. Kamehameha there engaged them in a naval battle off the coast near Hilo and forced them to retreat. Following up his success, Kamehameha in his victorious canoes pressed on, gave chase to the fleeting ships, and after reaching Oahu and disembarking continued the pursuit on land. Kamehameha's enemies, their ranks strengthened by numerous reinforcements and now defending their ancestral lands, were halted in formation and stood awaiting the king in Nuuanu Valley. It was on this site of an ancient battlefield, behind which yawned a precipice 1,200 feet deep and cleaving the island into two parts, that Kamehameha and his warriors met his foes face to face. There, where every route of communication to the rear was cut off, the enemy forces decided either to conquer or to perish.

These allied kings of Maui and Oahu had aligned their men at a certain enclosed spot among the valley's cliffs with their backs against the stony wall. Kamehameha was between his enemies and the sea, into which they hoped to drive him along with his troops. The struggle was heroic on each side. Kamehameha personally took part in the fighting and was several times brought to the brink of defeat. Ultimate victory was his; but rather than lay down their weapons in surrender, the vanquished chose to kill themselves on the spot. Surrounded on all sides, several hundred of the surviving warriors hurled themselves over the precipice.

By this brilliant victory, celebrated in the proudest annals of Hawaiian history, Kamehameha achieved control over the islands of Maui, Molokai, and Oahu. The island of Kauai alone still preserved its independence. The distance separating it from Hawaii, unpropitious winds, and an always rough sea constituted almost insurmountable obstacles for an invading army. Furthermore, the numerous inhabitants were quite prosperous and deeply attached to their king, Kaeo. All these difficulties merely delayed without discouraging the ambition of Kamehameha. He devoted several years to planning his strategy of attack and in 1804 assembled on the beach of Waikiki 7,000 well-trained veteran warriors, not counting fresh recruits, a fleet of 27 schooners armed with cannon and artillery, more than 500 war canoes, and a gunboat carrying 20 cannon, above which his ensign floated in the breeze. Just when he was on the point of embarking, a terrible epidemic broke out among his men while they were concentrated within a single area. He himself very nearly died. Although he had scarcely recovered, he busied himself finding replacements for his depleted ranks, renewing his stores, and patiently awaiting the first favorable wind.

Kaeo meanwhile had died. Warned of the military movements of Kamehameha, who in no way disguised his intentions, the Kauai chiefs and their people had rallied around their new king, the youthful Kaumualii. Active, energetic, and brave, the latter made preparations for a desperate resistance; his fiery-spirited warriors vowed that if necessary they would kill themselves at his side. Disturbed all the while by a melancholy presentiment, Kaumualii ordered a schooner to be built and loaded with provisions, resolving if he survived his defeat to embark along with his wives and his liege men and trust himself to the salty flood. Somewhere in the Pacific he would discover a distant land where he might live in safety sheltered from his rival's ambition.

Kamehameha, meanwhile suspecting resistance, kept himself well informed by spies about what was happening on Kauai. He conceived of a daring plan, truly original and worthy of his genius. He wanted to meet Kaumualii, personally confer with him, and through the power of persuasion achieve a success still very doubtful if pursued by force of arms. He sent a messenger to the chief, warning him that he was prepared to attack; but in the same message he also invited Kaumualii to visit him on Oahu. Despite the advice of subordinates, the ruler of Kauai accepted the invitation, and as a way of publicly displaying his complete trust in the good faith of his enemy, Kaumualii crossed the sea and with only a small suite proceeded into the very midst of Kamehameha's encampment. By acting in this fashion, he virtually was sacrificing his life, and so he took care to leave behind him one of his most devoted comrades to serve as regent. In the role of a man who has nothing more to look forward to, he eloquently addressed Kamehameha, asked him for an explanation of his aggressive designs, and reproached him for his unjustifiable hostility toward himself and the people of Kauai. He concluded by adding that his life depended on the mercy of his adversary, if, without regard for a sworn oath, he was seized and held captive; but, "Realize well, Kamehameha," said he, "that though I may be dead my people still live and stand on their own feet, and that their desire for revenge will double their courage. If you turn me free, I will do battle as their leader against you."

This speech deserved the most careful consideration by the audience at whom it was aimed. Kamehameha listened to Kaumualii without interrupting. Finally, speaking slowly, and in a voice touched by emotion, Kamehameha thanked Kaumualii for his trust. "You are free," said he. "You may leave, but first listen to me." Then he told in a few words but with animation about his persecuted boyhood, his threatened inheritance, and the need he had felt first to defend himself and then, finally, to initiate strategic attack in order to put a stop to endless and ever-burgeoning dangers confronting him. The gods had favored his cause; his victorious forces had triumphed over every opposition. Thanks to him, anarchy had been halted; peace reigned throughout his empire, and along with it security and the safety of persons. Ancient barriers separating tribes who spoke the same language, who practiced the same religion, had fallen away. In order to complete and consolidate his work, it was imperative that the entire archipelago should have a single master, and that one should be a king. Circumstances compelled him to rule, and he wanted to rule. If indeed he should consent to abandon his plans of conquest, his successors would only take them up where he left off. Kauai could not continue independent: the struggle, though deferred for this day, would break out again on some other. In this struggle Kauai would surely collapse. Could that island alone resist the combined efforts of the others of the chain? In order to give Kaumualii a proof of his moderation, Kamehameha proposed to allow Kaumualii to go free and govern peacefully his ancestral kingdom: provided, however, that he, Kaumualii, on his honor would promise to bequeath it by testament to Kamehameha or to Kamehameha's successor, and by this means assure an imperial unity and political consolidation in Hawaii which he was powerless to forestall.

These arguments, dictated by strong convictions, illustrate Kamehameha's increasing moral authority. They show how the conqueror of so many chiefs was able to conciliate Kaumualii by appealing to his desire to cooperate and share likewise in a grandiose political plan, and so spare his people a dreadful struggle. Thus was the king of Kauai reduced first to silence and then to admiration: Kamehameha did not omit any seductive appeal to draw Kaumualii along with him; he treated him as a friend and obtained his total support. The two chiefs gave each other their sworn oaths; and as long as Kamehameha lived, Kaumualii remained his friend and had nothing to fear concerning him.

This peaceful victory won for the conqueror the whole of the archipelago. The Kamehameha dynasty was founded and thereby was Hawaiian solidarity achieved.

Kamehameha was as skillful as an administrator as he was adroit as a politician and great as a military leader. The prestige brought him by his many successes made it possible for him to organize his campaigns with care and to eliminate all resistance. On each island his cohort chiefs received from him rewards in the form of land. These dividends distributed among various districts formed for them a generous recompense for their services, but did not allow them to establish at any particular point a position strong enough to resist the royal authority. Magnanimous toward the chiefs he had defeated, when he could be so without danger, he pardoned the descendants of Kahekili, who received lands from him and enjoyed high rank at his court. By wise ordinances conceived in a liberal spirit he regulated the coastal fishing rights and the exploitation of the mountain forests. Foreseeing the future prominence of Honolulu, he very regretfully abandoned his favorite residence at Kailua, on the island of Hawaii, in order to set up an establishment near the newly important harbor of Honolulu, which was becoming a frequent haven for foreign vessels.

The one-time seaman, John Young, designated by Kamehameha to live at Kailua, received as reward for his services the rank of governor of the island. The king was generous and truly royal in his dealings with naval vessels and their officers and enterprises. He proved likewise to be just and freehanded toward the traders and sailors attracted to the island by the news of his success, humanity, and desire to exchange the products of the country for European articles and goods. His meticulously organized army, under the command of tested lieutenants, was kept under rigorous discipline and was always ready to obey his orders, thus maintaining everywhere an uninterrupted state of peace.

Kamehameha was no less bold as a trader than he was efficient as an administrator. He enjoyed taking stock of the least sources of revenue and profited from the lessons of experience. One small example among a thousand displays his character, which was at one and the same time that of an intense man of action and also a man of ideas. Lured by the profits being made by the ships that bought up his sandalwood for resale in China, he turned ship chandler and naval factor. He acquired, at a jacked-up price, an American brigantine, loaded it with sandalwood, and dispatched it to China. These ill-considered measures resulted in a commercial disaster: deceived by his dishonest agents, he lost the cost of the ship, as well as its cargo, and found himself in debt to the amount of $3,000 (15,000 francs).* This was his sole traffic in foreign commerce; but in checking his accounts he noticed in them the high duty charged at Hong Kong for the privilege of bringing in imports. A few days later, he imposed by royal edict a modest duty on articles being imported by foreigners, and the Hawaiian treasury was enriched by an important source of revenue.

Two ideas dominated his thoughts during the last years of his life. The first was his desire to see the coming of missionaries as promised by Vancouver. He was impatient to learn from them what actually was that Christianity, which he knew only at second hand but never failed to inquire about when meeting the foreigners who landed at Honolulu. The vague answers of these persons, who were themselves usually without education and ignorant otherwise in every way, did not satisfy him. He sensed that the religion of his forefathers was tottering; it was a repugnant conglomeration of bizarre or shameful practices, concerning which he scarcely managed to conceal his scorn. His second thought was to extend his conquests still farther abroad. A new Alexander, he turned his gaze toward the south and dreamed of hegemony over Tahiti, from which he was separated by 800 marine leagues. It would have provided a curious spectacle if this barbarous king, surrounded by his war vessels, had audaciously sped them across the Pacific and conquered by sail such a vast distance, braving the storms and calms of the equator in order to add one more island to his kingdom, in which he was now beginning to feel rather confined. But this was only a dream that he was

---

*Throughout Varigny's book, the French franc in the dollar value of that day was worth twenty cents. [A. L. K.]

never allowed to fulfill. On May 8, 1819, Kamehameha died at his Waikiki headquarters, near Honolulu.

Waikiki is today a charming little village where the people of Honolulu like occasionally to spend several weeks at a time for the pleasure of sea bathing. I can still see the cottage I often occupied there, the property of one of my friends, Mr. E. H. Allen, later member of the United States Congress, a naturalized Hawaiian citizen, and for eighteen years chief justice of the supreme court of the kingdom. This marine villa was situated only a few steps away from what was once the royal residence of Kamehameha I, ruins of which could still be distinguished, shaded by handsome coconut palms and covered with trailing periwinkles. It was there under the perennially clear sky and facing an ocean always blue that this great and noble savage passed away, laden with glory and years, leaving behind him a venerated name and a nation where none had existed before except as a hodgepodge of warring tribes.

In 1863 the ruling king, Kamehameha, the fifth of that name, shared with me in that same spot his desire to found an order of merit, designed as a reward for services rendered to the state. We had just been considering the character of the award and its requirements and regulations, to which he wanted to give the name of his ancestor. I asked him whether or not he had chosen a motto for it. "Don't you think," he answered, full of memories of the head of the dynasty, "that his last words when he lay on his deathbed would do?" And he told me of the following incident. Behind the pallet couch of the dying Kamehameha stood Kaahumanu, his favorite wife, and his son, Liholiho. The chiefs, posted at the foot of his bed, were weeping. Addressing him, one of them asked, "After you, who will govern and command us? Who then will be our father?" He replied, "After myself, the kingdom will go to Liholiho, if he proves himself worthy of it, and Kaahumanu will be Kuhina Nui (vice-regent)." The death pangs were mounting. Liholiho, his eyes full of tears, kissed his father's hand. Kamehameha turned his head toward him and said: "*Hookanaka*, be a man!", and died. This is today the motto inscribed on the cross of the Order of Kamehameha.

CHAPTER 3

MISSIONARIES AND OTHER AGENTS OF CHANGE

Kamehameha II.—A regency.—Suppression of tabu.—Energy of the regent.—The first missionaries.—The kanaka language.—Schools.—Visit of Kamehameha II to England.—Revolt on Kauai.—Success of the regent.—Her excesses.—Her conversion.—Death of Kamehameha II in England.

The wishes of Kamehameha I were as much respected after his death as they had been during his lifetime. Liholiho, his son and successor, inherited the sovereignty without any of the conquered chiefs ever attempting to oppose him or to recover on the battlefield the independence they had lost. Kaahumanu shared the royal authority, just as Kamehameha had wisely desired, who well appreciated her unusual energy and almost masculine traits of character.

Born in 1795, Liholiho, better known under the name of Kamehameha II, was twenty-four when his father died. Solely interested in his pleasures, he was at that time squandering his youth upon his wives and courtesans. Passionate, unstable, surrounded by a dissolute court of young men his own age, he was popular for his generosity but also dreaded because of his unpredictable moods. He nonetheless loved his father as much as he had feared him, and now appeared to be deeply affected by his death, news of which had shocked the entire archipelago. Public criers sent at Kaahumanu's behest scurried everywhere announcing the catastrophe and proclaiming the accession of Kamehameha II. His first act was to see to it that his father was given a magnificent funeral. Following Kaahumanu's advice, he avoided openly offending the religious beliefs of the natives, for the assembled priests had prescribed a strict program of tabus extending over weeks. Wailing voices and chanted dirges echoed from one end of the kingdom to another; numerous victims were sacrificed upon the altars; and all the tributes that affection, gratitude, fear, and superstition could inspire were offered up in commemoration of Kamehameha I. His body was given over to the priests and carefully dissected; the bones, stripped of their flesh, were tied in a bundle and wrapped in the richest of fabrics. Then they were buried with the greatest secrecy at some spot unknown to this day.

The Kanakas fear above all the profanation of the mortal remains of their chiefs. If there are any still alive today who may know where the bones of Kamehameha now repose, the secret will die with these persons. I have all grounds to believe, however, that the present king alone knows where his grandfather lies buried, and that (like a new Attila) Kamehameha the Great rests beneath a torrent whose waters, after being diverted for a time from their proper streambed, have now rediscovered their original source.

The funeral celebrations for Kamehameha marked the last showy triumph of paganism in the Hawaiian Islands. Like a flame a little before it is extinguished, the event cast a brilliant popular light; but orgies, massacres, cruelties such as were occasioned by these several weeks of mourning, caused the chiefs themselves to feel disgust. Kaahumanu above all, who up to that point had been struggling simultaneously with her desire to respect the native traditions and her urge also to flout them, ended by choosing the second course. Her mistrust finally inspired in her a religious faith cleansed of both bloodshed and sensual vice.

Very soon after his father's funeral, Kamehameha II hastened to change his seat of residence to Kawaihae, on the island of Hawaii, in order to obey a superstitious notion that considers the residence of a king who has just died as tabu. On the one side, a group of foreigners who had easy access to Kamehameha II, and opportunity for encouraging him in his growing skepticism, were prodding him to break away from paganism; another group of priests and sacerdotal officers were trying to rekindle in him the superstitious instincts of his race. They urged him to mingle more with his people, and especially to beware of foreigners, whose black magic, as they believed, had caused the death of his father. Between these two parties, the foreigners and the native priests, Liholiho hovered indecisively, leaning one day toward this side and the next day toward the other, sometimes playing his role in the sacrificial mysteries, and sometimes deriding beliefs he only pretended to share. Weeks passed by in this fashion when, on August 20, 1819, the armed corvette *Uranie* visited the archipelago. Two of the leading chiefs, Kalaimoku, whose functions corresponded to those of prime minister, and his brother Boki, a man of daring spirit with a taste for adventure, yielded to the persuasions of the chaplain of the *Uranie* and allowed themselves to be baptized. Their example in no degree influenced Kamehameha II, but it did induce Kaahumanu to take an important step. She presented herself to the king, insisted with great eloquence on the evils entailed by the superstitious native practices, reminding him of the recent debauches, and pointed to the spectacle of his people being destroyed, indeed decimated, by these appalling human sacrifices. She concluded by advising him above all to abolish the tabu: for the violation of tabu, especially when punishable by death, was an exceedingly burdensome shackle for the chiefs as much as for the people. As an immediate response, Kamehameha arose, betook himself to the royal veranda where the chiefesses were eating, entered, sat down among them, and proceeded to eat. No more public occasion could have been devised for breaking the tabu that forbade the men, on the most solemn penalty, to consume food prepared for the women. A long wailing cry, "The tabu is abolished!", echoed throughout the entire island. It was a cry of liberation.

Within a very short period all the harsh barriers imposed down the centuries were overturned; but, as usually happens in such situations, license unreined soon followed upon a religious despotism that had known no bounds. Everyone in the circle of the king and the regent hastened not only to imitate but also to surpass the example of their superiors. Indignant priests and soothsayers, scolding at everyone, withdrew into the hinterlands, where they labored to reawaken the hatred of conquered tribes, stirring up the ashes of religious passion and attributing to the advice and example of foreigners the disenchantment of the chiefs with their ancient gods. The divine wrath, they declared, would not be slow to manifest itself and its results would be devastating. While this storm was gathering, Kamehameha II held feast after feast, lighthearted as ever and interested only in his revels, frivolously wasting all the treasure amassed by his father. The burden of governing the kingdom was carried on by Kaahumanu; but, deaf to her councils and sunk in pleasure's embrace, Kamehameha took no steps to avert the perils threatening him.

Kaahumanu alone remained vigilant. Though she too had plunged into all manner of extravagances, unsurprising enough in one of her sensual and passionate disposition, she nevertheless did not fail to follow events with an alert eye, for she was not solely preoccupied with her sordid love affairs. When in February of 1820 the revolution struck, the enemy found her to be quite prepared to resist. The battle was long and very terrible. Incited by their priests, by whom they had been led to believe that they were obeying their old gods, several thousand natives rebelled and threatened because of their numbers to exterminate the paltry array of royal troops that Kaahumanu had united in behalf of the king. In order to protect the son, the veterans of Kamehameha I performed prodigies of valor. Thanks to the foresight of the regent, they had in their possession numerous rifles, a circumstance which assured them a splendid victory at Kuamoo. At this time, fighting among the ranks of the royal troops, there happened to be a young warrior-chief who later was to play an important role in the history of the Hawaiian Islands. His name will recur often in these pages, and even more within my memories. He was called Kekuanaoa. The father of two later kings, he died only recently at Honolulu, at an advanced age, honored by the tributes and regrets of all. When I left Honolulu on July 22, 1868, he came aboard my ship to bid me farewell. It was not without deep feeling, and a sad intuition of his approaching death, that I clasped the loyal hand of this old man for whom I felt such keen affection and sincere respect.

Hardly known before this period, Kekuanaoa proved in the bloody battle of Kuamoo his rare courage combined with calm judgment. As reward for his services, he was given the rank of king's treasurer and inspector for the sale of sandalwood. Kamehameha's policy of restraint assured him of military success. The defeated enemy, having acknowledged their submission, were not executed but proceeded to report back to their home districts concerning the fearsome military strength of the king and their experience of his magnanimity.

While these events were taking place in the islands, a ship flying the American flag, the *Thaddeus,* whose arrival marked the beginning of a new era, was slowly approaching the shores of the archipelago, bringing aboard it the first Christian missionaries sent to the Hawaiian Kingdom. The adventurous spirit of the American people was just beginning its maritime competition with the commercial genius of the English. American fishing vessels were sailing northward as far as the polar seas in search of whales. Though whales had been hunted for centuries in the North Atlantic, by 1820 the Americans were pursuing them in the famous region of the Northwest Passage and into the mysterious waters along the Gulf of Ocholk [Okhotsk] and the Behring [Bering] Straits. Kamehameha's victories, together with the relative security that was their consequence, had made the Hawaiian Islands an admirable rallying ground for reprovisioning the hardy whaling crews. Their tales had called attention to these new parts, for the men were not silent regarding the marvels of the Hawaiian climate nor its health-giving virtues and various local products. At Boston one had heard talk of the conqueror's wish to know more about the Christian religion, his dislike of the barbarous rites of paganism, his kindly outlook on foreigners, and the delay shown by England in sending to him a band of missionaries as he had entreated.

The religious societies of New England were ambitious for the honor of evangelizing the islands. The shipwrights of New Bedford and New Haven speculated about the enormous advantages to be afforded them by the harbors and roadsteads of the Hawaiian chain of islands, situated so conveniently near the new fisheries, where their ships would find awaiting them a natural haven for use as winter quarters. The merchants of New York, whose enterprising zeal increased with each success, hoped to open up new markets for their trade. As a consequence, the government of the United States, having advantageously concluded the War of 1812 against England, was now striving for the honor of outshining its rival and extending its political influence into ever more distant spheres. Religious sentiments, commercial instinct, patriotic ambitions—those powerful impulses so characteristic of the American temperament—all coincided and harmonized in favor of such a project, of which the groundwork and support, in the form of human sympathy and Christian devotion, never for one instant faltered.

The *Thaddeus* dropped anchor in the roadstead at Kailua on Hawaii on April 4, 1820. The missionaries on the same day were informed of the recent death of Kamehameha I and the succession of his son to the throne. If the news of the defeat suffered by the supporters of paganism struck a note of encouragement, the scandalous tales of the king's debauches, his religious skepticism and his love of pleasure, caused the missionaries to deplore the death of his father, whom they had expected to depend on for their protection. Circumstances had indeed changed mightily since that day when, full of hope and new-kindled yearning, they had left the United States bringing with them their wives and children. Above all, they trembled for the sake of their little ones amidst such a dissolute people as those they beheld, just before disembarking, indulging before their very eyes in orgies and outrages of every possible description.

Before leaving the ship, in order to conform to the laws of the country, they sent a message to the king and to the regent Kaahumanu asking their permission to remain in Hawaii for the purpose of providing education for native children; instructing them in the knowledge of the true God; and teaching the Kanakas various skills and trades: in short, everything was to be just as Kamehameha I had so long and so earnestly desired. The king assembled his council of advisers for study of this request. The leading members held divergent opinions. A certain set of foreigners, who had hitherto enjoyed easy access to the governing chiefs, and especially those settlers and traders who had so pleasantly prospered by catering to native vices and accepting chiefly generosity, viewed with distaste the arrival of the newcomers. These members of the foreign community deeply distrusted the consequences of missionary influence and example, and overlooked no means of arousing the apprehensions of the chiefs. To the younger ones, they predicted the end of their licentious ways and their pleasures; to the older folk, they made out that the English missionaries requested by Kamehameha I, at his meeting with Vancouver, would arrive any one of these days and that to admit these intruders from America, citizens of a country only recently at war with England, would mean offending their powerful protectress. And they recalled finally the desire of Kamehameha to cultivate the friendship of England, the benefits from Britain he had received, the promises of further support, the assurances given.

Only Kaahumanu argued and fought for the admission of the American missionaries. It was her persistence that at last triumphed over the irresolution of the king and the objections of the chiefs. When the requested permission was conceded, the American missionaries landed in these islands where they were to play so noteworthy and so diversely appreciated a role.

When in 1857* I visited the island of Hawaii for the first time, I stayed for a while at the home of an old settler, John Parker. I shall have occasion to speak of him again later on. He passed along to me some very odd historical details about the arrival of the missionaries in the islands. In reply to my question about the attitude of the natives concerning the newcomers, he told me of the astonishment of the Kanakas as they watched the missionaries landing at Kawaihae. He depicted these good people as they appeared at close quarters, coping with the practical difficulties of first getting settled. The white women in particular, he told me, left the natives absolutely dumbfounded. Accustomed to seeing their own women so very lightly clothed, with bare throat and naked breasts, the natives attributed the high-necked gowns worn by the foreigners to their fear of the cold. The desire of the natives to put the ladies at ease led them to make certain investigations that greatly alarmed the strangers, who misunderstood the purpose of these attentions. The chiefs therefore were obliged to forbid such excesses in curiosity and zeal. Yet this unsophisticated scrutiny was the principal hardship that the missionary wives had to endure, for at no time either then or since has a single example occurred of a white woman being molested by a native. I regret to add that the same claim cannot be made concerning the behavior of their American compatriots.

The king was indifferent to the fate of the missionaries, whom he tolerated only out of respect for Kaahumanu; he considered he had done enough in allowing their band to remain. At the beginning, he paid them little attention. However, true to his hospitable temperament, and moved by his own sympathy for the missionaries, my host, Mr. Parker, went to great lengths to help them. He sent them food, cattle, and fruits. By his example he attracted the natives to do likewise, who for their part set about building cottages to provide shelter for the newcomers, and finally a large barnlike hall, which served the double function of schoolhouse and place of worship. Though they were hardly settled down, and had only a little recovered from the first painful impressions produced by a welcome so different from the one they had been expecting, the missionaries began to teach the children, and on their own part they set about studying the language of the country.

As I have mentioned, writing and consequently reading were unknown to the natives. The chants alone preserved the memory of past events. Having

---

*See footnote at the end of chapter 5. [A. L. K.]

originated in Malaysia, the kanaka language was a variant of languages still in use in the great islands and archipelagoes of Southeast Asia. Rich in vowels, poor in consonants, with a total of only seventeen letters, simple in appearance and extremely complicated in reality, the language gave the missionaries much difficulty. It demanded of them a plodding perseverance amounting to heroism to triumph over this obstacle to their educational projects, and to transform this primitive language into a written one with its own principles, rules, and grammar. Their devotion was equal to the loftiness of their task; and if later, in the course of this account, I should seem to pass a severe judgment on certain attitudes of missionaries and their successors (while entirely respecting them as men) and should also later find myself obliged to disagree with them along political lines, I still do only pay homage to the truth when I add here my own testimony to that of other contemporary witnesses. Here I would speak, first of all, in profound admiration of the immense services which these folk, isolated as they were in the middle of the Pacific, have rendered to the cause of civilization and humanity.

Five legitimate wives (of whom three were his father's daughters by another wife) plus an army of concubines were not enough for Liholiho. Seizing upon one of his father's ideas, and rashly excited by a desire for an ocean voyage, Liholiho dreamed of traveling to Tahiti to marry Queen Pomare and thereby add a new chain of islands to the one he was governing so wretchedly. His approaching departure served as a pretext for innumerable farewell feastings, and for those habitual orgies by which he was exhausting his treasury. Kaahumanu, however, though spasmodically forgetful of her recent missionary protégés, little by little drew nearer to their orbit and followed their progress with benevolent curiosity. Education obsessed her. Deserting the playing cards that had become her liveliest passion once age had cooled her more lascivious enthusiasms, the regent often sat perched on a school bench and, gravely bowing over her lessons and manuscripts, forced herself to learn to read. When at last she became impatient with the confusing characters traced by hands little schooled in such exercises, she did not rest until a printing press was established by the missionaries. On January 7, 1822, the first page proof in Kanaka was lifted from the mission presses. On the following August 11 was celebrated the first Christian marriage. In September no fewer than 500 scholars of all ages and ranks were to be found in the commodious shed now grown much too cramped for its educational purposes.

The chiefs observed, some with satisfaction and others with indifference, the progress the missionaries were making; but hostility had now disappeared. Wholly submerged in their tasks, the newcomers carefully avoided becoming involved in the dissensions among the chiefs, and they shepherded their new disciples by force of kindness and sound methods. One unforeseen circumstance helped them to dispel the unfriendly atmosphere which some of the foreigners had succeeded in generating against them by predicting that England would cast a disapproving eye on their admission into the islands. The British ruler sent a gift to Kamehameha II, a sailing schooner fully armed, named the *Prince Regent.* This vessel arrived in September and afforded the king much pleasure. He received with high honors the commanding officer charged with presenting him with the schooner and seized upon the occasion to ask the British emissary whether there had not been some delay in the arrival of the missionaries from England. On this point it was not possible to give a precise answer, but the commander assured Kamehameha II that England had noted without the slightest jealousy the welcome bestowed upon the Americans.

The subsequent arrival of the Reverend William Ellis, an English missionary from Tahiti, and of Messrs. Tyerman and Bennet, authorized by the London Missionary Society to visit the islands of Oceania, and more particularly the good relations which reigned between these gentlemen and the Americans, calmed all suspicions. Reassured on this matter and grateful for the evidences of interest he had just received, Kamehameha II abandoned his project of a voyage to Tahiti. He now thought only of a journey to England in order to thank the regent. Above all, he wanted to visit that Europe which he had heard mentioned so often and whose celebrated wonders so much excited his eager imagination.

Kaahumanu, who had tried by every device to dissuade Liholiho from the Tahiti expedition, did not oppose this new idea, which was debated in October at a solemn session of the high chiefs. The majority were of the opinion that Kamehameha would do well to carry out the plan. An English vessel, the *Eagle,* was immediately chartered and the regency was placed in the hands of Kaahumanu, who was to govern the kingdom during Liholiho's absence. Kauikeaouli,* a son of Kamehameha I, was named heir apparent.

Kamehameha II took with him to England his favorite wife, Kamamalu, her brother Boki, Liliha, Boki's wife, and Kekuanaoa. Preparations were speeded and on November 27, 1823, the king and his suite embarked at Honolulu. Thousands of natives were present at this leave-taking, which they watched with sorrow. The most lugubrious prophesies circulated among them, for they considered their king already as good as dead. Disturbed by

---

*A younger brother of Kamehameha II, Kauikeaouli (1813–1854) reigned as Kamehameha III until his death, which occurred on December 15, 1854, only a few months before the arrival of the Varignys on February 18, 1855. [A. L. K.]

sad premonitions, Kamamalu embarked last of all. At the moment of stepping aboard the shallop which was to take her aboard, she turned around and according to native custom, as her eyes welled with tears, chanted an impromptu elegy upon the land she was never to see again:

> Farewell to all you skies and lands!
> To all you mountains and now this sea,
> And, O, to you my companions and subjects,
> Farewell! Farewell!
> Land for which my father struggled,
> Land of his most zealous care,
> We now bid you perhaps forever
> Farewell!

Only wailing and sobs were heard in reply. The *Eagle* hoisted sail and disappeared into the darkling night.

At the moment Kamehameha II left Hawaii to sail for England, Kaumualii, former king of the island of Kauai, lay at the point of death. Conquered by Kamehameha I, he had received in reward for his submission the title of Governor of Kauai. In his last will and testament, Kaumualii had been faithful to his sworn word and had named Kamehameha II as his heir and assigned to him all the lands which Kamehameha I had permitted Kaumualii to keep. A populous and warlike community dwelt on Kauai, the most remote island of the group. Never until recently, and then only indirectly, had Kauai known the yoke of the conqueror. Less afflicted by intermittent warfare, and as a result more rich and productive than the other islands, Kauai was linked by only a very flimsy chain to the rest of the archipelago. Now the death of the chief had broken the weak tie, and communication with Honolulu was infrequent. In fact, news of the death of Kaumualii had barely reached the queen regent when the high chiefs of Kauai, meeting at Wailua, the main settlement of the island, already agreed unanimously to ignore the will of their late king in order to proclaim the independence of the island and to offer the royal headship to Humehume, son of Kaumualii. They had dispatched a message to Humehume, the gist of which was as follows: "Join with us. You will be our king. This island will be yours, just as in olden times it was your father's."

Kalaimoku, who was serving the queen regent as her prime minister, was at that time on Kauai. An energetic and resolute man, he followed as long as possible a policy of resistance and delay in order to give Kaahumanu time enough to come to his aid. He locked himself up in the fort at Waimea, where he would be secure for a while, and sent a schooner to Honolulu bringing news of the rebellion. Upon his advice, Mr. Bingham and Mr. Whitney, who had recently been sent by the mission to carry on their work on Kauai, embarked from that island for Honolulu with their families. At the moment of their departure, a young rebel chief was officially escorted aboard the vessel, having been seized by Kalaimoku as a prisoner. Off the north coast of the island, the native captain ordered that the chief be brought up to the bridge. He was a very tall young man of imposing presence. He climbed to the deck slowly, saying to the men around him, "I know what to expect." At the moment he placed his foot on the last step of the stairway, the captain struck him down with a knife wound, remarking: "With the compliments of Kalaimoku." The young man's body was dumped into the sea. Some other prisoners of the lowest rank were massacred in the same manner. Thus were treated prisoners of state after the abolition of human sacrifice.

Immediately after receiving the message sent by her faithful minister, the queen regent dispatched a first enforcement of 1,000 elite warriors under the command of one of the finest lesser chiefs, Hoapili. Kalaimoku's effective resistance disconcerted the besieging forces, who found themselves fighting in the open, without cover, and handicapped by the loss of many of their members. The arrival of Hoapili permitted the besieged warriors to regain the offensive. Realizing his defeat, Humehume sought refuge in the mountains. A little later, when he was captured, he was brought to Honolulu and there died. Kaahumanu, accompanied by various chiefs of Hawaii, Maui, and Oahu, and escorted by a war flotilla, arrived to take possession of the island in the name of Kamehameha II. The vanquished chiefs were sent into exile on other islands, and their lands were distributed among the friends and favorites of the regent.

The determination of Kaahumanu, admirably seconded by the courage and devotion of Kalaimoku, had saved the kingdom from a great danger. She had proved herself worthy of the trust of Kamehameha I, who died believing he could not have assigned the fulfillment of all his labors to more valiant hands. Her return to Honolulu was a genuine triumph. More than ever, all heads bowed down to the very ground before the haughty and imperious queen regent, whose pride knew no boundaries. This Semiramis of the Pacific was surely one of the oddest and most astonishing characters in the entire history of the islands.

Tall like all the chiefs, who are easily recognizable because of their height, Kaahumanu, who had been lovely and graceful in her youth, during the period we are concerned with was a colossal mass of flesh. Its cause was not merely her hearty meals but also her habits of constant repose. The greater part of the day she passed semicouchant on her native mats, playing cards, reading, or chatting with her ladies-in-waiting and male courtiers. Her corpulence was a distinctive badge of her rank. Losing it, she would have been destroyed. She walked but rarely. Whenever she grew weary of rest and wished to visit one of her numerous properties or take a turn about the town, her stalwart bearers transported her in a litter. During her progress everyone removed headgear and bowed low. Everyone trembled at her slightest gesture, her lovers most of all, for she crushed them equally whether with her scorn or her overwhelming favors. They did not approach her except by crawling on their knees when, at the very most, she would nonchalantly deign to extend a single finger to chiefs of highest rank.

At the palace in Honolulu hangs a portrait of Kaahumanu (painted it is true by an untrained hand) which successfully captures the queen's air of hauteur together with her lively, intelligent eyes. She is dressed in a long tunic falling loosely in generous folds around an enormous body; the carriage of her head is handsome; the nose prominent and commanding, rather flat; the lips very full and sensual; the swarthy hair abundant and slightly wavy, like that of all the native women, caught up at the back of her neck and thus reminiscent of the European fashion of the period. It is impossible when seeing this portrait not to recognize a woman of regal power and voluptuous presence, brimming with aristocratic pride and endowed with a rare force of character.

If I insist on the distinguishing traits of Kaahumanu at this epoch of our concern, it is because there was then at work in her an amazing transformation, symptoms of which had already shown themselves on various occasions. Indeed, these were now about to express themselves with that impassioned energy which she poured into all her revolutionary achievements. She was pondering nothing less than whether or not to break entirely with paganism and to sweep all her people along with her toward the new religion which the missionaries had begun so humbly to preach. Used to regarding her merest wishes as laws, and her mere personal example quite as authoritative as the settled beliefs of others, she never suspected that they would hesitate to follow her along the path she wanted to lead them. She quite expected that the pressure of necessity would extinguish any resistance if, improbably, as she believed, any resistance should raise its head. She began by reforming her own conduct. She pushed away her lovers as one might push away lackeys; her ladies-in-waiting set about imitating her, so far as they were capable, but with regret. The card game had ended and she gave orders that the cards be burned; thus were the openly defied idols smashed. She summoned the soothsayers, and adepts in sacrificial mysteries within her entourage, and informed them that they must cease dreaming dreams and abandon their bogus magical exercises. Kalaimoku, impressed by her example, was likewise converted. Together they compiled severe laws against immorality, gambling, the drinking of fiery spirits, belief in the native gods. Incontinence would be punishable by death; enormous penalties were to be levied against persons who touched brandy or rum. Finally, the summary order was given to break up and burn all idols, and to worship in the style of the new religion. These laws were all put in effect simultaneously, so that the people learned at one and the same time that Kaahumanu herself had now accepted the Christian faith, and that therefore they too, the people, must likewise become Christians.

What was the role of the missionaries in this new-model coup d'état that decreed a change of religion as one would decree a police ordinance? It would be hard to say. But I believe their responsibility was not so grave as their enemies are pleased to insist, and that rather than rushing to urge Kaahumanu into her violent measures, the missionaries had tried to hold her back. Furthermore, the Queen Regent was never the woman to negotiate or confer; and even had she done so, she would probably not have made much sense of their arguments and sage advice. She acted on this occasion as she had acted throughout her life: she detested delays, the dull time-consuming business of arrangement-making in human affairs. What she wanted she commanded: *Hoc volo, sic jubeo, sit pro ratione voluntas.* *

For a period, at least, the facts justified her actions. Used to complying with the wishes of the chiefs, whom they regarded as infallible, the Kanakas were for the moment overcome by the daring of the innovators. Suspended between their fear of distant gods and the formidable immediacy of Kaahumanu, they trembled and obeyed. Thus they commenced the labors of destruction just as they had been commanded to do. Down tumbled the idols, and the gods said nothing. Here and there, however, whispered curses greeted the new decrees; but dissimulation (that spontaneous resource of the weak and the oppressed) became the watchword of the malcontents. Nevertheless it was not among the advocates of paganism, nor peculiarly among the priests and soothsayers who lived by virtue of the common superstitions, that the fiercest angers were expressed. Foreigners already settled in the islands, such as agents for whaling vessels or factors in the sandalwood trade, but most of all the sailors who came to Honolulu for rest and recreation, and who there had acquired a taste for liberty without check, hailed Kaahumanu's edicts at first with general disbelief. Later, however, after they had witnessed barrels of the illicitly unloaded brandy being emptied publicly onto the beach, and then finally when the sailors encountered the severe legal

---

*This is my will, thus I command, let my wishes be reason enough. Juvenal, *Satires* VI, l. 223. [A. L. K.]

penalties imposed on their lusts by the authorities, they turned their anger directly against the missionaries. To missionary intrigue the sailors attributed the sudden, and totally unexpected, veering about of the moral weathervane in the Sandwich Islands.

The storm gathered. Kaahumanu, unmoved and unyielding, saw to it that the decrees were executed. The pagan priests fled for refuge to Hawaii, to the volcanic home of the goddess Pele. There they awaited the return of Kamehameha II, upon whose volatile imagination they hoped to have an impact. Meanwhile, the disgruntled foreigners offered for the benefit of the natives the example of their continuous grumbling complaints. Such was the state of affairs when, on March 20, 1825, a whaling schooner, the *Elmira*, brought the news that Kamehameha II and Kamamalu had died in London from measles, on June 8 and 14 of the preceding year, and that the English frigate *Blonde*, dispatched posthaste by the British government, was now on the high seas carrying the body of the Hawaiian king back to his islands. It had taken nine months for the news to arrive from England.

Having sailed from Hawaii on November 27, 1823, aboard the *Eagle*, the king, his wife, and suite had refreshed themselves at Rio de Janeiro, where the emperor of Brazil received them with the highest courtesy. On May 22 the vessel arrived at Portsmouth. The king was greeted by the Honorable Frederick Byng and conducted to apartments for himself and his entourage at the Osborne Hotel. It was some while before tailors and modistes were able to prepare the royal party for their presentation at court. When at last they appeared for this event, if one is to believe the chronicles and newspapers of the period, the impression that they produced was entirely favorable. Feasted and entertained by the English aristocracy, promenaded from ball to ball, invited to numerous official dinners and banquets of state, propelled so abruptly out of their habitual orbit and moving without transition from the calm, indolent life aboard ship to the feverish activity and commotion of a world capital, the Hawaiians were naturally affected in health. They were already indisposed when their majordomo came down with the measles. The next day the king in turn showed symptoms; the queen, Boki, and Kekuanaoa were also attacked during the epidemic, though in a day or so these last two were out of danger. Kamehameha himself made a partial recovery, and indeed on June 4 he was well enough to hold an audience for Mr. Charlton, appointed by the British government as its commissioner in the Hawaiian Islands. The next day the king suffered a relapse. The queen lingered just this side of death. Kamehameha II had himself brought to her side; and she died holding his hand. The king died four days later, his grief having completed the work of his disease. Before his death he commanded that his body and that of Kamamalu be taken back to Honolulu and there be entombed.

The king of England, George IV, when informed of these melancholy events, summoned Boki and Kekuanaoa to Windsor Castle. He told them how deeply sorry he felt, announcing that he had fitted out a ship, the frigate *Blonde,* to sail them back to their islands, carrying with them the bodies of their dead sovereigns. He further entrusted to their charge messages for Kaahumanu and the young king, recommending them to give their cordial welcome to the American missionaries, and to follow their suggestions and advice, and he promised them his own protection and friendship. On September 28, 1824, the *Blonde,* commanded by Lord Byron,* hoisted sail at Portsmouth, and after calling at Rio and Valparaiso to replenish stores arrived in sight of Lahaina on May 4, 1825.

The principal chiefs, followed by throngs of Hawaiians, went to greet Boki and Kekuanaoa on the beach. All bared their heads as they stood weeping at the sight of the coffins enclosing the bodies of Kamehameha and Kamamalu. The chiefs immediately joined together in council to hear from Boki's lips the details they were so eager to learn. Boki told of the illness and then of the death of the king; the courtesies with which they had all been honored by George IV; the messages with which he had charged them; and the recommendations which he now wished to transmit at the king of England's behest. The next day the queen regent received in solemn audience Lord Byron, who presented to her the gifts for the young Hawaiian king. The funeral ceremony was held on May 11. Following native custom, these rites continued for a period of days and it was not until June 11 that the council of chiefs proclaimed Kamehameha III as king of the Sandwich Islands. Kaahumanu was declared regent, and indeed it required hands as powerful as hers to exorcise the dangers multiplying on all sides, not the least of which was the succession to the throne of a little boy nine years old.

*The commander of the *Blonde* was Captain the Right Honorable George Anson, Lord Byron, R.N. (1789–1858), a cousin of the poet. [A. L. K.]

CHAPTER 4

BIRTH OF CONSTITUTIONAL GOVERNMENT

Reign of Kamehameha III.—Attempt at moral reforms.—Opposition of foreigners.—The Dolphin.*—A new Jason.—Death of the queen regent.—Religious rivalries.—The prime minister.—Political intrigues.—Death of Kamehameha III.*

Carried away at first by their immediate emotions, and grieving deeply over the death of Kamehameha II, the high chiefs were quite swept out of their usual reserve toward the American missionaries. After they had heard the recommendations of George IV, as explained by Boki with all the fervor of his intensely emotional character, the chiefs adopted a proposal submitted to them by Kaahumanu. Her plan was to invite Mr. Hiram Bingham, the most influential member of the Protestant mission, to be present at the council meeting at which the succession of Kamehameha III was to be officially approved. By this device, of inviting the most esteemed among the missionaries to share in their deliberations, the majority of the chiefs simply wished to acknowledge their respect for the advice of the king of England and simultaneously to give proof to the missionaries in general of their trust in them.

As a new and impetuously earnest convert, the hopeful Kaahumanu was also desirous of something more. She pursued her program of reform without a moment's pause. Accustomed to prompt and unquestioning obedience, she dreamed of transforming the moral attitudes of the Hawaiians by force of governmental decrees. She believed that she could rely on the support and counsel of the Reverend Mr. Bingham—an ardent missionary, a believer in coercive methods, a man used to seeing the natives obey without a murmur the wishes of the queen regent and the chiefs. Like all his coreligionists, Bingham was profoundly pained by the licentious behavior of the Hawaiians, which presented so formidable an obstacle to propagating the mission's religious and moral aims. For his benefit, Kaahumanu drew a vivid picture of the character, unfortunately all too true, of traditional kanaka practices; she attacked particularly, and with eloquence, the way Hawaiian women regularly visited aboard the trading vessels and the native gunboats, the orgies that took place in the harbor, and, above all, the terrible effects in the country of venereal diseases, hitherto unknown, but already threatening to exterminate the native population. She imperiously concluded by demanding from the council drastic laws to suppress such excesses. A law was at once passed to ban visits to ships by native women and to punish all transgressions with severe penalties.

Among the sailors this law, so just and reasonable in itself, caused much grumbling and indeed a potentially fierce resistance. It interfered with one of their most accustomed forms of license, for with shameful laxity they had accommodated themselves to wickedness and had come to regard the islands as a sort of "free city" where they could flaunt their vices and abandon themselves, far from family and home, without the slightest moral restraint. They did not forget how many times the missionaries in writings and preachings had focused attention upon their evil ways. The sailors knew that it was the missionaries who originally had presented to the notice of chiefs and governors the countermeasures needed. When they realized that Mr. Bingham himself had attended the council meeting that had approved the decree, the sailors joined forces with the whole floating population of Honolulu and Lahaina which made a living off them and profited from their corruption. Angrily objecting to the council's recent action, the troublemakers said that this law tore away the mask and revealed how the missionaries behind the scenes were exploiting the power of government in order to promote their own religious designs. Not being able to succeed by persuasion, the missionaries now wanted to command. From this period, in fact, dates the influence openly exercised by the Protestant missionaries upon the Hawaiian government: an influence often calculated to aid a good and just cause but a cause that also sometimes ended in serving blind and intolerant religious passions.

My readers are no doubt surprised that some Europeans and Americans, persons presumably brought up according to Christian principles, thoroughly familiar with civilized laws and standards of conduct, ventured to object when these half-barbarous natives, in league with the missionaries who sought to convert them to the true God, now attempted by legal means to prevent the prostitution of their wives and sisters and daughters. One blushes in shame at the notion that a naval officer, in the uniform of his service moreover, would claim it as a right to bring on board ship a certain number of women to slake the brutal appetites of a crew. Nevertheless, such incidents actually occurred. Civilization does not always manifest itself before the wondering gaze of primitive people in its fairer aspects. If one were to examine closely the causes of innumerable conflicts that have arisen in the still unfamiliar islands of the Pacific Ocean, collisions which have given several of these places a forbidding reputation, one would find very often that the aggression, injustice, and violence were initiated by white men and that the natives, though accused of the attack, acted only in self-defense.

On June 14, 1826, a man-of-war of the United States, the *Dolphin,* sailing under the order of Lt. Comdr. J. Percival, arrived at Honolulu. When warned of the strictly enforced laws, he scorned the regulations and succeeded in violation of them in bringing on board a number of native women. When these returned to shore they were arrested and jailed. Lieutenant Commander Percival demanded that they be freed. At first fearful and uncertain of their prerogatives, the chiefs seemed inclined to give way. Kaahumanu, however, refused, and her resistance was blamed on her missionary advisers, whose influence supposedly could be detected in every act of government. The sailors of the *Dolphin,* encouraged by their commanding officer, armed themselves and went ashore, heading for the residence of Mr. Bingham, where they attempted to force an entrance. A riot broke out involving sailors and natives; only the intervention of the chiefs prevented bloodshed. The next day, the commander of the *Dolphin* announced that he would do nothing to restrain his crew if the present law were enforced. The intimidated governor, fearing a bloody confrontation, gave way, and numerous boatloads of women continued to board the vessel. The *Dolphin* remained at Honolulu one month, and for one month the orgies aboard ship continued. One of these occasions was especially outrageous, and when Kaahumanu who had been out of town learned of what was taking place, she informed the governor of her sharp disapproval and set out straightway for Honolulu. Whether the commander of the *Dolphin* did not care to risk his chances in a dispute with a woman as strong-minded as the queen regent, or whether he was himself disgusted with the misconduct of his crew, he hoisted sail before Kaahumanu returned. Her presence on the scene restored order and validated respect for law, but still failed to bring such conflicts to an end. After the precedent set by the *Dolphin,* the execution of the law became a simple question of force. Everywhere, when a ship arrived in port, the captain would insist on the shameful privilege of permitting women aboard.

Nevertheless, the struggle could not long continue on this ground. In proportion to the development of more direct and frequent communication between the Hawaiian Islands and Europe and America, the facts of the Hawaiian situation became better known, and even the most stubborn supporters of absolute license fully realized that public opinion would rapidly turn against them if they boasted flagrantly of their sins and selfish desires. Disregarding for a while both the law and the government, they turned their attacks against the mission itself. What was most unfortunate was that their religious adversaries likewise entered the contest.

As their influence increased, the missionaries marveled at the ease with which the natives, obedient both to the decrees and to the personal example of the queen regent, were being converted to the Protestant faith. Without knowing exactly what they were doing, I would say, and perhaps without even desiring it, but impelled by their strong convictions, they were seeking to rule over Hawaii with a Bible and to inaugurate an experiment in government-by-theocracy. Though presumably Christians, the natives were by no means truly converted, but simply grafted hypocrisy onto their other vices. Excessive penalties imposed against minor pleasures made law enforcement impossible or repelled an honest conscience. Nevertheless, after banning immorality and misrule, the missionaries now unwisely intensified their campaign of purification. They showed no understanding of the errors of the past, ignoring the fact that one does not transform the character of a people by means of legal texts, and certainly not within a period of several months.

At this time of exacerbated feelings, of both foreign and domestic antagonisms, the tense situation lacked only a leader. The malcontents found him in the new British consul, Mr. Richard Charlton. Apparently alarmed by the rapid progress of the American Protestant mission, jealous of the influence of Mr. Bingham upon the chiefs, and convinced whether rightly or wrongly that the United States was yearning to take possession of the Hawaiian Islands and that the missionaries were preparing the way, Mr. Charlton declared himself as their adversary. A thorough Protestant himself, he attempted to add to the missionaries' difficulties by setting himself up as an advocate of a Roman Catholic mission. This idea was not at all a new one and had already reached the stage of execution. In 1826, Pope Leo XII had appointed the Reverend Father Bachelot as apostolic representative in the Sandwich Islands, and the latter arrived at Honolulu on July 4, 1827. During the preceding March, Kalaimoku, faithful friend and right-hand man of Kaahumanu, had died; she alone continued as regent and Boki, brother of Kalaimoku, had been appointed guardian of the young king and named governor of Oahu.

At that time the Hawaiian laws prevented any foreigner from becoming a permanent resident in the islands without first procuring an official permission to do so, signed by the governor of the island where the foreigner wanted to settle. Father Bachelot accordingly made application to Boki. The queen regent, warned by the Protestant mission of the ecclesiastical role and the intentions of the newcomer, notified Boki that he should absolutely refuse. In reply to his request for an explanation, Father Bachelot was informed that a Protestant mission had already been established in the Hawaiian Islands for several years, and that to admit the Catholic mission would excite religious disputation. This would only weaken in the native mind the sense of moral responsibility and the inward conviction required for their conversion. Boki went on to say that in the opinion of the queen regent and the chiefs, such religious arguments would create rival political parties in the kingdom and thus lead to civil strife. He finally instructed Father Bachelot that the priest could remain in the islands no more than two months and that he would urgently advise him to leave Hawaii by that time.

There is no doubt that at the period of this incident the queen regent and the chiefs were merely echoing the ideas of the Protestant mission. Nevertheless, they would never have admitted (as some parties insisted) that this exclusion policy had been dictated to the missionary leaders by the United States government in Washington. In my judgment there seems to be no question that the decree had been suggested by Mr. Bingham, and that his energetic and well-received appeal had been made primarily to the chiefs' prejudices and fears.

Though he found himself merely tolerated during his restricted stay, the Reverend Father Bachelot nevertheless established himself in a Hawaiian grass hut. He managed to have a shed constructed of branches and leaves beneath which he celebrated mass. A scattering of Spanish and Portuguese sailors attended these services, together with a small number of natives lured by their curiosity. Throughout all parts of Hawaii the Protestant pulpits echoed with denunciations of the new form of worship. They compared it to those rites used by the natives in olden days to pay homage to Pele, the volcano goddess.

These accusations were as exaggerated as they were unwise. Their only result was to pique the curiosity of the natives further, who on the following Sunday flocked into the Catholic chapel. Among the foreign population, a certain sympathy was expressed for the new missionary in their midst. Some upheld the rights of liberty of conscience; others asked if the accident of being a Roman Catholic is a legitimate justification for an exclusionist policy.

So the weeks slipped by. When summoned to leave, Father Bachelot claimed that there was no available naval vessel sailing for South America, where he wished to journey although he was quite without funds. He had a feeling, however, that supporters of his cause existed in Hawaii. Kaahumanu, whether mislead by her zeal or poorly advised by the missionaries, redoubled her strictures. Not daring to work directly against the foreigners, whom Charlton in his capacity of British consul had taken under his protection, she ordered that the same laws invoked against the natives who practiced pagan worship should henceforth be applied to the natives who took part in the Catholic services. Boki refused to give way when urged by Kaahumanu to carry out orders that he believed to be unenforceable. Disappointed when he saw his advice being ignored and his objections unheeded, Boki became still more alarmed when he realized how much Kaahumanu was dominated by the American missionaries—in fact, she hardly turned more than one distracted ear to the advice of the high chiefs. But Boki was unwilling to submit. As royal guardian and tutor, he won the support of the young king and openly declared himself in favor of resisting the religious ordinance. All the dissidents rallied around him. Boki was well liked and popular, and the disaffected natives were weary of Kaahumanu's iron yoke. Every one of her acts was attributed to the influence of the Protestant mission, which mission was only longing, according to some of its critics, to sell the country to the United States.

Indeed, the kingdom was on the brink of revolution. Kaahumanu had assembled the royal army in order to march against Boki, whose posture, more and more threatening, foreshadowed immediate trouble. The warriors themselves remained hesitant, for the presence of the young king in the opposing camp had shaken their loyalty. The chiefs, meeting in council, decided that Kekuanaoa should approach Boki and attempt to calm him in order to avoid an armed struggle. Kekuanaoa acquitted himself skillfully in this delicate mission, and by his shrewd persuasion led Boki, if not to yield completely to the orders of the queen regent, at any rate to assume an appearance of submission. This at least delayed the looming dangers.

Kaahumanu attempted next to persuade Boki to promise the young king that he would refrain from employing force. Yielding once more to the high chiefs, she decided that the king, who was at that time about sixteen years old, should himself be allowed to take part in the affairs of government. His weak and undecisive character promised certainly to make him a willing instrument in Kaahumanu's hands. In fact, she had no trouble winning his support for those same laws for whose abolition the king's governors had been on the point of running up the banner of revolt.

But while Boki had submitted, his cohorts had by no means all done so; nor, above all, had the foreigners who were urging him on and who were resisting with all their might what they described as the unjust arrogation of authority on the part of the Protestant mission. Encouraged and strengthened by the forbearance of the chiefs, as also by the attitude of the British consul, the foreigners no longer limited themselves merely to blaming and criticizing the new decrees. They sought to undermine their enforcement. Arguing on legal grounds of their nationality, they denied the competence and judicial prerogatives of the local courts and authorities. One recent law inspired and publicly promulgated by the missionaries, when they found themselves powerless to check the licentious behavior of their compatriots, declared that any person who after a certain date lived with a woman as his mistress, and in a state of concubinage, should be considered as having contracted a marriage and assumed civil responsibility *for her and in her behalf*. The truth is that this law applied virtually to almost all the foreigners in the islands, excepting only the missionaries. The measure was unenforceable and remained unenforceable, but it aggravated the ill-feeling toward Mr. Bingham and his colleagues. Fresh efforts were made to persuade Boki to take up arms, depose the queen regent, and seize absolute power in the name of the king—her very recently liberated pupil. Boki perhaps would have bowed to these solicitations, had a new emergency not occurred to divert his restless, vacillating mind away from politics.

Like several other high chiefs, but to an even greater degree, Boki was deeply in debt. A friend of his, one with a taste for adventure, proposed to him a scheme for repairing his fortunes. He told Boki of a Pacific island located somewhere in the southern hemisphere and covered, he said, with sandalwood forests. Sandalwood, being very much prized in China, was becoming quite scarce in the Hawaiian Islands, where it had been the object of extremely shortsighted exploitation. The experience had taught the chiefs to appreciate the value of sandalwood, but not before it was too late, for they had foolishly squandered this source of wealth. Boki's warm imagination kindled at the thought of the treasures awaiting him. Deaf to advice and to the protestations of his family, he fitted out a schooner and accompanied by 179 natives set sail. Nothing further was ever heard of either him or his companions. It is known only that there was a very considerable quantity of gunpowder aboard the vessel and that the ship supposedly had an accident and exploded on the high seas. However, careful inquiries carried out in the regions where Boki was known to have been sailing shed no light on his fate.

Kaahumanu had made no effort to dissuade Boki from his project. She had watched with pleasure as her danger-loving ally made his farewell. His departure having left a vacancy in the office of governor of Oahu, Kaahumanu summoned to the post Liliha, the young king's sister, who was even younger than he. By this step the queen regent complacently believed she would avoid any challenge to her authority, but Liliha followed in the tradition of Boki and refused to inflict upon the Catholic natives the stern laws Kaahumanu had attempted to impose. Determined to have her own way, Kaahumanu did not hesitate to relieve Liliha of the governorship and to give it instead to Kuakini, one of her own faithful supporters. A few days after this last development, the Catholic missionaries received an order to leave the kingdom, and three months later they were forcibly placed aboard ship and transported to San Pedro, on the coast of Baja California. Their converts were treated still more harshly: thrown into prison, condemned to the heaviest labor, placed in chains along with criminals, they were victims of a persecution that only the unexpected death of Kaahumanu, on June 5, 1832, brought to an end. This notable woman, who played so great a role in the history of the islands, at the time of her death was only fifty-eight years old.

If her death meant a deliverance for the Catholics, it was equally a release for the young king, who mourned in the lost Boki the companion of his wildest revels. Certainly Kauikeaouli had never adapted himself to the austere regime prescribed for him by the queen regent. Now free, he flung himself into all the dissipations his pliant character was capable of, after having been so brusquely cut off from his pleasures. Sunk in debauchery, he surrounded himself with Boki's old comrades and repealed Kaahumanu's iron-bound laws. The results were prompt. The people, abandoning themselves utterly, carried on the most brutish orgies. The disturbances at last reached a point where the king himself, appalled by his own actions and their consequences, decided to revive and vigorously enforce those same severe edicts which, as the recent episodes well demonstrated, suppressed immorality without quibbling over principles of justice.

Ironically, the opposition to the religious program of Kaahumanu served all the more to encourage the hopes of the Catholic missionaries. Exiled though they were, these watched events in Hawaii with an attentive eye. Powerful support on high did not come amiss, as when the pope himself exhorted them to persevere and predicted a successful result for their efforts. Their first attempt to stage a return occurred in 1835. In that year, the Reverend Father Walsh, an Irishman whom I saw much of in the islands (he died there only recently, in 1869, head of the Catholic high school, Ahuimanu, a few leagues from Honolulu), disembarked at Honolulu and was able because of his status as a British subject to escape the ostracism to which he was liable in his capacity as Roman Catholic priest. The British consul, Mr. Charlton, always intensely hostile to the American mission and to its head, Mr. Bingham, approved the request of Father Walsh, who was finally authorized to remain in the islands, but on the express condition that he would abstain from preaching Catholicism and from attempting to make converts.

It goes without saying that Father Walsh did not accept this stipulation and paid no attention to it. His presence revived the zeal of the Catholics, and in 1837 the exiled papist missionaries all returned to Honolulu. This audacious act in defiance of the law brought to a climax the displeasure of the Protestant mission and its disciples. Excited by these persons, the chiefs officially ordered the Catholic priests to reembark. They refused to do so. The king then published a royal proclamation banishing the priests forever from the Hawaiian Islands, and they were herded aboard a schooner by force. The captain refused to hoist sail, however, and simply abandoned his vessel to the Hawaiian authorities, thus making them the guilty party for having interfered with his property without his permission.

The arrival in port of a French man-of-war, the *Vénus,* brought the conflict to an end. The commanding officer, M. Du Petit-Thouars, having been informed of events, insisted on an audience with the king. It was a lively session. Among those present were Mr. Bingham and the British consul, Mr. Charlton, who insulted Bingham by declaring that the American missionary was responsible for all actions taken and attributed to Bingham's intolerance the persecutions of which the Catholics were complaining. In order to terminate these tactless and arbitrary decrees, Commander Du Petit-Thouars negotiated with the government a treaty guaranteeing French nationals treatment in keeping with France's status as a most favored nation. Finally, wishing to avoid the wearisome annoyances of a religious debate which threatened to degenerate into a web of political complications, Du Petit-Thouars sailed away after his brief Hawaiian visit. On the third of November following, Monsignor Maigret, vicar apostolic for the Sandwich Islands, arrived at Honolulu with the Reverend Father Bachelot. On November 23, they were forced to reembark and to leave the islands. Father Walsh, always protected by his rights as an English subject, alone remained.

During the next two years the Roman Catholic natives found themselves the object of constant harassment, if not of outright persecution. The spirit of intolerance was triumphant. On July 10 the corvette *Artémise,* commanded by M. Laplace, arrived to request the reason for the banishment of Maigret and Bachelot. M. Laplace further demanded their free readmission, religious toleration for Catholics, and also as a guarantee the deposit aboard his ship of 100,000 francs, a sum which would be returned after the Hawaiian government gave proof of having lived up to its promises. M. Laplace framed his demands in the form of an ultimatum, threatening to bombard the fort in case of refusal. Too weak to resist, the government gave way, and the Reverend Father Walsh celebrated for the first time and in public the ceremonies of the Catholic form of worship.

The reinforced struggle between the two missions thus came to a climax at the very period when paganism was collapsing throughout the islands. The death of Kinau, the last representative among the chiefs of the religious beliefs of their ancestors, confirmed the victory of Christianity. Basically the rival missions were pursuing the same goal: the destruction of the ancient religious teachings and the conversion of the natives to Christ's words.

While they agreed about what was to be torn down, however, they failed to agree about building up. The Protestant mission accused the Catholic priests of idolatry. The latter, however, contended that the Protestant mission was ambitious for power above all else, and that it busied itself primarily with political goals, aspiring rather to add a new domain to the American union (already so expansive) than to lead the Hawaiian people into the fold of the true God. If these charges were to some degree valid ones, for indeed certain members of the Protestant mission did resign from it, apparently, in order to accept paid appointments in the government of Hawaii, nevertheless there was another side to the case. Tahiti was an illustration, for events had happened there recently which had great reverberations throughout the Hawaiian Islands. The Protestant missionaries made the most of these events, according to their own interests. In the eyes of the chiefs, the situation in Tahiti symbolized the ambition of France, and the arbitrary and extreme methods that had, in particular, deprived a small country of its nationality in order to transform it into a colony of a foreign power with which the Tahitians had no affinity whatsoever of race, language, nor even religion.

These discussions, with their bitterness and contention, of which a feeble echo is still heard in Hawaii today, continued throughout the entire reign of Kamehameha III. The Protestant missionaries, heavily predominant in his cabinets, persuaded the king to decide in 1840 to present his people with a constitution. Cast in biblical style, this organic act became nonetheless a great milestone of civilization and of progress beyond anything that had existed in the past. It declared certain civil rights and, more particularly, it established orderly government on a foundation of statute law. Though greatly modified since that time, this enlightened instrument remains one of Kamehameha III's principal claims to the gratitude of his people.

In order to organize the new government, it was necessary to draw upon the talents of persons of experience, with knowledge superior to that possessed by the native chiefs of the time. Dr. Gerrit P. Judd, an American medical missionary, left that post to assume the office of minister of finance. A Scotsman, Mr. R[obert] C[richton] Wyllie, recognized for his various public activities in the islands, became minister of foreign affairs in the new government. Both these men have played prominent parts in Hawaiian history. The first is still living,* though fallen from power, and still wields considerable influence in the country; the second died several years ago. Although I must count Dr. Judd among my political opponents, and sincerely deem it an honor to have always found Mr. Wyllie a faithful friend, I

---

*Dr. Judd's death occurred July 12, 1873. [A. L. K.]

shall try to be fair in my appraisal of both these men. As I have withdrawn from the party struggles which divided us, this task will be a more easy one and I hope to state the truth while remaining impartial.

A man of strongly dictatorial character, deeply emotional under his seeming composure, Dr. Judd is and will continue to be the same kind of North American he was in the year 1840. He arrived in the islands as a young man, after the coming of the earliest Protestant missionaries. He studied the country closely for several years before turning his hand to the business of government. A hard worker, dedicated and authoritarian, with the kind of stubbornness often characteristic of men of limited ideas, Dr. Judd played a very important role in the critical early years of the Hawaiian Kingdom. He indeed labored hard to build on the ruins of a decaying despotism, of a feudal system by then battered and broken, the groundwork of a new political and social order. During the preceding thirty years, the customs and behavior of the natives had become markedly more softened and civilized. Christian doctrine and its teachings, by abolishing human sacrifice, had simultaneously subdued or driven underground the particular brutal traits of character that had served to prop up the old superstitious practices. In 1840 the authority of the high chiefs apparently remained intact, but the common people had observed and well digested the fact that the chiefs themselves had much to learn from the foreigners. The intellectual superiority of the latter had to be admitted, a superiority the natives were even inclined to exaggerate. Everyone became fired with a burning desire for education, a lively curiosity to comprehend and master this new form of civilization, the products of which were beginning to pour into Hawaii from all parts of the globe. During this period the whale fisheries of the North Pacific were attracting numerous whaling vessels to Hawaiian waters; the crews spent their winters mainly recuperating at Honolulu. Ships of trade likewise were calling at the islands, coming or going from Asia or America, and regularly these would pause at Honolulu in order to sell some of their cargo. Finally, a few naval men-of-war were beginning to visit this country, hitherto so little known. Now, however, startling news of Hawaii's progress was receiving wide circulation around the globe through the evangelical labors of the religious societies of Massachusetts.

The institutions of the past had seen their day, as everyone understood, and no one realized this better than did the Hawaiian monarch. Kamehameha III readily assented to giving up some portion of his power in order to carry out the counsel of his missionary advisers, all of whom were strongly imbued with the republican ideas of New England. It was unfortunate that the councillors had so little understanding of how to manage the social and political problems bound to arise during the necessary period of transition.

A Scotsman by birth, Mr. R. C. Wyllie had traveled extensively and acquired a considerable fortune from commercial enterprises in Mexico and the East Indies, until mere chance and his taste for adventure brought him to the Sandwich Islands. What held him there was the appeal of the incomparable climate and the opportunity to study a new civilization in its early stages of development. Equipped with an observant and inquiring mind, Wyllie had compiled and published, under the form of "notes," the results of his sytematic excursions through the several islands. He carried out statistical surveys of Hawaii, including a census of the population, the agricultural products, and the receipts and expenditures of the government. These miscellaneous findings, which one can still consult with profit, and which concluded the generalizations and judgments whose soundness time has verified, had drawn attention to himself and won him the favor of the king, who selected him for a ministerial post in the newly established regime.

In fairness to both Mr. Wyllie and Dr. Judd, it must be stated that neither accepted public office from motives of self-interest. The ambition to serve, the wish to play a public role, alone persuaded both men to accept: by Dr. Judd the post of minister of finance, and by Mr. Wyllie that of minister of foreign affairs.

The native chiefs willingly retired into the background. Their ambition did not extend beyond the desire to assist in a task they regarded as beyond their capacities, but to which they all wanted to lend their loyal cooperation. They had but one goal, that of establishing an orderly system of government, of abandoning anarchy and despotism, of winning through their moderation and wisdom the kind of respect they realized they could never attain by the mere exercise of force.

Kamehameha III was a man of naturally decent character, accommodating and easygoing, though somewhat weak-willed. The older he grew the more he realized the difficulties of his position, and also the flagrantly covetous intentions with which his kingdom was regarded, particularly by the United States. In the eyes of that nation, in point of fact, the philanthropic problem of Hawaii had now become a political problem. After loudly singing the praises of the missionaries, their qualities of devotion, abnegation, and disinterestedness, American authorities and political interests proceeded to employ this assessment of the missionaries as a tactical device, a stratagem for staking out a claim and exercising, under the cover of a deceptive policy of protection, a type of political domination which in the more or less immediate future would result finally in annexation. For a fairly long period the missionaries had already been accused of tending in that direction. I believe that originally the charge was unjust; but I am also convinced that it ceased to be so particularly during the period here under scrutiny.

On the one hand, the American missionaries hated the Catholic missionaries; on the other, they resented the exercise of French power in Hawaii, in particular the quite tactless conduct of our French official representatives, who had displayed toward the king and his chiefs not the slightest delicacy of insight as to the national pride and sensitivity of the Hawaiian natives. These anxieties of the Hawaiians were now joined with the added fear, on the part of the Americans, of eventual military occupation by a French squadron, as had already occurred in Tahiti. For these reasons, members of the American mission saw no prospect of safeguarding their interests except by immediate annexation to the United States. Under the protection of the American flag, they reasoned, they could continue and complete their work of religious propaganda without having to fear the national jealousies of their rivals. They estimated that they had much to gain from such a change. Certainly the natives had nothing to lose by trading an obscure and contemptible claim to national status for the title of citizens of the United States.

These were the somber complexities and intrigues that darkened the last years of the reign of Kamehameha III. Public opinion accused the Protestant missionary party of having initiated and directed the annexation movement. The missionary spokesmen denied the charge. They insisted that the idea of ceding the kingdom to the United States was emanating from the king and had no other source than the fear of seeing his realm share the same fate as Tahiti. Whatever the truth of these various assertions, a petition swarming with signatures, among which figured those of the heads of the missionary party, had been presented to the king. The petition recommended annexation by the United States as the sole means of avoiding forcible seizure of the islands by France. A treaty of cession had even been drafted. The Hawaiian Kingdom was thus on the point of extinction when Kamehameha III suddenly died, on December 15, 1854, before he had signed this document. It is certain that alcoholic excesses, indulged in each day as he kept putting off the signing of the agreement, sometimes on one pretext, sometimes on another, hastened the king's end. It is also certain that the disgraceful methods of intrigue resorted to by the missionary party were ironically turned against their authors.

CHAPTER 5

THE "NEW ERA" OF KAMEHAMEHA IV

Kamehameha IV.—His visit to France.—His cabinet.—Foreign affairs.—My arrival in the islands.—The French consulate.—A legislative session.—A difficult negotiation.—The king's marriage.—Queen Emma.—Princess Victoria.—A courtly tale.—The French treaty.—An urgent reform.

The period of transition ends with Kamehameha III. The struggle between ancient barbarism and emergent civilization ended in the victory of the latter. A young, energetic king, immersed in European ideas, enters on the scene impatient to break with the errors of the past and to free himself from both the yoke of the missionaries and the guardianship of the high chiefs. In preceding pages I was obliged sometimes to consult oral tradition, sometimes incomplete archives. From this point forward I draw upon my own notes and memories. I have seen, I have known personally, the individuals and events remaining to be described. The history I am about to relate is that of the recent past, of yesterday and of today.

Kamehameha III became worn out before he was old. The excesses of his dissipated youth had exhausted him, along with the troubles of his twenty-nine-year reign. He was only forty-one when he died. He left no direct heir, but some years earlier he had adopted as his son and successor his nephew, Prince Alexander Liholiho, younger son of Kekuanaoa and Kinau, herself a daughter of Kamehameha I.

Born on February 9, 1834, the new sovereign was only twenty when the premature death of his uncle called him to the throne. Like all the nobles he was tall, but obesity (another characteristic of nobility) did not disfigure his slender, athletic frame. His features were regular, his forehead high, his smile delightful. Lively, intelligent eyes lent brightness and animation to his very sympathetic facial expression. His manners were those of an English gentleman of aristocratic birth; he gladly adopted a similar style of grooming and dress. Easy and informal in his manner with inferiors, he nevertheless kept them at a definite distance. His mind was more quick of perception than wide-ranging, more aware of surfaces than of depths. His most prominent quality was his imagination: he caught on to an idea very quickly, but he was easily put off and discouraged, and his volatile imagination detracted from his stability and from his firmness in carrying out his plans.

His brother, Prince Lot, his elder by two years (and since then king, under the name of Kamehameha V), presented a conspicuous contrast. By nature less favored, but more sober and reflective, Prince Lot possessed all the qualities lacking in Kamehameha IV, save that gift of personal charm which in the latter made up for all that was missing. The two brothers were united by a most tender and sincere friendship; and indeed, though he was the elder, Prince Lot looked on without the least feeling of jealousy when the partiality of their uncle singled out the younger brother as heir to the throne. He was perfectly contented to become merely his brother's first subject, and this attitude was never, even for a moment, contradicted.

In 1848–1849 the two princes, then respectively fifteen and seventeen years of age, made a trip to Europe. They had successively visited the United States, England, and France, where they had been granted an audience by the prince-president of the Republic. These travels engraved upon the memory of the young Hawaiian princes some very vivid impressions, probably very different from those they had been expected to experience by Dr. Judd, charged with accompanying them on their journey. In the United States they were deeply hurt by the very evident social prejudice aroused by their color, and much offended by the slight distinction drawn between their own copper-hued race and that of the Negro. In England, on the contrary, they received a fine welcome. There they were feted by court and aristocracy; in France, however, political and not social concerns ruled everything. People were polite to them, but nothing more. Thus they returned home profoundly imbued with English ideas and predilections, enthusiastic admirers of a political system whose stability appeared all the more pronounced because of its sharp contrast with what they had seen in revolutionary France and the republican United States. These memories and impressions from his travels abroad permeated the whole reign of Kamehameha IV and powerfully influenced his policies and political alignments.

At the time Kamehameha III died, the Hawaiian cabinet was made up of the following persons: Mr. Robert Crichton Wyllie, minister of foreign affairs; Mr. Elisha H. Allen, minister of finance; Mr. W. L. Lee, chief justice of the supreme court; Mr. John Young, minister of the interior; and Mr. Richard Armstrong, minister of public instruction. In 1852 Dr. Gerrit P. Judd had been obliged to relinquish the post of minister of finance. His partiality for the Protestant missionary party, his disregard of public opinion, and his dictatorial style had aroused a strong dislike for him. An epidemic of smallpox happening to break out on Oahu that same year, resulting in many deaths among the native population, served as the occasion and pretext for his fall from power. He was criticized for having done nothing to arrest or control the progress of the disease, and indeed for having observed with secret satisfaction the rapid decline of the population which, if continued, would quite foreseeably lead to the extinction of the race and the annexation of Hawaii to the United States.

Mr. Wyllie had openly broken with Dr. Judd and yet had managed the breach in such a way as to appear to have had no hand in Judd's fall, and in particular to have gained nothing from it.

Mr. E. H. Allen had succeeded Mr. Judd as minister of finance. Very popular and much respected, an outstanding member of the Hawaiian bench, Mr. Allen was able to work harmoniously with Mr. Wyllie. Though he was thoroughly American, Allen had a capacity for winning the assent and sympathy even of his opposition. Mr. W. L. Lee, chief justice of the supreme court, and Mr. Armstrong, minister of public instruction, both born in the United States, represented in the cabinet the purely American element, having strong ties with the missionary party. Mr. John Young, a son of the Young who had figured in the conquests of Kamehameha I, was the single native chief serving the government in a cabinet role.

Conforming to custom, the ministers handed over their resignations to the new sovereign and received from him an order to continue performing their duties until he had taken the royal oath of office, as required by the constitution. The diplomatic exchanges concerning annexation were suspended at once, and attention was concentrated on assuring that the funeral ceremonies for Kamehameha III were conducted with all due solemnity. They took place on January 10, 1855. The next day there was an official reading of the will of the former king, and Prince Alexander was proclaimed ruler under the name of Kamehameha IV.

Though the young king had not the slightest intention to revive the annexation project broken off by his uncle's death, he nevertheless had a strong desire to avoid conflict with the United States. He accordingly appointed Mr. W. L. Lee to report to Washington the necessary explanations and to substitute for further negotiation, in place of the annexation proposal, a tripartite treaty between the United States, England, and France, by which these three great maritime powers would guarantee to respect, and to ensure that others would respect, Hawaiian independence. The treaty would also commit the three nations to support and preserve the Kamehameha dynasty.

The Hawaiian government made a serious effort to assure the success of this highly problematic project. In order to win the influence and goodwill of France, the government declared that it was ready to discuss the working draft of the treaty which, since 1852, M. Émile Perrin, the French commissioner in Honolulu, was urging as a substitute for the earlier treaty with France of 1846. According to the terms of this agreement regarding international tariffs, the Hawaiian government could not impose upon foreign imports a duty rate exceeding five percent ad valorem. On the other hand, brandies were admissible at a rate of five dollars, or twenty-five francs, per gallon (3½ liters). Moreover, France's imports in the islands were not limited only to brandies. The result therefore was that the United States and England, which because of a parity clause benefited from the rate stipulated by the treaty, imported their manufactured products at a considerable profit, paying only a trifling duty of five percent ad valorem. The French, meanwhile, according to our own articles of agreement on imports, paid an excessively high tariff. Truly, French diplomacy could not possibly have discovered a formula more advantageous to other parties and to whomever had least concern for French interests; but in this matter our negotiators had remained faithful to their traditions. Indeed, our supreme indifference regarding economic questions, the magnificent disdain of our consular agents for all matters touching on trade, were here, as elsewhere, given free play. Nine years of experience had accumulated ample evidence that we were making fortunes for our rivals, while rendering it impossible for Frenchmen to trade in the islands.

In 1852 our government finally decided to take up negotiations again; but what had been easy to stipulate in 1846 was difficult to attain in 1855, when we found ourselves faced not only with the distrust of the local authorities, but also with the conjoined interests of England and the United States, both of which hoped to profit substantially from our new treaty.

For three years M. Perrin awaited a favorable occasion for the opening of negotiations. The accession to the throne of Kamehameha IV, and the mission of Mr. Lee, had provided M. Perrin with an opportunity, and he hastened to make the most of it. He was a devoted and conscientious consular agent, but he had almost no knowledge of English, the single language in which one could communicate with the local government. Having been chosen for a delicate diplomatic mission, probably because he had served for a number of years in Central America, where only Spanish was spoken, M. Perrin could not escape feeling some embarrassment when faced, as now he was, with the assignment of having to draft protocols in English and to translate from English into his own tongue the innumerable communications being transmitted to him by Mr. Wyllie.

I arrived in the islands on February 18, 1855. M. Dillon, the French consul at San Francisco, with whom I had been closely associated in that city, had given me letters of introduction and recommendations to M. Perrin. I was likewise the bearer of similar letters from M. de Mackau* in Paris, a former minister of the navy and one of the friends of my family. I received an exceptionally kind welcome from M. Perrin, who immediately familiarized me with the present consular situation, including his own special difficulties. At that time, however, I had no intention to remain in the islands, but simply wanted to continue on my return journey to France by way of China and the East Indies. M. Perrin pleaded strongly with me to change my mind and remain at Honolulu. He explained to me his need for an assistant and offered to arrange with the French foreign office to have me attached to his legation with the title of secretary. Since action on such a request, including time for a reply, would require several months, he asked me while awaiting it to take up my duties at once and collaborate with him on the negotiations just about to begin. I accepted his proposals.

The first practical difficulty raised during the treaty discussions concerned the local customs duties. The Hawaiian Legislature alone had the authority to change the tariff rates, and as its sessions occurred only every two years, it was imperative to obtain from the current legislature in session the necessary alterations. The combined influence of the king, Mr. Wyllie, and Mr. Allen succeeded in overcoming the opposition of the other foreign interests involved, and finally on April 28 the legislature voted a new tariff rate, scheduled to go immediately into effect after the projected treaty was completed.

Defeated thus on one ground, the American party achieved its revenge on another. They managed successfully to persuade a majority of the legislature to hold up the vote on the budget, managing by this device to keep the cabinet at a stalemate for several days. The king, deciding that the only remaining course was to dissolve the legislature, scheduled a special meeting for July 30, with the definite purpose of voting on the budget and approving necessary revenues. It was very evident throughout that parliamentary procedures were being scrupulously observed, but only with a strange admixture of artlessness. Indeed, two days after the assembly had been dissolved, a statement signed almost unanimously by members of the House of Representatives was delivered to the king at the palace. Kamehameha IV was requested to revoke his order of dissolution, and in exchange he was promised that an immediate vote would be taken in the House of Representatives upon the rejected bill, and in the form moreover in which the House of

---

*Ange-René-Armand, Baron de Mackau (1788–1855), was appointed vice-admiral of the navy by Louis-Philippe in 1837. During the 1840s he served as minister of the navy and of French colonies, taking measures to increase the number of ships and build up France as a maritime power. In 1847 he was made an admiral, but lost his post in the February Revolution of 1848. He became a delegate to the Senate in 1852, under Napoleon III, but died three years later. [A. L. K.]

Nobles had already endorsed it. The king refused this transaction, which suited neither his dignity nor his plan of action. He reproved the representatives, insisting on several occasions, in language colored by his strong feeling, that he would remember all his life that the unflinching minority who had supported the cabinet had remained loyal. His remarks served as a threat to the majority. This they understood, and the legislature thereupon adjourned to await a new election.

The results of the election were favorable to the government. Though composed of very disparate political elements, the government's new substantial majority was able to control its opposition. The extraordinary session lasted one month and ended August 30. In the interval preceding the special session, a committee had been established on the king's order to make certain changes in the constitution. The purpose of such a reform was to regulate procedures when, after an election resulting in a badly splintered and unmanageable House of Representatives, it might become imperative to dissolve a legislature and attempt a coup d'état: to find a means of escape, in short, from a very dangerous political situation. Fortunately, the ease with which the government had achieved an electoral victory and overcome its opposition made it possible to reject so radical a change in the Hawaiian constitution.

Indeed, the king had discovered that he could count on the assistance of the legislature. He accordingly ordered that discussions should begin with M. Perrin on the subject of the new tariff treaty, and he appointed as his representatives, with plenipotentiary power, Mr. Wyllie, minister of foreign affairs, and Mr. Allen, minister of finance. The conferences began August 21, when I was named secretary for the negotiations, with the joint approval of the French and Hawaiian members. Although I had no other official title, I was permitted to participate actively in the discussions. Altogether four months were swallowed up by the interminable meetings. Despite all the reciprocal goodwill on the part of the negotiating officials, it proved impossible to speed up the proceedings. Finally, in January of 1856, an understanding was achieved and Messrs. Wyllie and Allen received from the king his order that the treaty could be signed.

At that moment, however, the unexpected return of Mr. Lee from Washington threw the whole treaty matter again into the arena for diplomatic questioning. The sole result of Mr. Lee's mission to the United States was that he returned to Honolulu even more imbued with American views and leanings, more convinced than before that the preponderant influence in Hawaiian affairs should be American influence, and altogether more hostile to the interests of France and England.

As chief justice of the supreme court and as chancellor, Mr Lee's role in the king's council was merely advisory. Actually he would have liked to be prime minister. His position was a strong one because of the friendship and support of Mr. [William L.] Marcy, the current American secretary of state; particularly strong, in fact, because of Mr. Lee's permanent post in Hawaii as chief justice. He devoted himself to reminding his colleagues that in the future no important business could or would be conducted without his presence. He considered it a very bad sign that during his absence the government had embarked on so critical a project as negotiating a French treaty. He fully realized that the United States in particular was profiting from the restrictive clauses contained in the treaty of 1846: that to this treaty, in fact, they owed in large measure the growing importance, day by day, of American commerce in the islands, and that they had much to lose and nothing to gain from the substitution of a new treaty.

Messrs. Wyllie and Allen informed Mr. Lee of current developments and turned over to him their records and notes on the conferences. From the very first session of the treaty committee, Mr. Lee fiercely attacked what he called the inadmissible claims and expectations of France. With skill he seized upon the weak features of the treaty, dwelt upon the vague and ill-defined ideas contained in certain articles, and with little regard for the dignity of his colleagues, he proposed to break off negotiations and to limit his support to the terms of the treaty of 1846. Neither Mr. Wyllie nor Mr. Allen cared to follow him that far: the king himself had formed a working arrangement with the French commissioner, M. Perrin, and he gave Mr. Lee a full account of the progress of the negotiations and likewise passed on to him the minutes of each earlier meeting. To break off negotiations in these circumstances was virtually to abdicate in favor of Mr. Lee and to submit, in consequence, to the wishes of the American element. The king could not do this, and indeed he was weary of Mr. Lee's insistent demands. Kamehameha IV lacked, however, sufficient vigor and will to convey to Mr. Lee his views in the matter. He trusted that the passage of time would rescue him from the diplomatic straits in which he found himself.

Furthermore, all this while Mr. Lee was gravely ill from tuberculosis of the lungs. He could not live many more days. There was nothing for others to do but to wait, and up to this period waiting had been the traditional foundation of Hawaiian political strategy. Impatience, an enthusiasm for progress, has been throughout history the character of races that inhabit cold and temperate climates. To await the passage of time, to fall back upon patience, to employ the tactics of resistance as one might exploit the force of inertia, has always been a characteristic of people dwelling in tropical zones. Indolence is the consequence of hot climates; the relative ease of the living conditions enervates and diminishes energy while apathy itself becomes a system.

In other respects certain quite personal concerns, in which politics played only a minimal part, were absorbing the attention of Kamehameha IV. He was tired of the easy pleasures to which he had devoted his youth, and now he sincerely wished to reform his conduct and take care of his already threatened and uncertain health. He was even more concerned with passing on his throne to an heir, and so was thinking of marrying and settling down. After some months of hesitation he found his choice for a wife in Miss Emma Rooke, a direct descendant of John Young, the trustworthy and esteemed friend of Kamehameha I, and of a chieftainess of high rank. Emma was the adopted daughter and heir of Dr. Rooke, an English physician who had been a resident of the islands for the past thirty years and, without children of his own, left to Emma his entire fortune. She had received a good education and in addition possessed uncommon personal attractions, including a sweet disposition, artistic interests, dignity, and a marked grace of manner. The king could not have made a better choice. His request had been favorably received and on June 19, 1856, he took as his wife one who since, under the name of good Queen Emma, became for many unfortunate natives in the islands an agent of Providence. Her benevolent influence soon found expression in the charitable and religious institutions she helped so much to found.

At that time, in addition to the king and queen, the royal family was made up of Kekuanaoa, father of the king; Prince Lot Kamehameha, his brother; and Princess Victoria, his sister, about twenty years of age. Victoria was one of the wealthiest landowners in the kingdom, but her great inheritance and rank condemned her to a burdensome spinsterhood. Among her brother's aides-de-camp was a certain young Englishman, a handsome gentleman-rake and *beau cavalier,* whose friendship with the king and official duties allowed him ready access to the palace. He was married. One day, following a rather prolonged dinner where the toasts had been abundant, the aide-de-camp made his way to the princess's private quarters. There his insolence reached a point at which the princess was obliged to cry for help. The king and his brother immediately ordered the arrest of the guilty courtier and, waiving the death penalty, banished him from the kingdom. In vain the foreigners, the English in particular, protested against this summary sentence and threatened to set the culprit free. The king remained firm and M. M.* was forcibly persuaded to embark aboard a merchant schooner and was thus transported to California. Several years later, however, as a result of his wife's pleas, he was allowed to return to the islands, but without permission to appear again at court.

---

*Marcus Monsarrat (1829-1871), born in Ireland, was a surveyor and landowner, and a naturalized Hawaiian citizen. [A. L. K.]

The health of Mr. Lee continued to fail and he died on May 1, 1857. Mr. E. H. Allen, at that time minister of finance, was welcomed as his appointed successor. By order of the king, Mr. Allen on June 4 assumed the duties of chancellor of the kingdom and chief justice of the supreme court, posts which he still holds today. His conciliatory spirit, his friendly charm, above all his probity and finely balanced judgment, fully justified the king's choice. The high chief John Young, old and ailing, stepped down from the ministry of the interior, and the king appointed in his place Prince Lot Kamehameha, who was also placed in temporary charge of the ministry of finance.

The death of Mr. Lee meant the disappearance of the principal obstacle to the conclusion of the treaty with France. The negotiations were taken up again on August 12. Mr. Wyllie and Prince Lot were appointed as the Hawaiian representatives on the committee. From this period date my earliest relations with the prince who was later to become king under the title of Kamehameha V, and who made me his minister of state and his friend. Nothing at that time foreshadowed such changes in our lives. Kamehameha IV was young and brimming with vitality; his wife gave promise of producing an heir to the throne; and I, a mere consular secretary at the moment, dreamed of nothing better than the immediate routine advancement I could expect after ten years of service, depending very much, however, on a rare combination of favorable circumstances.

I loved this country where I happened to be living. I had no wish to change my home. I read a great many books and applied myself, above all, to making an accurate survey of the agricultural potentialities of the islands, the conditions of commerce, the laws regulating it, and Hawaii's economic prospects. All about me people were predicting the inevitable, and by no means remote, decline of the native race, ending in their absorption by the United States. I, on the other hand, was seeking to determine whether or not racial decadence was actually the Hawaiians' necessary and fated course. I was deeply concerned about the future of this people whose virtues, like their defects, are so strikingly plain to see, and whose hospitality toward foreigners surely deserved some better reward. A sincere friend of Hawaiian independence, I had little by little become wedded to the idea. I passionately believed, and on the basis of study estimated, that the Polynesian race was capable of progress; and I totally rebelled against a type of political and religious fatalism that condemned the Hawaiians to death and oblivion, for the sake of adding one more star to the Union flag.

An aboriginal race, cradled within a group of islands protected on every side by an expanse of ocean 700 leagues wide; a Polynesian people, offering to anyone its friendly shores as a homeland, and now timorously requesting entry among the ranks of civilized nations—these Hawaiians seemed to me to have incontestable rights to live their own lives and maintain their own place in the sun.

My ideas were a mystery to no one. I was looked upon as an inveterate foe of annexation, but my opinion at that time carried but little weight. More a matter of feeling than of knowledge, my views were not yet based on experience or solid argument. The former required time, the other hard work. Therefore I patiently began assembling an arsenal of facts and observations, a storehouse upon which one day I could abundantly draw and thus erect and defend a clear and soundly conceived political system.

The negotiations, begun on August 12, 1857, ended with the signing of a new treaty on October 29. Discussion had been lively on both sides, and the objections of the Hawaiian representatives to certain details seemed justified. The French government was insisting on some specious concessions of only theoretical significance. As only one example, I would cite article 3 of the treaty, which at this period aroused endless objections and was for a long time a major stumbling block to understanding:

> It is agreed that documents presented by the French representatives in their own language will be accepted in every instance in which documents in English are presented and accepted, and that matters of concern treated in the documents composed in these two languages will be taken up and disposed of promptly with the same good faith and with equal care. In any instance when the accuracy of the translation of one of these aforesaid documents becomes a subject of controversy, the translation will be submitted to the French consul who, after examining it, will certify its accuracy.

If one keeps in mind that there were not at that time fifty French citizens in the islands (and still are not many more), and that among these few there was not a single import merchant, and that all imported French products were brought in by English and German firms, and that no one in the islands spoke French, and finally that our own consuls knew no English, one readily comprehends the absurdity of the propositions set forth above in article 3. People speak English in Hawaii because the commercial activity is English and American; because numerous English and Americans have settled there; because the foreign imports arrive in English and American ships; because England and the United States are the chief exporting countries; and, finally, because almost the entire whale-fishing fleet is made up of American vessels, manned by American sailors. In 1855 there were 300 American vessels that stopped at Honolulu, but only six French ships arrived during the same period. In 1862 I saw our last French whaling vessel; for ten years not one other French whaler has entered any island harbor.

Now what is there left to say about this clause stipulating the French consul as a last court of appeal in determining the correctness of a translation, when it is widely admitted that nine times out of ten our consuls are ignorant of the language of the country to which they are accredited? The same is true of Europe itself, where consuls of equal caliber prove themselves unable to write a letter in a foreign language. Not long ago I read in the newspapers that for the first time in many years the French ambassador to Berlin understood and spoke German.

The rules and practices that govern our recruitment of foreign representatives are wretched. This fact has been demonstrated only too well in recent years, when two scandalous lawsuits brought the matter to public attention. These unsavory cases, at a time of grave danger and supreme national effort, revealed how the French have frequently entrusted their commercial interests to very dubious or incompetent consular agents, and our political interests to court diplomatists usually ignorant of the language of the country to which they have been assigned.

There are three indispensable qualifications that a minister of foreign affairs should insist upon, above all else, in the consular officials appointed to represent France in foreign countries: tested moral character; perfect familiarity with the language spoken in the country to which they have been posted; finally, a thorough knowledge of our commercial interests. As not one of these conditions has been required, it is a matter of lucky happenstance when one does encounter them—or, indeed, due solely to the determination of a particular individual, who himself sets the proper official standard in the absence of effective rules.

Is it not true that in Europe, Asia, America, and Oceania, those individuals among our consuls who speak English, German, Spanish, or Italian are accidental exceptions, and that before these were appointed no one bothered to find out whether or not they knew a particular foreign language? Everyone has heard how decisions concerning geographical assignments and stations are influenced by considerations of personal interest and convenience, as when a representative is shifted from the Far East to the United States, and from there returns to Russia, or departs for Oceania, according to such arbitrary criteria as the number of leaves permitted, the perquisites attached, and the prestige of the post.

How many of our consuls possess any fundamental knowledge of commercial matters? No one asks them to give proof of it. When they do acquire such knowledge, they derive it only from one area of experience. Their common ambition is to mix into matters of politics. Most frequently they display a great disdain for economic affairs (though legally they are the responsible agents for shaping commercial policy)—the disdain of men who would like to deny the importance of economic realities.

The need for reform is urgent. We have far too many consuls-general, consuls, and vice-consuls. Their salaries are inadequate more frequently than not, and invariably inferior to those of English or American officials of the same grade, who are much less numerous than ours but better compensated. It is necessary in this area as elsewhere to reduce the number of officials, and also to increase the salaries and perquisites.

In a great many second-class seaports, as in towns situated well within the borders of a country, we have salaried consuls whose functions could be carried out more economically, and with greater benefit to the nation and with genuine advantage to our commerce, by French merchants who have retired from active business. These should be men of independent means, known and esteemed in the foreign country, speaking its language, familiar with local practices, and possessing social influence of a sort that an agent can acquire only at the cost of a long period of residence. Many of these men would discover in the title of consul a reward for their probity of character. Thus the gratuitous honor of serving as their country's commercial representative would become the crowning distinction of an industrious life and the confirmation of their success.

A single diplomatic official accredited to the capital city of a foreign power, having under his orders and direction a cadre of assistants selected in this way, would amply fulfill the responsibilities he would bear. Given better remuneration and more prestige, the diplomatic representative would be able to make important economies and eliminate from the funds at his disposal many scattered, frittering expenses.

As a general rule, a consul rarely remains more than three years at the same post. When one reflects upon the fact that many of the consuls have wives, children, and servants, and that they all travel at the expense of their government, one gets an idea of how much their travel costs the country. Furthermore, no matter how intelligent a consul may be, he cannot meet the demands of his post, the problems and conflicting interests there involved, except after a fairly extended period of residence. It is no exaggeration to say that he is usually sent elsewhere just at the moment he begins to prove effective. England, the United States, Germany, Russia, and all the second-class powers of Europe have adopted the system we are recommending, and are well satisfied with it. What are we waiting for before we follow their example? Are not the results of our defective system glaringly obvious to all eyes?

Under our method of recruitment, every consul remains a bureaucrat—that is, his supreme goal is to achieve promotion. But to be promoted one must be visible and known, and by no means permit oneself to be forgotten. France is far away; the minister in Paris, the source of all favors, is deaf to pleas. It is necessary to catch his attention. To achieve this aim there is only one method. Instead of solving his government's problems, the official creates problems for his government. He launches a difficulty, exaggerates it, begins to shout; he pulls down his flag, when a gunboat arrives he runs it up again, and the Paris newspapers, badly informed, speak of the incident as an insult to "la France." Everyone knows the rest of the story.

Has everyone already forgotten, in this country of ours with so short a memory, the incidents that preceded the Mexican War? Has everyone forgotten our innumerable troubles in Asia, Central America, the farthest reaches even of Oceania?

All that is yesterday's history. Will it also be tomorrow's?

But let us return to Honolulu and resume the course of our story.

At last, by virtue of conference after conference, and repeated threats of breaking off negotiations, article 3 was retained. It is still in effect today. Yet the slightest reduction of the tariff rate on French products would have been worth twenty such articles. I would even be willing to say that after all tempests in a teapot on questions of theory, there has never once occurred an occasion when article 3 was applied in practice—a situation indeed that could only embarrass the consular official charged with upholding article 3 and enforcing its execution.

The treaty was sent to France to receive there the required ratifications. I profited from the resulting leisure that fell my way by taking a trip to the island of Hawaii and visiting the famous Kilauea Crater, celebrated as the largest active volcano in the world. In my correspondence of that period I find a detailed account of this excursion and its incidents, which are of a sort likely to interest my readers. Unfortunately, what follows are not the notes of a scholar, but only those of a tourist—they have not the slightest scientific value. All the same, they are authentic and exact, and as I reread them today I discover anew my impressions and feelings of the moment.*

---

*All Varigny's "correspondence" presented in chapter six is headed as having been written in November 1857, and throughout the rest of his book he continues to mention a first trip to the volcano region of the island of Hawaii in that year. However, his visit to Hilo appears almost certainly to have been made in 1861. Mme de Varigny's memoir (see Appendix 2) clearly justifies such an inference, as does also the fact that no steamship operating on the Hilo route existed before June 1860. In like manner the subsequent narrative in chapter six describing travel in the Kohala district in 1857 appears to be based upon a second family holiday in that region in 1862 (see Appendix). Varigny's reasons for assigning the trip to 1857 are possibly explainable on both autobiographical and rhetorical grounds. For Varigny the months after the treaty negotiations were apparently uneventful and barren. Furthermore, chapter six may simply have seemed a strategic point for introducing a change in narrative pace and rhetorical tone, between the more sedate expository chapters. The epistolary genre here employed by Varigny, a mode well understood by his French readers, allowed a certain element of fictive inventiveness and dramatic license. Even Varigny's anonymous Honolulu reviewer, the longtime resident writing in 1884, saw nothing amiss in Varigny's travelogue manner and style: "The best parts of the book are undoubtedly those which are neither political or historical. M. de Varigny is a sharp observer and has a happy faculty in description. The account of his visits to the other islands interspersed through the book are bright and pleasant reading." [A. L. K.]

CHAPTER 6

EXCURSION TO THE ISLAND OF HAWAII

Lahaina.—Hilo.—Snowy summits.—The volcano of Kilauea.—Descent into the crater.—A surf of fire.—Waipio Valley.—A precipice.—Waterfalls.—An amorous guide. —A Hawaiian ranch.—Jack Purdy.—His exploits.—Ascent of Mauna Kea.—A pagan temple.

The volcano of Kilauea
November 5, 1857*

MON CHER AMI,

I hardly know how to tell you the latitude and longitude of my present lodging, but that doesn't matter much. Certainly it's on the messy side. One can't escape a stench of stale weeds and moldy grass; the smoke, missing its outlet through the roof, drifts prosaically and meanly out by a single door; and we are converting ourselves, slowly but surely, into the condition of Westphalia hams. Our furnishings consist of the two mats we lie on, for we are still too civilized to prefer the bare ground. The bottoms of a couple of tins of preserved food do duty as plates and tumblers. An antique pot sits in the corner, and inside it we do our cooking and, when required, also brew our coffee and tea. Heaped-up saddles and bridles complete the accommodations. We are down in the tropics, but the weather at this moment is intensely cold. At last we find ourselves watching the most astounding spectacle in the world.

But my pen runs away with me. I forget to tell you exactly where we are and to mention who are "we." *We* stands for your old friend and his constant companion, Mr. Von Holt, a Honolulu merchant, a bold explorer, and a no less bold horseman—earlier I visited all Oahu with him. Naturally, he was unable to resist the temptation to sample the pleasures of the independent, humorous traveler—I was about to say tourist, but that species or genus doesn't exist in these parts. We are on the island of Hawaii, atop the steeper slopes of a mountain called Mauna Loa—that "great mountain"—in

*See footnote at the end of chapter 5. [A. L. K.]

full view of the crater of Kilauea, inhabited or haunted, however little you may believe it, by the goddess Pele!

> Do you regret the time when heaven walked the earth,
> And a race of gods lived and breathed?*

Or to say the same thing (and with all proper respect for the poet), does a feeling for the materialistic worship of nature turn you into a pagan? The specimen of paganism at this moment before my eyes would remove the temptation if I felt it—or if I ever should feel it.

What I really regret is that I've begun, as I see now, where I ought to have finished. I've not followed (but I don't know why) that popular method of modern composition which consists in holding the reader in suspense, so that he has no notion whether he will ever arrive at the point an author claims to be leading him. But perhaps you would gladly have me spare you these acrobatics. So I must explain that I'm simply being faithful to the program I sketched for you at the end of my last letter, when I mentioned that my friend and I left Oahu aboard the best steamship Honolulu boasts of. We embarked Monday evening and on Tuesday morning dropped anchor in the roadstead of Lahaina, a delightful little town on Maui, where after landing we stretched ourselves out lazily beneath a great green dome of Maui's splendid foliage. Slender coconut palms line the beach at Lahaina, towering in silhouette against the dense groves where the dark green of the orange tree weds the paler shades of *hau* and *kukui*.

Although no more than a village, Lahaina is with the exception of Honolulu the most frequented port of call in the islands. It adds up to no less than seven or eight shops. What goes on during the off-season I couldn't say. Merchants, utterly idle, kill time as best they can, and on this account reach such a stage of boredom that they can only chase after the travelers arriving here twice a week from Honolulu and try to extract from them the news of the day. As the latter bring no news with them, they invent some, which does just as well. I can still see the shop where I went to buy a pocket knife, having left my own behind. I do indeed believe they would have given me one for nothing, if I had cared for the job of chatting with them an hour. I preferred to pay 7 francs 50. As you well know, I'm a chap with a taste for economy.

After our two-hour siesta at Lahaina (a call that might have been limited to ten minutes, as there was absolutely nothing to load or unload) we continued our seafaring and for the whole day coasted along the shores of Maui. We called at two other ports: at Kalepolepo, a tiny bay, exceedingly unin-

---

*Alfred de Musset, *Poésies nouvelles*, "Rolla," I. [A. L. K.]

viting, where one gazes upon nothing but sand and one huge, solitary shop, the very sight of which turns the spleen, and a little farther on, at Ulupalakua, hardly any better, except that there is less sand, a great many rocks, and no shop. After nightfall, when this chore was disposed of, we entered the channel separating Maui from Hawaii and on the next morning just at daybreak dropped anchor on the western coast of Hawaii, at Kawaihae Bay, 150 miles from Honolulu.

Kawaihae is a village situated in the hollow of the sizable cove that bears its name. The village consists chiefly of a single large wooden structure which serves as a country store and warehouse for the products of the district. Around the shop are clustered several makeshift buildings providing annexes for further storage. Scattered along the seashore are a few kanaka grass houses, about twenty. The setting is desolate: not a blade of grass, not a tree, except for the infrequent coconut palms, nor a stream. Enormous volcanic rocks, jagged and cinder-black, lie strewn across the ground, and a fine dusty sand covers the beach. A small wharf serves for the departure and landing of travelers. At a short distance from shore floats an old stripped-down vessel, its melancholy hull balancing at anchor and providing storage for products arriving from Honolulu. It was difficult for me to imagine a more arid and barren setting, and this introduction did not augur very favorably for our excursion to Hawaii. But the sun, once risen, revealed to us a landscape far surpassing our expectations.

Above some light clouds, resembling indeed smoke clouds, rose two mountain summits of dazzling white: the snowy crowns of Mauna Kea and Mauna Loa, twin giants of Oceania, whose height matches that of Mont Blanc. The contrast was stunning. A stifling heat, an already parching sun; but under the tropical sky our eyes, grown unaccustomed to the sight of snow (for we had seen none for more than seven years), could not tire of admiring that cold splendor. Little by little the last clouds disappeared, and we were able to contemplate three regal mountains, each of quite different form and aspect.

Before us, at a distance of thirty-five miles, rose Mauna Kea (the mother mountain), 13,000 feet high. The precipitous slopes, forest-covered to their middle reaches and capped with snow, formed a strange contrast to Mauna Hualalai, which on our right barred the sweeping curve of the horizon forty miles away. Hualalai, a mountain of lava and scoria, 11,000 feet, appeared to the eye quite somber and wild: no trees, no vegetation at all, clothed its black slopes. Huge rocks, such as one would have said had been hurled by the hands of Titans, were piled one on top of the other in frightful disarray, encumbering the outlying plain as far as the eye could see. Even the ocean shore had been sown with such weird stumbling-block shelvings. On the flanks of the mountain, quite clearly visible, were a number of extinct volcanic cones that from the distance where we stood resembled the mounds of earth piled up by ants. Actually, several of these cones rose more than 500 feet high.

Between Mauna Kea and Hualalai, on the far center of the horizon about a hundred miles away, stood Mauna Loa (the large mountain), whose snowy summit overlooking gentle, rounded slopes, tree-clad for the most part, formed a true amphitheater of verdure. With the help of a telescope I distinguished a black line running down from the summit of Mauna Loa, crossing valley and range, ending in the sea not far from Kawaihae, where it formed a menacing headland. Scarcely a year ago, though it had been quiescent for a long period, Mauna Loa all at once awakened and from its no longer snowbound heights spewed forth a river of lava. The black band formed by that outpouring was what we now beheld. For fourteen days the volcano had ejected the mass of lava and scoria that flowed like a tremendous river ninety miles long and three miles wide (thirty leagues by one). For several days the lava, still boiling, despite the distance separating it from the crater, struggled with the ocean, heating the waves over an area several miles wide. During all this time the molten current flowed at an average speed of forty miles an hour, destroying everything in its course, swallowing up a village, including several of the inhabitants. The glow was so intense that at Kawaihae one could easily see to read on the darkest night.

On our left began the mountain range of Kohala, wooded up to the top ridges and covering the northwest portions of the island. Finally, between Kawaihae and Mauna Kea, stretched the rich pasturelands of Waimea, which continue as far as the accessible slopes of the mountain. Such a landscape made us quickly forget whatever could be unattractive about the visual aspect of Kawaihae.

After a two-hour rest, we returned to the seashore and embarked once more, following a northward route in order to round Honoipu Point. The coastal areas of the Kohala district which we were now ranging are rich in fishing grounds. At this quite early hour in the morning, the sea was covered with small native canoes, shaped from hollowed logs and balanced by a cross-beam, or outrigger, and nearly all equipped with triangular sails. Each of these craft, so incomparably light that they drew only four or five inches of water, was manned by two Kanakas. Their catch had been abundantly successful, to judge by the number of the fish, especially the flying fish, which loaded down the canoes. Three hours after our departure from Kawaihae our ship cleared Honoipu Point and continued south en route for Hilo.

While the coast we were leaving behind us was monotonous and bare, the one now taking shape before our eyes became monumentally picturesque.

Our vessel skirted the shore for fifty meters. The coastline, cloven into deep ravines, gave glimpses of hills reaching ever higher and higher, wooded to their very crests, especially along the narrow ridges looking out to sea. In proportion to our progress, the ravines were transformed into full-scale valleys, the hills became more and more lofty, gradually attaining an elevation of 13,000 feet. From each ridgetop fell a cascade of considerable size, dwindling to a slender silver ribbon as it ended some few feet above us, dissolving into delicate rain, the merest veil of mist. The golden sunshine fell upon the silver rain, sending across it entrancing shimmers of light; sometimes it caught the reflection of a rainbow, and sometimes a single shaft of piercing sunshine lent the rain the appearance of a crystalline cloud.

For four hours our ship wove its way opposite these waterfalls, forty of them. The last, called Waipio, plunged from a height of more than 2,000 feet into the depths of one of the most gorgeously inviting valleys one could ever view while standing on the deck of a moving ship. We would gladly have stepped ashore to visit this noble landscape; but it is difficult for a small boat to land on this beach ruled over by a violent riptide. We shall return there later by an overland route.

On the following night, at 2:30 A.M., we dropped anchor in Hilo Bay, the most distant port of call for the interisland coasting vessels, after a fifty-eight-hour journey covering about one hundred leagues.

At Hilo we hardly had time to glance about us and admire the fine bay and luxuriant tropical vegetation. We were to return to Hilo later, and so rushed to complete our arrangements for the excursion to Kilauea. At that moment our miseries and frustrations began. In Europe there is no difficulty about engaging guides and mounts, but here nothing is simple. What with the natives and their interminable parleys, and the mules who here join to the vices they display in all countries the added distinction of being three-quarters unbroken and still wild, there are enough accursed troubles to cause the traveler to lose his temper twenty times a day.

Finally everything is ready; the mules saddled (no minor operation); the guides at their advance-guard posts; the porters loaded. We leave—which means we should very much like to leave, but the mules are not interested when they guess where we want to take them. Neither whiplash nor spur has any effect; they start to balk, refusing to budge a step. To our great embarrassment, since we fancy ourselves to be first-class riders, we ignominiously advance at the pace chosen by our mounts, while a pair of Kanakas armed with long pointed sticks of bamboo belabor the procession from the rear. Thus we cover the first ten miles. I blush merely thinking of it.

We left at 5:00 A.M., and our sole concern was to arrive before nightfall. I must also confess that I paid only moderate attention to the superb landscape unfolding in panoramic stages before our eyes. I recall some tropical forests, some plains studded with cactus and tree ferns; but our anxious eyes constantly questioned the horizon. I persisted, just as my companion did, in imagining that a volcano has the shape of a mountain crowned with flames, blazing light, smoke, cinders of lava. I saw nothing resembling such. Before me only the snow-blanketed summit of Mauna Loa rose in the distance. Between this and us, an ocean of trees; not the slightest hint of smoke.

We continued in our saddles for thirteen hours and in this short span of time achieved the utmost frontiers of skepticism. Did our guides actually know where they were guiding us? Wasn't the volcano much farther away than people had said? And did a volcano actually exist? All this goes to show that definitions are not like saddles that fit all horses, and that writers who call a volcano a mountain do not always know what they are saying. This was our first conclusion, and the only one that was right.

Dusk came on, the forests reappeared. There was not the smallest hill on the horizon and we began to struggle seriously with the problem of choosing an appropriate place to camp, when our weary mules gave a last tug on their collars. We sped them on at a gallop and emerged from the forest. Instinctively, we stopped them. It was time. Having denied the volcano's existence, we were on the very point of diving into it headfirst.

November 6, 1857

I take up this letter—or rather my interrupted journal. To it I dedicate these hours, frequent during travel, when rest is needed but sleep is not yet welcome. However pleasant it may be to sit dreaming before a spectacle such as the one I have before my eyes, I consider it more worthwhile to stamp it firmly upon my memory. Later, revery will overflow and fill up the numerous gaps in my narrative.

The more one resorts to imagination the more one exaggerates. During my life of travel I have often realized that imagination is a frequent source of disappointment. But if experience has often served me fairly by keeping me levelheaded and rational, it played me false yesterday evening. What I saw, what I still see, was not what I had merely envisioned. I was quite ready to marvel, to be astonished, but not to receive so profound a feeling of shock—and why not say so?—of terror. I should like to cause you to feel that terror too, but I shan't succeed. You'll read me in your nook by the fire, your feet toasting before the firedogs, surrounded by all the comforts of a civilization that banishes us from the unapprehended shores of existence, not permitting us to approach their mysteries except for purposes of entertainment, as in the playhouse or by reading a novel. Therefore I lay aside imaginative pretensions. I limit myself to being truthful and exact. Listen, and see what I have seen and heard.

Night is just about to fall. Only a few rays of fading sunlight wrap in their rosy reflection the distant summit of the great mountain. Behind us, to our right and left, is a dark forest where a light mist descends upon the leaves and sinks in silent droplets at our feet. We are in a narrow clearing. On both sides the trees extend almost to the edge of a precipice, leaning over the chasm as if curious to plumb its mysteries. The abyss is shadowy, but the remaining daylight allows us to trace its enormous contours, more than ten leagues in circumference, which vanish from sight in the dim distance. Now the whole immense circus, to a depth of a thousand feet, finds its double in the recesses of my present mind and mood. The rim is jagged with peaks. In the deep floor a reddish light burns more brilliantly than any star lighting night's firmament. A huge pillar of flame springs up at the center, illuminating with baleful reflection the cindery rocks surrounding it. Puffs of filmy white smoke escape in spirals from the thousands of open crevices that furrow the black and hardened crust, barely discernible from above. Beside us, in half shadow, a windowless hut, whose only door consists of several badly fastened pieces of bamboo, offers uncertain shelter, as if ready to crumble to bits along with the undermined soil that supports it. A low, continuous rumbling, which I can only compare to that of the sea at night during a storm, resounds from the yawning gulf.

I remained in that same spot there with Von Holt, not approaching, not withdrawing, feeling myself a plaything in a world of dreams. A thousand fantasies, a thousand confused images, rushed through my brain. I seemed to behold from on high a conquered Sebastopol, annihilated in that hell-fire celebrated in the annals of war. Those smoke clouds were from the bivouac fires of our victorious troops. Then, all of a sudden, I was present at the fall of Sodom. The facings of walls collapsed, leaving them blackened and smouldering. The earth cracked open to swallow the accursed city. Let the Dead Sea sweep in: here its basin has been excavated and made ready: its waters here will perpetuate forever that acrid taste of sulphur and bitumen choking my throat.

But night is coming on. Finally I realize I feel very tired. I'm cold, hungry, and thirsty. I get off my mule, mechanically tie him to the trunk of a tree. Our guides have remained in the rear. As there was only one pathway, we didn't need them ahead of us to follow it. The food supplies and bed covering are with them; nothing can be done except to wait. Von Holt suggests lighting a fire. The notion seems an absurd one atop a volcano, but there's something to be said for it. We gather dead branches. I heap them in a hole; the charred grass around us indicates an earlier camp. I try to start the fire but the wet wood doesn't easily ignite. I persist, when up out of the firehole leaps a blast of steam and hot smoke which puts out my matches and ruins my hearth. After a moment's hesitation we lean over, ears cocked, and distinctly hear the underground rumbling of the ocean of fire for which our hole is only a safety valve. There are other such rumblings coming from all directions. Everywhere beneath our footsteps the same phenomena are being repeated.

We abandon our post and seat ourselves at the sill of our hut to await our guides. They arrive finally at half past nine. Lacking candles, feeling cross and famished, we take possession of our night's shelter. It is from here that I write to you. But supper is still delayed, Von Holt is sputtering in exasperation, and I too am gripped by hunger's claw.

Thanks for helping me forget all this, up to the pleasant moment when I shall look back in remembrance.

Hilo
November 9, 1857

I am now at Hilo, *cher ami,* and return to the narrative of my journey. For the time being, I'm installed here in comfort but aching all over, just this side of collapse. The little strength I still have has settled in my fingers—and in my stomach. Thanks to the regimen I follow, which consists in daily downing a good number of substantial meals and abandoning myself to the pleasures of sea bathing and being lazy, enjoying the *far niente* life, it won't be long before I'll be in shape again for the road.

My letter left us in the hut by the volcano. We were dead tired from riding, stunned by what we had only caught a glimpse of, impatient to see more. I've rarely felt a sharper secret joy than that which caused me to wake up at sunrise the next morning. All night long we had found ourselves almost freezing. Even in the tropics a wide-open house, 4,500 feet above sea level, is not precisely the *ne plus ultra* of comfort, above all when it is occupied as was ours. But now daylight allowed us to inform ourselves a little about our geographical position, and to determine that we were on one of the slopes of Mauna Loa, although still about twelve leagues away from our goal. The mountain's snowy crest emerging from the fogs of night revealed in outline its pure, light-filled, terraced ridges under an incomparably clear sky. Birds in their trees were singing around us. Everything borrowed from the first shafts of daylight a peculiar seal of beauty, calm, repose. The appearance of the crater itself seemed to have altered, and now our eyes plunged freely downward and without fear into the abyss we were about to explore. Its austere grandeur now allured us as much as it had intimidated us the night before.

Breakfast, such as it was, gave us ballast and so revived us. Accompanied by our guides, and equipped with long staffs like alpenstocks, we set off down a kind of path very similar to a stair-ladder, but far more steep, which brought us after three quarters of an hour—I shall not say of walking, but of gymnastic exercises—to the bottom of the crater. There we realized that we were upon that blackened plain which from above had appeared to be so very smooth, but which now at close hand wore a quite opposite aspect. Nothing could give a more accurate image of it than the sea itself. Picture the waves of the sea suddenly solidified, preserving all their marine shapes intact, their rounded contours, their rippling folds turning backward upon themselves, even the foam that wreathes their crests. We entered upon that motionless sea by crossing from one wave to another, testing with the points of our staffs the firmness of the vitrified, but still warm, crust. Numerous crevices of all sizes and depths furrowed the plain. Some extended only several feet, others reached down as far as the sea of fire, and we could discern at the bottom a blaze of light resembling the zigzag of aerial lightning. Out of every dead crevice warm steam escaped, strongly impregnated with sulphur.

From wave to wave, crevice to crevice, we thus picked our way for more than an hour, before arriving at Lua Pele, the Temple of Pele: that supreme deity of the Hawaiian Archipelago, goddess of those subterranean fires that have created the islands, she whose furies have so often deranged and rearranged them. For my part, I have never known for what good reason the Egyptians deified the onion—or if I've known, I've forgotten it—but I'm no longer astonished, after what I saw, that the Hawaiians submerged in their paganism chose to deify and worship fire. Certainly no goddess of antiquity ever possessed a more appropriate dwelling than this one displayed beneath our eyes.

What is called Lua Pele is a pit, or a lake, a league in circumference, about seventy feet deep. At the moment we drew near the edge, our Kanakas removed their shoes and bared their heads. After muttering several words in a low voice (the sense of which escaped us) they tied stones to a few small objects evidently carried for that purpose from Hilo—necklaces, glass beads, and so on—and threw these into the echoing abyss, as they called out three times this cry: "Aloha, Pele! I salute you, Pele!"

I swear I was tempted to follow their example and to uncover myself in turn, but not before the pagan goddess: only before the power of the Almighty, whose hand reveals itself to us in the delicate petals of a flower as well as in this chamber of horrors.

In the lake I mentioned a moment ago, out of which radiated an overwhelming heat, a black liquid mass tossed and flung itself in all directions, resembling the waves of a tormented sea that pitched itself against the walls imprisoning it. After several moments of fierce convulsions, a larger wave than all the others raised itself up several feet high; the froth then divided as a result of the effort, exposing a red mass of liquid fire that crept forward with slow, regular movements from one side of the crater to the center, sweeping in its passage all the scum before it. On the opposite side the same phenomenon took place, with waves of the same size, so far as we could judge them at that distance; then another fiery wave pushed onward to overtake and collide with the first. One could have said that the mantle of black foam, which only a little while ago had covered everything over, had been rent through like a flimsy veil. The sound filling our ears did not, however, much resemble the roar of the sea. It was easier to imagine oneself surrounded by hundreds of mountain torrents rolling avalanches of gravel and stone. We stood transfixed, our eyes pivoted toward these two waves, awaiting with mingled curiosity and dread what would result from their inevitable collision.

The two moving mountains, more than twenty feet tall, seemed to rise up as if to measure one another's forces. A horrifying sound like that of an immense invisible earthquake heralded the moment of their encounter. The earth shook under and around us. At the very center of the pit, the two waves mounted in a pyramid of fire more than sixty feet high, hurling their molten volcanic spume in all directions. Then the stronger of the two waves subsided, withdrawing from its rival, and spread itself out like a red sheet beating furiously against the black walls, melting them under the embrace of the terrible heat. Finally the wave disappeared into the basin, like a sandy cliff which the sea saps and undermines until everything becomes liquefied. This spectacle lasted nearly a quarter of an hour, and was followed by a period of calm; the sheet of blackened scum reformed, split here and there into zigzag flashes of flame; the mass then repeated its slow and regular movement like that of a gathering tide. Pele, so say the natives, is recovering her forces, preparing new manifestations of her power.

It is difficult for me to describe the sensations I felt at the sight of these astonishing phenomena occurring on so vast a scale. In the immediate presence of the event, I had found it hard to analyze my responses. To each of us it was clear that we were in no immediate danger, at least from any eruption of unexpected violence; but my curiosity was still not satisfied. I was especially interested in my chances of collecting several handsome specimens of lava and sulphur. Although thousands of examples lay all around, these were not enough for me. I wanted to go down and get some from the fire-pit itself. I questioned the Kanakas and after some objections based on the indignation Pele would feel, with which I was only moderately concerned, and several other doubts about the hazards of crossing through the sulphurous fumes, which bothered me far more, I was able to persuade one of my guides, the youngest and most agile, to accompany me as far as the rim of the lake. There was one spot where the projecting rocks leaned out over the mass of molten lava, yet where the spectator was protected by a distance of about ten feet. Profiting from a moment when the volcano was at rest, we began our descent. Aside from the problem of facing the excessive heat, we found only one area of approach which with some difficulty we were able to penetrate. In this space about ten meters wide, we had to pass through some sulphurous steam impossible to breathe. We therefore inhaled a good supply of air, breathing it deep into the lungs; and then, speeding our descent as much as the breakable character of the ground would allow, we reached the proposed vantage point safe and sound. Beyond it no degree of curiosity could have lured us.

The descent took us about ten minutes. We arrived just in time to be present at the second rehearsal of the events I have just described. The great question for us, in the spot where we now found ourselves, was to determine which of the two fiery mountains would provide the drama, and if the great mass would head toward us or in the opposite direction. Just as Kanana, my guide, had predicted, it was toward us that Pele was decidedly racing. The waves, after a struggle whose shifting reversals and outcome we followed with anxious curiosity, looked from our side as if they were already well on their way. Our position was no longer tenable. But neither was it prudent to beat a hasty withdrawal, inasmuch as we had succeeded in sheltering ourselves behind a low wall of lava which served as a protective shield. We evidently did not have time enough to climb out. Indeed, within a few instants the rock we were just about to abandon was swept by a tempest of molten stone and fire. A second calm interval followed this eruption. We profited from it enough to gather hastily some pieces of "Pele's hair," but not without burning our fingers, and then to regain the summit. "Pele's hair," as the Kanakas call it, is a delicate, silky substance resembling in every way fine threads or fibers of glass. The volcano ejects it in only very small quantities. It is all the more rare because one must descend into the deeper pit in order to gather it. I likewise collected some extremely lightweight—"floating"—stones. But I'm ahead of myself. I was choking from heat, and it was only when I was some distance from Lua Pele that I was able to catch my breath and savor the blessing of fresh air. Meanwhile, nothing could remove the awful taste of sulphur that seized me by the throat. Pele had avenged herself in her fashion.

Afternoon was well advanced when we returned to our hut. It goes without saying that like typical tourists we were carrying, in the form of specimens, a load big enough for a mule. We arrived just in time, furthermore, to prevent a catastrophe. Our mules were about to break loose from their tethers and head down the road without us, back to Hilo. A thirty-mile chase on foot on such roads, though it would be picturesque, offered nothing to tempt us. We succeeded, however, in capturing the beasts; but when my companion asked about the cause of the panic, I heard only an outburst of profanity, which appeared to drive our Kanakas into a state of quaking alarm. I quickly stepped in and managed to restrain Von Holt just in time, for he was deliberately preparing to make one of our porters swallow a basin of boiling water. He explained to me the cause of all the fuss. He told me that our men, too lazy to go any distance to fetch some fresh water, had found nothing better for our haltered animals than to bring them some water from a sulphur spring. Von Holt strongly sympathized with the rebellious mules. I could not agree, and a sharp rebuke to the men brought the affair to an end.

Next morning we set off down the road for Hilo. The return trip took four hours. We found it necessary to leave our mules behind us while en route and to exchange them for some horses, who were hardly an improvement. Finally, at eight o'clock in the evening, we reached our home base and settled down to our suppers, with the proverbial appetite of travelers.

Waipio
November 14, 1857

I am at Waipio but I shall not make the trip again, not because the valley isn't worth the trouble, but really, as good old Horace says, because enough is enough—*Est modus in rebus.* The *pali,* or precipice, of Waipio was not created with this axiom in mind.

We are here, at any rate, in a room ten feet square, containing a bed from which we have dislodged its honest proprietor, who now sleeps stretched out on the floorboards. We have had a meal of eggs and *"hard grub"** and this "hard grub" (composed of boiled taro, sticky and fermented) *"plays the devil with our constitution,"* as our neighbors overseas express it. I shall not make the trip again, as I told you at the beginning: never again—but who knows?—and, anyhow, I'm happy to be here at all, for there are ten chances to one of arriving head first, and by a drop of 2,000 feet.

We left Kawaihae yesterday morning in the care of a guide who gave the impression of saying, "I'm their head man and therefore the proper thing for me to do is to follow behind." And yet, he hasn't followed us anywhere at all. Though I don't know where he is at this moment, I swear it's all the

*Varigny supplies the American idiom. [A. L. K.]

same to me—he can do just as he pleases. He began by reporting to us two hours after the time arranged for leaving. Next, instead of a strong mount in condition for the journey, he presented me with a mare who to my eyes looked exactly like a white cow, and who dragged behind her a dirty gray foal who stopped her at every step to tug upon a nipple. However it was my fault that the little creature transferred his fantasies of nourishment onto me —he sucked the tip of my boot and wore off the leather. I held my patience as far as Waimea, but there I made Halemakule dismount (such is the guide's name), shifted my saddle to the back of his horse, and let him make the best of it with the white mare and the gray foal. Since then, we've seen no more of Halemakule and his nag, and I'm in no hurry to see him reappear.

From Kawaihae, where we arrived by water, to Waimea, chief settlement in an area of fine grazing lands and cattle ranches, the road is very forbidding, constantly uphill and across an ocean of stones and volcanic boulders. Once at Waimea the landscape changes and also the temperature. One smothers at Kawaihae; at Waimea the weather is chilly. We next reached the district of Hamakua, traveling through shady, picturesque forests, a refuge for thousands of wild beef cattle who watched our passage with an unflattering look of surprise. I forgot to tell you that at Waimea we found a Kanaka to replace Halemakule and guide us through the labyrinth where we would still be wandering, if it had not been for this precaution.

I can't remember any more who it was that said all forests look alike. No doubt all of them are full of trees, but it does not follow that our authority was right. The sizable trees that we passed through displayed a striking singularity I have observed nowhere else. Vines hung from them in picturesque festoons—here forming the design of an arcaded vault; farther along the ogival shape of a Moorish window; and elegant pilasters everywhere, the ruins of Palmyra, so to speak, swathed in flowing green mantles of vegetation. From time to time mammoth tree ferns, more than thirty feet tall, shot upward their trunks cloaked with *pulu,* a kind of silky vegetal wool, which has become the object of considerable commercial development. Along our route we also frequently came upon the whitened skeletons of wild cattle who had strayed into these solitudes to find a lair in which to die, or who had fallen in their tracks shot by some bullock hunter in search of their hides.

So we clung to the road for the whole afternoon, observing, not without a certain uneasiness, the daylight as it rapidly waned. The virtual absence of dusk, for twilight in subtropical countries can slip by almost without transition from burning sun to deepest night, filled us with doubts on the question of descending the *pali* of Waipio. We were aware of its reputation as one of the most dangerous spots in the whole chain of islands. Furthermore, we did not then have even the resource of cowards, the capacity to retreat; not a sign of a sheltering hut, nor yet a mouthful of food. But our guide could hardly have appeared less concerned. He did not interrupt his silence except to regulate by gesture or voice his horse's pace. We stopped trying to control our own mounts; nothing could be done with them. Meanwhile, the sun had long since vanished from the horizon when finally we arrived at the summit of the *pali*. There our Kanaka pointed a finger at a sort of will-o'-the-wisp, which momentarily appeared and disappeared, blinked and vanished, 2,000 feet below. "There's where we bunk," said he.

We promptly grasped the ironic dimensions of the remark. We felt like men perched upon a rooftop without any notion of how to climb down. An almost perpendicular path, squeezed in between the rock on one side and the void on the other, scarcely a meter wide, tumbled rather than descended into a black cistern where we could just distinguish the distant sound of the surf pounding the rocks below. We could, but only dimly, make out a ghostly white strip and a glow of phosphorescent seafoam flecking the waves. I managed a suggestion that we should give our horses a break, but our guide stubbornly insisted that this kindness would accomplish nothing. His pretext was that rest would only give the horses stiff legs. I did not feel equal to disputing the question. Putting foot to ground, we looped our bridles on the pommels of our Mexican saddles, then pushed our animals in front of us; but they recoiled in fright and refused to budge. The guide found an explanation for their behavior, saying that probably because they had never traveled this way before and did not know the road, they would not keep on going except with us upon their backs. It was a gracious proposition. We made a mental calculation of the value of the animals, saddles, gear, and of the chances that we should need to replace them. We came to the conslusion that we had to make the best of our bad luck and try, at least once more, to descend by means of our mounts.

Reassured that they would take the leap in our company, we set off on our horses at a walk. We let them manage in their own fashion. They continued to insist, in the most positive way, on shaving the rocky side of the pinnacle as closely as possible. We left there several pieces of our trousers (but it is better to lose the part than the whole). With imperturbable calm our phlegmatic companion estimated how much distance with each step our horses diminished the length of our fall—as if some ten-foot stretches, or even several of a hundred feet more or less, along a trajectory of 2,000, with hard rock at the base, offered any guarantee which a fairly conscientious insurance company would stoop to consider.

Before we were halfway down, and while there still remained (according to Von Holt's calculations) a *mere* 1,200 feet to descend or fall, we found that the narrow path had suddenly shrunk to less than half its earlier width. Directly in front of us a landslide barred the way and prevented our hugging the cliff. Our horses took a fancy to acting skittish, and I was well convinced that we would reach the bottom far sooner than one ought. I directed some quick curses at my fellow traveler for his mathematical deductions, as he had not even left me to the comforts of my illusions; but my horse, frightened at feeling one foot already planted in a vacuum, pulled himself back, recovered his footing, and then kept himself tightly aligned to the rock, which from that time on he quitted no more.

At nine o'clock we reached the floor of the valley; at a quarter past nine we were eating all the eggs available at the house of our host; and at ten o'clock I was falling asleep, prisoner of a bizarre confusion of ideas. Our host had promised us that he would give us an opportunity the next day to admire the celebrated Waipio waterfall, where, said he, it is not mere water but a whole river that drops from the summit—in fact, a river of stones comes pouring down; and, then, a tour of the valley itself, through which flows a river that loses itself in the ocean and runs a course, he assured me, below the sea level of said ocean. Which is below sea level—the valley or the river? . . . Both of them.

I understand nothing, but I see that I have not come to the end of my geographical paradoxes.

P.S. 10 o'clock in the morning

I visit the waterfall and find that it pours down stones—definitely—even sizable rocks. My skepticism nearly resulted in my being crowned with one. The sight is no less impressive for all that, and perhaps the place borrows an added charm from the risk one takes when receiving such lapidary treatment. Imagine a foaming torrent leaping over a towering cliff edge 2,000 feet high and spending itself in a light mist just above your head. The large fragments of rock it loosens from the summit and drags with it do not dissolve so easily; but they are visible and one can dodge them with a little practice. As for the valley, it is the most green, the most secluded, the most felicitous I have seen; unquestionably the enclosed garden dreamed of by the misanthrope: where to have liberty is to be a rich man.

I shall not do you the disservice of informing you that the valley's altitude is above sea level, although in fact it must be, if only by a very little. However, I have not cared to contradict our host on this point, the sole white man dwelling in the valley. The Kanakas around him who have been converted to his notion would show him less respect if they found him convicted of error; and, besides, I would be imposing on myself a case of conscience if I should rob the poor devil of an illusion dear to him, a discovery which he can boast about, quite authoritatively, as its author.

Halemakule has just appeared. He is delighted with himself, but we cannot share his satisfaction. He bravely passed the night at the top of the *pali* and complimented us warmly on our courage in risking the descent in the dark. When we remind ourselves that thanks to him we were reduced to such an extremity, we are tempted to give him a sound drubbing; but that would delay us too much. He was punished quite enough when we ordered him to saddle our mounts. The clown has gambled on his delay, hoping by this means to persuade us to spend the whole day here, where he is acquainted with a young Hawaiian beauty, as dark and statuesque as the shepherdesses of Virgil, though far less savage and wild. He invents a thousand tales to make us change our minds, but we are immovable and we congratulate him on his courage, at seven o'clock in the morning, to descend a *pali* such as this one which he will have to climb up again at ten. Our revenge is very innocent, and he resigns himself to his lot, among other reasons because he cannot do anything else.

We are leaving for Manaiole and Laumaia. I shall write to you from the first place where I can find a pen, ink, and some paper, rare articles here. I shamefully confess that I regret still more the scarcity of foodstuffs. We cause a famine everywhere we stop, and I do not envy those who will be following us.

Manaiole
November 16, 1857

We left Waipio yesterday morning and yesterday evening we arrived at Laumaia, where we were welcomed by the hospitable Mr. Kenway, an American who settled in this country many years ago. From Waipio to Laumaia, the road skirts the sea, looking down upon it from a height of several hundred feet. The ocean stretches on the right, calm and blue as an exquisite Swiss lake; to the left, some thick groves of trees, advance guards of the inland forests, providing, from one lap to the next, a haven of shade which the unbearable heat beating down from the sun makes one search for thirstily. Monotony is the single blemish of this landscape, in which there are united so many of the elements of perfect beauty.*

---

*There is much that is confusing in this account of the Waipio-Laumaia-Manaiole trip, and some hints that it may have been made during the family stay in Hilo in 1861. Note Mme. de Varigny's reference to Laupahoehoe in her narrative in Appendix 2.

After leaving the valley at ten o'clock in the morning, we arrived at Laumaia at four in the evening, the end of a short enough stint. The road was excellent, and we abandoned ourselves to the pleasure of galloping over a thick grassy plain and in this way stirring up around us an artificial breeze. Mr. Kenway received us in his best style, and we did ample justice to his hospitality. His ranch is situated about a mile from the sea, on a bluff where the unbroken view reaches out to the very limits of the horizon. We there again met with the painful spectacle the traveler encounters at every step in the Hawaiian archipelago: I mean the rapid decrease of the race, in early times so numerous, which originally peopled these islands. Everywhere one comes upon uncultivated taro patches now invaded by parasitic weeds, ruined enclosures, dilapidated huts over which nature spreads a luxuriant cloak of vegetation. Nevertheless, everything still evokes the image of a vigorous people, by necessity hardworking, but today groping their way hit or miss through perils which have practically destroyed them, all as the result of their contacts with a foreign civilization.

The dense forest land between Laumaia and Manaiole took on a spacious grandeur. We passed through several clearings where we caught glimpses of the snowy summit of Mauna Kea. The tang of cool air as we drew it deep into the lungs formed a delightful contrast to the oppressive heat of the days preceding. We found ourselves at this stage 7,000 feet above sea level. Here the atmosphere of these upland plateaus has an exceptional power to carry the sound of the human voice, making ordinary tones audible a mile away; but there are no traces of inhabitants. Only some great wild cattle, recognizable by their curly hair, trouble the silence of these solitudes when during their wanderings a dead branch is broken. Like Hippolytes of the tragedy, we loosened our bridles and let them hang listlessly on the necks of our horses, who on their part were taking things very easy. Halemakule was struck by the unfortunate idea of testing the effects of his Hawaiian chanting as it reverberated among the mountain echoes. Still one more point on which we failed to agree. We preferred the song of the native birds to his slow, monotonous *melopoeia*.

Several hours ago we arrived at Manaiole, the ranch of Mr. Parker, an English settler.* We find here a completely patriarchal way of life. Ten Kanakas rushed to us on our arrival to take over the reins of our horses, who doubtless would have been quite ready to let us dismount without this medieval courtesy. Several young girls, attracted by the sounds of excitement, have followed along after them, some to find berries for us, *ohelo,* and bananas, some to look after kitchen and dairy supplies; and you can be

---

*John Palmer Parker (b. Newton, Mass., 1790; d. Waimea, 1864) was of American and not British origin. [A. L. K.]

sure that, like Paul-Louis, I shall be leaving you for their company as soon as they return. Cattle bellow, horses (not ours) whinny, sheep bleat, and a gentle fragrance of dinner titillates the olfactory nerves. Halemakule watches others while they perform the tasks that are rightly his. Squatting on his heels, he regales a circle of chattering Hawaiian matrons, who break into peals of laughter at his account of our travel adventures. We are all lodged in a sort of box (or, if you prefer, in a house) whose various compartments are sealed tight and entirely built of *koa,* a wood of the region resembling mahogany, and the *koa* has been highly varnished: roof, doors, partitions, floor, parquet, inside and outside alike, all glistening and insisting on being admired, all shipshape, very neat, clean, and exactly right. One might speak of the place as a gigantic toy.

Our host, Mr. Parker, is a man of cosmopolitan background. After many travels, he settled on this island where he had been captivated by the charms of a young and pretty native girl. He made her his wife and she presented him with three children. By his energy and enterprise he has built up a considerable fortune. He was already established on the island of Hawaii several years before the arrival of the earliest American missionaries. He possesses today a store of curious details concerning the behavior of the natives and the customs of old times. You should especially hear him tell of Kamehameha I. The account he gave to us of the battle fought on the plains of Kuamoo in 1819, an event that dealt a blow to idolatry from which the old paganism has never recovered, lends to the storyteller no less than to the geographical setting of the battle an extraordinary magic. We spent an entire evening with Mr. Parker and I swear I have experienced few so agreeable. His reminiscences evoke the romance and color of legend. Sprinkled thick with native sayings, proverbs, fragments of chanted poetry, they are nevertheless told without pretentiousness. If I had seen nothing at Manaiole except himself, I should never regret my trip to the island of Hawaii.

November 18, 1857

Our friend Taine in his account of his journey through the Pyrenees* has described wonderfully that powerful spell, an attraction in some degree physical, exerted on one by the propinquity of a high mountain. I have yielded to that spell and, indeed, both of us giving way to its irresistible dominion, Von Holt and I have decided to climb Mauna Kea. For eight days we have been scouring the slopes, and for eight days we have gazed in wonderment up at that curving dome with its bedazzling whiteness. Snow awakens in us delicious sensations of coolness. How good it can be to feel cold! Thus reason

---

**Voyage aux Pyrénées* (Paris: Hachette et Cie, 1855). [A. L. K.]

the denizens of the tropics, *cher ami,* envious of what they lack, but strongly appreciating whatever they have. Our ascent decided upon, we beat about the countryside organizing our means of carrying it out. First of all, there is the problem of a guide; second, the horses. The Kanakas we questioned urged us to talk to Jack Purdy.

Jack Purdy is a curious specimen of the kind of life some people lead in these Hawaiian Islands. He settled in this country about twenty-three years ago. He camps rather than lodges in a huge house situated in the very middle of a plain—there's not a tree, not a spot of shade, not a flower inside Jack Purdy's compound, constantly trampled by twenty horses as little civilized as their master. He is English by origin, age forty-five. He sailed from Liverpool as a cabin boy at the age of ten. He was a twenty-year-old sailor when a shipwreck washed him to shore on Hawaii. There he has stayed.

Jack is the best rider in the island, the most daring hunter of wild bullocks, the man who knows best the forest trails and the mountain passes. A tireless hiker, he covers enormous distances without turning a hair. Thanks to his rifle and hatchet, when in the woods he is always sure of finding food and shelter. He is usually accompanied by four large ugly dogs, well broken to this style of life, whose numerous scars attest to their bellicose dispositions. Jack is not alone in this kind of existence. There are many others who hire out their rifles and their stout arms to large-scale ranchers, who purchase government franchises for permission to raise wild cattle for commercial purposes. But for sheer daring no one surpasses Jack Purdy. When he has nothing better to do Jack will get a bit tipsy, if he is not already roaring drunk. It is his way of relaxing.

Only on one occasion, when he met a worthy rival, has Jack ever seen his laurels in danger of wilting. The rival, Mr. Brenchley,* was also a compatriot. Strong as Hercules, with courage enough for any kind of test, Brenchley was a man obsessed, an explorer whose adventures read like a novel. He was one of the first persons to cover on foot the American continent from Saint Louis in Missouri to British Columbia. Eventually, he arrived in the Hawaiian Islands, where he found the climate and the beauty of the scenery so alluring that he spent several years in Hawaii, devoting much effort to the study of the native language and familiarizing himself with the manners and customs of the Kanakas. He visited every part of the kingdom. He was as good a sailor as he was a skilled horseman and a first-rate walker, and by choice he traveled by the oldest schooners, the worst roads, the wildest

---

*Julius Lucius Brenchley (1816–1873), British traveler and author, educated at St. John's College, Cambridge. His travels took him to the United States in 1849, where he lived among the Indians. After arriving at Fort Vancouver, he sailed for the Hawaiian Islands and there in 1850 fell in with Jules Remy, the French scientist and ethnographer. Brenchley's adventure on Hawaii in the company of Jack Purdy presumably occurred in the early 1850s. [A. L. K.]

horses. He finally reached the island of Hawaii, preceded by a reputation honestly acquired, adored by the natives among whom he had spent the income of a sizable fortune. What he had heard about Jack Purdy gave him the idea of securing Jack as a guide. The result was a contest in courage and daring that lasted several months, but in which neither Purdy nor Brenchley finally came out the victor.

Purdy proposed to his companion to spend several days on the yonder side of Mauna Kea. However, they were not to take anything with them (as they normally would have done) besides their rifles and their blankets. The invitation was at once accepted, and our two rivals set forth along the road. On the first day they camped at snowline. Then they crossed the mountain and continued in the direction of Mauna Loa. The wild duck, the goose, and the plover provided them with food; but whether through some malicious trick or perhaps just a failure in foresight, they soon exhausted their gunpowder. Furthermore, they were not equipped with lassos, and the same was true of their horses, who should have carried lassos on their saddles. Jack was not dismayed. When Mr. Brenchley asked him how they would manage to eat, he answered that by a forced march they could reach a spot where wild bulls abounded and where he, Jack, was quite accustomed to finding an excellent dinner.

It never occurred to Mr. Brenchley to demur; his *amour propre* and curiosity had been whetted. After tramping more than twenty miles they came upon a stretch of swampland. There they bravely entered the hazardous terrain, sinking down at each step up to their knees. "The road's poor," Mr. B. appropriately observed. "Poor?" replied Purdy. "There are worse ones." —"Where are your wild bulls?—"There, in the woods."—"And how shall we tackle them?"—"There are lots of ways," answered Purdy. "You'll see, you don't need to worry. I'll just turn the bull over to you when he can't any longer defend himself—the rest will be up to you." "So be it," said Mr. Brenchley. Purdy headed for the dense thicket and disappeared among the trees.

After only a few moments, the familiar sound of breaking branches and trampling feet told Mr. Brenchley that a wild bull was approaching in his direction. In fact, a magnificent animal with eyes blazing and tail as stiff as a rod emerged from the brake to a distance about fifty paces away, where he attempted by a single leap to cross the muddy trail where Mr. Brenchley himself was standing half-submerged in the mire. But the leap failed and the bull fell into the bog, at its deepest and stickiest point. After several unsuccessful efforts to free himself, he remained a prisoner. "There's our dinner," said Purdy, when he returned a few moments later. "All you have to do is kill the beast and slice off a piece." "But," said Mr. Brenchley, "if the bull is so hopelessly stuck that he can't pull himself out, how can we possibly get to him and back?" "I thought you had more gumption than that," said Mr. Purdy, with a smile of triumph and the superior tone of an expert. Then he gathered two bundles of marsh rushes, knotted them tightly together and threw one bundle in front of him into the mire, mounted it as if on horseback, pushed the second bundle in front of him, and then hitching himself along from the first to the second, did exactly the same thing with the first, and so on until he reached the bull, which he thereupon killed with a single thrust of his hunting knife. After removing a slice of meat from the bull, he made his way back across the mudhole, washed his hands, lighted a fire, tossed the bloody piece of steak down upon the stones that rimmed his fire pit, and dined with his comrade. The following day Mr. Brenchley set off alone on the return trip to Hilo and caught the next schooner for Honolulu.

Such was the tale, notably unadorned, that Purdy shared with us on the night before our departure, tossing down his throat slug after slug of gin, which seemed to have no effect on him other than to cause him to lay aside his normal taciturnity. We had come to terms with him, settling on 250 francs plus a tip (left up to our generosity). He provided us with two sturdy horses and placed himself at our disposal for three days.

The next morning, as dawn was breaking, we left for Kalaieha, situated between Mauna Kea and Mauna Loa. From that approach the ascent of the mountain presented less difficulty. Our horses were fresh, the plain was level, the pleasure of our frequent gallops indescribable. The cloudless sky and the clear, transparent atmosphere made objects appear so close that our undertaking seemed an excursion for a party of children. We continued in this way for about fifteen miles. Then we called a halt in a cluster of pandanus trees to rest our mounts and eat our lunches. The view was superb. The road, or to speak more accurately, the direction we were traveling, spiraled along the sloping sides of the mountain, hovering at an elevation about 2,000 meters above the sea. On our right, the long rolling landscape slanted steadily downward to the shoreline; on our left, Mauna Kea; before us, at the horizon, the somber mass of Mauna Hualalai; and, circling all around us like a glassy azure ring, a sea of blue so intense that each feature, each detail, defined itself with a glorious purity of outline—the headlands, the coves, the cliffs. A day of perfection—and how we made the most of it!

At five o'clock in the evening we reached Kalaieha, where we were planning to camp. Kalaieha is neither a town, nor a village, nor even a huddled corral of grass huts. It is an immense plain which sprawls between two mountains. At certain periods of the year, especially in July and August, the plain abounds in wild geese attracted by the *ohelo,* small red berries with a rather insipid flavor. The shrub bearing this fruit is more plentiful at Kalaieha than anywhere else. Moreover, during the period of our excursion, sportsmen and amateur hunters looking for game pay frequent visits to Kalaieha for the pleasure of shooting. Unfortunately, the wild geese begin to spoil very quickly and cannot stand being shipped to Honolulu, since the journey takes three days. It is accordingly only on Hawaii that one can gourmandize on the birds. When we were at Kalaieha the season had just passed. The plain was entirely deserted and the bushes were stripped of their fruits. In compensation, though the geese were missing, the wild bullocks, boars, and stray dogs who had reverted to a state of nature were present in hordes. The place swarmed with wild boars. The ground, churned up over large areas by their tusks and snouts, gave our horses very uncertain footing, causing them to stumble in the furrows excavated by these hungry creatures in their pursuit of the *ti* root and the sweet potato.

Within this whole enormous mountain plateau, measuring not less than ten leagues in length and four in width, there is not a single stream. Here and there in the twists and turns of the rocks the traveler comes upon an occasional large pool or several meager springs, which are enough, however, to slake the throats of the wild animals that wander in these lonely pastures.

Near one of these springs, under a dense umbrella of pandanus and *kukui*, stood a spacious native lodge. Its four walls built of unmortared stones set upon the ground supported a roof framed of tree branches, quite adequate to ward off the rays of the sun, but unable to provide more than miserable shelter against the rain. Fortunately the weather was fine and steady. Our camping arrangements were quickly carried out. With saddles for pillows, a single blanket for the night, and several tins of preserved food for our supper, our living accommodations took up minimal time. When we had looked after our horses, making sure that they were strongly tethered with ropes long enough to let them forage, we gathered together sufficient firewood to last the night. After our meal we lighted up our cigars and made small talk, until sleep consigned us to silence. The only sound which disturbed our solitude and slumber was the far-off howling of wild dogs, warning one another from one distance to the next of our invasion of their territory. The fire, however, was enough to keep them away, and we knew that so long as they could see the light of our campfire, they would not approach within a mile of us.

The next day at dawn we were on our feet again, refreshed and ready, after washing ourselves generously at the spring's expense. We ate our breakfasts and then at five o'clock set forth on our ascent of the mountain. Our plan was to reach the summit and then descend by the other side in the direction of Manaiole, which we hoped to reach by six or seven o'clock in the evening.

We left the plain behind us and entered thick forests of *koa (Acacia falcata)*. Here and there stood enormous tree ferns *(Cibotium chamissionis)*; but as we continued to climb, the trees became more scarce, more thin and stunted, until finally they ceased altogether. Bushes took their place, at first vigorous and close-growing, later puny and sparse. The ground was carpeted with strawberry plants covered with their fruit, which our horses crushed at every step, sending up a perfume that reminded us of Europe. Grass became rare and short; after it appeared the *Ranunculi*.* Our horses sank down into the cindery soil or stumbled upon small stones that rolled under and behind them. We found it necessary either to be first in line or else keep a distance between us and our neighbor, in order to avoid these vexatious avalanches. We climbed and continued to climb. At 10,000 feet we began to note the first tufts of *Ensis argentea*,† a last but marvelously hardy vestige of plant life. This spectacular creature, which I have never observed elsewhere except on the high mountain tops of Hawaii, is a veritable miracle. Clinging to the ground by its very deep roots, in form it resembles the aloes. Its sword-shaped leaves are whitish gray, covered with a light down. They glitter brilliantly as they catch the rays of the sun. From the center rises a stalk reaching as much as ten feet high, which bears a silky plume similar to that of sugarcane during its blossoming period.

At last we sight snow. The air is so transparent that we believe we are much closer than we are. Our horses, panting, catch their breath noisily and want to stop with every step. Their flanks swell and diminish with a movement like that of the bellows of a forge. We feel pity for these poor weary beasts and to relieve them take to our own feet; but after ten steps we drop down exhausted. Jack has not followed our example; he has kept to his mount. After several moments of rest, we want to resume the march, now leading our horses by their bridles. Impossible—we have absolutely no strength at all. Whence comes this weakness? We attribute it to the rarefied atmosphere, and Jack, who rejoins us, confirms our hypothesis. We shall find it impossible, says he, to cover a mile in an hour. Our horses suffer from the same cause, but less than we do. We easily allow ourselves to be convinced and remount our animals.

The summit seems to retreat before us, to escape all our efforts. But we are climbing, always climbing, and snowfield follows upon snowfield. At last we reach the final plateau. The glare of the sun reflected on that great white expanse dazzles us. The solitude and silence—how deathlike everything is! No sound is heard, no living creature stirs. We take our bearings as we cast our eyes into space, and space here seems immeasurably vast. Far down, at the lowest level from where we stand, stretch the forests we have

---

Ranunculus hawaiensis, the native buttercup, *makou*. [A. L. K.]

†'*Ahinahina*, the silversword *(Argyroxiphium sandwicensis)*, is found only at higher altitudes on Maui and Hawaii. [A. L. K.]

just crossed, the plateaus, the hills, all the varied undulations of the terrain; in front of us, Mauna Loa and its dome of snow; then, over and across the channel separating us from the island of Maui, we confront Hale-a-ka-la (House of the Sun), Maui's great mountain. Twenty leagues as a bird flies divide us from that overwhelming mass, the huge crater that engulfs our fascinated gaze. At the right the hills of Kohala lose scale as they become lower and smaller until, finally, they vanish into the sea. The horizon ranges out of sight. We feel ourselves the plaything of a dream.

Jack shares with us neither our emotions nor our sense of wonder, of metaphysical mystery. Him the stunning landscape stuns not at all. He is preparing our midday meal. We have sore need of it. We had set out at five in the morning, and it is now two in the afternoon, and we perish from hunger. So our lunch is delicious—and likewise our savory two-hour rest! At four we return to our saddles. The sky continues to display its incomparable purity, but a bank of light fog moving upward from the shore evidently does not suit our guide, because he is hurrying us to get started, chides us for being so slow, so loath to tear ourselves from our fit of contemplation. Finally we leave. The mist thickens, forms long cloudlike strands of vapor that writhe like serpents at our feet, break into fragments against the rugged slopes of the mountain, then roll by in heavier tufts along what, momentarily, we perceive as the lower plain. But these moments gradually become rarer and more brief. When we reach the elevation just opposite the one we earlier climbed, the entire mountain is encircled with great white clouds that make it no longer possible to distinguish anything, as they crawl along 2,000 feet below our own level. The ridge we stand on is flooded with warm rays of sunlight, bathed in an atmosphere of exquisite purity. In the distance, however, we no longer identify anything except the three summits of the three mountains that still dominate the ineffectual clouds below them. The panorama is beautiful always, but today it is more noble than usual, more imposing in its majesty. We feel ourselves to be at one of those moments when the human mind aspires toward the infinite, believing it comprehends the infinite because of having yielded to its ineffable presence.

The descent begins, at a rate more rapid but also more painful than the ascent. We make excellent time as far as the girdle of surrounding clouds; but then, submerged in a dense fog which pierces to the very marrow, we notice also that daylight is beginning to wane, and realize we shall not reach Manaiole by seven or eight o'clock.

In point of fact, it was almost midnight before we reached our base, soaking wet and completely worn out, ready to collapse. We were nevertheless still trembling with the thrill of our experience, quite ready to repeat it someday under better conditions when we could take more time. At Purdy's ranch we sat down to a supper we did full justice to, with a good fire to dry us, a couple of straw slippers, and *two* blankets. A man needs no more to discover happiness.

Kawaihae
November 20, 1855

Here we are again, *mon cher ami*. Tomorrow morning we board ship for Honolulu, and I must set aside this last evening to bring to its conclusion this narrative of a trip which I shall always recall with delight. After leaving Manaiole yesterday morning astride the excellent horses supplied by our host, we quickly covered at a gallop the ten miles between there and Waimea, where we arrived in one hour. The road lay along a level plain that stretches from Mauna Kea to the hills of Honoipu.

At Honoipu we stopped for several hours at the house of Mr. Frank Spencer, manager of a considerable ranch, where he raises great herds of beef cattle and thousands of sheep. Under his hospitable roof we enjoyed a fine bath and a Homeric midday repast. Mr. Spencer, who is used to setting a handsome table, was so persuasive when inviting us that we took him at his word, even though it meant delaying our journey. Afterward we gladly accompanied him on a tour of his enormous agricultural enterprise. Surrounded on all sides by the finest pastureland, Waimea is *par excellence* the district for stock grazing; but there, as in many other areas of the Hawaiian Islands, one notices numerous signs of deterioration and ruin. Noxious weeds, above all the wild indigo, have invaded the most fertile plains and each year have taken over land where in earlier times hundreds of thousands of beef cattle could wander for forage.

After spending several hours at Waimea, we took off down the road to Kawaihae, where we arrived yesterday evening. Since I find myself here again, I must not forget to tell you of two peculiarities of this region, in other respects already so remarkable. The first weird phenomenon occurs at night; the second must be searched out by daylight. I mean the *Mumukou [Mumuku]* and the *heiau*.

Imagine yourself quite tired and very ready to put in a night's sleep. What occurs is like nothing so much as the play about *The Bear and the Pasha*—in fact, it is precisely the same thing. You go to bed. It's so hot that it would be suicide to shut the door or window. You fall asleep. All goes well for several hours. But towards two or three in the morning, you are awakened all at once by an infernal knocking. One would say that gusts of paving stones were flying through the air, whole boulders were being rolled through your room, you can hardly breathe because of the dust, the roof rattles and reverberates like a drum—say a two-headed Basque tambour—in a deafening hailstorm. You jump from your bed, and if you have a neighbor, you call out to him to find out what's the matter. If he hears you amidst all the racket, and especially if he has already spent several nights at Kawaihae, he will reply phlegmatically that it's the *Mumukou,* otherwise known as the wind of the mountain, which springs up periodically, lasts an hour or two, and ceases before dawn. The best thing to do is try to go back to sleep and pay no attention to it. Von Holt and I are convinced that we could live ten years here without achieving this result.

The *heiau* has the advantage over the *Mumukou* that it doesn't come looking for you, and that you can choose whether or not you care to pay it a visit. *Heiau* means "temple" in kanaka speech, and the temple of Puuapa, situated about a mile from Kawaihae, is the largest and most intact still in existence in the archipelago. Its length is 350 feet, its width 150. The walls are 50 feet thick at the base, 8 at the top, and not more than 20 high.*

The materials used to construct this huge barbaric monument were brought, according to tradition, from the valley of Pahulu [Pololu], about twelve miles (three leagues) away. The whole population of the island was assembled for this purpose, and the stones were passed along by hand from one toiler to another, so that the work was completed, so it is said, in three days. The exceptional interest of this architectural triumph, the last relic of paganism in the Hawaiian Islands, consists entirely in the fact that innumerable human sacrifices washed these stones with their blood, and that numerous human bones are still found among the loose and scattered fragments of the *heiau*. In the northeast corner of its precincts, open to the sky, lies an enormous flat stone on which the victims were killed. It was there that they were dissected, the bones stripped of their flesh, picked clean, then tied in bundles and buried among the rocks which formed the foundations. At a short distance from this stone one notices several others of the same shape, with a shallow incised griddling, on which the flesh was burned. These stones have vitrified surfaces, a result of the fierce heat. There are still living a few Kanakas who were present at these dreadful tragedies when they were small children; but though they speak of the scenes they witnessed with utter naïveté, they deny energetically that the flesh of the victims was ever eaten by the executioners. There is nothing in the history or traditions of the Hawaiians to justify the charge of cannibalism so carelessly brought against them.

When I touched with my hands these repositories of human bones, with

---

*Varigny seems to have confused two important *heiau* in the area: Puʻu Kohola near Kawaihae, and Mookini Heiau at the northern tip of Kohala, the stones for which, it is said, were carried from Pololu Valley. There is a hill in North Kohala called Puʻu Apaʻapaʻa. [A. L. K.]

their wrappings of fine network now almost turning to dust, I felt a profound sadness. I pictured to myself the hideous scenes of bloodshed and carnage: the resigned victims, paralyzed with superstitious terror; the fanatic priests; the crowd so rapacious to watch the last twitchings; so eagerly listening for the last shudders of one of their own fellows. Today the site of all these deeds lies under a curse. Nothing grows, nothing lives at the ruined temple of Puuapa. No human being dwells near the bloodstained walls, no step approaches to tread upon the stones where paganism so long held its odious assizes and celebrated its infamous saturnalian rites.

However oppressive and sad these last emotions were, they did not diminish the many fascinating experiences I shall long recall from my visit to Hawaii. At the moment of leaving the island, I consoled myself with the idea of returning one day, of reviving at first hand my impressions of those splendid scenes. But it is not merely memories I am concerned about: it is also notes, observations, facts. I love this land where my own volition and destiny working together have led me, this people who are so hungry to become civilized, so unsuspectingly trustful in their attempts to assimilate themselves to another mode of existence, and who so timidly petition the Great Powers for the right to live under their own kings and chiefs and to join the family of nations. I sympathize with their desires. I believe they can and should be realized. In my own modest measure I shall be happy to contribute to the fulfillment of their hopes. But I do not see at all clearly how it may fall to my lot to do so. Quite the contrary. I see only too vividly the opposing obstacles, which the ambition of the United States, the indifference of France, and the jealousy of England place in the way of Hawaiian aspirations. It will take years, many long years, and above all it will require very far-reaching political changes, to accomplish what the Hawaiians seek. As I await that time which I probably shall not see, I reach out to you a cordial hand. . . .

CHAPTER 7

PERILS OF AN ISLAND ECONOMY

Birth of the prince of Hawaii.—New ministers.—A seductive offer.—A royal crime.—The Anglican church.—Death of the French commissioner.—Political and agricultural condition of the country.

As I mentioned earlier, the Hawaiian government did not agree to a new treaty with France without sharp reluctance, nor did the government believe that its case had been wholly lost. Before the treaty had been agreed upon and ratified, the Hawaiian authorities were hoping to obtain concessions. At the same time that Hawaii was pressing its interests in Paris officially before France's minister of foreign affairs, in Honolulu every appropriate step was being taken to increase the number of the government's supporters and to profit as much as possible from every shift of events. One of the most important developments, so far as the nation and the dynasty were concerned, was the birth on May 20, 1858, of the prince of Hawaii, son of Queen Emma and Kamehameha IV.

The joy of the royal household was shared by the entire country. It was evident that the birth of an heir to the throne would serve to preserve and consolidate the Kamehameha dynasty, already recognized and accepted by foreign powers, and very precious to the natives. Several splendid public festivals celebrated the happy event, and the young queen, greatly loved and respected by everyone, received the clearest proofs of this sincere sympathy and esteem.

During the same period, a change of administration in the United States resulted in the recall of the American commissioner, Mr. David L. Gregg, and his replacement by a new representative, Mr. James W. Borden. Mr. Gregg was popular in the islands despite his intemperate habits, and the king felt for him a real liking. Without being exactly hostile to France, Mr. Gregg was known for his personal antagonism toward M. Perrin. The opponents of the treaty habitually took advantage of this combination of circumstances. Urged by the arguments of this group to enter the service of the Hawaiian government, Mr. Gregg gave his consent. After several interviews the king offered him the post of minister of finance, vacant at that time. The king's brother, Lot Kamehameha, had held this office during the interim.

These actions were approved with great satisfaction by the American party, who saw in Mr. Gregg's membership in the cabinet a personal victory and a checkmate to the French representative. M. Perrin revealed that he was very much aware of this situation. It became quite apparent both to him and to me that the final signatures would not be secured without serious difficulties.

In August, we received from Paris the treaty in the form in which it had been ratified by the emperor. We were ordered to conclude without delay the long and burdensome negotiations. M. Perrin duly informed Mr. Wyllie that he was ready to get on with the exchange of signatures. To this communication, his excellency the Hawaiian minister of foreign relations replied that the king, in accord with the nation's constitution, would first seek the advice of his ministers. It was a little late for him to want counsel concerning these formalities, but the Hawaiian government was in effect the prisoner of the constitution and its precisely worded text.

The privy council, a body without much real responsibility, whose membership was controlled by the cabinet ministers, had to knuckle under to its superiors on all matters of importance. For several months, however, the privy council members, particularly the natives among them, being much plagued by the opponents of the treaty, openly expressed their objections to the altered conditions that adoption of the new treaty would bring about. The significance of these changes had been greatly magnified by critics of the treaty, yet with the best of intentions the treaty's friends had found it hard going to demonstrate to the privy council the benefits to Hawaii the treaty could reap. The Hawaiian negotiators, very much embarrassed by their predicament, asked for nothing better than to conceal themselves behind the votes of the privy council, and in this way evade their responsibilities. In the eyes of the French government they had given proof of their own goodwill; other interests paid little attention to them. Under such circumstances, there was no doubt about the votes of the privy council.

Mr. G. M. Robertson, the chairman-elect of the treaty committee and also justice of the supreme court, who was one of the most vehement enemies of the treaty, presented his report recommending rejection. After a two-day discussion, this general conclusion was adopted with a single change, introduced by the few supporters of the French point of view. This modification consisted in inserting into the treaty an additional article that expanded, but in the emotional language of popular harangues, the text proper of the treaty. In doing so the revision deprived the document of any value it might have had in the judgment of the French government.

M. Perrin was infuriated by this unexpected development. In his dispatches to Paris, he had given the impression that the success of the treaty was assured. Not only had success eluded him, but in addition the opponents of the treaty were spitefully celebrating their victory with a cannon salute of 101 volleys. The Honolulu populace, worked up to this state by the leaders of the American party, were milling in the streets, jeering outside Perrin's windows, exactly in the manner customary in the United States for celebrating the triumphs of their political parties. Nothing was missing, not even the classic frontier "shivaree."*

There was no alternative for M. Perrin save to confront fortune's turnings with courage. He was concerned above all with the need to get the signature of the king. He declared accordingly that he was ready to approve the treaty with the additional article—this last, however, to be *"ad referendum"* only; or, in other words, he would defer on this point to the judgment of his government. Under these conditions the king gave his signature, and the treaty thus approved was returned once more to Paris for final study.

Early in 1859 we received from the French ministry the reply to this communication. Just as could have been easily predicted, the French government flatly rejected the article. The original matter of the treaty itself was confirmed, however, the signature of the king being considered as valid and final so far as the text proper was concerned. Thus called upon to adopt the treaty in this shape and put it into effect, the Hawaiian government gave way. There was nothing else to be gained, and there seemed to be no cogent reason to risk a crucial break with France.

Thus relations between the two countries became more and more strained with each passing day. Questions in themselves not very significant became exceedingly complicated, causing constant clashes and ill-feeling between the French commissioner and the principal members of the Hawaiian government. The king believed he would be able to smooth over the difficulties by presenting to M. Perrin and the French authorities in Paris a token of his goodwill. He accordingly revealed to M. Perrin his desire to appoint a Frenchman as a cabinet minister, so that French nationality might be represented in his government and make its voice heard. I was the official whom the king singled out by name. M. Perrin welcomed his proposal with pleasure, as he promptly let me know, enthusiastically urging me to accept the offer. He had no doubt about the corroboration of the French foreign office.

Certainly this was an inviting proposal. To exchange my modest position of secretary for a distinguished official role, one providing me a means to appease dissent, an opportunity above all to support the ideas and prospects

---

*Varigny uses the English word. [A. L. K.]

which a careful study of the country and its resources had led me to envision —this was a powerful temptation. But further reflection quickly pointed to other conclusions.

I was too new in Hawaii, too little known, therefore without influence and authority. I admitted to myself that I had still too much before me to achieve, and very much more to study, if I were to sort out from the chaos of my confused and contrary impressions the clear and firm concepts to which I instinctively gravitated by nature, but which I could not as yet claim to have made my own. Furthermore, I needed only to glance about me to realize that I could not depend on anyone else, and that it was necessary for me either to settle myself into the preferred job at once or else withdraw completely. I accordingly decided to refuse the appointment, very much to the great astonishment of M. Perrin, as he watched with regret the collapse of a scheme which his friendship for me had sanctioned, even though his vanity and personal interest as a diplomatist had desired the post for himself.

The sole consequence of this affair was that I set about working with redoubled ardor. I studied, I observed, I overhauled my practical education; I immersed myself in a more thorough study of the English language, which hitherto I had learned only by necessity and by ear. I developed an intense interest in political economy, in agricultural and commercial problems, and finally in all things relating to the country and to its prosperity. I ignored at the time the question whether or not any of this would someday prove useful to me in the islands, but I was fully convinced that there, or later somewhere else, I should find employment for my knowledge; that nothing one has mastered is in vain; and that, in the final reckoning, time devoted to intellectual pursuits is never time wasted.

Circumstances would later prove that I was correct. At the moment, however, nothing was less clear in my mind than my future career. Without seeking to wrest from it any secret promise, I contented myself with my official task as it had been assigned. Fortunately, my duties as secretary of the consulate left me scope for many leisure interests. The negotiations came to an end, politics were taking a rest, emotions overexcited by the conclusion of the French treaty were calmed, at least in appearance; the reorganized ministry was settling down to work, when a sad misfortune befell the royal family.

Among the familiar figures at the palace, the old boon companions in pleasure of the youthful king, there was a certain Englishman,* Neilson by

---

*Henry A. Neilson (1824–1862), who arrived in Hawaii from San Francisco during the early 1850s after the Gold Rush, was not of British but of American origin. He was the youngest son of Dr. John Neilson, a surgeon of the War of 1812 and a prominent medical man of New York City during the 1840s. Henry A. Neilson first emerged in the newspapers of Honolulu as a rep-

name, who lived on the most intimate terms with Kamehameha IV. He accompanied the king on many of those excursions in search of change of scene and climate required by Kamehameha IV because of his chronic asthma. Now despite his marriage, the king had not entirely broken with the habits of his bachelor days; he had, in fact, continued a liaison with one of the ladies of the court, who after his marriage had even become a lady-in-waiting of the queen.

On August 3, 1859, the king, accompanied by the queen and his suite, together with several secretaries including Neilson, left for a trip to Lahaina on the island of Maui. A total lack of serious occupation, combined with more than usual poor health because of his asthma, led the king to indulge his old drinking habit, something he had rarely done since his marriage, but which now he carried to a point of even greater excess. On August 11, close on the heels of a brief meeting with the favorite, and after hard and prolonged bouts of drunkenness, the king boarded his schooner to return to Honolulu. After nightfall, when the vessel was several miles offshore, he gave orders to turn back to Maui, landed at Lahaina, headed for Neilson's sleeping quarters, and called out to his secretary. When Neilson opened the door, the king fired a revolver at him point-blank, and Neilson fell to the floor.

What was the motive for this crime? The name of the queen became involved, although quite unjustly, for she had nothing to do with the matter. It was alleged that the king's paramour had worked upon the jealousy of Kamehameha IV in order to revenge herself upon the queen, who was beginning to suspect the adulterous connection of the favorite with her husband. The truth was that the royal mistress was herself jealous of Neilson, because the latter had urged his close friend the king to break with the lady and keep faith with his marriage vow. Kamehameha IV even accused Neilson of making amorous overtures to his mistress, hoping thereby to supplant the king in her favors. Drunkenness rather than love caused Kamehameha IV to seize the revolver. The crime had hardly been committed when already that volatile and impressionable soul suffered overwhelming pangs of conscience, a state of remorse so bitter and prolonged that ultimately it shortened his life.

The injury to Neilson was not in itself fatal, but his constitution, undermined by the indulgences of his wild bachelor days, could not bear the shock. For some little while he lingered on as an invalid, but finally died.

---

resentative of the New York Board of Underwriters. Up until the shooting tragedy, he served in various capacities as aide, secretary, and business agent in the royal household of Alexander Liholiho, Kamehameha IV. [A. L. K.]

Meanwhile, driven by his regret, the king had only one thought: to return at once to Honolulu, abdicate the throne in favor of his infant son, and devote the rest of his days to the expiation of his crime. In fact, he returned to Honolulu on September 30 and informed his councillors of his plan. The latter advised him to reconsider his decision. Accordingly, but troubled by dark presentiments, he considered it wise to proclaim the prince of Hawaii heir to the throne. A little later, he revived an idea of his ancestor, Kamehameha I, and drafted a letter for dispatch to London, requesting that a branch of the Church of England be established in Hawaii under the auspices of an Anglican bishop and English clergy. The king's emotional temperament was ill-adapted to the puritanical forms of Methodist worship.* As he had been brought up a Protestant, he opposed the spread of Roman Catholicism. The queen, however, whose family background was Anglican, strongly urged the establishment of a church with which she was in perfect intellectual agreement. Thus both husband and wife in the end hoped to entrust the education of the young prince of Hawaii to the requested bishop. Kamehameha IV strengthened his letter of request with an offer of land to be occupied by the future church building, and also with the promise of an annual subscription sufficient to defray in large part the costs of the new clergy. The king's proposal met with a very favorable welcome in England, and received at once careful official study.

But it was not merely in matters of religion that the king was disposed to move more closely within the sphere of British influence. The same tendencies were revealed in his governmental policies. Little by little the American party lost ground they had gained from the abortive negotiations with France, and from the appointment also of Mr. Gregg to the Hawaiian ministry. The latter gentleman succeeded only in damaging his reputation through his intemperance, and henceforth played but a very dim role in public office. His supporters abandoned him, and Mr. Wyllie a staunch advocate of the British alliance, strongly encouraged by the queen, regained all his former power. Acting under Wyllie's orders, Sir John Bowring, a veteran English diplomat attached at that time to the service of the Hawaiian government, submitted alike to the authorities in London and to the Tuileries in Paris a draft for the international treaty. It was hoped that this instrument would in turn rally the support of the United States and so, as the tripartite

---

*By "Methodist worship" Varigny apparently meant the absence of liturgy and ancient church ritual in the services of the early American missionaries. The latter came out of Puritan New England and had their institutional roots in Congregationalism. In general, they emphasized the Protestant evangelical principles of winning converts through preaching, teaching, and printing. [A. L. K.]

treaty's grand goal, guarantee conjointly the independence of the Hawaiian Kingdom and the preservation of the Kamehameha dynasty. This last objective was later abandoned in the course of the negotiations, for in reality there was no need for such a provision in a country where the dynastic question had not arisen, and where no competitor for the throne existed.

The object proposed by Mr. Wyliie was a just one in theory, but difficult to attain. So far as France was concerned, where serious thought was being given to the outcome, Mr. Wyllie's plan had to surmount two hurdles, one of which alone was enough to prevent success. The first was the chronic ill-will of M. Perrin; the second was the newly formulated policy of the French government, which at that time was proclaiming, through its spokesman M. de la Vallette,* the French minister of foreign affairs, the prime need in the world for great imperial nations and, accordingly, for the dissolution of small independent countries. No one in France at that time realized all the harm that would result from this declaration of controlling principles, only bound to alienate the feelings and sympathies of weak nations.

The overtures of Sir John Bowring were naturally received with great coolness by the imperial French officials. In England, however, Bowring's efforts met with a better reception; but in view of the indifference of France, there was a reluctance to embark on negotiations that required the simultaneous agreement of three powers, one of which opposed the drafted treaty simply by ignoring its aims, while the other, the United States, was actively hostile toward its goals. The administration in Washington thus remained faithful to diplomatic and political precedents, refusing to ally itself by means of a *tripartite*† treaty, since such would throttle liberty of action and forestall the advantages to be derived from future eventualities, a possibility and promise the United States had always expected to reserve for itself. The negotiators limited themselves therefore to inconsequential conversations, and these were wholly abandoned when war was declared in America between the North and the South.

Such was the condition of affairs when, on March 29, 1862, M. Perrin died, carried off within a period of four days by tetanus poisoning, the result of a fractured right arm caused by his falling off his horse.

I assumed at once the direction of the consulate, in keeping with standard

---

*Charles-Jean, Marquis de la Vallette (1806–1881), French diplomat, politician, cabinet minister. A supporter of Napoleon III, as ambassador to Rome in 1861 he urged the unification of Italy. Serving briefly as minister of foreign affairs in 1866, he published an influential article arguing the case for the unification of German states under Prussia as a means of preserving peace. [A. L. K.]

†In English. [A. L. K.]

regulations and procedures. I sent a report to Paris and awaited the foreign minister's orders. In 1855 I had been named chief secretary* of the consulate, and so by this time had accumulated seven years of experience of its functions. Ministerial rules required ten years of service for the post of consul, however, of which at least one year was to have been spent in an administrative capacity. I was hoping, understandably, that the foreign office in Paris would reserve the interim directorship for me, permitting me thus to fulfill an indispensable condition for my advancement. This is what in fact occurred, for the minister of foreign affairs kept me on as administrative head of the Honolulu consulate until the appointment of an incumbent, which did not take place until the end of 1863.

Acting in a managerial capacity during this eighteen-month period, I especially applied myself, as in the past, to the investigation and analysis of commercial questions. The records of the Honolulu consulate were in this respect woefully deficient. I labored to fill in gaps and to transmit accurate reports and precise information to the ministry in Paris. Meanwhile, from a political point of view, the atmosphere was becoming comfortably calm and pleasantly relaxed. The personal friction between M. Perrin and the Hawaiian government was not of the type that creates bitter permanent conflict, but instead faded away with M. Perrin's demise. It was also realized that, despite the intimacy I had shared with my superior officer, I had not agreed with all of his ideas. Like him, I was a supporter of Hawaiian independence, but I believed more strongly than did M. Perrin that the preservation of such political autonomy depended on international understanding, indeed on an entente as strict as possible between Hawaii and Great Britain and France. M. Perrin feared almost equally the influence upon Hawaii of England and the pressure of the United States. As circumstances might vary, he leaned sometimes in favor of the one, sometimes in favor of the other, in order to maintain a balance of power. I, on the contrary, considered that the sole danger threatening Hawaiian independence was to be found in the United States; and therefore that the French consular agent should cooperate closely with the foreign policy of England to dispel that danger. This is exactly what I did, and with sufficient success to attract the ferocious enmity of the American annexationist party.

I was now free to concentrate my efforts in the direction I believed to be most useful for carrying out the duties with which I was charged. I found in the field of studies I had chosen, in economic conditions and commercial affairs, an inexhaustible source of factual knowledge. The ocean fisheries were

---

Chancelier, or "keeper of the seal," referring to one who holds secretaryship of a consulate, embassy, or honorific order—e.g., "chancelier de la Légion d'Honneur." [A. L. K.]

in a state of rapid decline. The whales, after so many years of their pursuit in the Sea of Ocholk [Okhotsk] and along the Behring [Bering] Straits, betook themselves farther and farther to the north, where the fishing fleets could not follow after them. The commercial prosperity of the Hawaiian Islands was profoundly affected by this development, for up to this.time Hawaii's livelihood had depended on the whaling industry. Everyone was inquiring anxiously what could be done, and for the first time some thought was being devoted to Hawaii's scarcely developed agricultural resources. Several feeble attempts at large-scale farming had been begun here and there, but these enterprises were mostly haphazard affairs which collapsed, lacking sufficient capital and offering only pitiful precedents at best.

Cattle ranching alone had succeeded, but the problem was not merely one of breeding; it was necessary to market the products. Our closest customer, California, was 700 leagues distant across the sea. The pastures of California were as handsome as ours, but immeasurably more vast. The beef cattle of California sold there at a comparatively cheap prices, and salt pork and bacon were accordingly diminishing as an object of consumption. Furthermore, cattle grazing required great areas of cheap land, whereas the acreage at our disposal was extremely limited, while everywhere else in Hawaii the overwarm climate was an obstacle save on the mountainous high plateaus.

Several enterprising planters had attempted to raise sugarcane and coffee trees, but they had not managed to succeed. Sugar production entails elaborate and costly equipment, and in a country in which loans fetch twelve percent interest and large sources of capital are very rare, where does one find the necessary funds to construct mills and factories? Above all, where does one go for the cheap field labor without which successful sugar production is impossible?

In the long run, it was not money alone that was lacking; the workers were also at fault. The natives either sailed the seas with the whaling fleet, or else they did nothing at all. Apart from their strong emotional attachment to the whaling industry, and to the opportunities for profits it offered, the Hawaiians confined their activities to cultivating their taro patches. Thereby, in exchange for but a few days of rugged labor, they secured table provisions for an entire family. Their bundles of taro also furnished a surplus that they could exchange with the coastal fishing folk for a few dried fish.

Then, too, there was the question of clothing. The women took care of the earning problem, some by entering the employment of the *haoles* (foreigners), others by less mentionable means. As for the feasibility of asking the natives to leave their well-beaten paths, to abandon their old indigenous traditions and boldly adopt new methods of agriculture, this was out of the question. The whites who had tried it had nearly ended in bankruptcy.

Yet it was quite evident everywhere that, sooner or later, agricultural development would provide the only solution of the Hawaiian economic dilemma. Careful investigation indicated that sugarcane production appeared to be the crop that offered the best likelihood of agricultural success. Already in my rural excursions on Oahu, I had made note of the favorable conditions of soil and climate, especially the facilities for irrigation and transport. However, I required additional factual evidence, and wanted very much to study the results already being achieved elsewhere in the country on a fairly extensive scale.

The occasion I was hoping for occurred, and I did not allow it to escape. Mr. Wyllie, the minister of foreign affairs, who was also the owner of a large tract of land in the Hanalei Valley on Kauai, urged me to visit his farm there, which he had recently converted into a sugar plantation. Furthermore, one of my fellow countrymen, who had settled in another part of Kauai, had made me promise to spend several days in his neighborhood. As a result of this kindly arrangement, I was enabled to realize my wish to explore this island still unfamiliar to me. In Honolulu I had been tied down by my professional duties, and up to this period had not accepted invitations from compatriots. Now, in August of 1863, when I found myself at last able to profit from a bit of leisure time, I carried out the projected excursion.

CHAPTER 8

IDYLL ON KAUAI

Excursion to the island of Kauai.—An interisland voyage. —Wailua.—A French farmer.—Visit to Hanalei.— Sojourn at Princeville.—A drama.—The Haena caves.— Return to Honolulu.—Death of Kamehameha IV.

Kauai is situated at the extreme northwestern end of the Hawaiian Archipelago. The distance separating its nearest port from Honolulu is about a hundred marine miles as the crow flies, or about thirty-five leagues, but the prevailing headwinds and ocean currents make it a long and difficult voyage. It requires at least forty-eight hours at sea, and schooners often take seven or eight days to cross the channel. Accidents are frequent. During certain conditions of the wind the coast of Kauai is unapproachable, the seas are always heavy, and frequently, after several ineffective attempts to reach port, ships have to return to Honolulu to await a more favorable occasion before putting to sea.

I boarded the *Annie Laurie,* a schooner of respectable tonnage, moreover one which had recently been fitted out with a steam engine and a screw propeller. The captain was very proud of this innovation and did his best to land us at Koloa in twelve hours. We left at 5:00 A.M., negotiated very quickly the narrow harbor channel, and reached the open sea. So far so good. However, when it became necessary to bear to the northwest and to proceed against the headwinds and currents, unfortunately the screw propeller proved to have been installed far too high on the vessel. As a result, the *Annie Laurie* pitched frightfully, with its bowsprit almost always above water, the stern of the ship in the air, while the propeller flew about feverishly in the void. The choppy sea promised to become rougher still as soon as we were no longer sheltered by the coastal winds of Oahu. The captain concluded that the ship had been improperly loaded, and so we all hove to and piled chests and hogsheads at the stern.

Off we go!—the *Annie Laurie* beginning to move with prow in the air, the propeller plunging into the deep, but to no certain purpose despite its dashing style. After several revolutions the whirling blades halt dead, and the ship rolls and pitches like mad. The captain tells the mechanism to go to the devil, stokes up his little boiler, hoists sail, and we begin to beat up to windward, intending to double round the point at Waialua.

But this was only the start of our miseries. The rolling and pitching were so violent that there was no sense in trying to sleep in our tiny cabins, jammed in with luggage sliding from wall to wall. People spread their mattresses on deck and there lay outstretched, some twenty passengers, squeezed together like herrings and utterly delivered over to all the horrors of *mal de mer*. I had never before gazed on so desolate a scene. The breeze at last freshened. A smart patter of raindrops joined in. Within an hour everything was soaked—mattresses, covers, shawls; the women shiver and the men curse. Feeble remedy: the rain doubles, the sea breaks into foam against the bulwarks, and the *Annie Laurie* pitches and rolls about worse than ever. But we progress, or at least think we do, and await morning with feverish impatience. Finally, after a night of miseries, dawn greets us. "There's Kauai!" shouts a passenger. But alas, no, Kauai is not even in sight: what we are gazing at is the coast of Oahu! We've not even made thirty miles.

The night's rain is followed by a radiant sky and by a wind. But what a welcome wind—it blows from the northeast. By tacking closely with its course, we should be able to proceed. Our schooner, however, adapted to sailing when the breeze is slack, was not very well masted for hugging the wind. Seeking a very brisk breeze, we bear to the west and lean to the north, trusting in the Lord. Within an hour the sun has dried us so that now we parch, having no refuge from its cruel rays. The boldest among us try to keep ourselves active and upright, but very soon we give up. As for the others, they would rather die than get back on their feet. An insanitary and revolting Chinese, adorned with the title of chief steward, makes his entrance carrying an ancient zinc tray holding a half dozen badly chipped cups, swimming with a troubled brew he calls chicken soup. I manage to down a cup of this insipid beverage in which I can distinguish only the sort of dishwater left after boiling rice. Luckily, I had come aboard with a small tin of biscuits in hand.

The majority of the passengers refused any form of nourishment. They had reached the very acme of seasickness, in which the stupefied sufferer, lacking any capacity to resist finally surrenders. Two or three of the English ladies, the most prudish of all, lay sprawled out like sacks, rolling about right and left on their neighbors of either gender, and showing not the slightest concern. It had been an abominable night, but daytime was not much better. Nevertheless, we made a certain degree of progress. One more night of miseries and then another day should find us at last in sight of Koloa.

By the next noon we lay at anchor. The roadstead at Koloa is so exposed, however, that ships toss and heave about there almost as much as when at sea. For this reason, it was necessary to bestir oneself and disembark into the small bobbing boat that sometimes touched the topsides and sometimes dropped ten feet below. The unloading was managed in a manner suitable for handling a herd of beef cattle. After being lowered by whaleboat, the passengers were deposited, unconscious and soaked, sunburned and half-perishing from hunger, onto the sandy shore.

There, reader, you have an exact photographic record of the sea voyage from Honolulu to Kauai. All its wretchedness had been fully described for my benefit, but none had been exaggerated. Though the thought of having to face a return trip was not an inviting one, people fortunately do recover from seasickness with speed—torture itself fades quickly from memory. Though a man hastens to say he will never make the trip again, still he forgets his oaths and comes back to repeat his punishment.

Viewed from a distance, the island of Kauai presents an inhospitable and forbidding marine setting: an *iron-bound coast,* as the English say. Steep palisades; dark crags lifting their summits far above the water; shallow caves chiseled and worn away by the waves; headlands barren of vegetation and with no sandy beaches: such is the prospect of the entire southern and eastern coasts of the island. Koloa, situated on the south side, is a port for landing and loading, but it is accessible only under certain conditions of wind and weather, and there is nothing about its aspect that delights the eye.

While in the process of landing on the beach I was welcomed by M. B. [Bourgoing],* who had invited me to spend several weeks with him as his guest. An open charabanc, completely and comfortably fitted out and drawn by four stout mules, awaited us. Our luggage was installed along with ourselves, and I turned my back upon the sea, the *Annie Laurie,* Koloa, and all my recent sufferings with the greatest satisfaction.

M. Bourgoing's house was situated very near Koloa, only about twelve miles inland. I had heard it spoken of as one of the most enchanting spots on the island, but I confess with shame that, at the moment, the most romantic scenery had less charm for me than a slice of roast beef and a morsel of bread would have afforded. My imagination extended no further; and while it dallied with the delicious thought my host, entirely falling in with

---

*Varigny's book and his wife's memoir are almost the sole available source of information concerning the Bourgoing family, to whom Varigny refers only by the initial. M. Bourgoing seems to have left for California soon after the visit and is last mentioned by Mme de Varigny as living in San Francisco "near the Mission."

my mood, obligingly listed the menu awaiting me—fish, meat, vegetables, fruit. Brute appetite pricked up its ear in total sympathy, while even its opposite faculty, spirit itself, stirred as if willing to be seduced! Reassured on this point, the contemplative soul everywhere regained the ascendant and soon absorbed itself in the vision of the countryside surrounding me. It was fully worth the effort.

Leaving Koloa behind us, we were very quickly crossing a beautiful plain, smooth as a billiard cloth and sprinkled here and there with clumps of native pandanus. Well off in the distance, several high mountains took shape, like a scenic background in a dream, enveloped in a warm mist by the rays of the sun. It was as if a veil of translucent gauze had been stretched between the mountains and ourselves. We jogged off to the right, the road—always excellent—descending at first and then climbing again. The trees increased in number as we traversed long, handsomely maintained avenues resembling those of an English park. Then we approached a wide unruffled river where there was no sign of a bridge. Our horses boldly entered the clear water and made a diagonal crossing.

Suddenly our ears caught a low continuous roar, the sound of Wailua Falls. For at that moment, but a mile farther on, the river we were crossing dropped down to the floor of the valley and there formed a waterfall. Just off to one side of this exquisite spot stands the house of M. Bourgoing.

After we crossed the river, we reentered the parklike landscape. The trees linked their branches above our heads, mingling their leaves and blossoms. We quickly passed through two wooden gates, opened for our benefit by a Kanaka, and then abruptly rounding a curve we drew to a halt in front of a charming country residence, where Mme Bourgoing was waiting to greet us at the door.

For me it was intensely pleasurable to find myself at last among some compatriots. I could not escape the illusion that I was in France; but to do this it was necessary for me to close my eyes and limit myself to the magic circle of our little set of French folk on the island of Kauai. Although it had been many years since M. Bourgoing had left his native land, he and his wife had preserved their devotion to France and their love for her. Unfortunately, this quality is a rather rare one among our fellow citizens living in foreign parts. The majority of them assume what amounts to disdain for the mother country. In this respect they are just the opposite of the English and the Americans, who are always prompt in their loud insistence on their nationality and ready to boast about it, while the Frenchman abroad dissimulates his origin or admits to it reluctantly. His exile, whether voluntary or forced, leaves a bitterness in his heart that betrays itself in his casual remarks, as likewise in his unsuccessful efforts to adopt the customs, outlook, and ideas of those about him. This failing is characteristic of both our race and the Irish. It was also formerly a German attribute, until recent events rendered it no longer true, for the Germans are now proud of their nationality to a degree, as they hardly were before the war of 1866 and their first victory over Austria.

M. Bourgoing is an exceptional specimen of the French emigrant. Along with his wife, he left France to seek his fortune abroad, knowing he could do so more rapidly than in France. Simultaneously he wished to indulge a taste for adventure. First he went to Tahiti and there attempted farming. Like many others, he found himself much interfered with in that small country, burdened by the thousands of rules and regulations of every kind that our French passion for regimentation imposes upon this poor colony and its inhabitants. However, as he wanted to settle in a land at least French in name, he next emigrated to New Caledonia.

Thanks to his energetic enthusiasm and hard work, he there established a successful large-scale farm. Well thought of by the natives, who appreciated his fairness and consideration in all their dealings with him, he attracted around him a large number of laborers whom he employed both in his farming operations and in his cattle raising. His income and its profits mounted rapidly. In order to market his produce he bought first one and later two schooners, assigning them regularly to round-trip voyages between New Caledonia and Australia. The governor of French possessions in the Pacific was happy to see the problem of civilizing New Caledonia being solved by providing the natives with opportunity to labor. Indeed, up to that time most of the New Caledonians were still living as utter savages, either fighting or cannibalizing each other. In order to encourage M. Bourgoing's efforts, the governor entered into an agreement with him to establish a postal service with Australia. As he could now count on a subsidy large enough to defray part of the shipping costs, our host continued to expand his activities, and his influence spread throughout one whole area of New Caledonia. Abounding in courage as well as in energy, he even dared to intervene in the tribal wars and indeed helped some of the local natives to escape certain death. Among the latter he found a young girl, Wenga, and a youth, Warembe, who are still with Bourgoing as servants on Kauai, for they had not wished to become separated from his wife and him when the Bourgoings decided to leave New Caledonia.

Perhaps they would still be there today, had it not been for certain unforeseen circumstances. A dispute arose between M. Bourgoing and some of the zealous Roman Catholic missionaries. The latter wanted to organize a hasty campaign for winning converts, a scheme that to succeed would have needed much time and very adroit management. Soon M. Bourgoing encountered a good deal of priestly interference in the affairs of the numerous natives he employed. He refused to give his support to an unquestionably worthy cause, but one which was being promoted in a manner he did not approve. His relations with the missionaries became embittered. He accordingly realized he would be drawn into a wearisome struggle, and preferred to sell his interests and leave the place.

Having heard favorable reports of the Hawaiian Islands, M. Bourgoing decided to go there and settle. He arrived in Hawaii with a modest capital, bearing very complimentary recommendations from the governor of French possessions in Oceania. As I was at that time in charge of the French consulate in Honolulu, I welcomed M. Bourgoing and his wife, gave them such advice as my knowledge of the country suggested, and urged him before he undertook a project of his own first to get some practical experience for a while as manager of an already established farming enterprise. I recommended that he get in touch with a particular firm owned by foreigners, and he accepted its offer. So it was he arrived on Kauai, where I now found him acting as the manager of a sizable plantation.

He and his wife gave us a most eager and heartwarming welcome. They did everything they could in their considerate and friendly way to contribute to the comfort of my wife and children, as well as to my own.* We all very quickly forgot the ordeal of the *Annie Laurie*. Whatever other hazards the return trip might hold in store for us we hardly considered, absorbed as we were in our restful life, and enjoying especially the company of our hosts and the entrancing scenery spread before us at our feet.

The house of M. Bourgoing was situated on a level plot of ground with a panoramic view, looking down upon a steep and densely wooded valley. Along its base flowed the pretty Wailua River, the very one we had first crossed on our way to the Bourgoings, whose house stands only about a kilometer away from where the river makes its perpendicular leap down to the valley floor. From the terrace where we were sitting after lunch, we gazed down upon the foamy white cascade of the river, and then on beyond into the depths of the valley, where its silvery curves meandered through banana groves and coffee trees, whose pale green leaves contrasted sharply with the darker hues of orange and lemon orchards. As our eyes traced the river's ca-

---

*Varigny's abrupt departure from his practice of avoiding domestic details might make the modern reader wonder how Mme de Varigny and the children might have fared on the sensational voyage of the *Annie Laurie*. His wife's flat and casual mention of the uneventful channel crossing (see Appendix 2) is completely different from the "ordeal" comically described by her husband. Obviously, in this instance Varigny chose to borrow typical material from other travelers, whose miseries (as he explains earlier in the chapter) had been "fully described for my benefit." No doubt the actual voyage of the Varigny family was by old-fashioned schooner, because the *Annie Laurie* had been taken off the Kauai run at the time. [A. L. K.]

pricious windings, we watched it finally disappear into the thick woods at the far end of the valley. There in the distance it pursued its hidden course until it reached the invisible sea, concealed at the horizon several kilometers away by green hills of charmingly fanciful shapes, projecting skyward in the style of an ancient classical amphitheater. It was the most romantic and at the same time the most genial and friendly, location one could imagine, and it has enjoyed throughout the whole archipelago a rightly deserved renown. Only the famous Hanalei Valley, situated in the extreme northern part of Kauai, surpassed it, people said, in grandeur of scale and beauty.

Kauai is the most fertile of the Hawaiian Islands, the one where the volcanoes first ceased their activity and eventually became extinct. Just as in the rest of the island chain, one notices everywhere signs of subterranean disturbances that have lifted the surface of the earth above the waves; but here, strangely, the traces are not visible, save in the general configuration and makeup of the soil. Lava and scoria here have vanished under the slow, persistent action of the weather. Craters have been transformed into lakes or plains, cinders have been converted into humus, and under these benign influences of sun and rain this theater of terrible convulsions has acquired the demeanor and look of a peaceful, smiling countryside. No sign of this geological transformation is quite so visible on other islands as it is on Kauai, and one can see here what someday the most arid portions of Hawaii and Maui will become, when the same causes will have wrought the same effects.

The day after my arrival I visited, in the company of my host, this beguiling valley. We first went to Hanalei Falls, which I could not help but admire, and afterward made the trip down the Hanalei River by boat. The stream takes its course through the thick shade of lemon, orange, and citron trees (the latter larger than the lemon) which together form a kind of vaulted arch whose mingled odors embalmed the air we were breathing. Nothing could match for charm the path of this stream strewn with miniature islands, where fruits of the guava lay scattered about the ground, and where lemons and oranges hung at a hand's reach and seemed to invite the picking. Two kilometers from the house the banks of the Hanalei broadened: the river, swollen by a thousand small tributaries arriving in the shape of lofty waterfalls or cascading torrents, forms a vast circular curve at the foot of the hills. There it enters the plain, about to lose itself in the ocean, where a noble surf breaks upon a beach of finest sand, sparkling in the sunshine with minute grains of mica.

The plain, like the flat portions of Kauai, has unfortunately been taken over by a variety of grass called *pili,* which has become the despair of the sheep grazers. The larger cattle have become much better adapted to it, and move about quite unbothered by its sharp stalks, which lose their cutting edges when they come in contact with such tougher skins. The natives pay no attention to *pili,* but the Europeans in compensation curse it heartily. It is impossible to walk even for a few minutes among this grass without having one's legs prickle painfully from its unbearable stings. Accordingly, one does not do much walking on Kauai. Instead people spend their lives on horseback. The raising of sugarcane will have a beneficial effect on this scourge, for the extensive and varied types of labor required to grow sugarcane have already cleared several districts of the *pili* menace.

The sugar plantations are flourishing admirably on Kauai. As I mentioned earlier, the soil here is richer than on the other islands. The less mountainous terrain, combined with the thick bed of vegetable matter, offers advantages to the planters that usually they have been able to turn to account. The earliest experiments with sugarcane had been ruinous, but with perseverance the planters managed to achieve some worthwhile results. They chose to develop a type of cane introduced from Tahiti. The yield per acre reached two tons of excellent quality sugar (i.e., 4,400 American pounds), and the profits rose to $100 or 500 francs per acre. Furthermore, at present the planter is able either to market his sugar in Honolulu or to ship it directly to San Francisco. In either case he receives for it an average selling price of 25 cents a pound at the plantation. An acre of land, requiring about 500 francs in manual labor, thus brings 4,400 pounds of sugar, which at 25 cents a pound amounts to 1,100 francs. From this price it is necessary to deduct the interest of the capital tied up in machines and premises. The average size of a plantation is 300 acres, producing annually 600 tons of 1,320,000 pounds of sugar, worth 330,000 francs. After making deductions for costs, including labor and harvesting, the profit per acre of 500 francs rises to a total of about 150,000 francs, with the planter's total gross revenue running about 180,000 francs.

The initial costs of setting up and organizing a plantation naturally vary, depending on its location and the scale and importance of the enterprise. A 300-acre operation could require about 300,000 francs. As interest runs about twelve percent a year, it is necessary to deduct from this total of 300,000 francs about 36,000, plus an equal sum for costs of amortization, totaling perhaps 72,000 francs. The net profit of the planter would thus be about 100,000 francs per year. (These estimates are based on a theoretical yield of about two tons per acre; however, the figures are exceeded in a number of localities, and those given above represent indeed the most conservative average.)

The majority of plantations today have been organized as joint-stock companies. All pay rather large profits, except those operating on credit, which are obliged to pay out a good deal as accumulated interest, a cost that thus consumes all the profits. These are rare cases, however, for many of the plantations are free of debt and have already made their returns on their initial investment.

According to plan, my particular purpose in visiting Hanalei was to make a thorough study of this important question of sugar production. It so happened that Hanalei was the site of a quite large plantation very recently purchased and redeveloped by my ministerial colleague, Mr. Robert Crichton Wyllie. The distance from Wailua to Hanalei is about forty miles or fifty-two kilometers, and we were well mounted for the journey, accompanied by a native servant who looked after our provisions. We left early in the morning, in order to be able to pause for a rest at some midway point along our journey.

The route we followed was delightful, and one of the most picturesque. First it was necessary for us to cross two good-sized streams that at the moment happened to be fordable, though from one moment to the next they could become impassable because of the heavy rains that unexpectedly occur high up in the mountains where the streams originate. The water is pure and clear and makes a lively murmur as it flows over the pebbles. It requires only a storm cloud, however, to convert it into a foaming torrent that sweeps everything before it during its passage. We had seventeen rivers to cross in this fashion before reaching Hanalei, and not one of them provided a bridge. A traveler could find himself caught between two equally unnegotiable currents in full spate, and be forced thereby to wait until it pleased them to subside. One should add that although their rise is rapid, the rivers likewise diminish within a few hours, persistent rains being rare. Within two hours the cloudburst is ended, the sun has dried everything, currents have returned to their normal state, and the delayed horseman having regained his route quickens his pace.

The weather was favorable, even finer than usual. Not a cloud darkened the cheerful horizon charming our gaze, not a single raindrop forced us to hasten or cut down our speed. Around ten o'clock we decided to take a rest in a most inviting clump of *hau* trees *(Hibiscus tiliaceus),* of *kukui (Aleurites triloba),* and orange trees simultaneously loaded with flowers and fruits. Dense shade reigned under their thick branches. In fact, this was the spot where the Gospel was first brought to the natives of Kauai. In this improvised temple, the first Protestant missionary preached his first sermon in the native tongue, and it would indeed have been difficult to choose a site more appropriate for the newborn faith. Since that time, here as in the other islands, Christianity has made rapid progress. The chiefs rallied round the new religion, while the common people likewise welcomed it warmly. No objection, no obstacles of any kind, arose to hamper the work of regeneration, other than those resulting from the natural inclinations of the human heart, and from the painful effort required to resist the temptations of the flesh. For an entire year the Word of God was celebrated within this verdant grove. At the end of that time a fully completed chapel received the new converts.

To give a notion of the cooperation afforded at that time to the missionaries by the chiefs and the government, and especially by the imperious widow of Kamehameha I, the queen regent Kaahumanu, I shall limit myself to mentioning the following fact. The principal problem confronting the Protestant mission consisted in teaching the native women to be chaste. They had no knowledge of either the word or the state. Adultery, incest, fornication were at that time general, accepted by common opinion, consecrated by a shamefully pagan religion. Reform was urgently needed, but it is not easy to reform customary behavior by a series of decrees, and of course new ideas could permeate the minds of the common people only very slowly. The missionaries began by preaching chastity, and by recommending it to their flocks; they banned the *hula,* the licentious dances that were part of the legacy of paganism; but reform nevertheless proceeds slowly. They then invoked the help of the secular power. Kaahumanu, at that time approaching old age, after a tempestuous youth and an unconstrained widowhood, responded to the appeal of the missionaries that a law be promulgated against fornication. She assembled a council of chiefs and submitted to them the following program:

1. The property of any person convicted for the first time of the offense of adultery or fornication will be confiscated; the guilty male or female will be whipped in public and placed in irons for a year.
2. In case of a second offense, the guilty persons will be taken out to sea and held under water until they are nearly dead. Then they will be brought back and allowed to breathe. Then the same procedure will be repeated five times. If they have not by then perished they will be transported to another island.
3. In case of a third offense, the guilty male or female will be put to death, according to the law of God (Leviticus, XX, 10).

The chiefs approved; the law was passed and enforced; and it was not repealed until several years later.

We arrived at Hanalei in the afternoon. Never before had a more grand panorama unrolled before my eyes. I have since visited all the other islands of the Hawaiian group without beholding anything so wondrous. Mr. Wyllie's farmhouse, Princeville, is situated on a rise overlooking the entire valley, at a height of about 300 meters; below the sweeping terrace, extending in front of the house, lies the valley, encircled by steep mountains except on the side toward the ocean. Countless waterfalls descend in leaps and bounds down the mountainsides, forming a river that winds a wayward course amid rich fields of sugarcane and through cotton and coffee plantations. Navigable from its mouth near the shore as far as the heart of the valley, the river is covered with loaded boats carrying the produce to be hoisted aboard the sailing schooners that lie at anchor in the port. Other empty boats are moving upstream, and from the heights on which we stand we hear the rhythmic chanting of the natives as they accompany the rowing motions of the oars. Lumbering wagons drawn sometimes by four and sometimes by eight bullocks come and go between the plantation buildings fronting the river. Along the mountainside, at the extreme end of the valley and facing seaward, rise tremendous stands of timber. These carefully maintained upland forests, whose dark hues contrast with the pale green of the canefields, the silvery gleam of the river, and the radiant blue of the sea, provide a necessary source of fuel for the sugar plantation. Here and there native villages comprising fifty or more grass houses, picturesquely framed by tropical fruit trees, are clustered along the riverbanks. A substantial church lifts its steeple above the trees. Along the beach coconut palms hold aloft their ragged mop-headed crowns. Everywhere there is the stir and commotion of work, an atmosphere of solid prosperity, in a setting of marvelous beauty and calm. Unquestionably, Hanalei deserves its high repute, and I can detect no grain of exaggeration in anything I have ever been told about the place.

My host was pleased to listen to my reflections. He passionately loved this estate he had so recently acquired and from which he tore himself away with utmost reluctance to attend to his official duties in Honolulu. His dream was to return to Hanalei and there spend the rest of his life. He was planning to build a lordly country mansion on the same elevated site where his present dwelling stood. He explained to me his plans for improving his property, and also the working conditions of his employees. Wyllie was simultaneously an enlightened humanitarian and an exceptionally intelligent businessman. He was one of the first to grasp the idea that the development of its agricultural resources assured the Hawaiian nation a glowing future. He was the owner of the entire valley, having acquired it at a very moderate price from its preceding owner, a victim of missionary fanaticism.

Mr. Titcomb, English by origin, and a man of enterprise like so many of his compatriots, had introduced the cultivation of silkworms into the valley. His mulberry groves had prospered, and assured of an abundant harvest he had imported some silkworm eggs from China and Japan. To house them, he built extensive facilities suitably fitted out and well ventilated. At the start, he lost a good many silkworms through the inexperience of the local Hawaiians; next he had tried chiefly employing women as laborers. With much difficulty he succeeded, by his constant diligence, in bringing a number of silkworms to maturity and obtaining some superior cocoons. Encouraged by this initial success, he ordered a second shipment of silkworms. Everything was proceeding splendidly, and the kanaka women were carrying out their tasks well. He presented to each of them a bonus of several silkworms and he himself paid for their cocoons. The industry spread throughout the valley. On all sides Mr. Titcomb was being asked for cocoons, his silkworm farm was developing, natives and foreign settlers alike were sharing in the prosperity.

Unfortunately, silkworm culture demands constant watching, requiring surveillance even on Sunday, in order to renew the supply of mulberry leaves. The mission had recently persuaded the government to pass a law strictly prohibiting, under penalty of heavy fines, all work on the Sabbath. Mr. Titcomb, however, utterly ignored these regulations. Repeated fines were levied against him, to the point where finally the missionary of the neighborhood ordered the native laborers to stay home on Sunday. Because a single day of neglect proved enough to destroy this infant industry, the silkworms died and our Englishman was financially ruined. But not conquered: he returned to the job, abandoned silk production, and henceforth devoted his efforts to raising coffee beans. He succeeded, and today his fortune is assured.

If I mention this incident it is not for the purpose of delivering an indictment against the missionaries. I wish merely to illustrate the inevitable conflicts that occur, sometimes in the most unexpected manner, in a young country where all achievements demand pioneering; likewise to demonstrate the dangers that spring up when religion intervenes in the realm of legislation and politics.

It was largely through the efforts of Mr. Wyllie that the Protestant missionary party met its parliamentary downfall and that a liberal-minded executive cabinet was able to assume political power. Mr. Wyllie was essentially courteous in his dealings with the American mission, but he was at the same time no less a strong supporter of the civil government, its power and independence. Well loved by the natives, whose interests he defended with both enthusiasm and wisdom, he was wedded to the cause of Hawaiian autonomy, and unshakably opposed to annexation. He knew indeed how to hold the respect of his political enemies. His substantial private means, his fifteen years' experience in the foreign office and executive branch of the government, and above all the king's complete trust in Robert Crichton Wyllie gave him great authority.

During the period I speak of he was in his sixties, and looking forward to a restful retirement. He had only recently spent more than 1,500,000 francs for the purchase of a princely plantation property, along with the various installations he had introduced. Indeed, his sugar mills and machines alone represented an investment of a million more. He told me in detail what he wished to do when the day finally came that he could lay aside the heavy burdens of office. Already in 1858 he had urged me to enter the governmental service; he wanted me, in fact, to accept the ministry of finance, and he fondly hoped to see me become his successor. This done, released at last from official anxieties, he would enjoy a well-earned leisure.

Man proposes but God disposes. One day I would actually become his fellow official and successor; but he would never savor the repose he hoped for, nor would he die at Hanalei. Three years later, after a long period of illness, he breathed his last in Honolulu. His will provided that his nephew should be his principal heir, and he appointed me as mentor, guide, and legal executor in the young man's behalf. The nephew, having fallen in love with a young woman he met at my house, asked the lady for her hand and she had granted it. The heir thereupon returned to Hanalei from Honolulu, expressly in order to put everything in readiness for welcoming his bride. I was following with interest the happy course of their youthful love when, just eight days before his marriage, in the same room where his uncle had entertained me as his guest, the heir cut his throat in a fit of despondency. It became my painful task to break this news to his fiancée, settle the inheritance, and then watch the final collapse of that grand financial edifice erected by Mr. Wyllie that so often I had heard the latter describe with so much optimistic enthusiasm.

None of these sad apprehensions concerning the approximate future darkened the radiant morning of the day following my arrival at Hanalei. Since sunrise my host had been awaiting me for breakfast. There below us on the river floated a vessel, flying the brilliant stripes of the French and Hawaiian flags, which would make it possible for us to visit this immense estate without fatigue. Although the valley was everywhere awaking, one portion still lay in shadow so as to throw into relief the rosy gleams on the mountain ridges, already flooded with sunlight. We were on our way by six o'clock, ascending the course of the Hanalei River, overshadowed here and there by large willow trees that called to mind my own France. The entire morning was given over to visiting the facilities of the sugar plantation. Then, leaving behind us all signs of activity, of work and human life and the deafening roar of machines and the grinding of mills, we penetrated farther into the upper recesses of the valley. Our lightly built vessel, admirably navigated by the kanaka oarsmen, glided through the water with scarcely a murmur of sound. At some distance, at the head of navigation, a generous lunch sent up by the steward was awaiting us on a bluff, where the view as one's eyes scanned the contours of the valley embraced an expanse of beach and sea, and where the variegated blue of the water became lost on the far horizon when it blended with the blue of the sky.

Three days I spent thus at Hanalei, changing my walks, exploring the tablelands and flats that stretched behind the house and descended again in a gentle slope toward the ocean on the eastern side; but I invariably returned to the valley itself. This I admired each day all the more, and I never grew weary of submitting to its enchantment, especially to its fascinating diversity, in which sheer beauty combined with the busy works of man. However, Hanalei leaves impressions that the pen is powerless to describe and the painter's brush can only hint at; and so I must try not to weary the reader with words. I leave Hanalei, expressing my thanks to my host, and taking my farewell look at that lovely scene.

Mr. Wyllie had strongly urged me to visit the Haena caves. This sight involved only a side journey of a few kilometers, and everything I had heard about these caves from the natives had sharply excited my curiosity. My host himself only knew of them by reputation, but he had secured for us a reliable guide, accompanied by several natives who had already made this excursion. On departing I found myself among ten of them, all on horseback and well loaded with gear in the form of ropes, hooks, and strings of *kukui* nuts. All these preparations seemed to me at first rather strange, but since they had been carefully provided I concluded that they had their purpose.

The caves and subterranean passages at Haena are three in number. The entrance to one vast cavern appears at the base of a lofty hill, about 1,000 meters high. Ten horsemen could easily ride abreast through the opening. Inside the chamber immense stalactites project downward from a height of more than twenty meters, forming natural columns that seem to support a rounded cupola-like dome. This first cave encompasses a surface area of more than two and a half acres. On the right, a second fissure provides passage into a second cave. In order to enter it, the Kanakas lighted, in addition to their torches, the garlandlike chains of kukui nuts with which they had come equipped. From a nearby grass house they also brought a small canoe. This was certainly necessary for exploring the two caverns (underground lakes as they actually are) communicating with one another. The first lake measures about seven and a half acres. The water is unbelievably clear and quite deceptive as to its depth. I was astonished to find, after sounding for its bottom, a depth of forty meters about twenty meters from the bank. At one point I ordered the men to extinguish the torches. The place at first became pitch dark, but then by tossing several stones into the lake I proved that the water was phosphorescent. It gleamed like bits of mica, and the stones as they sank to the bottom trailed behind them a glittering path of pale light.

The natives have named this lake Wai-a-kapa-lae, literally, Water of Terror.* The last cave, which they call Wai-a-kana-loa, Water of Great Desolation, is perhaps still more curious than the second. It is reached by canoe, under a kind of Gothic arch moulded by volcanic upheavals. The water emits a strong smell of sulphur, and the interior walls are carpeted with a light yellowish subterranean vegetation resulting from the sulphurous oozings. The least word, the faintest sound, reverberates with a deafening echo. A native tradition holds that this fearful lake is the dwelling place of a god, a sort of basilisk or dragon, who devours everyone who ventures into his lair. The natives themselves laughed as they related to me these legends of long ago, and to display his disdain for such superstitions one of our guides began diving into the lake.

Not tempted to follow his example I was happy, after two hours spent in visiting these caves, to find myself once more outside in dazzling sunlight. We rewarded our guides generously before parting from them and then set forth again on our journey, arriving back at Hanalei after a speedy eight-hour gallop.

Kauai abounds in pleasant scenery, but after visiting Hanalei and Wailua a traveler, though he admires other spots, finds himself doing so with less enthusiasm. At these two places tropical nature seems to have exhausted all the rich colors and exquisite forms of her palette and brush. I beheld some lovely landscapes, deep-shaded valleys, inviting panoramic vistas, but without being myself much moved. Though I undoubtedly enjoyed them, the sense of wonder became dulled and I was soon involuntarily comparing everything I was seeing with the things I had seen a moment before. In general, during my tour of Kauai, I was seeking in memories and surviving traditions of ancient Hawaii, records and impressions of a different sort, and of such experiences I did indeed form quite a collection.

Among our various unfortunate fellow travelers aboard the *Annie Laurie*, there was a young chief named Kaeo,† an adopted son of Kalama, the widowed queen and heir of Kamehameha III. Albert Kaeo was a direct descendant of the ancient chiefs of Kauai. He still owned some large tracts of property on that island. Too young to be traveling alone, he was accompanied by an old man who dutifully waited on him and who had known, when he was

---

*Varigny's names for the two Haena caves are puzzles and not, as he claims, literal. "Wai-a-kana-loa" would appear to refer to the great Polynesian god identified with healing, Kanaloa. [A. L. K.]

†His chiefly name was Kunuiakea (1851–1903); he was a natural son of Kamehameha III and Jane Lahilahi Young Kaeo, Queen Emma's younger sister [A. L. K.]

still but a child, Albert's grandfather, the old reigning king of Kauai. Several days after my return from Hanalei, while I was staying at the Bourgoings, I received a visit from Albert and his elderly attendant. Both agreed to spend the day with us and not to leave before the next morning. Kanea, the temporary tutor of the young prince, belonged to that dying generation of natives who had carefully preserved memories and traditions of the Hawaiian past. His conversation interested me exceedingly. He knew the legends of his island birthplace thoroughly and expressed a sacred awe at the thought of the last king of Kauai, along with a sort of superstitious terror regarding Kamehameha I. The conquest of the archipelago as a whole had been the result of bloody battles whose names had long been household words. Details about these struggles were already known to me, for I had visited the various scenes of historic combat. However, the conquest of Kauai seemed to me more impressive than all the rest, considering the distance to be covered by canoes and the relative ease on that island of resisting a landing, and especially the reputation for bravery of the old Kauai warriors.

I had been fully informed of how Kamehameha I had overcome the island without a struggle, but I had heard little account of the exact methods by which this had been achieved. It was Kanea who told me the narrative I presented earlier,* in which the character of Kamehameha I is revealed in a novel light. He was not merely a supreme military leader and a wise administrator, but even more and above all else a masterly politician.

After a visit of three weeks on Kauai, I was recalled to Honolulu by consular dispatches from Paris notifying me of the approaching arrival of the newly appointed French commissioner. These communications not only confirmed, with special commendation, my interim handling of consular affairs, but also assured me in addition of a forthcoming promotion, one which would definitely transfer me to another consular station. I regretted this prospect because I felt strongly that I could be very useful in the islands, although I realized it was not my affair to discuss the orders I had received. In any event, I was granted a leave of absence and would thus be able to return to Paris. Concluding my official duties, however, and looking after my personal affairs would require me to remain in Hawaii for some little while longer. I was not planning to leave Hawaii until March or April of 1864.

Once more unforeseen circumstances were to wreck my plans and detain me in the Hawaiian Islands. I had arrived in Hawaii nine years earlier, with the intention of spending but a month or two. Now I found myself still in

---

*Chapter 2, pp. 25–27 [A. L. K.]

the kingdom, and it had been settled—at least it had been put into words—that I would remain now several years more.

On October 26, the new commissioner of His Imperial Majesty arrived at Honolulu aboard a French man-of-war. On November 2, King Kamehameha IV received him for an audience at the palace, along with myself, for the purpose of accepting official letters and credentials. The meeting was most cordial. The king, who had been suffering for several days from one of his attacks of chronic asthma, seemed to have recovered. He planned to give a banquet at the end of the month and then to leave afterwards for the island of Hawaii, where the climate was more favorable than that of Honolulu for persons suffering from his affliction.

A celebration and ball were scheduled to take place at the palace on November 28, the anniversary day commemorating the recognition by France and England of the independence of the Hawaiian Kingdom. Kamehameha IV, however, did not appear among his guests at this festive gathering because of a new and very threatening crisis in his health. The queen alone did the honors. She told me of her great desire to accompany the king on a trip to the island of Hawaii as soon as possible. The next morning I stopped at the palace to hear the latest word. His asthmatic disease had worsened severely, and on the morning of November 30 the king had died in the arms of his father and his wife.

Home of M. Charles de Varigny at Honolulu. Drawing by H. Clerget, based on a photograph.

Hawaiian sports. Drawing by Émile Bayard, based on a sketch provided by the author.

Honolulu, capital of the Hawaiian Islands, in 1855. View from the harbor. Drawing by J. Moynet, based on a photograph by I. Howland.

The village of Waikiki. Drawing by J. Moynet based on a photograph.

Group of Hawaiian horsewomen. Drawing by Émile Bayard, based on photographs by H. Chase.

Punahou School. Drawing by J. Moynet, based on a photograph by H. Chase.

Picnic party at the village of Ewa. Drawing by Émile Bayard, based on a sketch by P. Emmert.

Hawaiians in 1820. Kamehameha I and his warriors. Drawing by Émile Bayard, based on documents provided by the author.

Prominent Hawaiians in 1870. Drawing by Émile Bayard, based on assorted photographs.

Village of Waikiki. Drawing by H. Clerget, based on a photograph by H. Chase.

Waipio Valley. Drawing by J. Moynet, based on a photograph by H. Chase.

Hawaiian women. Drawing by Émile Bayard, based on a photograph by H. Chase.

Wild cattle on Hawaii Island. Drawing by E. Riou, based on a sketch provided by the author.

King Kamehameha V. Drawing by E. Riou, based on a photograph by H. Chase.

Setting off for Kilauea on mules. Drawing by E. Riou, based on a sketch provided by the author.

The landing of the king at Hilo. Drawing by E. Riou, based on a photograph by H. Chase.

Kilauea volcano, island of Hawaii. Drawing by E. Riou, based on a sketch by P. Emmert.

Mauna Kea and Mauna Loa from Hilo Bay. Drawing by J. Moynet, based on a sketch by P. Emmert.

Kilauea volcano. Daytime view. Drawing by E. Riou, based on a photograph.

Ruins of the Catholic church at Keauhou. Drawing by E. Riou, based on a photograph by H. Chase.

Cattle and goats caught in the lava. Drawing by E. Riou, based on a sketch provided by the author.

Distribution of supplies at Keauhou. Drawing by E. Riou, based on a sketch provided by the author.

Ruins of the village of Waiohinu. Drawing by E. Riou, based on a photograph by H. Chase.

River of lava. Drawing by E. Riou, based on a photograph by H. Chase.

Captain Brown near the grave of his wife. Drawing by E. Riou, based on a photograph of volcanic terrain by H. Chase, with illustrative figure added.

PART TWO
CABINET MINISTER,
THE HAWAIIAN KINGDOM,
1863–1870

CHAPTER 9

APPOINTMENT AS MINISTER OF FINANCE

Accession of Kamehameha V.—Organization of a new cabinet.—Offer of ministry of finance.—My acceptance.—First meeting of the cabinet.—Universal suffrage.—The elections.—Plans for constitutional reforms.—

The death of Kamehameha IV was quite unexpected even by his nearest relatives and came as an utter surprise to the nation as a whole. The heir presumptive to the throne, Prince Lot, was out of town at the time, unaware that his brother's life was in danger. Queen Emma, deeply shocked, grieved more for the husband she had lost than for the throne his death had snatched away, and old Kekuanaoa, the late king's father, watched in gloomy silence over the son once so brimming with life, whom he had believed was destined to survive him.

Alone among the cabinet ministers, Mr. Wyllie attended to first things first. With the greatest speed he sent word to Prince Lot and simultaneously summoned his ministerial colleagues. The new ruler hastened to the palace; his first concern was to share the sorrow of his sister-in-law and to complain bitterly about the carelessness of the physicians who had neither known enough to foresee the imminence of his brother's death nor had taken steps to avert the peril of a political crisis. In fact, none of the ministers was in the palace at the moment the king died.

After reaching the palace, Kamehameha V went to the council chamber where his ministers were expecting him and there he received their resignations. He requested them meanwhile to carry on temporarily with their duties and await his further instructions. At two o'clock the privy council convened at the palace, and at three an official proclamation announced to the public the death of Kamehameha IV and the accession of Kamehameha V. At the same time, Queen Emma received from the new sovereign an invitation to continue to reside at the palace, together with the assurance of his sympathy and fraternal affection. The next day the king settled down to work, interviewed his ministers, and then in closed session with the cabinet examined the fresh political situation resulting from the death of his brother, reviewing for them his own experience in government and especially his political associations and friendships.

Kamehameha V was an advocate of progress, liberal-minded in his convictions, but also by family tradition a believer in absolute monarchy, and somewhat by personal temperament an autocrat. Up to the present time, he had appeared to be in favor of the American party, which had lofty hopes of his reign. For several years, as a colleague of Mr. Wyllie, he had in fact often expressed and supported views contrary to those of the minister of foreign affairs, with whose verbose rhetoric and obstinacy, it was said, he had little patience. Now, however, he did not hesitate as king to call upon Mr. Wyllie's patriotism and wisdom, and to discuss with him confidentially his plans for reform and his projected legislative program. He revealed only to Mr. Wyllie his fluctuating uncertainties; and at the start, at least, Mr. Wyllie was the only person to whom he explained what he had in mind specifically, and what policies he intended to follow.

During this period the palace, thrown open to the public, echoed with the wailings of the natives, interspersed with the chanted dirges that were traditional on such occasions. The entire population of Honolulu, gathering hour by hour as new mourners kept arriving from the rural districts, crowded into the royal quarters where the body of the king lay in state. Both night and day the lamentations and the chanting continued, sometimes monotonously plaintive, sometimes piercing and shrill. It is impossible to describe the bizarre spectacle enacted all night long in the large courtyard enclosure immediately surrounding the palace. Thousands of natives filed past, row after surging row, while others rested themselves outside, scattered about and squatting on the grass. Ominous conflicting rumors swept through the excited crowd, fantastically illuminated by the hundreds of flaming torches held aloft by retainers of the royal household or by members of the palace military guard. Throughout the whole town aroused spokesmen for popular opinion were anxiously debating what political decision the king was about to announce. The American party, the largest, strongest, and most ambitious group, made great capital of their friendly connections with the prince. Some of these persons, the most audacious, loudly predicted the fall from grace of Mr. Wyllie, counting on the appointment of a ministry recruited exclusively from among their candidates. Numerous lists were being circulated from hand to hand, stamped with the same insistencies and desires.

The king spent the first four days of November conferring with Mr. Wyllie and determining, while the cabinet kept silent, upon his choice of ministers. On November 5, Mr. Wyllie stopped to see me in my office and announced that he had the king's official order offering me the ministry of finance. This proposal did not exactly take me by surprise. Nevertheless, as I still innocently subscribed to the prevailing notion that the persons selected to make up the cabinet would obviously be the leaders of the American party, I was astounded by an offer which apparently demonstrated inclinations on the king's part very different from those being generally attributed to him.

It was not at all a secret that I was, in fact, if not an out-and-out enemy of the American party, at the very least a sincere and open partisan of the independence of the kingdom. As a Frenchman I possessed neither the political sympathies of the Americans nor those of the Protestant missionary party. I answered Mr. Wyllie's offer by asking him to show me the list of the cabinet officers, and he sent it to me at once. In this arrangement, Mr. Wyllie kept the ministry of foreign affairs; Mr. Robertson, a justice of the supreme court and an Englishman by origin, became minister of the interior; Mr. Harris, finally, legal council for the crown, joined the cabinet as attorney general and minister without portfolio.

I requested Mr. Wyllie to grant me twenty-four hours to think over the matter, promising him an answer by the next day. It was still understood that in the event of my acceptance or refusal, I would consider myself honor bound not to divulge the names on the list shown to me. The king's wish was that the roster of the cabinet officers would be released only when the ministers had conferred among themselves and then, after receiving his formal message, had generally agreed upon the choice of the new slate of appointments.

I spent November 5 and the morning of November 6 scrupulously weighing Mr. Wyllie's proposal and making a precise assessment of the general political situation, including various party positions and alignments. My most important concern was neither to allow myself to be swayed by personal ambition nor to agree to the offer except with the conviction that I could assist the king in a substantial way and thereby serve the country in a manner warranting my trust.

As I have mentioned, already in 1858 I had refused, after thorough reflection, a similar offer from Kamehameha IV. This earlier rejection somewhat reassured my conscience. I did not feel that I ought to yield in 1863 to certain very personal considerations that I had been able to resist five years earlier. I had meanwhile acquired experience and more knowledge of the country; above all I had worked hard, and in some measure had digested and refined my ideas. Confidence had developed with the testing of my talents, and with the increasing sense of responsible obligation I had demonstrated in my official conduct. For several years I had made the most of the ample amount of leisure afforded me by my secretarial duties. Later, during the interim when I was head of the consulate, I had carried out systematic studies of the country, primarily from a commercial and political point of view. I had conceived an organized program of reforms, which I shall later describe in their appropriate context. The task which in 1858 seemed to me thankless and unrealistic, on the day after the treaty negotiations had been concluded, now seemed to me in 1863, if not easy, at least within the realm of possibility. The treaty agreement five years earlier had provoked a furious outburst of hostility against France, both in the privy council and in the public mind. The main obstacle I now anticipated was the uproar that would be caused by the admission of a Frenchman to the cabinet. I hoped I was correct in my judgment; granting certain favorable circumstances, I felt I could take care of my adversaries.

I was thus disposed to accept the king's offer. The continuance of Mr. Wyllie in office assured me of the cooperation of a colleague upon whom I knew I could depend. With Mr. Robertson I had maintained only very casual relations, but I knew him to be a hard worker and an intelligent man, who had won wide public respect. I nevertheless regarded it as a mistake to remove him from the supreme court, where it would be difficult to replace him. Moreover, I knew that I would perhaps find him objectionably dogmatic about certain questions, as well as sometimes rigid and narrowminded. All this was still true, but I was relying on the passage of time to bring us closer together, and on our mutual respect to eliminate particular sources of disagreement.

I was better acquainted with Mr. Harris, whose name will often appear in these pages, and I believed the king was acting wisely in drawing upon his judicial and administrative talents. He was a man of action, resourceful, persevering even to an excessive degree, combining the merits along with the failings of an American lawyer.

As a Frenchman and a civil servant, I could not accept the offer before me except with the approval of the French government. I accordingly made this a reservation concerning my appointment, though there was no reason under the existing circumstances to doubt that it would be permitted. Two days after he had spoken to me I informed Mr. Wyllie that, with one proviso, I would accept his offer. Mr. Wyllie forwarded my answer to the king, who duly summoned me for a personal interview.

I presented myself to the king at the palace. I had seen nothing of the new ruler for several years, our last conversation having occurred in 1857, when, as an official representative of the Hawaiian government, he had discussed with my chief, M. Perrin, and with myself the provisions of the French treaty. He now received me most cordially and then alluded to our earlier relations, of which he was kind enough to retain pleasant memories. He thanked me for accepting the appointment. I replied that if his offer had been a surprise to me, it had surprised even more the American party, which had counted so overwhelmingly on their assuming power. The king knew as well as I did the rumors circulating in town, the lists being handed about, the rewards the Americans were banking on as a sure consequence, they believed, of his personal sympathies. On this point he did not wish to leave a shadow of doubt. "I number the Americans among my friends," he said, "but there is a great difference between that fact and delivering the kingdom into their hands. When I was a prince I needed only to consult my personal tastes. As king I must have capable and intelligent advisers, above all men of determination, because I have important changes in mind."

He then asked me what I thought of my fellow ministers, and I told him my candid opinion, adding that I foresaw great difficulties finding a replacement for Mr. Robertson on the supreme court. The king informed me that the cabinet and Mr. Robertson himself would be consulted on this matter. On the subject of finances, when the interview turned to my own sphere of interest, he questioned me minutely and approved my plans. However, I was able to describe these for him only very briefly. For nearly a year, he himself had carried out the duties of acting minister of finance during the reign of his brother, and he quickly grasped the purpose of the reforms I proposed to him.

We then passed on to questions concerning the general political situation. He spoke to me of the approaching session of the legislature and of the method followed in electing representatives. On this point I neither could nor would conceal my beliefs. As a firm opponent of universal suffrage without restrictions of any kind, I explained my views with the greatest frankness. I said I regarded the franchise a grave danger when paper ballots were handed out to the masses without any stipulation concerning the voter's education and economic status. The king listened to me with close attention. "Here you raise a question that has long concerned me," he said. "I consider the present constitution to be in advance by many years of the traditions and needs of our population as a whole. We have barely emerged from a feudal system and already the Americans are hurrying us into a republican form of government. They are rushing things too much. Liberal though I may be, I have not yet definitely decided to swear on oath to uphold the present constitution. We shall talk about this legal problem again, but," he added, as he rose to his feet, "we understand one another on this point and I am optimistic about the future."

At the end of my interview, lasting almost two hours, I departed; my visit to the palace had roused no suspicion. I returned home, satisfied with what I had seen and heard, and ready to join my efforts to those of a sovereign whom I felt I could trust. From this day I mark the beginning of a friendship that has constantly supported me in my work, a friendship which neither my absence nor my long distance from Hawaii has weakened. My memory of the kindness of Kamehameha V will never fade.

On the following day we met again at the palace. Mr. Charles G. Hopkins,* whom I succeeded as minister of finance, was present. A personal friend of the late king, Alexander Liholiho, he was equally close to Lot Kamehameha, who though very grateful for his devotion considered Hopkins' administrative ability mediocre at best. For this reason, he removed him from his ministerial post and named him his chief secretary. Meanwhile, it was understood that Mr. Hopkins would continue to serve in the ministry of finance, until the dispatches from Paris arrived authorizing me officially to accept the new responsibilities offered. It was promptly agreed that, in order to secure secrecy in our deliberations, one of the several ministers should be especially designated to keep minutes. Meetings would be called by order of the king, and I was chosen to serve as secretary. In the event of the king's absence, the minister of foreign affairs was to preside over the cabinet.

We next turned our attention to filling the most important official posts. Mr. W. F. Allen was appointed collector of customs, a position he still occupies today and one in which he has rendered and continues to render outstanding service. Mr. Wyllie next proposed the organization of a special committee for public works, designated to develop, under the direction of the minister of the interior, necessary plans for the establishment of a modern road system, and for the chief public services. This measure was tabled. The board of health was then reorganized, and it was further settled that the agenda for the next meeting should include organizational questions of a

---

*Charles Gordon Hopkins (1822–1886) was a younger brother of Manley Hopkins (1818–1897), father of the Roman Catholic convert and poet Gerard Manley Hopkins. After the arrival of C. G. Hopkins in Hawaii in 1845, he served in the government in various capacities, first as a court reporter and police magistrate, later (and with journalistic talent and verve) as editor of the government-owned weekly newspaper, the *Polynesian*. Meanwhile, Manley Hopkins in London, head of a marine insurance firm, was appointed by Kamehameha III to the post of consul-commissioner and chargé d'affaires of the Hawaiian Kingdom, which he continued to hold down to the fall of the monarchy in the 1890s. Charles de Varigny's poor opinion of Charles Hopkins, as repeatedly expressed in this book, probably reflects an element of professional rivalry he felt toward Manley Hopkins, who was also a journalistic writer and an authority on the affairs of the Hawaiian Islands. Manley Hopkins' *Hawaii: The Past, Present, and Future of Its Island-Kingdom* (London: Longmans, Green, 1866; 2nd ed.), dedicated to Lord John Russell, was undoubtedly known to Varigny. Yet the works of the Englishman and the Frenchman, though both deal with many of the same events and share a common set of political concerns, bear very little resemblance to one another, except for their pervasive, and markedly contrasting, ethnocentrism. [A. L. K.]

strategic political sort, notice of which was particularly urgent because of the approaching session of the legislature.

It was now December and, as required by the constitution, elections for the House of Representatives were to take place at the beginning of January, for the session was scheduled to convene in April. It was true that the king had not as yet sworn the oath to uphold the constitution. We understood his feelings of repugnance about taking the oath, however, and we realized how strongly he desired to see that certain clauses in the organic act be changed —including, among others, the one we had discussed that made a fetish of universal suffrage, with no restrictions whatever, and thus placed the legislative power primarily in the hands of the plantation ownership.

The plantations had not as yet attained the degree of development and prosperity they would later achieve. But each day the sugar industry tended to acquire greater importance and to multiply its activities in every part of the islands. My past experience, shaped by my personal studies, had fully convinced me that we should exert every effort to encourage interest in agricultural enterprises, and simultaneously discourage the Hawaiians from whale fishing, an occupation that levied a disastrous toll upon the very finest flower of the native population. Every year several hundred whaling vessels, for the most part American, came to our ports for rest and recruitment, in order to purchase supplies, and especially to repair and outfit their ships. They did this by taking aboard several thousand hale and hearty male natives, attracted by the speculative opportunities of this system of seafaring, in which the sailor crews share in the catch: lured, one might add, also by the seductive advances in pay granted by the sea captains, riches that they squandered, even before setting sail, with all the heedlessness of their youth and race.

This constituted a severe threat to the future of Hawaii. Few Kanakas withstood the excessively cold climate of the arctic seas. Born in the tropics, they perished in those murderous latitudes; many others returned home sick and debilitated. Those who survived developed a taste for far-flung adventures, and clung therefore to a career that offered them no future promise. It was a system of conscription, profitable to none but the foreigner; and the population continued to decrease at an alarming rate. Native women, abandoned by their husbands, wrung from sexual vice the support they were deprived of by the absence of their natural protectors. Over a period of years, I had notified the French government in my dispatches, and likewise the local authorities in my articles in the Honolulu newspapers, of the dangers of this state of affairs. Everyone recognized the evil, but was afraid that, by changing the laws, the United States would become displeased and the American whaling fleets would take offense. Because the annual visits of the whalers were so profitable a source of revenue, people were asking who would purchase our products the day when the whalers began to buy them elsewhere, notably in San Francisco, or at various other Pacific ports available for reprovisioning.

It was vitally necessary, therefore, to stimulate and encourage this new agricultural industry that would put the native back on the land, help him to develop it to his benefit, and free the islands—as indeed the passage of time has proved—from the seasonal visits of the whaling fleet. On the other hand, the planters likewise would be confronted from the start by the same circumstances, the frustrating social conditions and practices already mentioned. There was a threatening labor shortage. Perhaps for a while one could manage with the limited labor supply at hand; but the time was not far distant when it would be necessary to seek the help of coolie labor from China and Japan. Furthermore, slavery did not exist in the islands; that ugly social plague was unknown. Indeed, every slave who stepped onto Hawaiian soil instantly became free. The generous and simple naturalization laws admitted the foreigner to exercise the rights of citizenship, after making a brief statement of declaration and completing one year of residence in Hawaii. Thus, in the not distant future, it would be possible for the planters to line up thousands of voters entirely at their wish, and hence inaugurate, under the shield of universal suffrage, the establishment of a foreign oligarchy with control over the nation itself. This was because almost all Hawaiian plantations were owned by foreigners. It was they alone who possessed the capital, and who had the experience required for this type of economic enterprise and exploitation.

Thus a new set of election laws was a crucial necessity. However, our hands were tied by the constitution, and if its ultrarepublican form was at many points an irritation to the king, on this particular point it represented a transparent danger which Kamehameha V desired to destroy. I agreed with him entirely. Although my cabinet colleagues and I understood each other's goal, we differed concerning the means of attaining it. The constitution provided a method of amendment borrowed from the United States. Article 20, in fact, stipulated that to achieve the force of law every proposed change had to be submitted to the House of Representatives, there must succeed in winning a majority of votes, next receive the approval of the upper chamber (the House of Nobles), and finally be ratified by the king. Furthermore, after a delay of two years, the proposed amendment had to be resubmitted to a new legislature, and there run the gauntlet of the two assemblies. The procedure was slow, the success more than doubtful. Meanwhile, as he continued to mark time, the king still refused to take the oath of office.

For a period of weeks the general public was unaware of the king's choices for his cabinet; nor was there any understanding of the causes of his hesitation, his scruples of conscience. Finally, on December 17, the government newspaper published the list of the new ministers. The result was widespread astonishment. The American party, considering itself to have been duped, concentrated all its indignation and anger upon me. That a Frenchman had been invited to join the cabinet; that his acceptance was dependent upon the approval of the French government; that as minister of finance he was charged with preparing and justifying the budget—all these were natural disappointments, skillfully engineered of course to exasperate certain persons who had believed they were sure to be restored to power. In Mr. Wyllie the Americans had recognized a long-standing enemy in the ranks of government. Now, in me, they discovered a new adversary arrived on the political scene.

Despite their ferocity, the attacks against me surprised me not in the least. I was expecting them, indeed I was ready to find them even more intemperate than they were, and I was not anticipating the remarkable change in my favor that occurred within less than a year: not because I deserved such favor, but rather as a result of altered circumstances. On numerous occasions I had never disguised my anxieties regarding the self-serving desires and ambitions of the United States. I was a staunch believer in the need to organize against the Americans and to consolidate all the European interests in the islands, in the hope of creating thereby a center of power capable of strengthening resistance.

For this reason I cultivated my connection with Mr. W. W. Follett Synge, who was at that time British commissioner, welcoming between us a social and political intimacy resting on a perfect harmony of ideas. During my term of office, I found him an intelligent colleague and a sincere friend: *Idem velle atque idem nolle, ea demum firma amicitia est.** We sought the same goals; we had the same enemies. For my part I have always had a liking for frank and clear understandings. If, on occasion, they have the inconvenience of increasing obstacles along the course, they have also the advantage of clarifying confusions, of putting one in a position favorable for distinguishing between friends and foes. Such relationships require more effort, but they also assure and confirm success: though the combat is fierce, the victory (if it is achieved) is more complete, and today's consequences are not placed in doubt when tomorrow's battle comes to be viewed from a different perspective.

---

*"The firmest friendship is built on an identity of likes and dislikes." Sallust, on the conspiracy of Catiline: *Bellum Catilinarium*, XX. [A. L. K.]

In short, I let the momentary clouds between us pass by without feeling disturbed. The newspaper articles bothered me not at all. Accustomed to the usual twists and turns of a public press that enjoyed unlimited freedom, I knew from experience that the brutality of the attack is likely to be in inverse ratio to its duration. I made no reply, for I had better things to occupy me.

My colleagues were by no means treated as harshly as I was. Only Mr. Wyllie suffered a few rather sharp assaults. Mr. Harris and Mr. Robertson received only compliments, as they furthermore deserved.

We were all well aware that it was now late December. The elections were scheduled for January 2. The opposition set to work with much energy. They made it their business, if not to overthrow the ministry, at least to be rid of Mr. Wyllie and me. In their ignorance of the cabinet's program, they had as yet found no political issue, properly speaking, suitable for organizing their campaign, whether for or against. They nevertheless instinctively guessed what such a question would be, and found one at hand in the king's continued reluctance to swear the customary oath to uphold the constitution. The opposition thus did not confine their activities merely to the task of getting their most zealous candidates elected to the legislature, or simply to making certain of the support of the American missionaries. In these matters they were fairly successful. Having been defeated in Honolulu, they took their revenge in the most remote districts, where the Protestant mission had the strongest body of supporters, and where they succeeded in electing a rather sizable number of their candidates. Busy with other current concerns, the government refrained from intervening significantly in the electioneering. By acting with such restraint, the government did no more than conduct itself in accord with local custom and its established institutions. Campaigning for office, whether in an officiously aggressive or a more pleasant style, was not the way things were done in Hawaii. Governmental activity was confined within the narrowest limits, and the administration took good care not to interfere in the contest of the ballots. Just as in the United States, the voter in Hawaii is excessively jealous of his rights; he willingly submits to the yoke of his party, and it often happens that he casts his vote for candidates he does not even know; but the least attempt on the part of government to instruct or influence his thinking is considered an unjustifiable interference.

The Hawaiian government, being administratively responsible for enforcing the laws, must by necessity report to the legislature on its handling of affairs. To seek to interfere in the choice of those persons who have been selected to control the acts of a government would appear to be a ridiculous anomaly, and would have the inevitable result of assuring the defeat of its own candidates and the election of its rivals. The party system rests on the assumption of responsibility: the burden of the conflict is shared by the competing parties, while the role of an administration is limited to assuring the complete honesty and good faith of its operations. At first sight, it would seem to a modern Frenchman very difficult to govern under such an arrangement, but actually it appears to me difficult to govern otherwise. In France, I believe, the experience of recent years has proved that campaigning, from whatever point of view one looks at it and behind whatever term one chooses to disguise it, has been an impossible burden for officials to bear, quite beyond the capacity of each and every successive government: in fact, intervention in elections has saved not a single regime, and their downfall in general has never been more imminent or certain than when the candidates of officialdom sweep the field.

In the Hawaiian Islands, as in all sparsely populated countries where agricultural interests predominate, the electorate is concerned above all with largely local issues. The building of a road or a bridge, laws favorable to farming interests, the improvement of transportation, the reduction of tariffs—these are objects of constant attention. Already assured of basic liberties, such as the full right of public assembly, of absolute freedom of the press, and of freedom of religion, the people of Hawaii talk over and argue their problems in public meetings as well as likewise in the several newspapers; and the selection of their candidates varies therefore, from legislative session to legislative session, according to the shifting pressures of circumstances.

As I have indicated earlier, in 1864 the commanding question was that of constitutional reform. The existing constitution dated from the year 1852. It was a charter granted by Kamehameha III to his people, with the advice and urging of the American missionaries, at that time an all-powerful controlling element. The king, my colleagues, and I were all in agreement regarding the constitution of 1852: certain changes were imperative, particularly in the requirements concerning the qualifications of voters.

The peril of the present system was increasing day by day and the need for reform was most urgent. One suggested remedy for the situation was to change the naturalization laws and require certain residence requirements for the exercise of political rights. This change, however, would serve only to evade the problem and defer it. The king did not disguise the fact that the monarchic principle and universal suffrage are, basically, incompatible ideas, and that the ultimate meaning and upshot of the one-man-one-vote equation is a republican form of government. Mr. Harris, born in the United States, and an American to the grain, was a republican, but he was too intelligent not to realize that this form of government was useless to a people still deeply imbued with the traditions and ideas of feudalism, a society scarcely advanced enough to master and manage a modern political system. Not only were we in agreement on this overriding question; Mr. Harris and I were equally convinced of the need for certain other changes, of less importance clearly, but bound to arouse hectic debate. We had no illusions concerning the arduous and very risky task we were undertaking.

To solve the inescapable problems of launching a new reign; to make radical alterations in governmental procedures; to combine with such goals the attempt to revise the constitution of 1852, a document very precious to the Americans—all this amounted to an outright challenge to partisan American interests in Hawaii, now so painfully humiliated—indeed festering—because of seeing themselves ejected from power at the moment when they had been most certain of their victory. It was to our advantage, in thus defying the Americans, to make our position quite clear and to state what we wanted; explain where we were going; and, as the conflict was unavoidable, decide upon our own proper battleground. The labor of constitutional revision, when combined with the conduct of our current business, consumed a great deal of time. Cabinet meeting followed cabinet meeting without interruption. It was very necessary for us to agree in detail on each of the changes we wished to introduce into the constitution of 1852. Otherwise we would not be able to submit for discussion and criticism by our opponents a complete and carefully prepared set of documents.

Steps were also being taken to fill the principal vacant offices. The most important undoubtedly was that of Kuhina Nui or vice-regent. The origin of this title goes back to the regency of Kaahumanu, after the death of Kamehameha I, who had declared on his deathbed that his kingdom belonged to Liholiho but that Kaahumanu should actually rule. Consecrated by local tradition, the functions of the Kuhina Nui had however become purely honorific, with the result that the administrative mechanism contained a useless wheel that could become dangerous. To avoid all possibility of conflict in filling the post, the responsibility was always lodged in one of the nearest relatives of the king. During the reign of Kamehameha IV, his sister, Princess Victoria, was invested with the office. Kamehameha V named his father Kuhina Nui. Meanwhile, it was generally understood that the new constitution would eliminate this bizarre institutional arrangement, as queer and quaint as it was ill-defined.

To Kekuanaoa the position meant a seat and a vote in the cabinet. His unquestionable authority over native Hawaiians, whom he influenced as much by his title of high chief as by his loyalty and famous courage, his practical experience, his diplomatic skill, and his deep devotion to his son, all made him a valuable ally. In all circumstances I found him a sincere and steadfast friend, and his trust in me never faltered.

The funeral of Kamehameha IV took place on January 3, 1864. Native custom disapproves of the burial or entombment of a chief's body except after a period of mourning, the length of which depends on the status and rank of the deceased. In fact, it is not uncommon for the casket containing the remains of a chief to be displayed for public view during a period of several weeks. While thus lying in state the chief is surrounded by attendants equipped with great fly brushes made of feathers, to be slowly raised and lowered again, while relatives, friends, simple curiosity-seekers, dependents, and other mourners spend long hours, motionless, kneeling or squatting, near the funeral bier. All marks of respect, including some of the most exotic as prescribed by native ceremony, were paid religiously to the remains of Kamehameha IV. His body, enclosed in three caskets, one of lead, and others of oak and *koa,* the island woods used in cabinetmaking, was continuously on view as he lay in state from December 1 to February 3. The splendor of the funeral arrangements was such as to satisfy the pride of the natives and minister to the sorrow of the queen.

Faithful in every respect to local custom, Queen Emma shut herself up for a period of days and nights in the royal mausoleum which her brother-in-law had ordered to be constructed for her husband. Not long afterwards, the coffins of the earlier rulers were transferred to the same sanctuary. This monument, situated along a mountainous upland plain overlooking Honolulu, and affording a superb panoramic view of the shore and ocean, is one of the special points of interest in the kingdom and deserves a visit by all travelers.

The two months of continuous work and daily cabinet meetings had a double result. They allowed the ministers to familiarize themselves with the difficulties of their task and to settle upon their program; and they equally brought into the open the points on which everyone was in agreement and those on which it was necessary to compromise. It was not to be expected that understanding would be complete in a cabinet composed of members of different nationalities. Indeed, on a number of questions our ideas and opinions are not exclusively those we hold as individuals, but rather are common notions deriving from the cultural setting into which we were born and where we have lived, notions or attitudes tempered by the lessons of experience and by our faculties for reflection and comparison. My colleagues and I aimed at the same objective, we desired the same result, but we also differed concerning the method of achieving it.

Always calm, coolheaded, reserved, the king invariably presided at our meetings; he spoke little and always last. He limited his role to summarizing discussions and moving them along to the vote. I have never seen him weary or impatient. In fact, he was grateful to us for defending our opinions and for persisting in pursuing a line of criticism or attack. He approved of men who held strong convictions and who marshaled clear and precise arguments.

I still recall one of our earliest discussions. It concerned the official newspaper of the government, the *Polynesian*. The minister of the interior, Mr. G. M. Robertson, had presented to the cabinet a report which announced that the funds appropriated by the legislature to pay the costs of this newspaper were almost exhausted. The law authorized the transfer of credit, but only for items listed under the same budget heading. In other words, the minister had the right to assign to the operating expenses or this newspaper, after its special appropriation had been expended, whatever money remained disposable by him under the funds generally allocated to his department. Being little inclined to take advantage of this administrative latitude, and not much satisfied with the results presumably to be obtained, Mr. Robertson neatly concluded his report by recommending the total liquidation of the *Polynesian*.

I supported him. I estimated that far from being an advantage and strength, an official newspaper was a burden and an embarrassment. I believed that since circumstances permitted us not only to rid ourselves of this organ honorably, but also to demonstrate clearly our respect for the legislature by calling for its decisive vote, we would actually reap a benefit from the timely opportunity presented to us. The other members of the cabinet, however, did not share this judgment. They believed in the soundness of the government newspaper; while admitting its failings and drawbacks, they clung strongly to its value and usefulness. They deemed it to be a poor policy to leave the journalistic field completely open to the opposition newspapers, and thus to deprive themselves of all independent avenues of communication with the public, especially during the intervals between legislative sessions. The discussion was brisk, at times even hot, but our argument prevailed. The official newspaper ceased publication, and did so on the very eve of a most difficult political campaign, a struggle in which, as our friends themselves agreed, the assured assistance of a newspaper legally identified with our program seemed indispensable.

However, our opponents were not mistaken about the matter. Some concluded that we believed ourselves to be in a position of power, since we disdained this means of support. Others were grateful to us for perhaps displaying an exaggerated respect for legality, as well as a concern for economy in the administration of the public purse. But the most unexpected result was the effect upon the opposition newspapers. They had complained bitterly of the competition they faced from the official newspaper, arguing that a publication supported by governmental funds should not be permitted to publish official announcements: this source of revenue, they had insisted, constitutes the principal profit of a newspaper. Indeed, everyone knows this who is at all familiar with the low prices of newspaper subscriptions in England and America. No longer was this greatly exaggerated grievance to be of any use to newspaper proprietors, now that the *Polynesian* had been abolished. On the other hand, a new problem had suddenly raised its head. How does one continue to carry on political controversy when the dispute all at once transforms itself into a monologue?

Alas, the opposition newspapers no longer had anyone to serve as a target for their editorial replies. They were reduced to making erroneous analyses, assertions whose falsities the facts themselves had already demonstrated. As for the public notices and broadsides, which we officials were legally compelled to convey to the people, we drove a bargain with the editor of the most prominent of the local newspapers operated by private interests. When the legislature later reestablished a government newspaper, designated the *Hawaiian Gazette,* I was obliged of course to give way; but I did so not without misgivings. I preferred that period between the demise of the *Polynesian* and the emergence of the *Hawaiian Gazette* when, freed of all official or officious ties with popular journalism, the government had accepted full responsiblity for its actions, yet never stooped to make itself answerable for the words and deeds of its overzealous, or simply inept, defenders.

CHAPTER 10

THE GOVERNMENTAL SYSTEM OF KAMEHAMEHA V

The privy council.—Judicial organization.—Dispatches from Paris.—Financial and agricultural situation.—The goal pursued.—Religious influences in Oceania.—A state without a state religion.

The time had arrived to take stock of the privy council and its organization. The commissions of its members expired when the king who had signed them died. Not that the law required this practice, for it is silent on the matter; but custom in Hawaii, stronger than law, decrees that when a ruler dies every important officeholder must submit his resignation to the new king and receive a new commission if he is expected to continue in his post. Thus had acted the members of the privy council on the day after the death of Kamehameha IV. The king reached an agreement with us concerning the appointment of new councillors, and we likewise settled the question of recommissioning certain former ones. Several notables had disappeared, and the new selections brought in some men, particularly qualified because of practical experience, whose ideas were close to our own.

The members of the privy council receive no remuneration, even though their duties are demanding and complex. The king convenes the council by request of his ministers, whenever such a meeting is deemed necessary. Purely consultative in function, the privy council is made up of thirty-five members who examine the questions on which the king and the cabinet wish to be advised. Depending on the nature of the business, the questions are assigned for study to a special committee that prepares a report stating its conclusions and settling as quickly as possible the problem under consideration. There are no standing committees and in consequence no vested interests develop: in other words, no precedents arise that stand in the way of free and unfettered judgment. The cabinet, if the matter is one of general interest, or otherwise the responsible minister when the settlement of the problem concerns entirely his own department, is not at all obliged to follow the advice of the privy council. The latter body has no legal responsibility for its recommendations, other than merely the obligation to give advice. It is therefore unable to impose its will upon a cabinet minister, who bears legal responsibility and must answer for his actions before the legislature. Free of the constraints of precedent, the privy council simply considers each case on its own merits. Moreover, the ministers do not seek the advice of the council unless the case is actually doubtful. In handling questions about which they feel no uncertainty, and where there is no need to read the pulse of public opinion, the ministers assume full responsibility for their decisions.

Actual responsibility on the part of ministers, critical responsibility, this is the key to cabinet government in the Hawaiian Islands. No power without responsibility, no responsibility without power: such is the solemn operative principle in the organization of the ministerial departments. Legal control is vested solely in the legislature, which exercises its power strictly, paying close attention to details. As soon as the legislature assembles, its first action after having heard the king's message is to proceed with the business of appointing committees. Corresponding to each ministerial department, there are one or more special committees equipped with all necessary powers. These bodies scrutinize budgets and bookkeeping, official correspondence, appointments of every stripe. They have the authority to investigate anything and everything, and no form of record or document can be refused them. About midway during the legislative session, although occasionally only at the close, the committees present their reports, concluding with censure or praise, and indicating any changes to be made. The minister then makes a reply. Finally, the legislature votes its acceptance or rejection, in whole or in part, of the committee's recommendations.

Such is the method of legislative control over the executive branch of the government. The exercise of political power by means of the party system takes a different form naturally, and I shall explain later some of that system's workings and results.

In 1864 the king's appointments to the privy council were quite favorably received. As I have mentioned, we took pains to select particularly qualified individuals from among the most dedicated supporters of national independence. The European element in the country was generously represented; Americans were included among the membership, but only in a limited number, and annexationists were scrupulously ruled out.

As soon as its makeup had been settled, the privy council was summoned to give advice on a very important issue. This concerned the replacement of Mr. Robertson on the supreme court. The king was very eager to appoint Mr. Robertson to the post of minister of the interior, for he was an effective, energetic, and experienced administrator. The king did not, however, conceal the difficulties involved in selecting a successor to Mr. Robertson on the supreme court: he had to be a man who, at one and the same time, would possess the professional qualifications of a chief justice, the respect of the community, and the confidence of the cabinet.

The judicial system of the Hawaiian Kingdom has been largely modeled on that of the United States. At the lowest level are the police magistrates, whose jurisdiction is limited to cases of petty crimes and misdemeanors. The magistrates are appointed by the king for a term of two years. Above them are the district judges, whose decisions when appealed are referred to the circuit courts. The Hawaiian districts correspond to our French *arrondissements*, the various circuits to our prefectural *départements*. Judges of the circuit courts enjoy permanent tenure and their salaries are fixed by law. They are appointed by the king, upon the recommendation of the chancellor, who is chief justice of the supreme court, subject to the approval of the cabinet.

Each year one of the supreme court justices presides over the circuit court and reviews judicial decisions that are under appeal. The supreme court holds its sessions in Honolulu. It is made up of three judges: the chancellor of the kingdom, who is chief justice, assisted by two associate justices. All three have permanent tenure, are appointed by the king, and receive fixed salaries. As a court of the highest jurisdiction, there is no appeal from its decisions. The attorney general, a member of the cabinet with the rank of minister without portfolio, represents the legal interests of the executive branch of government in matters relating to the judicial power. He authorizes and directs prosecutions, in the most important cases, himself defending the rights and interests of the state before the supreme court.

The chancellor of the kingdom was at this time, as he still continues to be, the Honorable Elisha H. Allen, whom I mentioned earlier. A distinguished lawyer and experienced political leader, he was respected by everyone. As he was elderly and somewhat frail in health, he needed as colleagues men who were relatively young and energetic. Mr. Robertson was his right hand, a man who had deservedly won Allen's trust, and the chancellor regretted deeply that he would now be deprived of the younger judge's assistance. Among the candidates for the vacant post, none particularly pleased Chief Justice Allen, and by his own request the cabinet deferred from day to day a decision that the mounting variety of problems was rendering ever more urgent. The chancellor insisted upon the need for a supreme court made up of strong appointees, elevated above party struggles. Although he never in fact informed us of his views, it was evident to us that Judge Allen believed that the return of Judge Robertson to the supreme court bench was an indispensable requirement; furthermore, he thought it would be easier for us to replace Mr. Robertson as minister of the interior than it would be to find another suitable colleague on the supreme court. We therefore agreed to present the matter to the privy council, Mr. Robertson having declared himself ready to return to his post, if such was the wish of the king and the council's advice.

The arguments of the chancellor prevailed: in fact, they were virtually unanswerable. Mr. Robertson soon took up his old duties, and Mr. Hopkins (whom I had only recently replaced as minister of finance) received from the king the portfolio of minister of the interior. This was not an ideal choice, and Mr. Hopkins as it turned out did not hold the post very long.

Presently it was April. The reply of the French government to the message I had sent gave no cause for further delay. M. Drouyn de Lhuys, French minister of foreign affairs at that time, informed me that the emperor had signed an order, on the preceding twenty-fourth of February, authorizing me to accept the high position offered by Kamehameha V, without losing my French citizenship. Another imperial order, dated March 5, awarded me the Legion of Honor; and, finally, the foreign minister entrusted to me the stewardship of French interests in the islands, as a distinction and reward demonstrating the highest goodwill. There was nothing for me to do but set to work and assume the task whose difficulties I did not disguise, however attractive they appeared as a challenge to my ambition and my young hopes.

I had lived in the islands for nine years and—I say this with no false modesty—I had worked hard. True, I had received little enough credit for doing so. I had studied the country, its language, its beginnings, its history. I had carefully investigated Hawaii's agricultural resources, natural markets, political characteristics, and the prospect for governmental reforms. Like all those who labor away in solitude, I had arrived at certain conclusions. These were perhaps a shade too idealistic, but they had gradually become transformed in my mind into convictions, firm hopes that strengthened me in my search for their fulfillment. I was not easily put off by inevitable difficulties in matters of detail.

When a man is young he rarely questions his capacity. When the results of his hard work join with his fixed ideas, his preconceived (and possibly uncritical) judgments, he achieves by easy stages a pitch of self-confidence that can stimulate the spirits of others and rally the hesitant and more timorous to his side. Even self-confidence, however, one must admit, sometimes possesses no other distinction than knowing only too clearly what it wants to achieve, and of desiring today what it desired yesterday, and will continue to desire tomorrow.

In any event, the cabinet was eventually organized. Mr. Wyllie was its head. For the past twenty years he had been in charge of the department of foreign affairs. His age and experience gave him great authority; but, unaccustomed to being contradicted or having to listen to argument, and always moving at his own pace, he was rather astonished by the novel ideas of his new colleagues, and preached to us often (though without converting us) the advantages of deliberate procrastination—that is to say, of a system of delaying tactics—which, in his case, had served him so well but which, in our own judgment, had outlived its time.

He was rather dissatisfied with his minister of the interior, Mr. Charles G. Hopkins, who constantly caused him trouble and required administrative supervision at every turn. An intelligent but also an unsteady and very idle man, Mr. Hopkins cheerfully shifted his responsibility onto his higher staff, allowing his accumulated knowledge of things Hawaiian to serve as a substitute for solid work.

Mr. Harris, on the other hand, the attorney general, who was a very hard worker, but with an overpositive and unbending mind, was always ready to do battle. Excessively persistent, unconcerned with personal popularity, he fought for his ideas inch by inch, and compelled attention to them by sheer force of conviction.

At the time I took over the ministry of finance, the budget, although not in a state of total collapse, just barely managed to maintain a balance. The customs receipts for Honolulu, which had risen to 800,000 francs in 1850, had dropped to approximately 600,000 in 1863. The number of whaling vessels in port had totaled 446 in 1851, but now was no more than 88. Agricultural products alone had increased: from 1,500,000 francs in 1851 to 3,700,000 in 1863. Sugar, molasses, rice, hides, and coffee were our most important products. Agriculture, however, was in its infancy, and it was therefore to agriculture that I turned, not only in search of a substantial increase in our commerce, but also to quicken the moral and physical regeneration of the Hawaiian people.

It was a favorable moment for steering the efforts of our farmers and our investors in this imperative direction. The decline of the whaling fleet was not difficult to explain. The discovery of oil wells in Pennsylvania was partly the reason; in addition, the substitution, in numerous types of manufacture, of steel for baleen, a horny substance obtained from the jaws of whales, had markedly reduced the demand for all whaling products, whether bone or oil. The whales, having been relentlessly pursued in the Sea of Ockostk [Okhotsk] and Behring [Bering] Straits, were abandoning these regions and penetrating farther and farther into the glacial solitudes adjoining the arctic circle. French shipowners, who were the first to become discouraged, had entirely turned over this type of exploitation to the Americans. Even the latter grew more weary of the search year by year and so gradually cut down the amount of their shipbuilding and outfitting. The whalers, the principal source of profits for local merchants, were threatening the nation with bankruptcy. It was clearly necessary to find some other market elsewhere and to produce on a large scale agricultural items that could find a ready sale.

Several types of crop farming had been successfully attempted in Hawaii, but for one cause or another these had been abandoned. An epidemic of insects that plagued the coffee plantations had discouraged the growers. Cotton provided only a meager yield in Hawaii. In addition, one result of the Civil War in the United States was to assure the Southern states a monopoly on cotton during the immediate future, an advantage they had lost but temporarily during the recent hostilities. Some attempts at rice growing were being made, but as yet very tentatively. Competition with China, where the cost of manual labor is wretchedly low, was impossible. We in Hawaii were growing superior rice, which the Californians were buying from us at a rather high figure. Would it be the same when North or South Carolina again began to export their rice?

There remained, then, the promise of the sugar industry. Our soil was wonderfully suited to growing sugarcane, but unfortunately there was on the one hand a lack of labor, while on the other existing manufacturing facilities left a great deal to be desired. We possessed only a small number of steam-operated machines, and substantial sources of new capital were unavailable. The first difficulty was the more serious, and the one it was essential to resolve promptly. Capital investment would appear on that approaching day when land and labor would require only enough financial backing to produce profitable results. Experiments carried out on a modest scale had proved that we could manufacture sugar at a prime cost that would leave a sufficient margin of profit for the planter. There was really no question that the base cost of production could be kept lower still, if the day ever came when the plantations could increase their acres of cane, and when they could also utilize the very best machinery. California, and for that matter the entire west coast of America, provided us a sure market. Competition with China was inevitable, but we had an advantage over China by being closer to the continental United States by half. Ability to transport our sugar to San Francisco, assisted by a reduction in the cost of freight, would enable us to meet this competition.

These estimates, as experience has since proved, were correct. The question to be settled could thus be phrased: how to provide our planters with a plentiful supply of labor and also a good market, in a country where the going rate of interest was almost twelve percent? If I here again mention the steep rate of interest in Hawaii, I do so because of its usual correlation with the cost of labor, which generally is also higher wherever interest on loans is steep.

What countries are more favored in this respect than is ours? Where, indeed, should Hawaii turn for the labor supply we so badly need? It is no use thinking of Europe or America. Of course, I should have been most happy to see European emigrants pouring into the islands in order to develop their own commerce as well as ours, to cultivate our fields, and to swell the ranks of these persons who uphold Hawaiian independence. Yet the warm and humid climate, the distance to be overcome, the considerable costs of the voyage, served as so many insuperable obstacles to the flow of emigration into Hawaii. In America the cost of manual labor is much higher than in the islands, and likewise one finds in the United States a chronic shortage of manpower. Only Oceania and Asia could supply us with laborers. In my own mind I was partial to Oceania. My deciding reason was the affinity in racial stock. To bring into Hawaii immigrants of a similar racial background would be entirely a benefit, both to them and to us: a profit to them, for they would be readily assimilated to a population whose language, traditions, and manner of life had so many points of kinship with those of the Hawaiians; and an advantage to us, who would thus escape the introduction of a new, often dangerous, and always embarrassing social element, whose absorption into the local scene would be achieved only with difficulty.

The numerous islands of the South Pacific were inhabited by peoples either barely civilized or not at all, broken up into tribes, and constantly warring with one another. Famines were frequent, despite the fertility of the soil. Among these primitive peoples, the first beginnings of civilized society were colliding at every point with the same obstacles that the government of the Hawaiian Kingdom had encountered some twenty-five years earlier. I was inspired by the vision of carrying out, entirely by peaceful means, the task begun by Kamehameha I of unifying and attaching little by little these various island groups to the political life of the Hawaiian archipelago: of civilizing these people by providing them with an opportunity to engage in useful work and commerce. I hoped, in fact, that they would come to regard Kamehameha V, if not as their ruler, at least as their protector and spokesman in the great family of nations. To serve the common cause of progress, while extending our influence, to attract to Hawaii the surplus of their population, to send to them missionaries and schoolteachers of their own race, to place in their hands the advantages of peace, to preach to them through deeds and examples—this was my dream, which I was ultimately unable to realize, but which others will some day carry out, if the independence of the islands is preserved, and if the greed and ambition of the United States permit.

Possibly, of course, the country had as yet not given sufficient proof of its own capacity to overcome all these obstacles, of which the last—the issue of independence—in my opinion remains the most grave, the most formidable to surmount. Time alone will provide the answer. The great maritime powers, France, England, and the United States of America, watch Hawaii with jealous eyes. Though the group of islands I speak of is hardly known, these foreign nations exercise over it an ill-defined protectorate, the purpose of which is not so much to obtain outright possession of Hawaii as it is to prevent the islands from being occupied by any of the rivals. With the exception of Tahiti, New Caledonia, Raiatea, and several other islands solely administered (and at considerable cost) by France, the rest of Polynesia and Micronesia serves as a battleground for Catholic, Protestant, and Anglican missionaries, each jealous of the other, always prompt to transform their personal grievances into international issues. Up to the present, however, these religious activities have achieved only insignificant results, when one considers the efforts and sums of money expended by their respective churches.

I often ask myself, in the face of facts whose accuracy I can vouch for, whether or not this furor of doctrinal propaganda in remote regions does not owe its existence quite as much to the hostility that animates religious sects to quarrel with each other as it owes its justification to their commitment to do good. Of course, I do not question the personal devotion of the missionaries, and it is not them so much as their superiors and directors whom I have in mind. Unfortunately, I have seen too many examples of the sorry results produced by the zeal to proselytize not to speak my entire mind, even at the risk of wounding convictions that I deeply respect. I need hardly mention Tahiti, for its seizure brought about by missionary quarrels almost overturned the throne of Louis-Philippe. Consider how many other conflicts, more or less concealed, have had any other cause, any other origin! From Cochin China to New Caledonia, from the New Hebrides to the Hawaiian Islands and everywhere else, no sooner did one missionary set foot on the soil than competing sects dispatched their own representatives.

Is it fully realized what the result has been for the natives? Almost always hypocrisy; indifference frequently. They believe what the missionary tells them when these parties attack one another. They cease to believe them when one of the latter proclaims its own church to be the sole possessor of the truth. Throughout Polynesia and Micronesia, the Kanaka believes the Catholic priest when he describes the Protestant missionary as a wolf in sheep's clothing; but he also believes the Protestant minister who speaks of the Catholic priest as an idolator, and of his ritual as tainted with paganism.

It is invariably in this fashion that the dispute begins; next comes the day when the gunboat arrives. Grievances are not lacking; the commanding officer naturally backs up his fellow countryman. Armed force is exerted in the service of a religious cause. This or that tribe originally greeted the missionaries with an unpleasant welcome, drove them off, obedient to the pressures of other foreigners and the interests of the latter. In consequence cannons are brought into line; and in order to obtain satisfaction for wrongs that are all too genuine, villages are burned, inhabitants killed, and seeds of hatred sown—implacable hatred—towards the civilization that seeks to impose its will on others by force.

I do not in the least exaggerate. These are the facts, and only a blind man cannot perceive them. At the very moment I am writing these sentences, China threatens to expel all missionaries, and blood will perhaps flow on the banks of the Yang-tse-Kiang, in the name of a God of peace and love. This is none other than the very same China that we in Hawaii were being obliged to visit in search of laborers, for without them our canefields are doomed to remain uncultivated. For centuries Asia has had the advantage of furnishing workers for the entire globe. But let us limit our examples to recent times. It is Asia that, with the Chinese as its agents, makes possible the profitable development of the vast guano deposits of the Chinchas Islands.* It is the Chinese who have laid the great Pacific railroad that links New York to San Francisco by means of an iron causeway 1,200 leagues long. India has furnished the "Hill Coolies" for the Isthmus of Panama project. The placer mines of California are aswarm with Chinese; and already, in fact, despite every obstacle such as the unjust exclusion acts, the Chinese are streaming into New York and the Atlantic states. Europe and America vainly expect to open the ports of China by employing gunfire, so as to allow their merchants, their missionaries, and their products to move in. Yet, by a strange inconsistency, they refuse to grant the Chinese access to their own spacious land! Nevertheless, social and economic circumstances more forceful by far than immigration laws are speeding up this new mode of invasion by foreigners.

The king fully shared my ideas on the subject of introducing into Hawaii settlers from other Polynesian areas. He was obliged, however, just as was I, to bow to the facts and to admit, at least for the present, that we did not have time enough to win our case by utilizing the hesitations and delaying tactics followed by European diplomacy. On the advice of the cabinet, it was decided to establish a board of immigration, charged with investigating practical methods for encouraging suitable immigrants, and with preparing a report on the question. Once approval was gained from both houses of the legislature, our idea was to begin the task of introducing some thousands of laborers into Hawaii, laborers whose services were indispensable to our pur-

*Off the coast of Peru. [A. L. K.]

poses. I was appointed by the king to serve as a member of the immigration committee, which was made up of the minister of the interior, the attorney general, and two members of the privy council.

The accession of the king to the throne had left a vacant place on the board of public instruction. For several years, in fact, he had been a member of the three-man committee, in which he was joined by the chancellor of the kingdom and by the most respected of the high chiefs, Kekuanaoa, his father. From these three individuals one can judge the importance of the committee's functions. Indeed, among the various governmental departments, that of public instruction alone has no cabinet minister as its head. Its supervisory responsibilities are instead carried out by a board whose members serve without pay. A minister is honored when he becomes an appointee to this body, and there is no official title more envied or respected in the islands than that of member of the board of public instruction. This is because there is no civic question more debated, or studied with greater concern, than that of education. In all the annals of the Hawaiian Legislature one can find not one example of the legislative houses refusing—or even reducing—an appropriation requested by the government for public education. It is as if this magic word alone seems to possess the prerogative of loosening the public purse strings. Furthermore, the amount allotted in the budget to appropriations for this department has given it fifth place among the total expenses of the government.

The system of free compulsory education extends throughout all the islands. Parents are responsible for seeing that their children learn to read, write, and work sums, under the same principle that obliges them to nourish their offspring, lodge them, clothe them. In each district there are one or more schools for girls and for boys, depending on the number of the inhabitants. School facilities are constructed on a basis of shared responsibility: half at the cost of the local population, which usually supplies the manual labor and certain of the materials; the other half paid for by the board, which appropriates the funds. Once built, the schoolhouse is maintained at public expense. The schoolmaster is chosen at a meeting of a local committee, presided over on this single occasion by the superintendent of public instruction, and composed of the justice of the peace of the district, a resident of the district selected by the central board sitting in Honolulu, and the father of one of the pupils. The latter is selected by a majority vote of the parents. This committee inspects the schools, makes certain that attendance at classes is regular, and submits annually to the central board a report in which the committee's observations and ideas are recorded. The superintendent of instruction is appointed by the central board and receives a reasonably adequate salary, along with his travel costs. His duties include visiting at least once each year all the schools in the islands, presiding over the local committees in matters concerning the employment or dismissal of teachers, and investigating the various requests and criticisms of the local committees. These findings, like the reports of the committees, are submitted to the central board, which rules on the issues that require further appeal. What the law does not indicate, but which practice stronger than law consecrates, is the important role played on the local committees by the member elected by the parents themselves.

Public education is completely separate from religious instruction in Hawaii. The state, represented by the central board, in no way interferes in this last question of school policy, and all teachers are forbidden to instruct youngsters in any religion whatsoever. It is the business of the parents, and of the ministers of religion of course, to provide for religious needs. The central board permits religious authorities, outside the hours of class instruction, to make use of school premises, on the condition that the ministers of the various denominations will agree among themselves on a schedule for occupying the schools. Thus the schools open at nine o'clock in the morning and close at two in the afternoon. For children of Catholic parents, the Catholic priest is able to conduct his course of religious instruction from three to four o'clock twice a week. The Protestant minister and the Anglican priest are able in the same way to teach alternately. In case of a conflict or some misunderstanding, the school closes at two o'clock and does not reopen until nine the next morning; the ministers of the several denominations then conduct their catechism either at home or in their respective churches.

The state does not enforce any official religion. In vain the government has been urged to serve as intermediary (to centralize revenues and provide for expenses), but it has consistently refused to do so. The Catholics pay the costs of their church directly; and the Protestants and Anglicans do the same. It is a matter to be settled between them and their own clergy. The state does not interfere; neither does it subsidize. Acting simply as a treasury for public funds, the government does not collect revenues that it is not specifically empowered to expend, and it leaves to individuals the free management of as large a sum as the state is in a position to appropriate. It is assumed that, without coercion, individuals can be trusted to act more intelligently than the state would act. It is commonly admitted in theory that parents are better judges than the government concerning the religious instruction they wish their children to have, and prefer to receive themselves. Thus they build their own churches, they join them, they are responsible for keeping them in shape; but no one would consider it to be a fair arrangement if a Catholic were obliged to contribute even a minimal amount of money to the building of a Protestant house of worship, or to an Anglican minister's living and support. However, this is what would happen if the government were held responsible for the financial upkeep of the different religious denominations.

But, someone may ask, what if in a given district there are too few Catholics for them to be able to construct a church? They then do without—a simple hut substitutes for a church building, and the pastor of the next district comes from time to time to celebrate religious services and conduct the catechism. Energetic individual activity takes over and makes up for the lack of physical resources; and this inconvenience, though frustrating, is after all rare enough, appearing to be infinitely preferable to the complications which inevitably arise when the state interposes itself in questions of such subtle complexity.

The district schools are essentially primary schools. Above these are the secondary schools. The instruction provided by the latter is free only within limits—that is, free tuition is granted after an applicant meets competitive standards, and is available only to a restricted number of pupils. Others pay a modest fee. Over and above these schools, competitive awards are available for admission to Lahainaluna Seminary, a normal school, which accommodates about 120 pupils. It is from this group that the state recruits the district schoolteachers.

In addition to the instruction supplied by the state, there is also the education provided by the private schools. The profession of teaching excludes no one in Hawaii from its practice: anyone can open a school without being involved with the state in any degree. It is left to the parents to assess the qualifications and skills of the persons to whom they wish to entrust their children; the proper concerns of the parents guide them in their choice. If they do not wish to take advantage of the educational opportunities the state offers to the public in general, and if they prefer other ones better adapted to their own needs, they may do so. All that is required of them is to see that their children go to school and learn to read, write, and master the elements of arithmetic.

I do not believe one would find today in the islands ten persons of twenty years of age, man or woman, who does not have a full command of these basic skills. One will not find many highly educated people, but one will not meet many who are ignorant. The Kanakas read a good deal, especially their newspapers, of which the number, in proportion to the population, is rather large. The two principal newspapers, printed in the native language and in the format of Parisian newspapers, are published in Honolulu. One of them, *Kuokoa* ("The Independent"), is the organ of the opposition party, supported by American interests. Its circulation is about 5,000 copies. The other, *Au Koa* ("The New Era"), follows the policies of the present government and represents above all the idea of national independence; its circulation is a trifle less than that of its rival. Besides these political papers, which enjoy complete freedom of expression and which submit to no form of license or regulation, there are also several journals of lesser importance in the native language, mouthpieces of the various religious sects, which generally carry on among themselves fiery polemic contests.

Theological questions loom large in the Hawaiian Islands. As I mentioned earlier, the Catholic missionaries, the Protestants, and the Anglicans maintain a running battle with each other. I shall have occasion later to return to this topic and show how, at one stage, the unfortunate results almost made it appear as if religious bias had become an official policy of the Hawaiian government.

It was not until June 8, six months after his accession to the throne, that the king took steps to reorganize the board of public instruction. Yielding to the wishes of his royal son, Kekuanaoa despite his advanced age consented to undertake the duties of president of the board. Mr. Hopkins, the minister of the interior, and I were appointed to the other two memberships.

CHAPTER 11

A PLAN FOR CONSTITUTIONAL REFORM

Life of a cabinet minister in the Sandwich Islands.—A plan to revise the constitution.—A royal proclamation.— Meetings of the opposition party.—Journey of the king through the islands.—The constitutional assembly.—The royal commissioners.—Stormy sessions.—First success.

The reader will realize from the preceding chapter that a post as cabinet minister in the Hawaiian Islands is far from being a sinecure. In addition to my special responsibilities as minister of finance, I was a member of the privy council, of the committee on immigration, and of the board of public instruction. In my role as the youngest minister of the cabinet, it was my duty to record the minutes of the meetings, including the questions on the agenda, and to transmit to my fellow members a certified copy of the resolutions adopted at each session. In order to keep up with all these varied chores, I found it necessary to schedule my work with utmost care, for time is the very essence of daily life.

I rose at a very early hour, at five o'clock, and began my day with a horseback ride. At seven I had breakfast and at eight was in my office. From then until ten I read through my official correspondence and made notes for my replies. From ten to eleven I worked with my chief financial clerk. The king usually made his appearance between then and noon, on days when there was no meeting of the privy council. From twelve until two I received official callers, but on the rare occasions when I found myself free I composed my minutes for the privy council. From two until four, but on occasion until five, I attended almost every day a meeting of either the board of public instruction or the committee on immigration. Else I simply conferred with my immediate staff.

At four I usually returned home, dined early, and then went outdoors again on horseback or in carriage. The evenings, given over partly to social gatherings, left me still from seven to ten with several periods of leisure, devoted partly to the pleasures of family life and partly to the study of current affairs. During this stage in my career I very often managed well enough with only five hours of sleep, especially during the legislative sessions, which occupied the freshest part of my day, from ten in the morning until two in the afternoon.

Material life is very different in the Hawaiian Islands from what it is in our northern countries, where the periodic return of the seasons assures regular and always welcome changes in the pattern of existence. Winter and summer in subtropical countries are terms without much meaning. Trees are always green, various plants are continually in blossom, the sun is consistently warm, and fluctuations in temperature are almost unnoticeable. The following table of weather observations for the year 1868 will give a precise idea of the superb, but also somewhat monotonous, Hawaiian climate.

CLIMATE

Month	Average Temperature (Fahrenheit)
January	73
February	72
March	73
April	75
May	77
June	80
July	80.5
August	80
September	81
October	79
November	73
December	72

The average difference between the two extremes is eight degrees Fahrenheit. To be aware of it one must have lived for a long time in a hot country and have acquired oneself something of the character of a thermometer.

Though the months called winter in Hawaii are slightly less warm than those of summer, the compensating trade wind, which helps one to bear the summer heat, disappears almost completely during the winter season. It is for this reason that the numerical results on the thermometer tend to cancel each other and even out.

As for rains, these are perhaps a little more abundant in December and January, but this depends very much on the area and the proximity to the mountains. In the islands one entirely escapes those periods of incessant rain so frequent in coastal parts of the Pacific Basin and in China and the East Indies.

During the entire month of April, meetings of the cabinet were held almost daily. The king went on refusing, flatly refusing, to take the oath to uphold the constitution, and the work of constitutional revision we had begun led us quickly to decide that it was desirable to encourage public discussion of this complicated problem. In fact, we had generally agreed that it was necessary to hold a constitutional convention made up of representatives of the people, the nobles, and the king, as a means of modifying by a general consensus the constitution of 1852.

Several plans for constitutional reform had been advanced, but despite all the drawbacks involved, the calling of a special convention seemed to us to be the most legal, and at the same time the only appropriate and really effective, means of safeguarding the rights and interests of the three estates: the king, the high chiefs or nobles, and the people as a whole. Indeed, one could very soundly argue that the constitution, having been originally granted by one of his forebears, could now be altered simply by wish of the present monarch. Nevertheless, there still had been a contract: the king had granted, the people and the nobles had accepted, and from this mutual accord there thus flowed the obligation for both the one and for the other participants alike to respect the mutuality of the original compact. I believed, as did my ministerial colleagues, that there was a need to take a progressive step and to call upon the other estates, not merely to ratify decisions made without their help, but to voice their own desires, and especially to discuss in full detail the justification for those changes deemed indispensable. The king, in particular, held this same view, for he believed that constitutional changes of such importance as those he was proposing would entail a complete revamping or the old constitution. He quite realized that if he hoped to begin his reign with a vigorous program of reform, he would accordingly have to follow a liberal policy in choosing his means of action. He would need to assemble the high chiefs together with his people and in this way organize a public debate from which some promising results could be expected.

We had no illusions, however, about the antagonisms we were about to stir up among the missionary party: in fact, we had decided to face the struggle head on. The following proclamation formulated by the cabinet appeared on May 7, 1864:

> We, Kamehameha V, by the grace of God, of the Hawaiian Islands, King: To all our loyal and loving subjects, greeting.
>
> Whereas, the experience of all constitutional governments has shown that a written constitution needs revision from time to time, in order that it may be adapted to the changing condition of the people: And, whereas, it has ap-

peared to us that many provisions of the constitution of our kingdom have not been productive of that good to our subjects which had been anticipated: and since further provisions are required for the benefit of our people and the permanency of our dynasty:

Therefore, being moved thereto by our love to our subjects, it is our will to meet our Nobles and the delegates of our people, for the purpose of consulting on the revision of the constitution of our kingdom, and consulting upon the public good as well as to provide ways and means to carry on our government.

Therefore, we do proclaim our pleasure that delegates to our people do meet our Nobles and ourselves in convention at the Legislative Chamber, in Honolulu, on Thursday, the 7th day of July, next, at 12 M. Our minister of the interior will take the measures necessary under this proclamation.

KAMEHAMEHA R.

By the King and Kuhina Nui
   Charles Gordon Hopkins

A ministerial decree followed, summoning voters to an election on June 13, for the purpose of selecting delegates to a constitutional convention. These were to be the same numerically as the representatives from each district attending the regular legislative sessions.

Feelings ran high. The American party believed—or, at any rate, their emotions instructed them—that they were being threatened. They immediately fell into line as defenders of the constitution of 1852, a posture they had long maintained, and they did not overlook any device for stirring up distrust among the electorate, urging them to cast their ballots for certain declared opponents of any and all changes in the charter as granted originally by Kamehameha III. Since the particular character of these changes had not yet been announced, this part of their campaign left much to be desired, for they were arguing in a vacuum. On one other issue, however, they opened battle with no less heat but with rather more skill. Barricading themselves behind article 80 of the constitution as if it were a fortress, they insisted that any changes made by other means than those there defined were null in law and, in fact, unconstitutional: the delegates of the people, so they claimed, had only to remind the king respectfully that the constitution of 1852 had already anticipated the present situation and had provided procedures for dealing with it. Therefore, as they were bound by their constitutional oath, they could not follow the course along which certain irresponsible ministers were leading the king.

The opposition newspapers furthermore announced a *"public meeting"**

---

*In English. [A. L. K.]

for the evening of May 19, to be held in one of the Honolulu churches. There a whole series of resolutions were on that date discussed and voted upon. The first of these was phrased thus: "We completely disapprove of the method of revising the constitution proposed by the Royal Proclamation: we believe that the same end may be achieved, if necessary, by conforming to the terms of the Constitution itself, and that any other mode of action is unjustifiable."

The last resolution contained the following pronouncement: "We are loyal subjects of King Kamehameha V. We have confidence in his regard for us and his desire to guarantee the rights that have been granted to us by his royal predecessors. We shall continue to uphold and support him, but his ministers have betrayed his trust in them and we respectfully beg him to dismiss from his cabinet certain persons who have revealed themselves to be the enemies of our civil and religious rights."

This last phrase was actually an allusion to a serious suspicion then prevailing among the natives. There had been an attempt, to some degree successful, to persuade distrustful Hawaiians that the king, a supporter of the Anglican church, intended to make it the Established Church of the Hawaiian Kingdom. It is perhaps superfluous to say that nothing of the sort was involved. Had it been otherwise, I myself should have immediately resigned from the cabinet. The calumny was nonetheless skillfully contrived, as a means of alarming both Catholics and Protestants and consolidating their votes—in other words, producing an almost unanimous agreement among the electorate against the cabinet's position.

The astonished reader will perhaps question how such a popular assembly could be summoned and staged in the very capital of the kingdom: a meeting to initiate charges against the ministers, to organize resistance to orders of the executive branch, and to invite the rest of the nation as a whole to participate in the same proceedings. Would this conduct be legal? Would the government have any method of forestalling or controlling it? My answer to the question is that in Hawaii such a meeting is perfectly legal and that no one has the power to oppose it. It is the incontestable and uncontested right of voters to unite together and pass any and all resolutions they please. Such a public declaration is what is called a "party platform" in the United States. In contrast to the way we manage such matters in France, they begin in Hawaii with questions of principle. They arrive at agreed upon propositions through discussion, first stating what they want and likewise what they do not want. When this has been accomplished, they select from among those persons subscribing to such a program the candidates of the party.

The election campaign thus launched in Honolulu was conducted in a spirited style throughout the rural districts. Everywhere the same slogan was adopted, everywhere the ministers were denounced as being suspect of bias in favor of the Anglican church, and as hostile to the liberties granted by Kamehameha III. The goal set up by the opposition party was to overturn the cabinet and recapture the power which the ministers had briefly fancied they possessed, thanks to the support of the king: in short, they believed they could still depend on the king's personal goodwill. Yet the heat and excitement of combat led them on, and while at the beginning of the struggle they had been sufficiently shrewd and skillful to aim their blows solely at us, leaving the king out of the dispute, this tactic was now demanding more restraint and cool judgment than they could muster. Certain of their allies given to intrigue were pushing them into extreme tactical positions.

According to the terms of the proclamation, the convention was to be made up of the House of Nobles, numbering fifteen, and the delegates of the people, of the same number as the House of Representatives, namely twenty-seven. The king reserved the right to preside over the discussions. In all districts the most committed and intemperate candidates presented themselves, patronized and supported by the Protestant missionaries, among whom there were some who did not themselves disdain descending into the political arena and soliciting the approval of the voters. In thus behaving they were not merely exercising their right but were even going beyond it, by affirming from the pulpit an essentially false proposition. Pointing to the excessive zeal of the Anglican bishop as their authority, they accused the government of seeking to establish a state religion.

The king thought he should counter these constantly repeated allegations with a formal denial. Ever since his accession to the throne, he had been considering a plan to visit the various islands of the Hawaiian chain. The occasion now seemed a favorable one to make his wish an actuality and to reassure his subjects concerning the trumped-up intentions people were ascribing to him. The king consulted his cabinet, received their approval, and on May 24 sailed on the royal yacht to visit Kauai. Mr. Wyllie, the minister of foreign affairs, accompanied Kamehameha V, the king having accepted an invitation to be Wyllie's guest for several days at Hanalei.

The sea voyage from Oahu was completed without incident. The king successfully toured Kauai, Maui, and Hawaii, receiving everywhere a most friendly welcome. On every occasion he made it a point to explain his political goals and clear up misunderstandings, and in general to educate his subjects regarding their own interests. Unfortunately, our ministerial colleague, Mr. Wyllie, carried away by feeling and embittered by the slander of the opposition newspapers, often ruined by his furious tirades the good effect of the king's words, thus providing his adversaries, and therefore ours as well, with forensic weapons they knew how to use adroitly. Mr. Wyllie became so exasperated by the pompous eulogies his enemies were lavishing on the constitution of 1852 that he frequently lost all judgment in composing his lively sallies. Falling into the trap set for him, he loudly demonstrated his low respect for what was after all the law of the kingdom, faulty though it was. Certain sentences in Mr. Wyllie's speeches, carefully selected, lifted out of context, and then commented on in the opposition newspapers, gave these critics much sport, and greatly complicated our task by making us appear brutally insensitive, at any rate in our motives and intentions.

The royal tour thus proved only a middling success, for the balloting on June 13 showed that the majority of the voters were decidedly cool to our project and our method of constitutional revision. Of the twenty-seven popular delegates to the convention, seventeen belonged more or less to the American party. Among this group, however, were several whom we were hoping to persuade and win to our side. Ten, in the end, were in some measure to join forces with ours. The House of Nobles, on the other hand, was unanimously in favor of the ministerial plan, except for two members. We had agreed to submit to the convention the following preliminary propositions: every member should possess the right to propose an amendment; each house would vote separately on each amendment; no amendment could be adopted unless it received the successive approval of the two houses. There was little doubt that these stipulations were such as would win approval, although the systematic resistance of the delegates at large could bring to a stalemate the whole proceedings from the start. Indeed, it was upon this resistance that the leaders of the resistance were banking.

The convention opened in an atmosphere of solemnity. The king, accompanied by his equerries and staff, his ministers, and his father and sister, presided in person. The usual assembly hall would not have been able to contain the eager throng hoping to attend the meeting, and so it had been necessary to assign for this ceremony the largest public building in Honolulu. The king indicated briefly, in a speech prepared with the help of his advisers, the reasons determining his important decision, including the serious defects of the constitution of 1852. His address ended as follows:

> The sheer number of changes to be made, apart from their importance, have led me to summon this convention in which all constituent powers of the kingdom are here united: in which my people, being represented by you, gentlemen, as their delegates: my *Ali'i* and men of rank by you, the nobles; and royalty by myself. I hope that nobles and delegates will freely exercise their right to frame amendments. Pray receive my assurance that, for my part, I am

prepared to listen to them. I only ask that the same kind attention be granted those persons to whom I have delegated the authority to speak in my name during the course of the debates.

Those to whom the king had entrusted this difficult task were the attorney general and myself, both of us new to our official posts. Kamehameha V was counting on our calm good manners, in short our *sang froid*—qualities that would be entirely lacking in Mr. Wyllie's style of argument—and on our perseverance in surmounting obstacles.

From the beginning of the sessions, the strategy of the opposition was plain. They consented to revise the constitution, but they denied that the convention had any legal power to enact specific changes, granting it merely the authority to recommend to the legislature at its next session the adoption of such and such amendments.

The question of the convention's legal powers came up in connection with a subordinate matter of procedure. A committee had been named to draw up and present to the assembly for adoption a table of rules. Article 15 of the planned procedure had been worded as follows:

> The three estates of the realm—the representatives, the nobles, the king—will vote separately on the question whether or not they recommend the adoption of each amendment. The delegates will vote first; if their vote is negative, the amendment will be considered as rejected. If their vote is affirmative, the nobles will vote; and if the majority of the nobles approve, the king will be respectfully invited to cast his vote.

After the reading of this article, the king requested the committee kindly to explain what was meant by the words "whether or not they recommend."

> Mr. Dowsett (one of the committee members): We mean by that the act of approving or disapproving.
> The king: But to whom do you mean to address this recommendation?
> Mr. Dowsett: Several of us are of the opinion that our powers do not go beyond a simple recommendation to the legislature.
> The king: I do not recognize in any assembly other than this convention the right to decide—that is, to approve or reject—amendments. The convention alone possesses sovereign authority.

The question was nicely posed and the conflict was taking shape. If the theory of the committee prevailed, and if the convention was merely a political gathering with no other powers than those involved in framing recommendations to the Hawaiian Legislature that such and such amendments be adopted, then our necessary goal—the thorough revision of the constitution of 1852—would be indefinitely postponed. Furthermore, the king would either have to swear to an oath of office phrased in the style of 1852 or else surrender certain powers that he could not otherwise legally exercise. Mr. Gulick, a young Protestant clergyman, one of the opposition leaders, felt that the moment had arrived to marshal a strong attack. In an impassioned but effective speech, he set forth the views of his party and closed with the following resolution:

> According to the terms of the royal proclamation, and of the mandate they have received from their constituents, delegates hereby declare the convention has no properly constituted power. Whatever decision they may be pleased to reach has no force other than that of simple recommendation. The Hawaiian Legislature in session alone has the powers necessary to amend the constitution, in conformity with the terms of article 80. The legislature remains free to accept or reject the advice and recommendations of the convention.

Messrs. Green and Judd supported the same argument, which was hotly refuted by several of the other delegates and by the majority of the nobles. The attorney general, in the king's name, answered the stated objections, especially emphasizing the legal aspect of the question. The sessions of the twelfth and thirteenth were lively and high-pitched. On both sides, the members of the convention were frequently meeting in caucus, and the majority of the delegates, obedient to the pressure of the opposition leaders, were now threatening us with an irremediable defeat. The meeting of the fourteenth thus opened portentously. The king presided as usual. Since the eleventh, he had not spoken and contented himself with following attentively the progress of the debates. At the beginning of the session, he sent me the following note:

> Take the floor and lead the discussion. The time has come to inform delegates that the present method of revising the constitution was advised by the supreme court. Insist that the convention has sovereign power and show, if necessary, minutes for the meeting of the privy council held March 3, 1864. I'm going to address several remarks to the convention—take the floor after me and carry on.

Then, amidst deep silence, the king rose to his feet and spoke his thoughts:

> Nobles and delegates, the member representing Kona district has proposed a motion declaring that the convention does not possess the power to amend the

constitution. At the time the constitution of 1852 was adopted and proclaimed, the sovereign power was in the hands of the king. Now where is this sovereign power today? It is here, in this assembly, and nowhere else. The delegate from Kona asserted yesterday that he could not take his seat and vote conclusively on any article whatsoever of the constitution. In doing so, he was obligated to voice the opinion and wishes of his constituents. If such is actually the delegate's view, it is a matter to be decided between himself and his supporters. They can, whichever seems right, join their efforts with ours, or else abstain from doing so, which last judgment their delegate doubtless will consider proper. In any event, it will be his task to give his constituents a responsible accounting of the use he has made of his mandate.

My assignment from the king did not allow me to be particularly intellectual or subtle; the prolonged discussion was already becoming inflamed, and several of the later speakers had presented such precise and eloquent affirmative statements to the constitutional tribunal, or forum of justice, so to speak, that it was becoming embarrassing for them to cover again the same old ground. At the same time, it was necessary to kindle their hopes and offer a justification of such optimism. To achieve the first result, I thought I should emphasize above all the responsibility they owed to their constituents. I explained that the king, in summoning them to work with him in the exercise of the constitution-making power, was voluntarily abdicating a portion of his authority and inviting them to share in a political task from which they had been excluded by his predecessor. Did they mean to proclaim, by their apparent refusal to cooperate, that sovereignty belonged to the king alone, or to the king acting together with his nobles? So be it: it was up to them to say so clearly and to refuse, in the name of the people they were representing, a royal political concession which elsewhere people fought to achieve by force of arms. I then stated that I thought this present conflict was the result of a misunderstanding, a confusion that a frank and fair explanation ought to resolve. Furthermore, by order of the king, and for the purpose of putting an end to various honorable scruples, I said I was authorized to announce that the justices of the supreme court—who had been consulted by us in their capacity as guardians of the organic act—had in that very same capacity recommended the summoning of a convention as the sole legal and effective method of revising the constitution of 1852. Our purpose was to make of the convention a mutual enterprise of the three estates, thus stripping from the constitution the character of a royal charter granted by the power of the sovereign alone.

The attorney general next took the floor, directing his remarks skillfully to the legal aspect of the question. In vain the leaders of the opposition sought to stiffen the spirit of their adherents; it was evident that they were losing ground, while the delegates were shrinking from their responsibility, which we were resolved to persuade them to accept. Messrs. Judd and Gulick considered it desirable to adjourn the discussion until the following day. Each of the contending parties needed to pause and take bearings.

The session next day began with a speech by Mr. Robertson, followed by the reading of a letter from Mr. Davis, one of the supreme court justices. Both confirmed my statement of the day before. One of the delegates at this point proposed to call for a vote on the motion introduced by the member from Kona. This motion, when acted on, failed to carry by one vote. The debates continued vigorously. We needed more than two votes among the delegates for the motion to carry in our favor. As for the assembled nobles, we were sure of good support. The attorney general and I retraced our argument of the day before, pressing harder still on the heels of our adversaries. The opposition leaders felt the ground slipping way under their feet. They struggled manfully, but with little hope. At the start, they had twenty-two votes out of twenty-seven. The ballot just now cast gave them fourteen against thirteen. We finally demanded a roll call on the same motion; it was taken in an atmosphere of noisy excitement. The hall was packed with numerous spectators eager to discover the outcome of a discussion so close to the hearts and feelings of the masses. The victory was a total one: six delegates voted for the resolution, twenty-one against. The nobles voted unanimously against, and the king voted against.

Though our success appeared decisive, we did not forget the battles remaining to be won. It required no less than hours of discussion and tremendous effort to achieve this initial victory, due in great measure to the king's energetic leadership and to the tireless perseverance of the attorney general, Mr. Harris. All the burden of the debate fell upon his shoulders and mine, and we were not receiving from our colleagues the kind of assistance we were justified in expecting from them. Because we had been designated by the king to speak in his name (in other words to lead the debate), this temporary role of ours somewhat isolated and estranged us from both Mr. Wyllie and Mr. Hopkins.

The former, who had become very unpopular ever since his ill-starred campaign tour with the king, was now extremely put out by the attacks of the opposition press, and held the floor often and very irascibly. It was always with dread that we watched him ask to speak. His years as well as his rank allowed us to remonstrate only in highly respectful terms, to which he paid minimal attention. He was a dangerous ally, for he jeopardized our cause.

Mr. Hopkins barely disguised the displeasure he felt for not having been selected by the king as his spokesman. He very mistakenly envied us this perilous favor, which besides would have been ill-suited to his habitual indolence. A good speaker when he wished to be, popular among the natives, whose language he spoke fluently, and whose customs and style of life he had adopted, Mr. Hopkins was nevertheless not much respected as a politician by the white population. He attended with an air of indifference the sessions of the convention, affectedly holding himself aloof, or simply absenting himself at critical moments when decisions were called for. We rather candidly told him our opinion of his conduct, but this was the sole satisfaction we gained from doing so. Out of humor with himself and with us, he wanted to save his efforts for a better occasion, for he was counting, I have no doubt, upon our downfall, a denouement he believed to be inevitable.

Nevertheless, glimpses of the truth were beginning to reach the public at large. Having a better understanding of our goal, people were willing to credit our good faith. In fact, our arguments, so firmly shaped by our convictions, had rallied to our side from the mass of the population a substantial body of supporters, though they had been rather opposed at the beginning of the convention. In order to dispel misunderstandings, we arranged for publication, and then placed on the chief desk of the convention, the complete text of the revised constitution. This document demonstrated how carefully we had prepared our drafts and arrived at our decisions in council. It pointed out the modifying amendments we believed to be indispensable, and likewise it listed those we were prepared to leave open to compromise after further study and discussion. The American party, still feeling the effects of its recent defeat, offered some critical comment about various details, but reserved their judgment on the important issues.

Consequently there was nothing more for us to do except to settle down to work. The opposition, however, were spoiling for battle on another terrain: proposing an adjournment of six weeks, so they said, to allow the delegates to consult their constituents. On this point, the attorney general and I declared our decision—to cede nothing. We admitted the propriety of an adjournment before the final vote, if the delegates expressed a desire for such, but we saw no justification for breaking off deliberations before the floor discussion took place. Nothing seemed to us more appropriate than the urge to consult the wishes of the people. Yet there was still a need, we argued, for serious consideration on the part of the public, so that opinions might be expressed and positions clarified, in the light of all pertinent information. Nor was it merely in the course of the debates in camera for their own sake that we could explain the reasons that justified, in our view, the changes we were seeking. We insisted that the convention continue in session in order that our arguments could be fully made known and circulated. Above all, we wished to prevent the bare text of the revised constitution from being submitted to constituents—that is to say, to the public at large—without other elucidation besides the malevolent, injurious, and erroneous commentaries emanating from our foes.

Defeated once again in this arena, the opposition withdrew its motion for adjournment, for which we then substituted, with Mr. Robertson serving as our intermediary, a motion to adjourn six weeks after the close of the debates on the constitutional articles. Twenty-five representatives cast their votes to that effect.

It was now July 26, and twenty-one days had already been spent in all this preliminary labor.

CHAPTER 12

THE ROYAL COUP D'ÉTAT

Business of the convention.—Fierce conflicts.—Officials of the Sandwich Islands.—Speeches and votes.—A coup d'état.—Dissolution of the convention.—Public agitation.—Meeting of the cabinet.—Violence of the press.—Promulgation of the new constitution.

The convention finally settled down to work, with the result that between July 26 and August 3 thirty-one articles were discussed and voted upon. Quite vehement differences arose concerning several of these, but a steady though fluctuating majority made it possible for us to overcome the objections. At the session of August 3, Mr. Judd opened a debate examining the article on ministerial responsibility. I presented a complete analysis of the problem. At the same session we took up the abolition of the office of Kuhina Nui, whose origin and peculiar powers I mentioned earlier. Mr. Harris summarized the reasons why we considered it necessary to eliminate this useless piece of bureaucratic machinery, the equivalent of which exists nowhere else in the world except in Japan, with its dual system of Tycoon [Shogun] and Mikado. The majority agreed with our proposal to do away with the Kuhina Nui. The remaining items, up to article 43, were approved without opposition.

Article 43, however, marked a new phase in our proceedings. Up to this point the ministers sat ex officio in the House of Nobles; we proposed now to assign two of them in the future to the House of Representatives: the minister of finance and the minister of the interior. This modification of our practice raised fears among some of the more suggestible delegates. They believed that their independence as representatives of the people would be compromised by the presence in their midst of two members of the cabinet. The majority of the delegates did not, however, share this apprehension, but on the contrary understood the real motive at work: our desire to establish closer communication between the legislative and the executive branches, and to demonstrate a genuine policy of concession on the part of the latter.

We made such rapid progress that by August 6 we had succeeded in adopting sixty articles. Article 61 listed the conditions of eligibility for persons serving as representatives. We had expected to meet rather strong resistance to the adoption of this item, but our chief worries concerned article 62. This established property qualifications for the right to vote, though in a very moderate form. Nevertheless, the article sharply limited the franchise as it had existed for the past twelve years. Discussion of article 61 was spirited, but again we succeeded in making our view prevail, and it was decided that to be eligible to vote one had either to own property of a minimum value of $500 (2,500 francs) or give proof of a minimum net income of $150 (750 francs). It was difficult certainly to require any less.

Article 61 had carried by a majority of only two votes among the delegates, and it was clear to us that article 62 would encounter formidable opposition. Day by day our influence on the outcome of this particular dispute was wearing away. Although we continued to man the breach without respite or truce, Mr. Harris and I stood in bad need of reinforcements if we were to withstand the opposition's mounting attacks during the debates. We felt ourselves isolated; our colleagues were giving us almost no support; and to avoid the fatiguing exertion of the meetings, Mr. Hopkins, ostensibly for reasons of health, had recently retired to his country estate, and chose from that solitude to follow the turn of events. Each day a special courier reported to him the result of the session and he wrote to us to send congratulations; but his vote, his influence, and his word were missing. On the day preceding the discussion of article 62, we insisted that he return and join us. He did so, though in an ungracious manner.

Debate on article 62 began on August 8. We allowed the opposition to present their argument. I mentioned earlier the reasons why we had decided to require the adoption of certain qualifications for voters. Above all, it was necessary to strengthen our position against the sugar planters, for otherwise they would be able within a very few years to exercise complete control of elections, when their plantations would be manned by hordes of Chinese or other imported laborers. We therefore proposed that each voter be able to give proof that he was a Hawaiian or had been a naturalized citizen for two years; that he be able to write and count; and, finally, that he own property of a minimum value of $150 (750 francs) or have a minimum annual income of $60 (300 francs). One of the delegates substituted, in the form of an amendment, a provision to maintain, pure and simple, article 78 of the constitution of 1852. The adoption of this amendment would have amounted to the rejection of our proposal. The debates lasted five days, in the course of which one of the native delegates, Mr. Kauwahi, spoke in favor of article 62. I find among my stenographic notes a summary of his address, from which I quote several excerpts, in order to give my readers an idea of the manner in which the Kanakas handle abstract questions and comprehend them. Here is the opening of his speech:

> Sire, nobles, and delegates: The question to be examined is article 62 of the constitution, on the one hand as revised, and on the other as modified by the delegate from Puna.
>
> The new article submitted to us contains the same provisions as those in article 78 of the constitution of 1852, but with two important additions: first, the stipulation covering the property qualifications of voters; second, the requirement that the voter know how to read and write. The debate concerning these two points has lasted two days and still has not arrived at a decision. Speeches have been made for and against, with the result that two very distinct, very positive, opinions have emerged that still remain quite irreconcilable. This is no new development; such has been the situation since the opening of the convention. Those who today denounce article 62 in the most virulent terms are the same persons who at the start denied the constituent powers of this convention; they probably obeyed the same word from on high when they persistently opposed any change whatsoever in the constitution of 1852.
>
> They tell us that the adoption of article 62 will deprive the people of a sacred right. If I believed this, I would vote for the amendment of the delegate from Puna. But I hesitate to believe it, and my reason is that I do not hear any arguments that convince me. If there are any, let them be uttered! For my part, I have reached after long consideration a different conclusion. It is not true to say that article 62 has been drafted for the purpose of depriving the people of the exercise of a sacred right. The property qualifications for voting have been defined in such a way as to enfranchise all natives except those who are totally shiftless or who own no property worth mentioning. We are not required to legislate for the sake of such persons. On the contrary, we must fight laziness and vice, cut down at the very root the tree bearing such fruits.
>
> What was the king's desire when he submitted this article to us? Did he want to prevent his people from enjoying a sacred right? I do not myself think so. The king is a member of the same race as we are; he is the highest of our chiefs. In submitting this draft of a constitution for us to study, it is not as if he had said, "Here is a new constitution, now approve it because I approve it—your role is confined to saying yes." He has submitted to us the draft of a constitution so that we may discuss and amend it, inviting us to select this and reject that. Why then these feelings of hostility, as revealed in the speeches of certain delegates? Do these persons think they are the sole guardians of the rights of the people? Certainly the rights of the people are also the rights of the king, and of both reciprocally. They cannot be divorced.
>
> I beg the delegates to remember the words of our fellow member from Makawao district. Yesterday he said that his constituents knew very well how to override the cabinet ministers. But who are these ministers? Are they not those

same officials whose concurrence makes it possible for the king to direct the government? And are they not the servants of the people, of the people of Makawao, as well as of other districts? Are the voters of Makawao under the impression that they form a constituency quite independent of the rest of the Hawaiian Islands?

The adoption of this article, so we are informed, will exclude the poor from the franchise, and the delegate from Kanapali [Kaanapali] tells us that in his district there are a great many paupers. I know the district. Its inhabitants could very easily earn more than the minimum proposed by article 62. It is not true that they lack the opportunity to work. If they find no market for their labor at home, why don't they move to Lahaina? Laborers are now needed on plantations at Waihee, Wailuku, Makawao. Timber is plentiful on these same lands, and the sugar refineries of Lahaina are wanting firewood. The fields in all these areas are fertile and could feed numerous flocks of sheep. Wild cattle multiply in the mountains, and hides and tallow are being exported to markets overseas. I do not agree that the people of such districts are poor by necessity, nor that their poverty is the result entirely of their sloth. Manpower is in demand everywhere; our products find a ready outlet, for we are situated on a great ocean highway; the seas lie open to our fishermen, our forests await the axe of the woodcutter, and our plantations invite the plough. So why this hue and cry about Hawaiian poverty? Why bring it up and magnify it as a case against property qualifications? Let us, of course, commence by waging war against laziness and the misery it breeds, just as in the past we have done battle with ignorance of mind. Then, at last, we shall be able to extend to everyone what everyone will have earned and merited. It is imperative that the Hawaiians, our own folk as a nation, learn to appreciate and treasure their constitutional right to take part in the government of the country.

Mr. Kauwahi next took up the question of limiting the franchise to those able to read and write, pointing out that every native voter already fulfilled this condition:

The only persons who can complain of being affected by this clause are certain naturalized foreigners who have become Hawaiian citizens. But who is actually to blame for their condition? We are not responsible for the ignorance into which these newcomers have sunk.

After a detailed study of article 62, I conclude that it is to our advantage to adopt it. I will accordingly vote for the article and against the amendment of the delegate from Puna.

With the help of these extracts, the reader should be able to form a correct idea of the style of reasoning and argument used by native Hawaiians. Their logic is in general close-knit; they all speak with ease, many of them even eloquently. They acquire at an early age the habit of expressing themselves in public—at their *"meetings,"** which are exceedingly frequent in the islands, gatherings open to everyone and called for all sorts of purposes. The building of a church, the repair of a road, a bridge to be erected, a school to be established—everything is a subject for a meeting. The Hawaiians have a great gift for sharing their ideas of what concerns them—in short, for governing themselves—and by that I do not mean that they move abruptly from theory to action, but rather that they are not content to remain indefinitely within the realm of mere theory.

The result of a meeting is almost always a formal petition addressed to a competent authority. Furthermore, in all areas, and by the natural course of events, this sort of petition has chances in Hawaii of being favorably received. The familiar results ("not approved") of "putting in a claim," so common among us in France, where a swollen and powerful bureaucracy finds itself faced with all manner of individual requests and complaints, are not encountered in Hawaii. In Europe today the government is concerned, not merely with an array of isolated individuals, but with particular and distinct groups of persons, numbering sometimes in the hundreds or the thousands. Yet the official is in actuality, as Mr. Kauwahi said, the servant of these people and their interests and needs, not their master.

It is true to say that no law in Hawaii protects or guarantees the bureaucrat, the civil servant, against his own incapacity; neither can he lay claim to his post on the grounds of having acquired a "vested interest." In other words, the fact of having been a nonentity for a certain number of years is not a right that an official can invoke in order to continue being a nonentity for any specific period of tenure. Nothing is deducted and withheld from his salary, and the state is not required to provide him with a pension; insurance companies, however, are at his disposal if he wishes to be assured of an income during his old age.

It is fair to add that the civil servants in Hawaii are better rewarded than in France, but they usually submit to the same fate as the minister under whom they are employed. For this reason they do not, except in rare instances, remain long in one post. The reader will ask what a staff member can do when he finds himself without employment. Well, he does what is done in the United States—he finds himself some other employment. It is entirely his own responsibility. The state, in accepting the services of people, assumes no obligation to look after them later on, or to protect them against all eventualities. Fortunately, the fact that a man has served his government for a certain number of years does not mean, as so often happens in France, that the

---

*In English. [A. L. K.]

man is unfitted for some other post; on the contrary, his varied background is considered a circumstance in his favor, not an obstacle blocking him from entering a quite different career.

But these passing considerations lead me into digressions which, without being completely foreign to my topic, would be better treated in a special chapter. Accordingly I shall now resume my account of the convention and its labors.

Kauwahi's speech, and the succeeding arguments presented by the attorney general and by myself, had indeed served to shake up the convention majority, but not enough to produce a decision in our favor. Each night destroyed the progress we had been able to accomplish during the day, and each morning found us at a stalemate, with the very same point at issue. The principal leaders of the opposition felt themselves at this time on comparatively solid ground. They were fighting, they said, to uphold the rights of the people, and therefore of the provisions of the constitution conferred by Kamehameha III. Obviously, the ministers of the government intended to rob the poorer classes of their franchise, to drive them out of political life, and to establish an oligarchy of voters from which persons owning no property would be effectively excluded.

The king, wishing to put an end to these charges, spoke to the assembled delegates in his turn. His address was cogent and solidly constructed, pervaded everywhere by the speaker's strong intention, one felt, to achieve his purpose. He refuted the principal points of the opposition and did not hesitate, in a "disloyal" surprise assault, to describe the constitution of 1852 as a so-called charter designed by the leaders of the missionary party and imposed on the Hawaiians by Kamehameha III, who credulously had sanctioned it. Alluding to threats of revolution currently circulating against the present government, the king said he would not lower himself by examining these rumors—he attached no importance to them:

> The question has been distorted. Are the rights of the people threatened? No. The electoral franchise is first of all a privilege, next a duty, but in no sense whatever is it an absolute right. Under a constitutional form of government the people must be consulted, but who are the people? Is it the dregs of society, the ignorant and improvident, or is it the intelligent element who are appropriately to be consulted? Which are the groups who should exercise the right to supervise and lead? Speaking for myself, I would explain my final views on the matter: universal suffrage cannot coexist with a monarchic form of government. I have no more belief in the stability of a monarchy based on republican principles than I have in a republic based on monarchic assumptions. A choice must be made: monarchy or republic. In this matter the choice of a majority of

the nation has been achieved long since, and so well has it been made that the most fiery partisans of universal suffrage have not dared, not once, to match their actions with their principles.

At the close of his address he stated that if the majority of the delegates refused to adopt article 62, he would insist that the convention adjourn for twenty-four hours, in order that he and his cabinet might meet and confer on the next steps to be taken.

"What would these steps be?" asked members of the opposition. On this point I know the direction my own thoughts were taking, for in my frequent interviews with the king I had not failed to discuss the question as I saw it and to anticipate, in fact, the situation now facing us. I quite realized that he was resolved to take extreme measures and, if necessary, dismiss the convention, declare the constitution of 1852 abrogated, and hand down a new constitution of his own. I shared these same conceptions and purposes, insisting all the while on the need to maintain patience throughout: indeed, to explore every avenue of discussion, and by doing so throw discredit on our adversaries. Thus their refusal to cooperate would be revealed for what it was, sheer factiousness laboring to disguise itself as a burning devotion to the cause of the people.

The king accepted my views on our strategy, and for several days he attended the sessions without speaking a word. At last he broke his silence. I surmised that he no longer was hoping to see the convention brought round to our position, and that the occasion for action seemed to him now at hand.

I regretted this outcome, all the more sincerely because we appeared to be approaching a solution, just when all the other difficulties had been conquered, and because I had long hoped to be able to master this last one. But for the past two days I no longer harbored any illusions, no more than did the attorney general, who on his side had fought valiantly. Our two other associates, Mr. Wyllie and Mr. Hopkins, continued to keep their distance; they were watching for their own opportunities to wield influence and develop strategy.

A coup d'état had become inevitable. I was then convinced, as I am still, that a republican form of government is the ultimate outcome of universal suffrage. Furthermore, a republican form of government in the islands was, and will be for many years more, an unworkable form of government. Monarchic traditions are too powerful in Hawaii; republican institutions are too little adapted to the instinct and understanding of the natives. A Hawaiian republic is not possible except by annexation of the islands to the United States, and only then after a considerable influx of emigration from the American mainland; but such a political union had then no adversary more resolute than I. I was absolutely determined to oppose it by all feasible means; I did not believe annexation to be so close, however, as its supporters were claiming. Even today, in retirement from the party struggle and the administration of Hawaiian affairs, I suspect that, should annexation come about, it will perhaps do so only through a series of accidents. That time has not yet arrived. For that matter, annexation will not soon, in my opinion, be either a geographic or political necessity.

The king had proceeded too far to be able to withdraw from his position, and his driving energy and force of expression had intensified as the situation approached a climax. Neither Mr. Harris nor I advised Kamehameha V to yield. Mr. Wyllie and Mr. Hopkins, the latter especially, opposed extreme measures. In fact, Mr. Hopkins on many occasions had not been able to disguise his sympathy with the views of the opposition, whose members made very skillful use of the newspapers and, hypocritically, chose to magnify Mr. Hopkins' disagreements with them on minor points, but not on matters of major principle. As for Mr. Wyllie, disturbed from the start by the opposition's attacks, and always seeing himself as their prime target, he showed how deeply hurt he was to see his past services to the kingdom misunderstood and his popularity falling about him in ruins. He was afflicted by the disease that only a few months later would cause his death. Very much occupied with the management of his large estate, as well as dissatisfied with playing only a secondary role in the convention debates, he was not much seen and absented himself frequently from the sessions, all too willing to shift responsibility upon either me or Mr. Harris. This was a burden on me that each day grew heavier.

Our opponents doubled their efforts. On Tuesday, August 11, an amendment submitted by Mr. Bishop, member of the House of Nobles, in favor of universal suffrage, was put to a voice vote. Of the twenty-three delegates, sixteen voted no and seven yes. The action involved only the amendment and left the principal issue—universal franchise for males—still undecided. We spent the entire session of August 12 in arguing our case, but without profitable result. Dragging out the debates had no other effect save to provoke our assailants to more speechmaking, with ever increasing stridency. From the start we had hoped to win to our side the delegates who had voted against the proposed article, but who had done so without taking an active part in the discussion. The task was now becoming more difficult, however, for this group was diminishing in number. Indeed, each adversary one after another carried his argument to the speaker's rostrum, and these represented a vote won and registered against us.

The excitement outside the convention assembly was no less acute than within it. Everyone agreed that a crisis was at hand. Some were surprised by the king's forbearance and by our own patience, which they attributed to the fear aroused in us by the threats of our enemies. Convinced of our imminent downfall, others concluded that the monarchy was collapsing and that the anticipated annexation of the islands would follow. The exponents of this notion, their hopes bolstered by their apparent success and by their enthusiasm, were counting on strong support from outside Hawaii. This, they believed, would counterbalance the numerous persons in the country who opposed them, and therefore they became all the more bold in their partisan onslaughts.

On Saturday, August 13, the convention was called to order at eleven o'clock. The king had not yet arrived; his father, Kekuanaoa, presiding officer of the House of Nobles, accompanied by Mr. Robertson, acting in the same capacity in the House of Delegates, sat at their desks. The early discussion took up a new amendment proposed by a member of the House of Nobles. I was on the point of making some remarks when an usher forewarned me that the king was about to arrive, and that he was awaiting me in a small chamber reserved for his use. I left and joined the king. He asked me my interpretation of the turn the discussions had taken. I answered that I did not expect a happy outcome; that the proposed amendment would probably be approved by the delegates, but that the measure was still unacceptable and in no degree solved the problem of the franchise. The king next asked my opinion of a scheme Mr. Wyllie had embraced: to call for a six-week adjournment so as to allow time for emotions to cool, and to give us an opportunity to persuade the resisting delegates to adopt our views. I advised the king that I considered this plan impolitic and very risky; that in the present state of affairs for us to urge, or even accept under pressure, an adjournment would mean sending back to their districts a triumphant opposition. Encouraged by their success, they would set themselves up before the electorate as defenders of the peoples' rights and thus profit from the additional time by organizing popular resistance to the government. In short, they would achieve their goal by confusing public opinion. I added that in case His Majesty should adopt this plan of Mr. Wyllie's, it would be necessary for him to make changes in his cabinet and that, for my part, I would consider my presence there not only dangerous to His Majesty's interests, but also untenable for myself.

The king did not indicate whether he had mentioned Mr. Wyllie's proposal to Mr. Harris and Mr. Hopkins, nor whether he had taken their advice. Neither did I ask him. So far as Mr. Hopkins was concerned, I doubted it; as for Mr. Harris, I believed he had been consulted. I had reason to believe that Mr. Harris, if asked, would have given an opinion similar to my own; but at the moment I had neither a suitable opportunity nor the leisure time to confer in detail with Mr. Harris. Even later on, when I had occasion, I did not attempt to justify my views, since they no longer served any practical purpose.

The king listened to me throughout my remarks without interrupting me. Then he said that he had made up his mind to take action. He would address a final appeal to the convention and await the result of the vote.* I returned with the king into the hall. He slowly mounted the steps leading up to his presidential chair, and the discussion continued. The area for the public was crowded; the corridors were overflowing with spectators. One felt instinctively that a crisis was at hand. The excitement was not less intense outside the hall, while everyone was awaiting developments.

Just before the voting, the king took the rostrum. Once more he invited the delegates to take to heart the wishes of their constituents. Fourteen delegates voted against the proposed article, and seven in favor. The result of the vote was received in deep silence. The king then rose and in the Hawaiian language delivered to the delegates the following address, whose text I quote in translation:

> For five days this article has been the subject of your deliberations, and it is evident to me that the representatives of the Hawaiian common people reject it. In my estimation this article is the most crucial of them all. If it is not accepted my government ceases to be a monarchy and instead becomes a republic. I therefore declare to you that I now terminate the work of this convention.
>
> I thank the delegates for their ready willingness to answer my summons and consult together. The constitution of 1852 was granted by my ancestor Kamehameha III, who clearly stated that he granted it only for so long as it served the interests of the people, and reserved the right to take it away. That right now rests in me. So long as it pleases God to keep me on the throne, I am its sole defender. I accordingly declare the constitution of 1852 abrogated; I shall grant a new one to take its place.
>
> I invite my ministers to retain their portfolios; if, however, several officers or members of my government wish to give up their posts under the present circumstances, I am ready to accept their resignations.
>
> If my people at some later date, through their chosen representatives, express a wish to discuss with my nobles and with myself the terms of a new constitution, you will find me very ready to agree to so just a request.
>
> The tasks of this assembly are terminated, and the convention is hereby dissolved.

During the king's speech, I watched closely the expressions on the faces of the opposing delegates, and I saw there more astonishment than anger. They did not believe that their sovereign would take so extreme a step. They

---

*The vote, that is, on article 62—which would establish property qualifications for the right to vote and had the king's unqualified support. [A. L. K.]

had been expecting a simple announcement that the meetings were being adjourned, an arrangement that would permit them—while the government found itself at a standstill—to visit their respective districts and report to their constituents what had been accomplished concerning the constitutional question. None of them particularly disguised the fact that he had aligned himself more closely with the party opposing the king than his constituents would have approved. These adversaries knew full well that almost all the native population were on the side of the king, sympathizing with him and seeing in him, more than in his brother and his brother's predecessor, both Kamehameha IV and Kamehameha III, the true representative of their race, their ideas, their desires. The task of the opposing delegates was a painful one. They were not ready, whatever they might say, to confront the king with a show of force. Indeed, very few of them had had any training in that field—they had simply resorted to threats. To attempt to carry out armed rebellion would be to court certain defeat. But to hold back was an admission of impotence. They accordingly decided to wait on events and permit public opinion to define itself.

That people were much displeased with them the delegates could sense, from the moment they left the convention hall. Since the first words of the king's address, as these were repeated and passed along from person to person in the corridors, the report had spread through the town that the convention had been dissolved. Soon a considerable crowd had gathered around the verandas. Members of the opposition were welcomed with total silence, while numerous "hurrahs" saluted the king. After stepping into his carriage, Kamehameha V was driven to the palace, where at his own request I had invited my colleagues to join him immediately. Thus promptly reassembled, the cabinet took up for consideration measures suitable to the circumstances. In line with the proposal of Mr. Wyllie, minister of foreign affairs and minister of war, the Hawaiian militia was called to quarters, but this step was regarded simply as a precaution. Neither the king, nor Mr. Harris, nor I believed that any further action was required. We were convinced that the uprising was impossible, and that the opposition was incapable of employing military force.

Mr. Wyllie and Mr. Hopkins were not so confident. They would gladly have strengthened the precautionary measures, for they obviously only half approved the king's action in having so boldly seized the initiative by assuming responsibility for adjourning the convention. Fundamentally, however, this responsibility was more apparent than real. However one may interpret the principles embodied in the constitution of 1852, or in the constitution later proclaimed to replace it in 1864, the king in any case was not to blame: he was neither the cause of the course of events, nor could he be charged with ultimate official responsibility. It had to be one thing or the other. Either the ministers would continue to hold power, and by this fact alone would be completely to blame for the political situation; or else they would turn over their posts to their successors, who thereby would inherit this same responsibility. As for withdrawal, no one thought of it; and retreat was unthinkable. So far as I was concerned, I wholeheartedly endorsed the king's action. It was commonly understood that I was sincerely on his side, not only through deepest sympathy but also in point of hard political fact. The same was true of Mr. Harris. Our two other colleagues accepted this set of *faits accomplis* as to our mutual responsibility.

After the military provisions, the financial problems entailed by my ministerial duties required a prompt response. The appropriations voted by the last legislature had expired during the preceding April, and now the financial year had ended. Until new appropriations were available, no disbursements from the treasury could be legally made. Indeed, since April the treasury had paid no salaries. It was imperative to remedy this state of affairs. I accordingly submitted to the cabinet a resolution authorizing me to begin paying salaries again, on the scale voted by the last legislature, and to take care of current expenditures of the government, as the budget had anticipated. This procedure had the effect of returning into circulation idle funds that accumulated in the treasury, thereby ending the financial crisis, which had been worsening day by day. The minister of foreign affairs was requested to transmit to certified local officials and employees of the Hawaiian government, and likewise to agents and staffs in foreign countries, a circular explaining the recent developments in Hawaii. A royal proclamation had been drafted while the cabinet was in session, printed within a two-hour period, and then posted throughout the city. It urged the people to be cautious and refrain from involving themselves in troublemaking partisan demonstrations. The notice also announced the promulgation of the new constitution.

It was already nightfall when the cabinet meeting disbanded. I noticed on returning home a certain atmosphere of excitement in the town, but there was nothing about it to arouse alarm. During the evening I received numerous visits from friends who confirmed my impressions. Several members of the legislature also came to see me and I quickly perceived that, with two or three exceptions, none of them expected an attempt at civil rebellion, or that if such should occur it would have any chance of success. We had carefully avoided any display of military power, any similar behavior likely to stiffen resistance, any sign whatsoever implying that we considered an uprising likely. The proclamation of the king was consequently well received. Without hesitation, the native population rallied round their sovereign and loudly testified their satisfaction. The businessmen, along with commercial interests in general, recognized that the king's coup d'état provided a remedy for a political crisis which, if prolonged, would have paralyzed business and brought all financial transactions to a dead halt. Our success was no longer in doubt. The question was how to follow it up and consolidate our gains.

What was the opposition doing during this interlude? They were by no means slumbering, but they felt themselves isolated, without genuine taproots in the national life. Their followers did not wish to go to extremes, yet what could they do? They charted a middle course, hoping to safeguard the future while protesting against the present. The mouthpiece of the opposition party, the *Pacific Commercial Advertiser,* published the following article, which I here present in full to demonstrate how far liberty of the press was carried, thanks to the government's policy of toleration:

> The deed is done. The ministry have triumphed. The fears and exaggerated predictions of the friends of constitutional liberty have been more than realized, and the constitution of 1852—at once the gift and the monument of the beloved Kauikeaouli—lies a wreck, which no skill or cunning can mend. Hawaii no longer stands before the world as a constitutional monarchy, but as an oligarchy ruled by a ministerial cabinet of four.
>
> On Saturday last, as announced in our extra of that date, the convention was dissolved. It was proper that it should end as it began, by an exhibition of might over right, and by a blow at the vitals of the nation. . . . We have no heart to review in extenso this backward step, which no loyal patriot can think of without the blood boiling in his veins. But this we will say, that the foundation for trouble has been laid, and that it will surely come, as winter follows summer. According to the logic of the ministry themselves, no one estate can act for the whole, except by revolutionary power; therefore the new constitution—even though it be as pure and faultless as gospel truth—rests only on a basis of revolution. Apologize for it as you can, it has no other foundation. If then, the example which has now been initiated, shall in the course of time breed popular discontent—if five, ten, or twenty years hence, Princeville or any other plantation shall become the scene of popular outbreak, its buildings burned, its overseers and proprietor slain—at the feet of the present cabinet alone can rest the responsibility for civil war and revolution. May God grant that this day, if ever decreed to stain Hawaiian history, may be far distant.
>
> There is an overriding Providence in the affairs of states, as well as of men, and often times events are permitted to take place in order to bring about changes which in no other way could be readily wrought. The Southern rebellion is an instance of it, in which Providence has permitted civil war for a wise purpose, which will result in liberating four million slaves, though at a cost of money and life that could never have been assented to by peaceable overtures.

So too, in our present national crisis, infinite wisdom may, by apparently revolutionary means, permit the laying of the foundations for changes, now little dreamed of. We are taught by Holy Writ to believe that "the triumph of the wicked is brief."

The violence of their language revealed the impotence of the opposition party. Persons assured of the righteousness of their actions do not threaten in this style. The article made what amounted to a hateful appeal to the most brutal of impulses, the rebellious passion of the firebrand and his proneness to kill. Our rivals urged us to take extreme measures, but the cabinet decided to do nothing of the kind. No precedent exists in Hawaii for political repression. Indeed, freedom of the press is so completely accepted as a customary part of political life, a kind of national habit, that intemperate language scarcely excites. Restrictive laws are the prime cause of a dangerous public press; when the political writer runs no risk of official interference his wildest diatribes remain without effect, for then he is obliged to convince his readers by the cogency of his arguments. Indeed, the mass of people rarely heed the verbal proddings of a writer when they know pretty well that he is sitting safe and secure at his desk. By their petty harassments—or even by their injustices—officials do not necessarily confer true importance on journalists and other writers. It seems to me that in France it has been authority, the powerful voice of government, that has always been the chief promoter of the reputation and fame of its adversaries. A substantial number of the latter, if but left to themselves, would otherwise never have gained without such official recognition either notoriety or influence.

A novice at journalism came one day to see Horace Greeley, the editor of the *New York Tribune,* to submit to him a fire-eating article attacking some mutual enemies. After reading it, Greeley handed the article back to his visitor, but without saying a word. Our young man, who thought he had outdone himself, asked Greeley if he was dissatisfied. "Oh!" said Greeley, with an air of indifference, "I'll see that it's printed, but it won't change anybody's convictions—I'd rather have ten lines of careful and close-knit argument." "But," said the rather crestfallen author, *"it's so easy to write a slashing article."** "Exactly," replied Greeley, "I know it—and so does the public."

The article in the *Pacific Commercial Advertiser* was but the prelude to a whole series of such, even more heated and still more personal, in which each of the ministers was individually and very savagely attacked. It was all a

---

*Varigny supplies the English translation, following *"C'est si facile d'écrire un article furibond."* [A. L. K.]

good enough show, and we endured the volleys of grapeshot without much anxiety. We held daily meetings of the privy council, until finally, on August 19, all was in order and arrangements had been made for the proclamation of the new organic act. We had agreed to keep this ceremony as solemn and dignified as possible. On Saturday, August 20, the king, surrounded by his ministers assembled in the throne room, together with several members of his council of state and a number of leading citizens of the kingdom, read aloud the verbatim text of the new constitution and then swore to the oath of office. In turn, all the higher officials of the government likewise swore to the oath as administered by the king. That evening the text of the constitution was circulated among the people.

There was one moment when the king hesitated. He seemed undecided whether or not he would follow the text of the original revised constitution, in the form it had been submitted to the convention for its approval, without adopting certain other modifications in matters of detail, which in fact had been systematically debated and adopted by the convention. We insisted that he take into full account the actions of the convention itself. The king consented with little objection, inasmuch as the changes involved were of trifling significance, and also because it was wise as well as profitable politically thus to persuade the delegates themselves to accept some measure of legal responsibility. Article 62 and its several sections were alone preserved in the form in which they had appeared in the original royal draft.

CHAPTER 13

FIGURES AND FORECASTS

Elections.—Opening of the legislative session of 1864.— The king's speech.—My financial report.—Parliamentary tactics of the opposition.—The liquor law.—The budget. —The bill for public instruction.—Punahou School.— The immigration committee.

The new constitution was welcomed as favorably outside the Hawaiian Islands as at home. Newspapers in the United States, far from supporting the thesis of the *Pacific Commercial Advertiser,* readily granted that the king and his government had followed the right course, that the constitution of 1852 had had its day, and that the new organic act gave promise of stable and durable government. The native population was particularly aware of the importance of the king's coup d'état: it signified the liberation of the sovereign's power from the yoke of the missionaries, and it made possible a more complete separation between the executive authority and special religious elements in the community. No officials resigned their posts, and routine business although briefly interrupted by the political crisis got under way again with renewed vigor.

A royal proclamation announced September 29 as election day for members of the legislature, and the session itself was scheduled to begin on October 15. The polls were to be conducted according to the regulations of the new organic act. As provided therein, the House of Nobles and the House of Representatives were to meet in joint session; the cabinet members would continue to sit at the right of the nobles.

Between August 13, the date of the coup d'état, and September 29, the day appointed for elections, there was an interim of only six weeks. Some of our political friends believed we would have been wise to allow a longer time for emotions to cool, so as not to provide our opponents too soon with an opportunity to seek revenge for their defeat. On the contrary, my colleagues and I thought it preferable not to rest on our oars, but to take as much advantage of our success as possible. So far as I was concerned, I was in a hurry to move forward from the present makeshift methods of doing business and return to stricter, and legal, procedures. As minister of finance in charge of the Hawaiian treasury, I could not safely prolong a state of affairs that carried a heavy burden of personal responsibility and could, at any moment, jeopardize the public credit. The financial condition of the country was essentially excellent: I had been able to reduce the public debt substantially and assure the continuance of governmental services; and, moreover, I was greatly counting on systematic fiscal accounting and recording as a means of strengthening public confidence and winning us support.

The results of the election favored our cause. The opposition was able, but only barely, to elect a very few candidates running in backcountry rural districts. In Honolulu, Lahaina, and Hilo, the majority of voters came out for men who were sympathetic to the government. We needed this basic support, because the approaching session gave promise of being a tense and harried one. A number of laws needed to be amended and brought into line with the constitution. We were likewise planning to submit to the legislature certain important measures bound to become ready weapons when placed in the hands of our rivals. At the head of the list came the immigration bill. The development of our plantations was being crippled by a lack of field hands, and the only way to remedy the situation was to introduce foreign labor. Legislative action was needed to provide for the importation of an authorized number of Chinese laborers, and to appropriate sufficient funds to carry out such a project properly. The new law concerning public instruction was no less likely to arouse the anger and recrimination of the missionary party.

The king opened the session on October 15, 1864, in the same hall where the convention meetings had been held. His speech from the throne, quite firm in tone, contained not the slightest note of acrimony and wisely followed a policy of conciliation. After briefly summarizing the recent course of events, the king concluded this very tactful portion of his address as follows:

> I do not come here to declare that the new constitution is not susceptible to change, but instead to tell you that it has been designed with the greatest possible care, and has been the object of long and scrupulous study. I here reiterate the promise I made in your presence last August 13. Whenever my people, through the medium of their legally elected representatives, shall have expressed to me their wish to revise the organic act of the Hawaiian Kingdom with my help and by means of a constitutional convention, they can count on my aid and cooperation.

On the question of foreign affairs, the king said:

> Our relations with foreign nations have never been on a more satisfactory footing. I continue to receive from all directions the most positive assurances of

goodwill and friendship, and likewise the most cordial wishes for the future of my dynasty and the continued independence of the kingdom.

Kamehameha V next took up the problem of finance:

> I call your attention to the treasury report, as clear as it is encouraging, which my finance minister will present to you, along with the account of receipts and the budget for expenditures during the coming fiscal year. We find in the report matter for satisfaction, in so reassuring a state of affairs. As shown in the minister's report, you will note that our financial condition is prosperous and that we have no need to resort to borrowed funds and neither to increase the tax levies. Our exports are expanding and it will not be long before they meet the level of our imports.

The royal address next contained some remarks on the principal bills drafted by the cabinet to submit to the legislature for examination; the proposals ended with a strong endorsement of the new law concerning public instruction. We were expecting that the adoption of this law would involve serious difficulties. When the king stepped down from the rostrum, however, he was generally applauded by the audience; people acknowledged with cordial approval the forceful leadership he had demonstrated in adjourning the convention, and above all the generous moderation he had displayed in alluding to this event and its consequences.

After the king's departure, I placed on the desk of the legislature the report of expenditures for the past fiscal year, together with the budget forecast for 1864–1865. Some printed copies of this document were distributed to each member of the assembly.

I confess that I was not without certain doubts about the welcome this financial statement would receive. I had made an open break with one segment of established tradition: I was asking for several important changes in the fiscal regulations then in force. As I was very determined not to resort to borrowing loans, I was making every effort, should my ideas be accepted, to trim expenditures across the board and not increase taxes—provided, however, that the legislature would stay within the budgetary limits I was proposing.

For various reasons, of course, I expected fierce and bitter criticism. I had been long accustomed to the hostility directed against me as a Frenchman and as an opponent of the American party. It came to me as no surprise therefore that my ideas offended other men's ambitions, and that my enemies were only awaiting this occasion, after having been defeated on the battlefield of politics, to attack me on the grounds of my bookkeeping. Meanwhile, my deeper concerns were engaged elsewhere. Very certain of the accuracy of my figures and of the need for the reforms I was advocating, I had resolved to face the fire of my attackers and give them a very good fight. It seemed at the time impossible for me to fail to win over the majority to my ideas. In other words, I was convinced that my defeat, if I did not prevail, should be attributed to my faults as a man, and not to the ideas and principles at stake.

But the outcome proved quite otherwise than I had anticipated. Far from provoking the opposition, my report was received with such marked favor that my first impulse was to suspect a deliberate trap. There was none at all. The newspaper of our rivals, the *Pacific Commercial Advertiser,* which up to that point had never spared me its insults and sneers, subtly changed its line and ended its lead article thus:

> This report will receive a very favorable public welcome and enhance the reputation of the finance minister. If he continues to give such proof of his ability and fairness; and if he shows sufficient courage to carry out the program he presents, he will eloquently refuse the objections of those critics who, like ourselves, have regretted seeing him called on to perform the most important functions of government. If among our public employees we possess some men who are inspired with intentions so good, and who acquit themselves so well in carrying them out as the finance minister has done, the public will have no grounds for complaint against the government.

From then on, beginning with the opening sessions of the legislature, I noticed the same change in argumentative tone and style. I was able quickly to assure myself that the measures I was advocating would win an impressive majority to my side. Indeed, I was no longer the victim of the opposition's ill will. They were now attacking my colleague, Mr. Harris, and the most stubborn of those against him were none other than the persons best known for their American connections. They could not pardon the attorney general for the important role he had played at the time of the abrogation of the constitution of 1852. His share in the affair was apparently unforgivable, and their enmity increased in proportion to the amount of floating capital, in the form of high hopes, they had once invested in him.

The opposition newspapers began their campaign in complete unanimity, though seemingly ignoring my part in the picture. Their situation was a puzzling one, all the more so because the attorney general in his capacity as minister without portfolio could not be attacked except on matters of broad policy: in other words, he did not lay himself open to criticism targeted on specific questions and details. But with respect to general policy, and notably in the matter of the constitutional convention, it was impossible to attack him without attacking myself, so closely intertwined had been our two official roles. After several insignificant skirmishes, the opposition abandoned its strategy, and without burying any grudges ceased for the time being its political maneuvers, hoping nevertheless that some parliamentary incident would afford them opportunity to deal with the attorney general separately and turn him out of office.

The response of the legislature to the king's opening message provided the cabinet with a solid basis for operation. Approved by a substantial majority of both houses, the speech examined and emphasized the various points which the king felt required no apology. On the question of the new constitution, the representatives heartily congratulated the king for his forthright behavior, declaring that they were in complete harmony with his views. The opposition group was neither able to avert this statement of support nor soften its firm expression.

The legislature set to work. The drafted bills submitted by the government were all favorably received and handed on to the various committees, which successively presented reports recommending adoption. A loyal legislative majority approved these endorsements and cooperated with us, but the assistance was not as disinterested as one might expect. Among those persons who joined us there were some who were hoping, if not to enlist us on their side, at least to keep us neutral concerning the issue recently placed at the top of the agenda: the regulations governing the sale of alcoholic beverages.

For a number of years, a strict and rigorously enforced law had forbidden the sale of liquor to the natives. Initiated by the missionaries, the measure had originally applied alike to natives and to foreigners living in the kingdom. However, commercial treaties negotiated successively with France, England, and the United States had nullified the law so far as it concerned their nationals. The distinction was an offensive one, as viewed by the natives, who were unable to buy beverages containing alcohol without exposing themselves, purchaser and seller alike, to a fairly heavy fine. For some while the importers, like the natives, grumbled about the burdensome restrictions on their trade, depriving them of substantial sales and profits. They had easily persuaded the humbler element in the native community to share their point of view. A series of public meetings was held, at which vehement speeches played upon popular attitudes, and numerous petitions were addressed to legislators demanding repeal of the liquor law.

There is no way in the Sandwich Islands to suppress activities regarded as lawful agitation in a cause. Anyone at all can organize a meeting for the purpose of calling public attention to conditions that, in his opinion, militate in favor of maintaining or abolishing any statute whatsoever. The government cannot step in unless the meeting interferes with the orderly use of public thoroughfares, or unless such a meeting would entail a clear infraction of the law; but there is no means of preventing those who are subject to the questionable statute from discussing it, criticizing it, and urging its repeal. If the arguments are sound, something is gained; if they are false, they have no effect. In the last resort the legislature decides, and before that body the government explains and defends its position.

As for the particular case of the liquor law, the ministers reached no unanimous agreement. Two of my fellow officials and I were in favor of maintaining the present law; Mr. Wyllie was opposed. This divergence of views was known to the public, and discussion was accordingly brisk and heated. We succeeded in carrying the vote by a total of twenty-six in favor and eleven against. I personally had no doubt that repeal of the law would have further hastened the decay of the native race. The use of spirituous liquors is a deadly practice for inhabitants of tropical countries. I did not disguise the fact that the natives would find the law's restrictions damaging to their equal status as citizens; but I nevertheless tried to convince them that there was nothing humiliating in a prohibition voted by themselves and in no sense forcibly imposed upon them. When all was said and done, they could only admit the physiological truth, so miserably demonstrated by far too many individual examples, and forbid the indulgence of so dangerous an appetite. Equality does not consist in propagating the vices and excesses of the foreigners. Equality in this context only means equality in the face of ruin and death.

The vote was decisive. The measure was passed after we had finished examining the budget I had prepared with the help of my cabinet colleagues. The receipts, very conservatively estimated, came to 2,700,000 francs. Expenditures totaled 2,500,000, leaving a surplus in the treasury of 200,000 francs. Actually this figure came in the end to much more, and I was able to conclude my financial balance sheet with a surplus of 500,000 francs and a great reduction in the national debt, a decrease achieved by systematically redeeming public bonds. The budget was passed without alteration, and on January 8, 1865, the legislature notified the king that it had completed its work.

The prorogation of the legislature took place on January 10 at an impressive ceremony. The king in his address eloquently expressed his pleasure in the spirit of cooperation demonstrated by both the government and the representatives of the people, and he stated that he would approve all the measures that had been passed. The session disbanded in an aura of general goodwill.

The cabinet went their way greatly encouraged by this first test, from which the opposition had anticipated quite different results. Not one of the objections were heard that they had been hoping would be raised against the new constitution; on the contrary, a unanimous vote of approval hailed the altered state of arrangements. Our adversaries withdrew to their tents, awaiting some unforeseen incident, or some error on the part of the cabinet that would permit them to renew their hostilities.

One of the measures approved during the recent session increased the teaching staff of the Normal School at Lahaina. Certain important educational reforms recommended by the government were also introduced and authorized. I have mentioned elsewhere the principles followed in organizing public instruction in the kingdom, and I have also noted that our schoolteachers are largely recruited from among the pupils of the government-founded Normal School. They are admitted to that institution on a competitive basis, and are provided lodging and board there at the government's expense. At graduation they take a final examination and then begin their teaching duties. Those among them marked out for other careers, such as naval posts, public works, shop management, and the like, are required free of charge to take additional courses at Lahaina, and on completion these graduates receive special diplomas.

The government has also undertaken to establish on each of the islands a public high school, admission to which at a nominal fee is open to young people who are capable and wish to continue their instruction beyond the elementary level.

In addition to these public institutions, a number of other schools have been established by individual initiative and as private ventures. The most remarkable among these schools is at Punahou, on Oahu, for which the cabinet requested and obtained a public subsidy.

Built by the Protestant mission on an extensive tract of land granted by Kamehameha III, and situated a league and a half from the center of Honolulu, this school was originally intended for the education of the children of missionaries. Since that time the limited staff and facilities have been extensively enlarged, and the Punahou academy is now attended by children of all sorts of foreigners living in Honolulu. It admits, without discrimination between the sexes, both boarding and nonresident pupils in almost equal number.

One large building, devoid of architectural pretension, facing toward the ocean but about a kilometer from the beach, occupies the central portion of the school's property; this contains quarters for the principal and the headmistress and teachers in residence, along with classrooms and dining hall. Two adjoining wings at right angles are assigned as rooms for the pupils. The one on the right is allotted to the girls, that on the left to the boys. A handsome lawn planted with trees and shrubs, without any intervening wall, separates the quarters of the one from the other. Each pupil has a separate room, certainly small, but modestly homelike and comfortable. Classes are attended in common, and in the same room. This arrangement also holds true for meals, and likewise for recreation periods, which follow a uniform schedule. When I add that the age of these young people living thus as one community ranges all the way from twelve to twenty, I am sure the reader will wonder what type of results such an educational program can produce.

The results are better than one would expect, when judged by French views concerning such matters. This communal life, incompatible with our own customs and the type of education we in France provide for our girls, does not entail serious dangers, such as one so easily imagines and such as I at first assumed. As a member of the board of education, I was obliged to give a good deal of thought to Punahou School. I thoroughly investigated the question of the mingling of the sexes in the government-supported schools, and I came to conclusions quite contrary to those toward which I had been originally inclined because of my preconceived notions. I have never once heard of a single case of seduction or licentious sexual behavior among the students of Punahou. It should also be pointed out that all the young people have been brought up as Protestants, and from an early age have been accustomed to exercising their individual moral responsibility. While on the one hand the boys are imbued with a deep respect for womanhood, the girls are likewise in the habit of deserving, and insisting on the necessity of, gentlemanly respect. Among their own families the girls are not treated like beings apart, conspicuously frail creatures who require incessant chaperonage, but indeed like human beings endowed with rational minds, who later on will be called upon to become the companion and equal of a man, and to exercise freely their own right to choose a husband by themselves. If they do not possess that charming ignorance of evil we attribute, perhaps gratuitously, to our French maidens, at least their Punahou sisters are distinguished by their moral fiber and strength. Their feminine instinct, and the natural purity of their sex, are sufficient to preserve them from danger.

It is equally important to take account of the fact that the girls are in the habit of freely associating with boys from infancy, sharing their studies with them and taking part in their games. Thus familiarized with the opposite sex, mutual contact loses the attraction of novelty and ceases to be forbidden fruit. I am not at all claiming that the result of such education is to lead them, on both sides, to view one another merely as fellow comrades. By no means. Imagination does not abdicate its power in them any more than does the heart. While at Punahou, inclinations develop among the pupils and attractions gradually take shape, but they are honorable ones and the relationships are serious. Nothing prevents the young people from marriage in the due course of time. They realize this. No matter how well off the parents may be, they do not provide dowries for their daughters. It is the husband's responsibility to make a living for his wife; it is the wife's to be her husband's helpmate. Both belong to the same social class; or rather, to put it more accurately, there are no rigid classes. There are numerous instances of young couples who have been brought up and educated together, and then who marry one another several years after they have left school. After having become fully acquainted they decide upon marriage; and if their love stories may lack a certain poetic charm, the loss is amply made up for by the mutual trust and clear certainties that such a decision provides.

All of which means that the American style of education prevails in the Sandwich Islands. They do not merely teach their girls such subjects as history, geography, music, singing, drawing, and sewing. Above all, they seek to make them practical women, capable of setting up and managing a household. One example among various others reveals a good deal on this subject. Every fortnight the principal of the academy appoints a certain number of girls, as their turn comes, to manage the household under the supervision of the headmistress. The girls are systematically charged with the responsibility of carrying on the varied activities involved in domestic organization and direction. They plan the meals, supervise the cooking, themselves prepare a variety of side dishes, as well as the puddings, sweetmeats, and cakes. They take over the marketing, set the tables, see that the linen is in proper order, exercise authority over the domestic help, and in general are in complete charge of the well-being of the establishment. Each pupil makes his or her own bed, tidies and cleans the room, keeps it in proper condition. Once each month the principal and headmistress receive evening visitors, relatives or friends, who come over from town. Once a year a general examination is conducted, which the public is invited to attend. The exercises, lasting three consecutive days from ten o'clock in the morning to six in the evening, draw a large crowd. The presiding officer at these meetings is one of the three members of the board of public instruction. During the entire period of the examination the academy keeps open house; relatives and friends are invited to share the meals. The girl pupils serve the guests—in short, do the honors of the house—and vie with each other in baking the cakes they present to their friends. They are as earnest about the culinary contest as they are about their academic competitions.

Gardening, especially flower growing, is the chief form of outdoor recreation. Students' rooms, though rather small, are everywhere made cheerful and fragrant with bouquets arranged with considerable art. Horseback riding and swimming are a regular part of the curriculum. There is no shortage of outdoor space. Situated in an area sheltered from strong winds, and today irrigated by the water of a mountain stream (a work project carried out by the boys), the Punahou grounds present a most attractive sight. The agricultural activities expand every year. The Honolulu membership of the Hawaiian Agricultural Society has provided the academy with various grains, plants, and shrubs, which are flourishing healthily. Fruit trees abound and vegetables, together with other kitchen or culinary items, are also grown. Excursions into the mountains, conducted by the professor of natural history, combine exercise with study. In short, Punahou School represents a type of educational institution at which the Americans excel, and one I should like very much to see imitated in France.

The reader will excuse me, I hope, for lingering so long on this subject, which I have far from exhausted. Nevertheless, the importance given in the Sandwich Islands to everything pertaining to education requires that I go into some minute detail concerning an issue that has finally begun to arouse deep interest in France. Indeed, on our successful handling of this issue clearly depends the solution of so many other urgent problems facing the French people.

In Hawaii, I should add, the stimulus for school development came from the king, whose concern with all aspects of public instruction was so sincere that he felt obliged to share in our labors. In fact, despite the length and frequency of board of education meetings, he attended them regularly.

In accord with the legislation setting up a committee on immigration, we invited the sugar planters to form an association and prepare for us a statement of their needs and recommendations. Our request was acted upon, and after consulting with the association, we decided to send a special commissioner to Japan, China, Manila, and India, partly for the purpose of studying new methods of growing sugarcane, but also to look into the possibilities of introducing into the islands a limited number of unindentured plantation laborers.

Dr. William Hillebrand, a very versatile member of the community, highly respected throughout Hawaii, was chosen for this formidably difficult mission, and he carried it out quite successfully. The result was the arrival in the islands of several thousand Chinese, who immediately found remunerative employment and thereby contributed enormously to the increase of sugar production. New plantations were being established in all directions. Subsidies granted by the legislature made it possible for us to open new rural roads, an achievement bound to augment the agricultural and commercial value of hitherto undeveloped lands.

The increase in the sugarcane crop necessitated more elaborate and varied means of transportation. Honolulu, as a seaport catering to the needs of arriving and departing steamships, developed inevitably into a mercantile center with warehouses, thus becoming closely linked with the neighboring islands by means of local shipping lines. The government was obligated, however, to construct additional wharves, extend the customs buildings, and in short provide all possible facilities for the use of the new commercial enterprises multiplying every day. All these projects were encouraged and rapidly pushed ahead. Capacious docks, solidly built, replaced the old worm-eaten wooden landing arrangements, and in a very brief span of time Honolulu was able to offer coastal, interisland, and seagoing vessels, along with foreign battleships, safe and certain anchorage in one of the finest ports of the entire Pacific Ocean.

CHAPTER 14

APPOINTMENT AS MINISTER OF FOREIGN AFFAIRS

Changes in the ministry.—Visit of Queen Emma to Europe.—Death of Mr. Wyllie.—My appointment as minister of foreign affairs.—Elections.—Commercial prosperity.—Legislative session of 1866.—Death of Princess Victoria.—A tactful suggestion.—The ministerial program.—Close of the session.

The accomplishment of these varied projects required, in addition to constant hard work on the part of the cabinet, above all else a complete agreement in point of view; but, unfortunately, this did not exist. Our colleague, Mr. Charles G. Hopkins, was unhappy about the increased work load assigned to him, and likewise about the dim role in our business to which his chronic indolence had reduced him. For many years he had been accustomed to an easy and self-indulgent style of life, and especially to letting his subordinates assume the administrative burdens of his department. He did not at all conceal his displeasure with the new ideas prevailing in the cabinet. He kept much to himself, dispensed his more cooperative contributions in a competitive spirit, and sharply criticized our final decisions. This state of affairs could not last long. He himself realized as much, and when the opportunity occurred to remove himself from a difficult situation he took advantage of it.

For many months Queen Emma had suffered from nervous depression, so severe that her physical health was endangered. Finally, acting on the advice of her physicians to leave Hawaii and travel abroad, she decided to carry out a plan originally conceived by Kamehameha IV, but which he had been unable to realize. For several years the queen had fondly played with the idea of a European sojourn. Her husband, the late king, had already seen London and Paris, but the queen had never visited these cities. Now she was planning an extended tour through parts of the United States, England, France, Germany, and Italy. A personal invitation from Queen Victoria to visit her in England overcame Emma's initial hesitation. However, she would not undertake this journey alone, accompanied merely by her ladies-in-waiting. Mr. Hopkins, an old and intimate friend of the former king, offered to accompany her, and his suggestion was accepted. Mr. F. W. Hutchison, an Englishman highly respected in Hawaii, was appointed in Mr. Hopkins' place to serve as acting minister of the interior. Actually the appointment was a permanent one, but it was deemed important at the time not to diminish the prestige of Mr. Hopkins in his newly assigned post as member of the entourage of Queen Emma. In May 1865, Mr. Hopkins left Hawaii on the long journey over land and sea, which was to last a full eighteen months.

Mr. Hutchison, our new cabinet member representing the interior department, was a most intelligent and energetic man, completely dedicated to the cause of Hawaiian independence, and strongly opposed to the American party, which was quite disgusted by his appointment and regarded it as a fresh sign of our political intransigence. In that quarter of the community we had nothing to gain, however, nothing to look forward to, while on the other hand it was imperative for us to define our political program clearly and give no evidence of uncertainty.

It was thus when we had just reorganized the government, when the cabinet had barely begun its work, and when we were hoping to proceed without any new complications, that Mr. R. C. Wyllie became dangerously ill. His age, combined with a constitution ailing and worn out from his long career in Hawaiian politics, left us with little to hope for, and finally on October 19 he died. By his death we were faced with a crisis. He had been minister of foreign affairs for the past twenty years, and as such had been associated with all the most important events of that period. Indeed, the establishment in Hawaii of constitutional and parliamentary government was made possible largely through his persistent effort and sage advice. The king lost in him a faithful councillor, and I a sincere friend.

The vacant place in the cabinet caused by Wyllie's death was difficult to fill. His unmatched experience and the weight of his seniority made him the leader of the cabinet, and the Hawaiian constitution gave sanction to this privilege by designating the foreign minister simultaneously as prime minister of the kingdom. At the beginning of his illness, he had requested permission of the king to let him name me as minister pro tem. Aware that he was on the point of death, Mr. Wyllie had a long conversation with Kamehameha V, who came away deeply shaken.

As eloquent testimony of his sorrow and regret, the king arranged a funeral of state for Mr. Wyllie, which he personally attended. As further sign of his special favor, the king ordered Mr. Wyllie's body to be deposited at the Royal Mausoleum, near the two sovereigns—Kamehameha III and Kamehameha IV—whom he had served as minister and councillor.

For two months the king made no announcement concerning Mr. Wyllie's successor. It was commonly thought that Kamehamea V could not make up his mind. To those of us who were closest to him, however, it was clear that he had reached a decision but would reveal it only when the right day and hour, as he saw it, had arrived. Otherwise, we were completely ignorant as to the identity of the person he would name to fill the vacant post. According to the constitution, the choice depended on the king alone. Though a member of the cabinet was free to accept or reject the individual thus selected, in the case of rejection normal procedure required the dissatisfied minister himself to resign. This was the extent of our cabinet powers; only the legislature (not at that time in session) had authority to overturn by its vote the sovereign's decision.

On December 20, 1865, a message from the king summoned me to the palace. He explained his plans to me, asking me to exchange my post as finance minister for that of minister of foreign affairs. In conferring upon me the highest responsibilities and making me the leading member of the cabinet, Kamehameha V quite understood that he was asking of me a costly sacrifice. With great effort I had reorganized the department of finance. The present healthy condition of the treasury was, in part certainly, my achievement; I had overcome the prejudices of those who had doubted my capability. Aided by men I had selected, who had adopted my ideas and put them into execution, I was able, in large measure, to entrust to them administrative details and devote myself to the numerous special committees of which I was a member.

I raised these objections in my talk with the king. Above all, I understood the fact that my appointment to these new duties would arouse all the angry emotions and bigoted zeal of the American party, who accepted me in my present position, but who would consider my appointment as minister of foreign affairs as a hostile gesture directed at the United States government. The protracted illness and death of Mr. Wyllie left his department in disarray; everything needed to be reorganized. It would be necessary to start with some hard decisions which would exacerbate public opinion further still. The American party was hoping that the king's final choice of a foreign minister would be someone less outspoken, less implacable toward the annexationists.

I was not greatly worried about the struggle so far as my own personal interests were involved, but I questioned whether it was wise to provoke the opposition at this particular moment when, beaten and now voiceless, it appeared ready to lay down its arms. What concerned me now was my health, which was beginning to suffer from overwork. I had hoped, with the king's kind permission, to take a leave of absence in the very near future, to see again my native land, my family and my friends, and to enjoy a little dearly purchased rest. Now the king's new proof of his trust in me, his wish to assign to me even further duties, required that I lay aside and defer my deepest hopes.

Kamehameha V listened with his customary courtesy to these personal objections. He nevertheless insisted that he trusted his own good judgment and was counting on my services in the new, and more important, post to which he was summoning me. Whatever choice he made, he added, he could not expect to please everybody. The opposition, reduced to an insignificant minority, had not up to the present succeeded in shaking the cabinet, which in the last legislature had maintained an impressive majority. It would be several months before the next session opened, and the actions he would take between now and then would justify his selection of me as his choice. He intended to appoint Mr. Harris, formerly in the cabinet in the role of attorney general, to the post of minister of finance, permitting the cabinet to determine who should be the next attorney general. If I accepted his offer, as he hoped I would do, the king assured me that, out of consideration for my health, my faithful services, the friendship he felt for me, and always my personal and private desires, he would leave it to me to decide the time of my leave of absence. He was convinced, he said, that I would keep in mind in this respect the interests of the government. He wanted also to give me one very special indication of his confidence in me. He would authorize me to conduct the revision of our European treaties, and for this purpose would name me his ambassador extraordinary, thus transforming my leave into a very special diplomatic mission performed for the sake of the Hawaiian government.

I was deeply touched by the king's kind opinion, as he described his plans to me. Assured of his complete trust, and also of his personal friendship as displayed in so many ways, I accepted his offer, and the following day an official notice announced the changes in the cabinet.

The response of the opposition newspapers varied tremendously from what I was expecting. My appointment was received without surprise and with no intemperate reaction. On the other hand, Mr. Harris's appointment aroused the fiercest recriminations. His ability as attorney general was admitted, but his selection as finance minister was deplored. He was severely criticized for his private financial ventures, for the administrative chaos which reigned, so it was rumored, in the justice department, and above all for his handling of accounts in probate cases, for which he was legally responsible. None of these attacks was wholly true, but party politics is never scrupulously fair. Furthermore, as we were all used to bitter and highly personal criticism, such as absolute liberty of the press allows, we paid only moderate attention to the journalistic pandemonium, which soon ceased of its own accord.

The new task I was now assuming was, as I had anticipated, fraught with complexities. The records of the foreign office were in a state of utter disarray, and it took me not less than two full months to introduce within the department any semblance of system and order. One of my first steps was to staff the office with qualified and trustworthy persons. The king had given me carte blanche in this respect; I began by dismissing the chief secretary of the department, an Englishman by origin, who had held the post for the past decade. To replace him I selected a French compatriot, who had arrived in the islands only a year before, and though not well known, possessed just the qualities of discretion and loyalty I was seeking. This change was very badly received; I was accused of partiality, of wishing to staff the administration with French newcomers at the expense of Englishmen, Americans, and other nationalities who had resided in the country for many years and who were identified with its interests and requirements. I ignored the babble. In this post above all, I needed a man I could count on. I chose him where I found him. He had at present no reason to come into contact with the public, and would have no such contact in the future. In my opinion, the public had no reason to raise objections in the matter.

The attitude of the various foreign commissioners accredited to the Hawaiian government satisfied me completely. Of course, I could not expect great enthusiasm on the part of the minister in residence from the United States. His diplomatic colleagues, however, more or less devoted supporters of Hawaiian national independence, cordially assured me of their cooperation and expressed their delight in seeing me continue, in an even more vigorous and resourceful way, the traditional policies laid down by Mr. R. C. Wyllie.

Though the legislative chambers were not meeting until April, election time by now was well on its way. In conformity with the law, balloting in the race for the House of Representatives would take place on the first Monday in January, only fifteen days after the reorganization of the cabinet. The legislative majority I was counting on surpassed my anticipations. In Honolulu, a stronghold of the opposition party like all the larger towns, the four nominated representatives were not merely supporters of the cabinet, but also personal friends whose backing we were guaranteed. In the other districts, even the most remote, the defeat of the opposition party was across the board. It was just barely able to carry into office a few of its most moderate and flexible candidates.

This victory of ours was in large degree the result of the circulation, as widespread as possible, of the commercial statistics for the year 1865. The steps we had taken to develop the agricultural resources of the kingdom had produced wonderful rewards. The volume of sugar production, in particular, had increased astonishingly. Sugar exports, which in 1860 had failed to reach 600,000 pounds, exceeded 15 million in 1865. Growth in general, though less for other products, was registered everywhere throughout the economy. It was impossible, even among our most prejudiced and hostile critics, to deny this evidence. The stimulus to trade was visible on all sides. Laborers were in scant supply in all occupations, and no willing worker went without a job. Assured of finding a market for their products, the natives were working their acres and reaping a prosperity unknown among them up to that time. Everywhere comfortable dwellings, clean and healthful, were replacing their traditional huts constructed of bamboo and leaves. Their cattle fetched a better market price, and their lands rose in value. Now they had twenty different means of winning a livelihood, whereas earlier they could find no employment without leaving their homeland and risking their health aboard the foreign whalers.

Thus the legislative session of 1866 opened under the most promising circumstances. The king's address was confined to listing and making a matter of record the remarkable progress achieved, his own personal satisfaction therein, the hopes he shared with the legislature, and likewise the spirit of cooperation and unanimity he found prevailing among the several ministers.

Unfortunately, a sad event in the history of the royal family marked this session of the legislature, which opened on April 25 and continued until July 28. On May 29, after a short illness, the king's sister, Princess Victoria, died at the age of twenty-seven. Heir presumptive of the throne, in the event the king should die without direct successors, she was unmarried, and her death cast a somber shadow over the prospects of the Kamehameha dynasty, unless the present king should alter the situation by his marriage—a course I very much desired. Kamehameha V was not yet thirty-five years old. Earlier in our informal interviews I had often touched on this delicate question; I had pointed out to him the importance of marriage from a dynastic point of view. He did not positively reject the idea, but simply dismissed it with a laugh, urging me to find him a wife who combined the attributes necessary for his happiness, asserting his preference meanwhile for a bachelor's style of life.

The death of the king's sister imposed on me the duty to return to the question. I urged Kamehameha V to grant his subjects the pledge that they lacked, and that he could not withhold from them much longer. I thus seized the first occasion that had arisen to plead my case, hoping to persuade the king to make up his mind in the way I was convinced was indispensable if Hawaiian independence were to be preserved. I cited especially the significance the annexation party would attach to this latest sorrow afflicting his dynasty, likewise the poorly disguised satisfaction it stimulated in them. And, above all, I finally emphasized the urgent need to come to a decision. That he was still young was true, but his sister after all had been younger than he; and his brother, his royal predecessor, had also been his junior. I made the most of all the arguments I could think of in favor of the advice I permitted myself to offer—in fact, I took the liberty to insist.

The king promised to weigh my reasons very carefully. Without disclosing to me his most private thoughts, he told me enough for me nevertheless to guess the causes that thus far had prevented him from marrying. It was understood between us that we would return to this question on a later occasion, and I left his presence encouraged by our interview.

The session was not to end without the opposition party, although weak numerically speaking, calling upon me to explain to the legislature the policy I intended to follow in watching over foreign affairs. Naturally, I wanted to clarify the whole subject myself, and so I took the opportunity to pose an indirect question. I had completely approved of the course followed by my predecessor, Mr. Wyllie, and far from shifting from that course, I merely proposed to emphasize its character and direction more plainly. While entirely respectful of the text and letter of the concluded treaties, I did not evade the fact that several of them had been negotiated under conditions unfavorable to the Hawaiian government, during a period when the immediate security of Hawaiian independence appeared very doubtful. I believed therefore that these treaties should be modified, and for this reason I proposed to nullify the agreements each in turn, when their stipulated terms had expired. I further recommended a plan for renegotiating each of them, according to a single clear and precise formula, guaranteeing absolutely equal treatment for all foreign nations. I wanted, in other words, to eliminate various so-called special concessions. The type of concession I had in mind was a provision, originally applied to a single nation, but which had been permitted to extend in other treaties to other countries, in the guise of a special clause awarding preferential treatment to "the most favored nation."

Thus our treaty with France, signed in 1857, and intended to continue for ten years, was ending in 1867. I planned to profit from the occasion by nullifying it and introducing changes suggested by experience. As for relations with the United States, we were hoping later on to enter upon negotiations leading to a commercial treaty that would assure, if possible, the free admission of our sugar to California and Oregon markets. At the very least, we intended to insist upon a tariff law that could not be changed from one day to the next, according to the fluctuating decisions of the United States Congress. We faced a serious economic problem in that respect, for a rise in tariffs could easily, at almost any moment, transform the conditions determining our commercial existence, and thereby furnish a powerful weapon to the partisans of annexation.

These statements of mine were favorably received. Several days later, at a meeting on June 7, they were ratified by the legislature in a unanimous vote of confidence. On one point, however, the cabinet suffered a partial defeat. The new minister of finance presented to the legislature the draft of a law authorizing, under certain anticipated conditions, the issuance of bearers' certificates, serving as legal tender, and guaranteed by cash holdings in the Hawaiian treasury in the form of gold or silver. It was an ill-chosen moment to introduce such a measure. It was just at a time when the United States was in the midst of a protracted economic depression, a natural consequence of issuing too much paper currency, and the hot debate during the crisis had frightened off mercantile and capital investors in general. The Hawaiian paper money bill lost by a sizable majority. The government, however, convinced that the proposed currency bill had persuasive advantages, announced that it would permit its parliamentary defeat to become an occasion for reconstituting the cabinet. This simple declaration provided our political friends a certain liberty of action, and they decided to refer the question to the people and leave it to public opinion to determine ultimately.

The proposed budget was approved without debate. The legislature placed at our disposal the necessary funds for public works projects, likewise for speeding up the importation of foreign laborers, and finally for increasing significantly the funds to be appropriated for public instruction. On July 27 and 28 the legislature concluded its work and was formally dismissed by the king. His closing address, enthusiastically applauded, once more called attention to the good relations existing between the legislature and the executive power and the throne.

CHAPTER 15

MINISTERIAL FOREBODINGS

Return of Queen Emma.—Social life in the Sandwich Islands.—Opening of negotiations with the United States. —General Montague McCook.—Proposal of reciprocity treaty.—Hesitations.—An American battleship.—Complications.—A special session of the legislature.—A unanimous vote.—Elections of 1868.—A national disaster.

The return to Hawaii of Queen Emma several weeks later was greeted with general rejoicing. The United States government had placed at her disposal the American flagship that brought her to San Francisco, in the care of Admiral Thatcher, commander of the Pacific Fleet. Honolulu took on a festive air, and for more than three weeks balls and dinners followed each other without interruption.

As I mentioned earlier, hospitality is practiced on a lavish scale in the Sandwich Islands, and among all the naval stations of the Pacific Ocean the port of Honolulu is especially preferred by the officers of men-of-war. Material comforts are diverse and generous; social relations, among the foreign population and the native alike, are exceedingly friendly. People go out of their way to be kind to outsiders, and the great freedom of conduct enjoyed by the young women is not the least attraction to newcomers. After due allowance for certain distinctions, there is more easy and informal sociability in Hawaii than in Europe, in the sense that entertaining is less costly in Hawaii than in France and is not the prerogative of only a small number of wealthy people. Great fortunes are few in the islands; comfortable circumstances, however, are general. Each family has a house of its own, more or less spacious, depending on income, but invariably surrounded by a garden. Rooms are large, quite airy, simply furnished as a rule, and housekeeping is meticulously systematic and neat. Small hutlike structures, picturesquely grouped, are frequently seen scattered about the grounds of a main house.

As in all foreign colonies where the American element predominates, the young women are queens. Everyone considers their likings; everyone is much absorbed in their desires. Balls and picnics are very frequent, above all when the arrival into port of one or more warships introduces a new social component, one well able to arouse coquettishness and kindle feminine curiosity. Fearless Amazons and indefatigable dancers, the young unmarried women of Honolulu are nevertheless intelligent and well brought up; they know exactly how to maintain the respect of persons who otherwise, according to our European notions, would be tempted to believe that girls are inclined to push a flirtation rather too far and too fast. American officers are not so likely to be misled, being thoroughly schooled concerning the social modes and manners of their compatriots. In fact, it is our French officers who are sometimes prone to form quite mistaken ideas in the matter, and above all those who have not traveled in the United States.

The visit to Hawaii of Admiral Thatcher and his official staff was not a brief one. The king saw fit to show his gratitude to the United States government by bestowing upon the admiral a royal Hawaiian decoration, which by a resolution of Congress the latter was permitted to accept. This exchange of courtesies somewhat calmed the suspicions of the American party in Hawaii. The admiral, being an intelligent man, did not sympathize with the attitude of animosity displayed by a certain group of his fellow Americans toward the Hawaiian government, and his wise advice helped to temper their ill-feeling. I had several interviews with Admiral Thatcher in which I took pains to explain our political situation, and the absolute necessity for us to protect ourselves against the extreme tactics of the missionary party, in order to maintain among all the nationalities as firm and just a balance as possible.

I also took up with Admiral Thatcher the question of negotiating a reciprocity treaty. He had no specific authority to conduct such a discusssion, but he listened closely to our views and promised to inform his government about them in his dispatches. He finally did so several months later, and these overtures once received in Washington helped to launch serious official negotiations.

The end of the year was not distinguished by any other event of importance. The days passed quietly by, during a period when prosperity was steadily rising, with beneficial results touching all segments of the population. Our sugar exports exceeded those of the preceding year and attained a figure of 17,500,000 pounds. The importing of tariff-free machinery required for sugar manufacture, and likewise the introduction of foreign laborers, made it possible for planters to reduce the cost of sugar production to a phenomenally low figure. In fact, among plantations completely mechanized, the cost was reduced to fifteen centimes per pound of sugar. In San Francisco, our chief market, the sale price held at an average of thirty-five centimes, leaving a considerable margin for the costs of transportation.

The encouragement we had given to rice growing began to show good results. By preventing the importation of rice from China and India for local consumption, we were no longer contributing each day to the wealth of the Chinese exporters. Instead, we were now producing at home a surplus of more than 500,000 pounds of rice for our own export purposes. Flax, cotton, coffee, and orange trees were all equally represented in our foreign trade, and the rising total of our exports reached 10 million francs.

Early in 1867, the American administration in Washington, D.C., announced its readiness to begin discussions on the subject of a reciprocity treaty. The United States commissioner in Hawaii, General Edward M. McCook, was granted the necessary powers to carry on preliminary talks. The United States government, however, wishing to keep negotiations secret until agreement had been reached on major points, invited us to send to Washington an accredited representative as our special agent. Mr. C. C. Harris was assigned to this mission and left for Washington, where Congress was then in session.

General McCook had already preceded Mr. Harris, and the two plenipotentiaries first met one another in San Francisco, where negotiations then began. The result from a commercial point of view could only be to the advantage of the islands. The amount of sugar we exported alone exceeded the value of our total imports from the United States. Our importers preferably purchased goods in the commercial capitals of England and Germany, which offered very much lower prices than did New York and Boston. Since the Hawaiian tariff rate was only five percent, it was evident that the admission of American goods even free of tariff charges would still make it impossible for articles from the United States to compete successfully with imports from Europe, where labor was cheap and the manufacture of goods for overseas markets played a leading role in the national economy. The United States government was fully aware of its competitive interests in these matters.

However, the basic goal of the State Department was a quite special one. It was important, for domestic political purposes, to win California's approval because of the approaching presidential elections. Sugar in the United States is an article of prime need. California was complaining about the burdensome tariff fees, which added so greatly to the price of sugar, thus forcing the state to deal with the sugar refineries of Boston. These Atlantic Coast manufacturers were themselves being supplied by raw sugar from Cuba, as a result of the destruction of the Louisiana plantations during the Civil War. A treaty abolishing the sugar tariff and the opening up of the Pacific Coast to Hawaiian sugar imports would immediately bring about a considerable reduction in the price of sugar. Such a treaty would thus satisfactorily dispose of the endless grievances and complaints of the West Coast states, California and Oregon, and of their adjacent areas.

It was clear to us that a treaty of this type was bound to benefit our agricultural interests. On the other hand, I did not disguise my fear of the appalling dangers to which such a treaty would expose us. Suppose the tariff were in effect for a period of seven years, as suggested by General McCook, and thus assured us a remarkable prosperity for this period of time. What if, at the expiration of this term, the United States government should exert the right to annul the treaty and impose on our sugar a tariff rate of fifteen centimes per pound, as it was already doing at that moment? Would not such a shift in future policy result in a terrible commercial crisis? Threatened by imminent ruin, would not our planters all rally round the notion of annexation to the United States, if only that nation would assuage the planters' fears of the future by permanently abolishing the tariff on sugar? Such circumstances would be a formidable test of our political autonomy. How would Hawaii survive it?

I did not question the reasoning behind the action of the administration in Washington. But was it feasible to reject the overtures of the United States and, out of fear of possible danger to Hawaii, ignore the present and very positive economic advantages, contributing at exactly the right moment to the success of our own political program for Hawaii? Even if I had sought to refuse the proposed agreement, I could not have succeeded. I should have found it impossible to win over to my side—I do not say a majority—even a respectable minority. The king shared my hesitation, and arrived at the same conclusions as mine. The only course to follow was to alter public opinion, and in the meanwhile follow with careful attention the proposed negotiations and any developments arising from them. The final result would depend on a vote of Congress, while the public discussion preceding the decision would enable us to estimate clearly Washington's intentions. Furthermore, seven years would give us time to establish our sugar production on a solid basis. Above all, we would have an opportunity, through similar negotiations, to open up other markets that would compensate us for the loss of California, in the event that our gloomiest forecasts should be fulfilled.

Having finally reached this conclusion, we settled down to work. The two negotiators quickly agreed on principal points. A draft of their projected treaty was transmitted to Honolulu, and after approval by the Hawaiian government, except for certain changes in details, was returned to our colleague, Mr. Harris, who then continued on to Washington with General McCook. The treaty was there examined and approved by the president and his cabinet. Finally, it was turned over to the congressional committee on foreign affairs, to be forwarded by them to the Senate, which would render the deciding vote.

While the negotiations were thus following their regular course, an American battleship, the *Lackawanna,* was stationed in Honolulu harbor. It was commanded by Captain [William] Reynolds, who earlier had lived in the islands for a number of years before returning to active duty in the United States Navy at the outbreak of the Civil War. Residence of more than ten years in the islands had completely familiarized Captain Reynolds with the political parties and the general social and economic condition of the kingdom. He had made a number of friends, and had figured in the annexation movement that had coincided with the illness and death of Kamehameha III. In fact, he was a strong supporter of the annexation idea, equivalent to the downfall and end of Hawaiian independence. His reputation furthermore had been greatly enhanced by the recent Civil War, in which he had played an honorable role. He did not at all conceal his political sympathies, nor his hope to see the Hawaiian Islands someday become a state of the American union.

In our present circumstances, the assignment of Captain Reynolds to the Honolulu station, as commander of the *Lackawanna,* was to say the least an unfortunate choice. It took on added portent when we learned that his visit to Honolulu was not a temporary one, for indeed he had solicited and obtained orders from his superiors to remain with his ship in Hawaiian waters, and to carry out what he described as a "mission of surveillance." I have every reason to believe that the American authorities, wishing to be informed about the prospects of a reciprocity treaty—how much it would mean to Hawaii, how popular it would be with our citizens—had believed it a sound decision to charge Captain Reynolds with the task of gathering such useful information, in the absence of the regular American minister, who had been summoned to Washington. Captain Reynolds' thorough knowledge of the country naturally qualified him for his post, and his ties with the missionary party, a body very influential in Boston, had further recommended him as an official who could be trusted.

Although we were at odds on political matters, I had formerly seen a good deal of Captain Reynolds and had always been on amiable enough terms with him. I was sorry to interrupt this relationship, but I did not hesitate to do so. The official behavior of Captain Reynolds from the beginning left me with no other alternative, and his active participation in the maneuverings of the annexation party forced me to request a clarification from Washington. What I learned was not very satisfactory. The administration hesitated to disavow unequivocally the compromising actions of its representative. Indeed, the simultaneous arrival at Honolulu of a British man-of-war and a French corvette charged with keeping watch on the *Lackawanna* made the recall of the American vessel difficult and untimely. Nevertheless, to avoid international complications then threatening to become dangerous, Captain

Reynolds received from his government an order to sail for San Francisco and not return to Honolulu until several weeks had elapsed.

In August, during Captain Reynolds' absence, I received the first text of the treaty as drafted in Washington and approved by the American cabinet. The specific ratifications to be exchanged depended on votes of approval by both the Hawaiian Legislature and the United States Congress. We therefore decided to request the king for a special session of the legislature, for under the provisions of the new constitution, no commercial treaty could be ratified except by confirmation of that body.

The special session, a brief one, opened on September 1. I placed on the agenda the text of the reciprocity treaty, explaining our reasons for recommending its adoption and without suppressing the apprehensions it would arouse. My colleague, the attorney general, who in the absence of Mr. Harris was acting minister of finance, submitted a draft of the law regulating the proposed new tariff rates, by means of which we were planning to compensate for our loss of customs revenues, caused by admitting free of duty articles manufactured in the United States. On September 9, the legislature voted unanimously to approve the changes in the tariff, and granted us the needed powers for the exchange of ratifications with the United States government.

In Washington the legislative machinery did not move so swiftly. Support there rested on the cabinet, on the safe votes of senators representing the Pacific Coast states, and on the assent of several other legislators loyal to the administration. In William Sumner, however, chairman of the committee on foreign affairs, the treaty was faced with a formidable adversary. The senators from the Southern states obviously were ready to follow him; those of the Eastern states remained as yet undecided. The debates were protracted, periodically revived but then suspended, ending in the administration's supporters withdrawing from their position, convinced finally that they could not organize a majority. In fact, this goal was not achieved until 1868. The failure to ratify the treaty had been anticipated by everyone, however; and, for reasons I have indicated above, it left us with only moderate regrets.

The elections of 1868 in Hawaii, like those of preceding years, were exceedingly satisfactory. The state of public opinion, the final departure of the *Lackawanna*, the conclusion of negotiations with the United States, and the absence of all domestic and foreign anxieties gave me hope finally of persuading the king to grant me the leave of absence I had been promised. My health, weakened by years of uninterrupted work, greatly needed attention and a period of rest. Before approaching the king on this subject, I awaited the results of the new legislative session.

It was to commence on April 18, under favorable circumstances. The financial report of the customs office revealed a new peak of improvement in our export trade. The condition of the Hawaiian treasury was excellent; the revenue from taxes surpassed our expectations. Then, because of an unforeseen event, just when everything pointed to an era of increasing prosperity, suddenly the country found itself faced with disaster.

CHAPTER 16

KILAUEA ERUPTS, 1868

Eruption of Kilauea Crater.—Departure with king for island of Hawaii.—Threat of earthquakes.—Ruins at Hilo. —Harrowing sights.—Rainbow Falls.—Departure for Keauhou.

On the morning of March 29, 1868, a whaling vessel arrived at Honolulu from Kawaihae, one of the chief ports of the island of Hawaii, bringing letters to us reporting an eruption of the volcano. Details were vague and incomplete. The collector of customs at Kawaihae wrote to me that on the morning of the twenty-seventh a column of smoke more than a kilometer high was seen rising over Mokuaweoweo, the huge crater on Mauna Loa (the "long mountain"), 4,500 meters high and forty kilometers inland from Kawaihae, which had given no significant evidence of volcanic activity since 1855. I have mentioned that occasion in my account of my trip to the volcano in 1857.* At that time, the snowfall had obliterated all traces of earlier eruptions, and it was only much farther and lower down in the plain that one could discern the enormous lava flow that had taken thirteen months to cool and had only, after filling up valleys and ravines and running its fourteen-league course, finally halted when within four kilometers of Hilo.

The first letters of our correspondents seemed to indicate a considerable volcanic outpouring, but further information arriving the next day was more optimistic. The column of smoke had vanished and no fiery glow was visible. Several natives had been dispatched to ascend the mountain, but it took them at least three or four days to reach the summit and return. The king summoned his council of ministers and we decided, after examining the facts, to await further knowledge. It was not long in reaching us. On the evening of the twenty-eighth, several earthquakes were experienced in various districts of Hawaii, some light but others violent.

The island of Hawaii is the sole area of the archipelago where volcanic

---

*See footnote at end of chapter 5. [A. L. K.]

eruptions still occur. However, on the other islands traces of them are still apparent; there is not a hill nor a mountain that may not prove to be an extinct crater, but time has meanwhile performed its work. Under the combined action of sun and rain, the disintegrated lava has been converted into rich and fertile humus, nature has thrown her cloak of green vegetation over scenes of desolation, and at least within living memory there is no record of a full-scale earthquake. From time to time muffled underground rumblings still attest to the volcanic origin of the islands, but all the force of the compressed subterranean fires is concentrated within the island of Hawaii, where Kilauea Crater remains perpetually active.

Situated on the slopes of Mauna Loa at an altitude of 1,500 meters, Kilauea is one of the oddities of the islands and attracts a certain number of adventurous tourists. I have described it in the earlier account of my visit to Hawaii. Far from frightening the inhabitants of the island, the volcano as they view it is a warrant of security. They begin to tremble only when Kilauea is quiescent, for experience has taught them that this continually open valve is indeed for them a safety valve. In fact, all the great eruptions have been preceded by a period of inactivity at Kilauea Crater. Therefore we were impatiently awaiting the news from Hilo, the seaport nearest the volcano.

Since the discovery of the islands by Europeans, eight major eruptions have occurred on Hawaii. The first, in 1789, was largely an eruption of ashes; I have related elsewhere how it was also one of the principal causes of the military triumph of Kamehameha I, conqueror of the whole chain of islands. Details are lacking concerning the second eruption, which took place in 1801. All that is known about this occurrence is that it occurred on the mountain called Hualalai, 10,000 feet high, situated in the southernmost part of Hawaii and forming, with Mauna Kea and Mauna Loa at much higher elevations, one of the three mountain masses dominating this island, whose total area is roughly equal to that of Corsica.

Four later eruptions followed, in 1823, 1832, 1840, and 1843. Mauna Loa was the theater of all of them, and their damage was minor. The rivers of lava vanished into the sea, creating in their passage new headlands and bays. In 1852, a lava stream again flowed down from Mauna Loa for a month, traveled ten leagues, and likewise disappeared into the sea. The eruption of 1855, mentioned earlier, was more awesome. It narrowly missed annihilating the already flourishing town of Hilo. The inhabitants had completed their preparations for escape, carried their most valuable possessions with them aboard vessels in the harbor, and were all ready to move to Honolulu. Their precautions resulted in nothing worse than a good scare, however.

This same eruption directed toward Kawaihae a river of lava twenty leagues long and one league wide, which fortunately flowed merely into the sea, missing that port by several kilometers. The activity continued for six months, and the fiery glow was so bright that on dark nights at Kawaihae one could read print as if by daylight, while vessels ten leagues at sea were illuminated by the reflected glare.

The news reaching us from Kilauea Crater was not reassuring. Accompanied by the reported earthquakes, it augured that a large-scale eruption was threatening. Not only did Kilauea Crater itself show no sign of activity, but the level of the molten lava had also dropped so rapidly that it looked as if it were draining away through an enormous fissure. Finally, the lava of the crater disappeared entirely, leaving exposed a yawning chasm more than four kilometers in circumference. The quakes meanwhile increased both in number and in strength. In the Kona district, 50 were felt in twenty-four hours, but in Kau, closer to Kilauea, more than 300 had been noted during the same period. One of the scouts was stationed at the so-called Volcano House, a tourist hotel built on the summit overlooking the crater. There the shocks were terrifying. If one lay on the ground one could distinctly hear the boiling lava when it struck against the walls of the earth's crust. According to report, it was like being atop the soldered-down lid of an enormous caldron in which boiling water was being violently hurled about, sometimes in one direction, sometimes in another.

The proprietor of the Volcano House, long accustomed to the various manifestations of the crater, had held out for several days, but in the middle of the night when a violent quake shattered everything inside his place, he fled in the direction of Hilo, not caring whether he saved a thing. On April 2 a shock even more violent than any of the earlier ones was felt, this time extending throughout the whole length of the archipelago, even as far north as Kauai, an island situated more than 100 leagues in a direct line from the volcano and separated from it by 350 kilometers of ocean. In Hawaii the effect of the quake was instantaneous. Pedestrians and riders were flung upon the ground, all stone structures tumbled down, trees were rocked in all directions, fiercely shaking their branches and striking against one another as if beaten by a wild wind; yet there was not even at the time the slightest stirring of a breeze. An eyewitness from whom I gathered these details told me that it was impossible to remain on one's feet, and that he and his entire household, lying prone on the ground, experienced the most wretched seasickness. It seemed to them as if some heavy subterranean artillery were firing shells at them, volleys that rattled against the earth's crust and indeed seemed to be attempting to penetrate it before shooting off into space. Everyone I have since had occasion to question on the subject has drawn the same comparison, which truly conveys the way it felt, and to the accuracy of which I myself can swear.

The earthquake of April 2, occurring simultaneously with the arrival of this news, was experienced in Honolulu also. Accompanied by underground rumbling, it warned us that we were dealing with a more severe eruption than the earlier ones. On the same day, the sky slowly darkened and the sun turned a dusky red; a fine impalpable dust filled the atmosphere, although we were twenty-four leagues from the island of Hawaii.

When the cabinet reassembled it was unanimously resolved to take vigorous measures to determine the extent of the damage and to bring assistance and supplies to Hawaii. The minister of the interior was ordered to charter a steamer and to load it with foodstuff, clothing, and provisions of every kind. Convinced that the circumstances demanded extraordinary concern, I suggested that the king should visit in person the endangered island, knowing that his presence there would have significant effect. I added that since he was more fortunate than other rulers in not having to risk the perils of the battlefield, it was his duty to confront danger whenever it threatened a portion of his kingdom, and that his very presence would do more to encourage the natives, to stimulate the zeal of our officials, and to testify to his own love for his subjects, than all the material aid he might send. My advice was sharply challenged. There were those who alleged, not unreasonably, that my plan would only result in exposing the king to unforeseen risks and that we would be assuming a grave responsibility.

The king cut the discussion short by agreeing with my advice and thanking me for having expressed it. On my request, he appointed me to accompany him on his mission, and issued an order fixing the following day as the time of our departure.

Word-of-mouth report of this decision rapidly sped through the town, where it was received enthusiastically. Preparations were rushed. Besides food supplies and clothing, I saw to it that a considerable sum of ready cash was sent aboard ship, and when everything had been attended to we embarked on April 8 for Hawaii. By special favor the king authorized me to take with me my wife and son,* my eldest child. The king was aware of the courage and devotion of Mme de Varigny, who had offered to assume responsibility for distributing supplies and aid to the native women.

We were obliged first to stop over at Hilo. It was at one and the same time the most important town—actually the most exposed to danger—and the place where we could best gather the information we required. A large

---

*In Mme Varigny's laconic account of the mission to the island she states: "I begged leave to accompany my husband, and it was deemed that the presence of a lady would not be without its uses. Henry came along with us. He was a first-rate rider and a good sailor and would be no bother at all. . . . M. Bérenger and Monsignor Maigret were likewise granted permission to accompany the king on the *Kilauea*." [A. L. K.]

crowd was present in Honolulu when the steamer departed, and the royal ensign floated from the mainmast. One of the highest officials serving under the minister of the interior acting as his deputy, together with two departmental assistants, a physician, two members of the king's suite, along with the French commissioner, were the only other passengers on board. We left Honolulu at five o'clock in the evening, and plunging into a cloud of cinders promptly lost sight of the island of Oahu.

During the night the wind sprang up and turned soon into a gale. At dawn we vainly attempted to round the western point of Maui, and from there to keep to the side of the wind, so as to reach Hilo by the most direct route. It was necessary, however, to give up this effort and proceed down the wind. At noon, having reached the roadstead at Lahaina, we sent a boat party ashore to learn the news. None was to be had, as no ship had arrived from Hawaii for several days. The townsfolk were greatly disturbed and, knowing nothing, imagined the worst. We therefore returned to sea, and as long as we hugged the coast of Maui were protected from the wind in the northeast. The height of the waves and the general roughness of the sea made it quite evident that a storm was raging abroad.

Toward evening we left Maui behind and entered the channel separating that island from Hawaii. The sky grew ever darker and more and more laden with smoke; a buffeting squall assailed us throughout our passage; but our craft was seaworthy, we laid on steam, and continued all night on our way to Hilo, where at last we arrived on the afternoon of the following day.

On the beach a very large crowd was awaiting us. For several hours the steamer stood in full view, while the unaccustomed sight of the royal standard on its mast much excited the local population. The king was likewise moved when, on disembarking, he was welcomed with repeated hurrahs. Though the governor of the island was expecting us, her partially destroyed house was in no condition to take us in as guests. We then accepted the offer of Mr. Thomas Spencer, the leading merchant of Hilo, who went out of his way to place at our disposal his own slight frame dwelling, which had suffered little from the severe shock of the earthquakes. On my way to Mr. Spencer's I passed in front of the Roman Catholic Church, then in the process of construction. One portion had fallen totally to the ground, while the remainder, terribly riddled with cracks and crevices, was in danger of collapsing in fragments. At Hilo even most of the stone buildings had been demolished. The dried-up streams, the empty wells, the rubble heaps of ruins, all gave evidence of the extensive devastation. The following is what our host, Thomas Spencer, told us about the events preceding our arrival; I shall take up later the conditions we witnessed for ourselves.

April 2 had been an appalling day. Shocks from earth tremors succeeded each other with such speed that it was easier to note the intervals of rest than to count the convulsions of the ground. During the afternoon a temblor of utmost force shook the entire island, and it was this one that had been felt as far as Honolulu. Under the impact of the boiling lava, a deep crevasse burst open at Kapapala in the Kau district, about fifty kilometers from Hilo. Kapapala, which I later visited, was a valley of rich pastureland where many cattle were being grazed. The floor of the valley was covered with a fine grass, called *manienie* by the natives, much sought after by the livestock, and along the sloping hillsides frequent groves of trees sheltered the animals from the noontime heat. Settled by two or three prominent landowners and their families, the valley also contained a rather large number of native shacks inhabited by the Kanakas in charge of the browsing herds and flocks.

The eruption* had occurred at the far end of the valley, where the earth split open with an alarming noise and a mass of mud, water, and rock was hurled upward with such force that the first jet extended over a distance of *five kilometers,* engulfing everything that blocked its journey. Near the same spot where the earth cracked open had stood a native hut of bamboo. This had been overturned by the jolting current of air. However, the aerial stream of volcanic mud shot along overhead without covering the area in between, striking the ground only 300 meters from its takeoff. From there it rolled along the earth without stopping, at a speed greater than that of a bullet fired with full force. This river of mud, from the point where it landed to where it halted its flow, was more than four kilometers long and one wide. About one meter in thickness along the borders, it attained more than ten meters at the center; everything standing in its way was destroyed. The surprised animals could not escape, and along the banks the carcasses of beef cattle and goats were still visible where they had been seized by the moving flood and now lay imbedded within its thick mass of solidified mud.

Up to this time, thirty-one deaths had been recorded among the natives. Many of the latter, frightened by the horrible shakings that had preceded the cataclysm, had fled in every direction and thus escaped certain death. Nevertheless, several of these fugitives met their end elsewhere, and in some other form.

I studied closely the specimens of mud that some of the Kanakas delivered to us. It was composed of red, powdery soil, such as is commonly found throughout the islands in volcanic areas. Its consistency was that of hardened cement. When struck by a hammer it easily disintegrated, reduced to a fine, almost impalpable dust, similar to that which for several days had been darkening the atmosphere. I found no trace in it of scoria or lava.

*Varigny describes the well-known, and very destructive, Wood Valley mud slide, which was caused by the earthquake but was not itself a volcanic eruption.

This explosion was followed by a copious emission of boiling water, at first cloudy and yellowish, then bright and clear, which again diluted the viscous mass and permitted the flow to continue through the area. Its temperature dropped, ending by being no warmer than the surrounding air. This springhead still exists today. I am unaware of whether or not it possesses any special chemical or therapeutic properties, though in any event it has neither the smell nor taste of mineral water.

But this location was not the setting of the last catastrophe of this dismal day. At the same moment as occurred the terrible earthquake ending in the Kau district, with the explosion just described, another phenomenon, much more disastrous, took place along the coast. I heard of it from an eyewitness, Mr. Stackpole, proprietor of the Volcano House, and I was able two days later to verify for myself the thorough accuracy of his account. As I have mentioned, Mr. Stackpole had been forced to abandon his house when it was in danger of immediate collapse. In the middle of the night he rushed off and headed toward the sea. During the afternoon, at the very moment when the severest of the shocks occurred, he descended the Pali (precipice) of Keauhou. Astounded by the violence of the quake, he watched the rocky cliff and masses of earth crumble away from the shoreline in all directions. Luckily, he himself remained unharmed, and after several dazed moments he was able to get to his feet. Stretched out before him lay the Apua coast. The ocean had withdrawn from the normal shoreline for a distance of more than a kilometer. He could see it boiling furiously, covered over with red foam and surging columns of water, tossed hither and thither, propelled upward from the sea's floor by submarine volcanoes. At several places the quake-riven cliffs were spewing cascades of muddy lava that descended into the sea, while along the beach the inhabitants were fleeing in despair. After its movement of withdrawal, the sea began to flow back coastward again, rolling powerful billows into the shore, piling one wave upon another, so that, traveling with incredible speed, they finally broke against the island, submerging and engulfing everything. Indeed, this gigantic rush of seawater surpassed by more than ten meters the level of the highest earlier tides. The force was so frightening and the sound so resonant that it seemed as if the whole island were plunging into the abyss of waves. Men, women, children, canoes, dinghies, houses—all disappeared within the wink of an eye in a confused mass of uprooted trees, collapsing cliffs, boards floating at random, human beings and animals struggling against death like playthings in the grip of an irresistible power. Several times the sea subsided and then returned, hurling here and there all sorts of debris, in which cadavers collided and became locked with the bodies of the dying. Then, little by little, the ocean grew calm. As far as the eye could penetrate, one found no trace of fishing villages. Everywhere one saw only waste, desolation, ruin.

Throughout the whole coastal region of Hawaii the same awesome phenomena occurred, with more or less intensity, but in no part with such violent results as in the northern direction, closest to the spot where the explosion had taken place. There the ravages of volcanic activity did not cease. On April 3 the tremors and shocks recommenced; they again persisted up to the moment when we were assembled at Mr. Thomas Spencer's house, where we carried on our conversation through the night, accompanied by the sound of plates knocking against each other, partitions shaking, trees swinging, all because of that undulating motion of the earth to which no one ever really becomes accustomed

As soon as we landed, I requested the governor of the island to dispatch messengers in all directions, in order to forewarn the inhabitants of the arrival of the king, and to invite those nearest Hilo to meet with us the next day. I also arranged with the king to visit all the coastal areas. Notice of our intention, including the day and place of our landing, was sent to the most remote districts. The distress in these areas was heavy. Many persons had lost all their belongings, and it was imperative to provide at once for their most urgent needs. We had to meet the Hilo people accordingly on the following day and then, if possible, leave the town by evening in order to reach the worst scenes of disaster.

The district which had suffered least was Puna, off to the west, where the king owned vast properties and numerous cattle and domestic animals. As he decided to make his lands and animals available to the most unfortunate of the people, we spent the night working with the map, dividing his extensive holdings into lots sufficient to meet the needs of a family. Also we apportioned beforehand the number of animals suitable for their support.

On the morning of the next day, the first news we heard from two of our messengers was that a fresh rift had just appeared near the pleasant village of Waiohinu, in the Kau district. There again the hills had been rent by fissures through the force of subterranean fires, the village had been destroyed by earthquakes, and the desperate inhabitants had taken refuge like a flock of sheep upon a nearby hillock, where the soil was sliding down onto the plain. The obstinate villagers nevertheless refused to move elsewhere. Their terror had risen to such a pitch that they were ready to believe anything, blindly obeying the notions of a native fanatic; in fact, one whose unbalanced mind already dated back several years, and who insisted that Pele, the goddess of the volcano, had appeared before him and had informed him that she wished to avenge her repudiated cult by displaying the very power that the missionaries had denied. Waiohinu obviously was a demonstration of the worst symptoms of social disruption and poor morale. It was urgently necessary to bring these conditions under control, and more than ever I rejoiced in the presence of the king, whose steadying influence would more than counterbalance that of Pele.

The new rift had formed on the afternoon of April 7. Its presence became known to us at the Pali, at the cliff named Manuala. According to reports being forwarded to us, the lava was flowing out of four openings, and these were flooding the entire plain surrounding Waiohinu and plunging thence into the sea at the eastern end of the island. Details were unavailable, as our messengers were not able to see any of this for themselves, and were only reporting hearsay.

The next day I accompanied the king to the residence of the governor of the island. It lay almost in ruins, but within its spacious compound they had hastily run up a canvas tent to which they had carried several armchairs and a portion of the food and other provisions with which our vessel had been loaded. A crowd of natives was silently awaiting the arrival of the king. Almost all were inhabitants of the local coast and victims of the tidal wave. Among their number were several suffering from injuries, more or less serious. Some were being assisted by their relatives or neighbors, others were being transported in crudely constructed bamboo litters. This speechless crowd respectfully bowed to their sovereign, and then at his signal squatted before him awaiting his questions.

The native character displays remarkable respect for the chiefs, an unusual mixture of veneration combined with independence. In the presence of their superiors they speak very little, but their answers are clear and precise. They always *"tutoient"*—that is, use familiar modes of address; the more formal pronoun for "you" is never used by them except in the special plural sense when addressing two or more persons. But this informal way with pronouns does not imply a lack of respect or excessive familiarity; nor does it contradict in any way their general attitude and bearing in the presence of superior status. Their respect is in no degree servile; it is that of a people who accept social distinctions, particularly superiority of rank and education, but who feel that they are their own masters, and that no yoke of serfdom weighs them down. They revere the chiefs but they also judge them; they know that they owe obedience only to the statutory laws and that, however lofty may be the place of a chief, his authority is exercised only within the strict limits of his official attributes and privileges, provided he has been duly invested with them, or with other particular rights that every master possesses in relation to his wage-earning employees. The latter can leave him, and do so as they see fit. They are free to hire themselves out to him or to refuse him their services. It is a mutual contract and nothing more, in which the codified laws of the realm determine the obligations and their scope.

The king, as he addressed the natives gathered around us, briefly explained the object of his journey and the measures taken by the government to come to their aid; he then invited the listeners to tell us of the extent of their losses and of their needs. So as to avoid all confusion, he added that the heads of families would be heard first and would speak for all members, specifying their number in each respective family, also their sex and age, and indicate among them those who were dead or injured. A special ledger was to receive all such information. The king concluded by reminding this audience that the government's supplies were necessarily limited and were primarily designed to provide for their most urgent needs. As the legislature was about to be convened, however, the cabinet ministers would request from the two houses when assembled sufficient appropriations for distributing among the needy a second round of welfare aid. In addition, private charity was already at work. Several collections had been organized in Honolulu, lotteries were under way, and the receipts of these would be paid over to those most deprived. The victims should accordingly be as moderate in their requests as possible, and not forget that we still had to visit some districts even more cruelly afflicted than their own.

This speech, addressed both to their hearts and to their minds, was thoroughly understood; heads nodded in assent and one of the group, the eldest, served as their spokesman. I seem still to see this old bearded fellow with his white locks and his lively resolute eyes. On behalf of everyone, he thanked the king for visiting them and assured him of the deep gratitude of his faithful Hilo subjects. Then he described briefly the losses he had suffered among a family made up of twenty-two persons—the children, the daughters-in-law, the sex of everyone, the small babies. Six had perished. He requested clothing for the survivors, a piece of dress material for the women who would make their own garments, and a little money for purchasing necessary articles of food. However, if it were at all possible, said the spokesman, he preferred not to be given money but some food supplies instead, together with materials for replacing or repairing damaged fishing nets and smashed canoes. They would then gladly set about, without delay, to rebuild their bamboo huts and frame cottages.

The king acceded to the speaker's very reasonable requests, giving him permission to cut bamboo and other required wood from his royal lands. The old man slowly stepped forward, fell to his knees at the king's feet, and, taking him by the hand, lifted it to his lips. He did so with such a combination of dignity and gratitude that I found tears welling in my eyes at the sight of so much resignation and courage expressed in the face of such dire misfortune.

After the old man spoke, another elder presented himself and then another, each reciting the same sad tale with a few variations. The luckiest had lost only their possessions, but none of them failed to find a hearing. The most unfortunate were the widows, now left alone without support, very often without any children. As for orphans, the king generously announced that he would look after them; depending on their age and aptitudes he would see that they were well brought up by his own relatives or retainers, or perhaps else he would simply provide homes for them on one of his royal estates.

The entire day was devoted to this melancholy labor. Systematically, as soon as we had finished listening to a head of a family, the king and I would quickly confer about the case. Then I would hand to the native a written voucher indicating the quantity of articles, the meters of cloth, the amount of foodstuff, and sometimes the cash to be allotted to the person. The native would then present the voucher to an employee of the ministry of the interior who, with the assistance of several clerks, would hand over to the bearer the articles and the money. The governor's secretary was in charge of the ledger for itemizing the successive names, a summary of the claims, the amount of acknowledged losses, and the sex of the dead persons.

By five o'clock our inquiry had ended. The rest of the daylight hours I spent visiting Hilo and examining certain of the areas damaged by the earthquake. The effects were a bit less disastrous than I expected. Only stone buildings had suffered; the Roman Catholic Church, erected recently at considerable expense, and one of the most beautiful in the islands, had been severely impaired. One of its twin steeples had been overturned, the other was on the verge of tumbling down, and the entire edifice was badly cracked. The customs house was hardly in better condition, and a number of shops needed extensive repairs. As for family dwellings, almost all were merely one-story wooden affairs, so these had fared rather better.

Hilo is situated on the bay bearing its name. There is no spot more picturesque and inviting than the view of this little town lying in a seaside amphitheater, with the white cottages silhouetted against the background of green vegetation that frames them. Dense plantings, utterly tropical, wreathe the middle distance of the landscape at its upper levels, enveloping every house and yet extending shoreward to the very edge of the waves. The two projecting headlands of the curving bay, a vast horseshoe, drop to a gradual slope covered by thick forest, below which coconut trees gently sway their topknots of jagged leaves. Far off in the distance rises the snowy summit of Mauna Loa, crowned with fire and smoke. The direction of the wind had just changed and flung the column of ashes in the direction of Kau. The trembling earth continued its series of tremors, but these were growing weaker. They were supposed to cease as the lava gradually cooled.

That evening I received a visit from Father Pouzot, a Catholic missionary at Hilo. He came to pass on to me the information his brothers and fellow workers in Kau and Kohala were sending him. The news was calamitous. Only by intense effort had he and his fellows been able to escape death. Their churches, their rectories, lay in heaps of ruins; a number of their converts had been killed. Burning with resolution, Father Pouzot wanted to set forth and bring them his aid and comfort, but the journey overland was impossible and no schooner captain cared to take to sea to reach the endangered districts. I immediately offered Father Pouzot passage on our steamer, certain that the king would approve my proposal. The priest accepted with gratitude, and promptly arranged to have several packing cases of clothing and personal effects carried aboard, along with other provisions that his boundless charity had deducted from his modest means. The Roman Catholics of Hilo imitated his example and each, according to his ability, made it a point of honor to contribute to his priestly good works. It was truly touching to see these humble people bringing a calabash of poi here, a pig there, several chickens, a few eggs, any sort of old and valued object. But their sympathy was not confined merely to these modest offerings. All had welcomed into their homes one or another of the refugees, and shared with them their grass huts and their simple meals.

Hospitality is an inherent talent of native Hawaiians. They practice that virtue on a splendid scale and among them, as among all primitive peoples, it is greatly honored. Wherever in the world humanity has to struggle with the natural environment, wherever hunger and thirst are the immediate enemies, there hospitality figures as one of the innate human sentiments. Hawaiians give away today whatever tomorrow they will ask of others. But, alas, to the degree that civilization establishes its works in the Sandwich Islands, hospitality ceases to be thus esteemed. In Hawaii, as elsewhere, the people learn the value of money. The native who formerly found it quite simple and natural to lend a horse, so that a traveler could continue on his journey, or to invite someone to share a meal and spend the night, today offers the passerby only a mount for hire. And even if he does not yet stipulate the price for the hospitality he on occasion provides, he fully expects that it will not be given free. This is especially the practice in the most populous districts and in areas adjoining towns. Nevertheless, one still discovers primitive traditions surviving in isolated backcountry localities, but there too the old-time ways are slowly being abandoned.

So far as Christian charity is concerned, country folk demonstrate it. The latter do so, in fact, much more frequently than is often the practice throughout the islands generally. The exercise of true charity indeed requires special circumstances fortunately very rare, such as those we were encountering at the time of the eruption. Great catstrophes awaken great sympathies; and because the imaginative faculty of the natives is exceedingly lively and well developed, they open their hands bounteously on occasions of gift giving.

The departure from Hilo was scheduled for the next day. We planned to call first at Keauhou. However, a still very rough sea was to delay our progress. We realized that the necessity to hold the steamer offshore and well in the offing, because of the destruction of the coastal ports and landings, would make it impossible for us to drop anchor. We therefore decided to travel by night, in order to arrive at Keauhou exactly at dawn, and so be able to devote the entire next day to distributing aid. The natives, forewarned of our intentions by the messengers dispatched earlier, were all set to run up signals along the bluffs above the shore: tall bamboo poles topped with colored pennants, facing the least dangerous spot for landing our longboats. They had likewise been ordered to keep a bonfire blazing all night to serve as a landmark.

I spent the morning of the next day visiting the environs of Hilo, and above all the celebrated Rainbow Falls. At the time of my earlier visit to Hawaii, I had not been able to do this, being in a hurry to reach the volcano, the object of my trip. I therefore planned, with the occasion now offered me, to make up for this oversight. The falls are about five kilometers from Hilo. Ordinarily, one gets to them on horseback by a rather rough road, but it was unnecessary for me to consider this mode of travel. The ground crisscrossed with crevices caused by earthquakes was anything but safe and secure. I decided for this reason to visit Rainbow Falls on foot, in the company of a guide carefully selected for me by the governor. I allowed myself two hours at least to cover this short distance, and from this experience I can vouch that it would have been impossible to reach my goal on horseback. Everywhere there were fallen rocks, dammed-up streams forming impassable quagmires, uprooted trees testifying to the tremendous upheaval that had disturbed the whole terrain. I regretted nothing when I reached the foot of the waterfall, however, and felt more than recompensed for my troubles.

A huge extinct crater, with a steep cliff along one of its sides, forms a natural basin about a kilometer wide and 300 meters deep. At one end of the crater lies a channel accommodating the overflow. Opposite this, at the other extremity, a river leaps from the cliff in a straight plunge—a single white sheet of falling water. No rugged ledges break its descent. At the base of the vertical rock the swirling water has hollowed out an immense cavern in which, according to the imaginative Kanakas of old, there dwelt a fabulous creature, half-man and half-fish, who seized and carried off to certain death any visitor foolhardy enough to bathe in his waters. The truth is that the whirlpool caused by the waterfall is so treacherous that no matter how expert the native swimmers, even for them it is a very hazardous adventure to try to bathe there.

The king told me that when he was eighteen years old, on a visit to this same waterfall, his native companions still firmly believed in the existence of this ill-disposed demigod, though they professed to be converted Christians. To convince them of their error, he told them he was going to enter the cavern and take a swim. In vain they tried to dissuade him, even offering to deny the existence of the god they had only just affirmed, but he would not listen and began preparing to try his luck. Members of his suite could have easily restrained him, but there is no record of a Kanaka lifting his hand against a high chief; no prayers, no beseeching on their part, prevailed. The prince stripped and entered the fabulous mere. After swimming close enough to the waterfall to realize the impossibility of either skirting or passing through it, he made a very straight plunge downward, by which he succeeded in reaching the interior of the cavern. There he caught his breath for several seconds and then, making a second dive, he was able to rise to the surface on the cavern's opposite side. His strength was almost exhausted, however, and to return to the original bank meant still another dive. His companions, fortunately observing his present danger and persuaded that no maleficent god inhabited the pool, were preparing to swim out to join him themselves. At that instant, very luckily for him, he spied a tree trunk that had been swept along by the waterfall and was now floating on the surface of the pool. Quickly catching hold of it, and thanks to its support, he was able to swim to the opposite bank quite safely.

To accomplish such a tour de force it was necessary to be almost amphibious (as indeed the prince was); but I vow I was in no way tempted to imitate him. Since that earlier day the spell has been broken, and the Kanakas of Hilo bathe frequently in these pure translucent waters. Yet I know of none among them who ventures as far as the submerged cavern's innermost chamber.

When the rays of the afternoon sun strike against that expanse of white falling water, it shimmers with all the colors of a rainbow. This optical phenomenon, occurring every day, except on those rare ones when the sky is entirely overcast, has given its name to a waterfall visited by all travelers to Hawaii in search of scenic beauty.

I returned to Hilo in time to complete my preparations for departure. Several of our messengers had arrived and reported to me what they had seen. Their news confirmed the extent of the damage. Everywhere, according to their accounts, they had found great misery and intense fear. The announcement of the king's presence on the island had somewhat raised the people's courage, but the dead already numbered in the hundreds, and our envoys assured me of the severe hardship threatening the entire population of Waiohinu. I decided to journey there myself, relinquishing my earlier plan to dispatch a police constable from Punaluu to restore a sense of order to the stricken community.

CHAPTER 17

SCENES OF DISASTER

A hazardous landing.—Unloading food supplies.—Journey ended.—Need to encourage immigration.—Origin of the native race.—A dream of Kamehameha I.—Arrival at Punaluu.—A native prophet.

By six o'clock in the evening we had all boarded ship. After consulting with the king I gave orders to sail. We were quickly at sea, cleared Kapohe [Kapoho] Point at midnight, and at four o'clock in the morning had arrived offshore at Keauhou, island of Hawaii. Daybreak made it possible for us to catch sight of a flag hoisted atop a hillside. But of the village itself we could find not a trace. Neither our captain, familiar with the whole coast, nor our pilot, whose hometown was Keauhou, recognized any of it. The black rocks that normally served them as a guideline had disappeared. The coastline had been leveled and most of the cliffs had collapsed. Here and there along the beach remnants of roofs, broken planks, and tattered shreds of cloth were the only indications of where once stood fishermen's huts. Our ship maintained a full head of steam, as it waited offshore about two kilometers from the village. With my son beside me, I got into a landing craft manned by six expert oarsmen to reconnoiter for a spot to put into shore. When I thought I had found one, I told the men to row us back to the ship so as to take aboard the king.

We had much difficulty making our landing. We moved forward cautiously, avoiding the submerged rocks scattered everywhere in the shallow water. Sometimes we reached within ten meters of the beach, but then had to turn back upon our own tracks before making another try. A few natives standing on a remaining bluff, who had watched our boat take off from the ship, ventured to come down to the water's edge. One of these, bolder than the rest, began to swim toward us, diving and sounding the bottom as he swam, until he discovered for us a feasible channel. We finally disembarked among shouts of welcome on the part of the growing crowd of Kanakas, including those who had decided to abandon their perch on the heights and join our company.

Within a few moments we were surrounded by hundreds of these wretches, who were only too glad to shake our hands and pour out their troubles. All of them were hungry. I ordered some boxes of biscuits to be brought posthaste from the ship, also a barrel of salt pork, and finally a tent—I had instructed the men to bring one along in the landing boat. The sun beat down upon the beach unimpeded, for neither tree nor grass shack was available there for shelter. The tent was instantly put up and provisions were installed beneath it. I sent the small boat back to the ship along with my son, together with a list of supplementary supplies to be landed. Then, while awaiting the vessel's return, I saw to it that the boxes of biscuits and the barrel of salt pork were opened. Their contents I consigned for distribution to a dozen prominent Kanakas, those who according to the crowd were the heads of village families.

In excellent order, everyone found a place to sit down on the beach, with the exception of the women and children who, by my directions, enjoyed shelter within the tent. The distribution was handled without quarrels, without recriminations, despite the hunger felt by everyone. But these natives did not eat, they devoured. Unfortunately, no water for drinking was available, and it was necessary to go some distance to find any. I selected several of the youngest and strongest to bring back a supply. They obeyed unquestioningly, taking with them several empty biscuit boxes, whose zinc linings adapted them to serve as water containers—not very large, true enough, but the only ones serviceable. These unfortunate people had not even been able to salvage their own calabashes; and the ones that had been washed onto shore by the tide had been battered to fragments.

About ten o'clock the landing boat returned with the king and a load of supplies. No less than three such trips were necessary. We had surrounding us more than 200 natives, deprived of all their belongings, and especially of their food and clothing. They had absolutely nothing except what was on their backs, and it was a pathetic sight to see these small children and half-naked women under the blistering sun. The awaited arrival of the king was hailed with repeated greetings, welcoming alohas without end. When everything was again settled, we went ahead with the first distribution. The tent we left in charge of Mme de Varigny, who looked after the needs of the women and children. She was aided by several of the most active and intelligent native women, whom she had chosen as her assistants.

The king and I, accompanied by several clerks, then found a refuge in the shade among the rocks of this wild and rugged shore. Surrounded by the men, we there began our inquiries, proceeding to the distribution of supplies, especially food and money. Some men were already hoisting and hauling off ship and across the water a number of planks and light boards that had been under consignment to Hilo. The natives had fastened these boards to some rafts attached to the heavily loaded landing craft. The entire operation took three hours to complete, because of the distance separating us from our vessel. We selected a detachment of men to transport the planks from the landing craft to the beach. One man was directed to climb to the top of the cliff and bring back, with the help of his hatchet, a quantity of tree branches. Another fellow, having dug some holes in the sand, installed wooden posts and joined them to the plank boards, while others assembled together a number of the branches that their companions had tossed down to them from the cliff. With these branches a roof was constructed, ineffective in case of rain, but adequate to protect the people and the provisions from the sweltering sun. Within several hours twenty of these improvised shelters had been erected, and the poor natives, now decently dressed and relieved of their hunger and thirst, were thus able to get some badly needed rest. Despite their various privations and their fatigue, all the work was accomplished speedily and well. At one and the same time they had recovered their strength and their courage.

After making sure that everything was going well I rejoined Mme de Varigny. I found her surrounded by women and children. The distribution of cloth had been completed. All had needle and thread, some did the cutting, some took fittings, and all were making dresses with the greatest speed to replace their meager rags. The youngest children, with the carefree innocence of their years, were playing on the beach, gathering here and there bits of debris that the ocean had washed ashore. These they heaped in a single pile, which each person then could examine, hoping to find something that had belonged to him. It was a scene of activity, of approximate gaiety, and of orderly good sense that was a pleasure to observe. The anxious air of all these simple folk, and in particular their gratitude, moved me very deeply.

The day at last drew to a close. It had been a busy one. When the time came for us to board ship, we found ourselves in improved spirits. We had left behind us enough provisions for a month at least, and also adequate housing. The Kanakas assured us that forest wood and bamboo were plentiful along the upper ridges, and that it would be no great trouble for them to rebuild their huts, now that they had hatchets, saws and nails, and sufficient sheds for working in the shade and sheltering their women and children. On our part, we promised them that the steamer would return within eight days and bring in fresh supplies. The king authorized them to select some cows and sheep from his royal herds, a journey of only one day on foot. After making inquiries, we named as head man a particular native whose moral character and leadership convinced us that he was the best man to serve temporarily as business manager of the village. He assumed general responsibility and was given full power to choose his own assistants.

At six o'clock in the evening we were again aboard the *Kilauea,* with our landing boat hoisted on deck. We recuperated quickly, thanks to our evening meal. The night was marvelous. As we moved at a leisurely speed under little steam, making our way to Punaluu, we could easily distinguish in the clear moonlight, as we sat on the bridge, the sinuous and varying irregularities of the Hawaiian shoreline, only a few kilometers away. We chatted of the events of the day, we projected our plans for the morrow. We were painfully troubled by what we had seen of the destruction, up to this stage of our survey. The material losses were considerable (though these were not entirely to be measured in terms of money) and there were sufficient treasury funds to make me hope to remedy the worst of the suffering and physical damage. The legislative assembly was in session, and I had no doubt about being able to obtain a special appropriation adequate for helping the natives in their plight. Unfortunately, what was irreparable was the loss in human lives. Deaths numbered in the hundreds. The king was alarmed by the figures, for there were already too few Hawaiians left in their land to serve as a agricultural labor force. Now this last disaster had swept away not only young men but women as well, these in the best years of their lives. How were such losses to be compensated? If foreign immigration brings certain advantages, it also has its disadvantages. The mass of immigrants to Hawaii are drawn chiefly from the United States, and the predominance of this element poses a danger for the political future of the islands. We had already brought in laborers from China, and others more recently from Japan; but both of these groups have only slight affinity with the Hawaiians, and this mixture of races thus far has not produced any promising results.

We discussed with the king the question of importing native colonists from the southern islands of Oceania. This, I confess, is one of my favorite ideas, and the king shares it with me. For several years I had been much occupied with studying the problem of the origins of the Hawaiian race. I applied myself by investigating the analogous problem of language. Through careful study, I had traced the linguistic affiliations of various Pacific languages as far as the Malaysian peninsula and its archipelagoes, and from there observed the development step by step, as it were, along that extended pathway of migration which after leaving Sumatra next established itself in Borneo; from there crossing the straits of Macassar, 200 miles wide, and reaching Celebes. Then the long voyage moved on to New Guinea, situated eight degrees farther, but meanwhile the Bass Islands and Ceram served as points of rest and recuperation along the route of the long journey. From New Guinea the migration arrived at the New Hebrides, after a voyage of

1,200 miles along a course strewn with islands; 500 miles farther it encountered the Fiji Islands; 300 more brought it to the Navigator Islands; from the Navigators to the Hervey group, 700 miles; and from there to the Society Islands, 400 miles. The longest of the voyages, among the many between Sumatra and Tahiti, was the passage from the Hervey Islands* to the Society Islands, but a tradition among the Raratongans designates the Hervey group as the actual cradle of the earliest Hawaiians. The resemblances between the languages spoken by the natives of Tahiti and by those of the Sandwich Islands are exceedingly close. The common origins of these two peoples cannot be doubted.

There is no problem more interesting to examine in this manner, through the study of interrelated languages, than the probable various stages of migration that I have here sketched: to assign to each of these successive movements a definite date; to discern, in the slight alterations a related language has undergone, the residue of a more or less lengthy period of sojourn; to note the modifications effected in the language by the nature of soil and resources, by climate, and by the admission of foreign loanwords. During the period when I gave much of my leisure to the study of such questions, I had no other end in view except to contribute my share of knowledge to the solution of an ethnographic puzzle. But now, in 1868, I discovered in my conclusions a political implication. I had found a reason for seeking in these other island groups a class or quota of persons, with cultural attributes in common, who could help us to recoup our population losses, and who, sharing their origins with our own natives, could not escape becoming assimilated to them.

I succeeded in convincing the king. With the map before our eyes, he had followed with me stage by stage the sometimes slow and sometimes rapid pace of this vast migration of peoples. He had discovered in the languages of Malaysia the source and origin of his own; there indeed he found the birthplace and cradle of his race. Kamehameha I, his ancestor, had intuitively hit upon this same fact; despite his ignorance in many matters, he possessed the intuition of genius. Conqueror of his enemies and sole lord of the Hawaiian Archipelago, he had directed his gaze toward Tahiti and the Marquesas. He dreamed of nothing less than retracing the routes followed by that vast ancestral migration; in each region he rediscovered his own language, customs, people. What he had dreamed in his time we were envisioning again in ours; but now with different and far more effective means of realization. Though Tahiti and the Marquesas constituted a protectorate of France, and were accordingly closed to us, even so there remained certain island chains

*Now usually called the Cook Islands, of which Raratonga is the best known. [A. L. K.]

much less well known, groups less frequented, where the still primitive native peoples remained a terror for mariners and an obstacle to the progress of civilization. I hoped to convince both the Hawaiian House of Nobles and the House of Representatives by my arguments, for I believed them to be irrefutable. I hoped to obtain from the two chambers necessary funds for a large-scale importation of natives from islands of the South Seas, especially those areas badly depleted by their miserable conditions, their barbarism, and the effects of famine. In order to make possible the execution of my plans the king had recently named me member of a committee on immigration, and I hoped to win the interest and support of my colleagues.

We spent part of the night examining possible measures. Unfortunately there could be no doubt as to the question of timeliness. This crisis had been forced upon us. After my return to Honolulu, I decided to submit the problem to the legislative assembly and at the same time propose our solution.

Well before daylight we found ourselves opposite to what had once been Punaluu. A great bonfire blazed on the cliff top, warning our pilot of the village's presence. We tacked about at sea, after firing off several rifles to notify the natives of our arrival. While awaiting the dawn we retreated to our cabins and enjoyed some sound sleep. At sunrise we wakened. The ship was three kilometers from the beach. We gave orders to be brought closer to shore, but the captain was less than optimistic. This coast, so very dangerous at all times, was doubly so now. Extraordinary bubblings along with other agitations of the sea indicated the presence of submarine volcanoes, as did the points of black rocks projecting to the surface of the water, while a rather violent riptide swept along the shore. The cliffs were covered with natives, coming and going, who evidently hesitated to climb down to the beach. A landing craft was lowered, loaded with food supplies, and I set off for the shore.

If disembarking was troublesome earlier at Keauhou, here where the volcanic activity had been even more intense our landing was more difficult still. From our position thirteen kilometers from the crater we noticed to the south a stream of lava pressing onward to the sea, where its black and reddish billows were rolling over the perpendicular cliff. The air was scorching. Dense fumes of smoke hung heavily along the sides of the hills and broke away in a large bank of gray cloud. On the beach, portions of the cliff had crumbled because of the impact of the upheaved waves. The tiny port no longer existed. We made our way groping, as it were, to find a point for landing. None appeared, other than some smooth, slippery rocks, which we hooked ourselves onto with our very strong grappling irons. The Kanakas moved down to welcome us. Our presence persuaded them to abandon their cliffs, more dangerous for them actually than the beach itself, since the cliffs were in a state of constant tremor. But such was the natives' terror of the tidal threat that they preferred the risk of being crushed to death by the collapse of the cliff to that of being drowned by the invading sea. The latter danger no longer existed, but it was hard to make them fully understand this.

I landed not without difficulty and had the provisions and food supplies brought ashore, just as on the morning before. The small boat then returned to the ship to bring back boards, tent, and additional food. I found many more natives at Punaluu than there had been at Keauhou. A number of the inhabitants of Waiohinu, after their frightening ordeal, had arrived to join forces with the people of Punaluu, and from these folk I finally learned what had happened.

The village of Waiohinu is situated in the central part of the island, twelve kilometers from where we were standing. The river of lava had erupted near the village. The Kanakas thus confirmed the original reports brought to us in Hilo by our messengers. Waiohinu no longer existed. More than one hundred persons were dead. The inhabitants had sought safety upon a high bluff that overlooked the plain, but this elevation slowly crumbled to pieces as a consequence of the continuous earthquakes. A self-styled prophet, who was predicting to these people the end of the world, announced that only those would be saved who took refuge along with him upon the hill. He had received, said he, a revelation from heaven. In vain the missionaries tried to persuade the natives to listen to reason. The judge of the district, who first regarded the new prophet as demented, had a little later seen his own house collapse and his wife perish before his eyes. He himself, injured in the same disaster, had lost his mind, thus adding further color to the predictions of the seer. For several days these miserable villagers camped on the hill, finding nourishment in the form of weeds and roots, and singing hymns to Pele to appease her anger. Certainly, what they had endured was fit to deprive them of their wits; but now it was imperative to put an end to such a state of affairs.

I conferred with the king and he agreed that as everything was under control at Punaluu, I should turn over the responsibility for our investigation to subordinates and leave in the afternoon for Waiohinu. My wife and my son insisted on accompanying me, and I assented to their wishes. I announced my decision to the assembled Kanakas. They tried vehemently to dissuade me from my resolve, assuring me that the road was impassable, furrowed with deep crevices that would force us to make endless detours. They painted an alarming picture of the dangers awaiting us at Waiohinu. When they realized however that my mind was made up, several of them volunteered to accompany us. I chose from among them the sturdiest and most energetic. They immediately set out to find horses in the neighboring countryside, and with some trouble succeeded in bringing back several animals which had been grazing on the plain. These had neither saddles nor bridles, but I had our own brought from the ship, and in the afternoon everyone was ready.

During this interval we carried on just as we had done at Keauhou. Instructed by our experience of the day before, we proceeded with speed. By noon, four large sheds had been erected on the beach, and there the women and children were furnished shelter. Food supplies were distributed, and the women were set to work under Mme de Varigny, who had organized her own division of aid promptly.

At noon we boarded ship again to share a hearty meal and to stock ourselves with a variety of provisions. It had been agreed with the king that when the investigation was ended and our rescue work accomplished, the steamer should leave the same evening, if possible, and await us at Kahaulala [Kaalualu] twenty-five miles farther along the coast. Thus we might eliminate the return and the difficult landing at Punaluu, where our work had already been completed. I should furthermore be able to form an exact idea of the results of the disaster along the new route we were planning to follow. My informants, however, told me our revised itinerary was unfeasible, because a lava flow had chopped it into two parts. But sometimes it is wise to allow for exaggeration. Therefore I cling to my belief that we shall be able to make our way through this unknown terrain.

CHAPTER 18

MORE SCENES OF DISASTER

Departure for Waiohinu.—Interior of the island.—Appearance of Waiohinu.—A camp among the ruins.—A sad interview.—Departure for Kahaulala [Kaalualu].—River of lava.—The crossing.—A father at his daughter's grave. —Cascade of fire.—Return to Honolulu.—Vote of the legislative assembly.

At one o'clock in the afternoon we paid our parting respects to the king. Then we set off, accompanied by five natives as indifferently mounted as ourselves, though I was pleased by their resolute manner and air of competence. The road, insofar as it could be called one, followed along the beach for a short distance and then, rising abruptly on the left, ascended the face of the cliff. There our troubles began. At every step our horses had to slide along between crumbling rocks or bump their way among sizable stones. We followed each other up a steep ridge between two sharp drops, one on each side, which at every moment threatened to give way with us. The weather was scorching and there was never the slightest hint of a breeze. We continued in this fashion until we reached the plateau.

There the look of the landscape changed. The low rolling plain was covered by clumps of half-uprooted trees and furrowed by deep fissures. We paused for a brief rest to let our horses catch their breath. At our feet the devastation spanned the full length of the beach. The plain itself continued its modest ascent. In the distance we distinguished on the right the snow-covered heights of Mauna Kea and, directly facing us, the uplands of Mauna Loa, enveloped by a dense bank of smoke hanging along the sloping sides. The cloud formations as they shifted in the wind permitted us, momentarily, to glimpse the mountain's summit, glittering like a diamond in the full sun. On the left a moving black ribbon crept ever forward until it intercepted the horizon: this was the stream of new lava in its downward course to the sea, emitting as it flowed a heat so intense that it made the air shimmer, giving the illusion of hazy and much attenuated cloud. We had no time to lose in our wonder at this singular vision. It was imperative to reach Waiohinu before nightfall. On an ordinary occasion we could have finished the journey in less than two hours, but now we were being delayed by the latest upheavals of the earth.

With a last parting glance we bade farewell to those of our companions who had remained on the beach. Then, turning our backs upon the sea, we set off for the interior of the island. The first few miles presented no serious difficulty. We were certainly halted by some of the fissures, but our horses were able to clear most of them. We found it necessary to turn aside only from the very largest. To do this required us to note the direction in which their size was increasing, and likewise to find our bearings by watching the plain on the opposite side. We thus avoided the largest crevasses by making fairly extensive detours around them. The majority of the chasms measured about thirty feet in depth. Many were no more than a meter wide, but others reached three or four. From their murky recesses sulphur fumes were being expelled; trees wilted and bushes turned dry as they hung over the blighted edges, their branches and sickly, yellowing leaves lacking all sap and vigor.

Meanwhile we were progressing at a better speed than I had at first dared to hope. After an hour's further plodding, we began to distinguish the higher hillsides, at the foot of which lay Waiohinu. We were entering into a new region and a different type of landscape. On both the right and left side of the road stretched a broad plain, normally quite fertile and luxuriant, but now wilted and dried because of the heat. The area was thickly covered with intermittent stands of sandalwood. This prized wood, very much valued because of the China trade, had formerly been one of the greatest natural resources of the Sandwich Islands. However, excessive cuttings carried on between 1830 and 1840, as a means of raising revenue and settling dubious legal claims against the government on the part of foreigners, had long since exhausted the sandalwood supply. Sandalwood trees grow very slowly. This district where we now found ourselves was one where they had chiefly flourished. I am sorry to record that all the young trees were now dead. A fiery blast of heat had swept them away, and it would take many years to replace them.

The devastation became all the greater the closer we approached Waiohinu. Indeed, at Waiohinu it reached its apex. We worked our way into a ruined and deserted village, where neither a house nor a single inhabitant could be found. The church had been razed to the ground. Not a sign remained of stone laid upon stone; everywhere walls had been overturned, living quarters had crumbled. We walked over the roofs, tramped upon broken calabashes, trod upon the collapsed beams from which the calabashes had once hung. Bits of cloth and household utensils littered the ground. The fire had sprung up a little to one side, where partly consumed debris and live ashes were still smoking. At a half kilometer's distance rose a prominent hill, scooped out of its original setting. Elsewhere a track of stones and yellowed soil showed the route taken by a gigantic landslide, which had halted only at the doorsills of the last houses of the village.

Along with the natives of our party, I went about the neighboring countryside attempting to find among the ruins safe shelter for my wife and son. We finally discovered one house somewhat less damaged than the others. Though the roof barely held together, one room still possessed three of its walls intact. True, the fourth wall afforded a view of the landscape, since it no longer existed, and the collapsing floor was so uneven that it was difficult to walk upon. But one could, in a pinch, escape the rain, if any occurred, by sleeping as far as possible from the exposed side, and no other requirements much mattered. We slept fully clothed, primarily to be ready for any emergency, but also because there was no corner one would care to use as a dressing room.

When these arrangements were settled, there remained the question of food. One of our natives made shift for a meal by using what we had brought with us. Several others, primed with my instructions, went up the hill to inform the Kanakas of my arrival and to present my greetings to the district judge, requesting him to come down to village level to meet me and to bring along with him the local inhabitants. I admit I expected, and naturally dreaded, rather strong resistance on the part of the villagers. But I also counted on the eloquence of my native aides, who well knew that the king himself was at Punaluu, and who also had witnessed the measures taken elsewhere to help the sorely tried people. Furthermore, with their native gift for exaggeration, these messengers would give the impression that I had at my disposal certain possibilities of action I definitely did not possess at all. And I was not mistaken. Just when we were finishing our simple supper, I saw one of our guides come running up almost totally out of breath. He reported that the district judge was following at his heels, together with the majority of the Kanakas. A small number of natives had succumbed to the influence of a would-be prophet, however, and were still refusing to come down from their hill. With this remnant I would have to try to reach an understanding later on.

The runner quite convinced me of the importance of making the approaching interview a solemn affair. But this was not easy to do, even with the best will in the world. Seated on a chair minus a leg, with my back propped against one of the surviving walls, I awaited the worthy official. He soon arrived, his head bowed in the abstraction of sorrow, escorted by two or three hundred natives who gazed upon their ruined dwellings with expressions of fear and bewilderment. Many of them believed they were still in mortal peril. Would not Pele avenge herself upon them for their audacity, their rashness in disregarding her fury? I welcomed the district judge with chilly formality, notifying him that the king had sent me there to investigate his conduct. Without other sign, except a gesture of utter discouragement, he indicated the accumulated devastation surrounding us. His sole and best excuse was this mute spectacle. What we looked upon, harrowing enough for me, a mere visitor, must have been an excruciating sight for these forlorn people who were not only deprived of their belongings, but who had also lost among the ruins their dead relatives and missing friends. I myself could share their grief, but this was no occasion for tender sensibilities.

What was needed was to restore morale, silence superstitious fears, and persuade them to abandon their dangerous abode before they too could come to an unhappy end. The undermined hillside, riddled with fissures, threatened to collapse from another earthquake. Actually, for the past two days the successive quakes had diminished in force, but they were nevertheless continuing. At this very moment the ground was trembling beneath our feet, as the earth seemed sometimes to sway in one direction, sometimes in another. I turned to the surrounding crowd as they stared with stupefaction at my wife and son sitting at my side. I told my audience they could no longer remain in this spot, for it was impossible to provide them with food and assistance; and that we would do for them what we could, but they must begin by helping themselves.

As for their prophet, I chided them for their credulity. I also announced that I had authority to arrest him and take him off to court. Tomorrow the steamer would be leaving for Kahaulala. I was returning by that route, and I urged all those listening to me to come along. There they would receive food, tools, and clothing. They could settle down to work and build themselves new houses, whether at Kahaulala or in some other district to which they might immigrate. These proposals tempted them mightily; but could one even get to Kahaulala. They thought the road was blocked by lava. Was it not? I had not the least notion, but in any event the road to Punaluu was passable, as I had just come up from there, and Punaluu had been stocked with adequate provisions. They welcomed my arguments with numerous expressions of approval, but when I insisted that they should spend the night at Waiohinu I had no luck persuading them. In vain I promised to stay there myself, along with my family and guides. They answered that this would expose me to certain danger. All that I could get out of them was that they would come down again the next day and at that time return with me to Kahaulala.

Once the ice was broken, the women and children swarmed round Mme de Varigny, who for their benefit repeated the sensible advice I had just given. As I mingled among the men, I systematically tried to make them ashamed of being so gullible and superstitious. I told them of what we had achieved at Keauhou and Punaluu, of the zeal and energy with which their fellow countrymen had rebuilt their grass houses and applied themselves to their tasks. These miserable folk needed only to be convinced. It was clear that the local judge, stunned by the death of his wife, had completely lost control of his wits during this critical time, paralyzed by his despair. Little by little, the bravest of the men asked themselves whether, after all, it might not be better to spend the night at Waiohinu. They had been there for the past two hours and as yet Pele had devoured no one. I myself was obviously staying and my guides likewise, and we did not look the least bit frightened. About a score of the men decided to imitate us, and some of the women felt the same way. At sunset the timorous contingent trudged off up the road to the higher elevation, followed by the jeers of those who chose to remain in the ruined village, together with me and whoever else appeared to have survived their former terrors.

Our arrangements for the night were quickly completed. A curtain was strung up to take the place of the missing wall and we were reasonably well protected. Two sleeping pads dumped on the ground, several saddles for pillows, and that was the extent of it. Our virtually demolished lodging was so unattractive that we stayed awake until quite late, sitting outside at the doorsill, chatting, inhaling the cool evening air stirred by a sea breeze. The tremors gradually lost strength, though they still caused the beams to creak and loosened even more the wobbling posts of the foundation; but this did not greatly disturb us. To say that we slept all night would be stretching the facts, but finally we got some rest without too many wakeful interruptions. We were on our feet again at daybreak.

Naturally, our Kanakas were quite surprised to find us in the morning still among the living, but for that reason they were all the more reassured. An even greater throng of them appeared than on the day preceding. Their tales had aroused the spirits of the reluctant natives, but their prophet remained perched on his promontory, together with his band of about a dozen fanatic disciples. Our success was total. I had not hoped for anything better nor even expected as much. The distaste they had shown yesterday for traveling to Kahaulala had now given way to an eager urge to go and join their village friends, gaze upon the king, and receive finally the food reinforcements and other help they needed most of all. Their children had suffered great hardship, and the deaths had been numerous among these poor little ones among a dwindling population, deprived for more than ten days of roof over their heads and proper nourishment.

I deliberately delayed our departure. Earlier I had ordered several of my guides to go on ahead to determine whether or not the road was cut off or blocked by lava, and I was now awaiting their return. In the event we should not be able to reach Kahaulala, I would instead fix upon Punaluu as our goal. My natives would return at ten o'clock. The road was difficult but appeared to be negotiable. Although the lava flow crossed it, one could avoid the barrier by making a detour. Accordingly, we finally set forth, under orders to head directly for Kahaulala. I decided that I would myself visit the lava stream, carefully examine the direction of its motion, and ascertain exactly the extent of the damage. In fact, it was claimed that a number of Kanakas whom the eruption had taken by surprise had already sought safety on various small hills and rises. Surrounded by molten or hot lava, they had then found themselves unable to leave their precarious points of refuge. If this report proved true, there would be little likelihood of finding these persons still alive. The heat and the sulphurous fumes could have asphyxiated them. Supposing they were able to escape these hazards, starvation would have finished them off. I kept my guides of yesterday at my elbow. I could trust both their energetic zeal and their courage.

The road was such that no one could ride at a gallop. An hour and a half at walking pace brought us to the lava. By standing on a rise and looking down upon the river's dark course, I was able to estimate the direction of its flow. Its origin lay several kilometers to our right, along the sides of the mountain. Moving as a compact mass, the lava had first streamed downward as far as the plain. There it divided, turning aside from the knobby hills and elevations, sometimes meandering as if at random, leaving here and there vast flats or plateaus intact. One could speak of these plateaus as islands of various sizes and shapes in the midst of a black and burning sea. The heat was furious. A hazy white smoke below floated along at ground level.

The surface of the lava having hardened, this exterior crust seemed firm enough to support the weight of a man. We descended to the edges, after leaving our horses in the care of one of our guides, and made ready to cross over the first of several spurs. Using some handfuls of dried grass and weeds, our Kanakas equipped themselves with a kind of thick sandals to protect their bare feet. We armed ourselves with long pointed staves, made of sturdy tree branches, to help us walk and to test the solidity of the crust. I went on ahead with the Kanakas. My wife and my son, who insisted on following us, trailed along behind. We proceeded slowly. Along the edges the lava was strong enough to support us, but as we advanced the thin crust became less resistant to our traffic. In the middle of the streambed, we felt it yield at our every step, like newly formed ice on a river. When I poked it, my stick penetrated the soft layer and as I drew it away I could see its tip glowing from the fierce heat of the interior. The temperature was so intense that it singed the soles of our feet, and we found it necessary to make haste. By one last effort we reached the opposite side safe and sound. Our shoes had not been able to stand the heat of the surface, however, for their leather was badly scorched. We ourselves, gasping, were hardly able to breathe.

The lava formed an expanse about 300 meters wide. By examining the contours in relation to the surrounding ground I was able to judge approximately the thickness, which was not less than 50 feet where it flowed between two globe-shaped hills. We were on an island encircled by lava. Ahead of us, at a kilometer's distance, another more narrow fork, being more enclosed and confined, turned off from one of the hillocks and flowed away to the right. Farther still, the white smoke indicated the presence of similar branches and tributaries. Everywhere there were islands and islets whose withered trees and singed plant life presented a vision of desolation. A few islands larger than others had maintained at their centers some bits of greenery, which gave them the appearance of an oasis in the midst of a desert. Within these last areas we noticed several nebulous figures weaving about through the shimmering atmosphere. My field glasses enabled me to identify these mysterious figures. They were bullocks and horses, who had managed somehow to reach these plateaus, and who now were successfully devouring the meager grass that they found there. On the smallest and nearest islands, skeletons of such animals lay scattered on the ground. Heat, hunger, and thirst had killed them. It was an excellent opportunity for a panoramic view, but I could make out no human shapes. If any Kanakas had managed to take refuge there, they must have perished for lack of water.

Our guides went on ahead to reconnoiter another fork. It was impassable. The crust of even the most substantial patches was not solid enough for us to pass over. We explored our island in every direction. As we found it impossible to continue, we could only turn back in our tracks. The reader should not jump to the conclusion that we had primarily crossed the earlier lava stream because its flow had ceased. It had done nothing of the kind, but was in constant interior commotion immediately beneath our feet. It was exactly like the surface of a river frozen to ice, but at varying depths of solidity. The liquid currents were circulating under the hardened layer, and thus were continuing their downward journey to the sea. The total amount of lava contained in the volcano was not identical with the amount ejected at the time of eruption. The quantity of lava in movement was diminishing, and the thickness of the crust as it cooled became greater in the same proportion. At certain points in its pathway, as I verified later, the lava flowing across the plain was not deeper than about one meter but at those areas the width of the stream reached more than a kilometer. At some other points the depth must have exceeded thirty or forty meters. When observations were made at the time of preceding eruptions, and notably during the activities of 1838, it was concluded that a lava bed thirty meters thick requires not less than one year to cool completely.

As we now found ourselves forced to abandon the scheme of continuing cross-country and then ahead, we returned to the roadway and started descending in the direction of Kahaulala, skirting the lava spurs and obstinately searching the horizon to discover whether there were any human beings alive atop the various hillocks. We could find not a one. Later, when the eruption had ceased and one could explore more thoroughly, here and there among the skeletons of animals appeared the corpses of a few natives; but at the time I was making my survey, these persons had evidently been dead already for several days, and at the moment no mortal could have rescued them.

Along this road I visited also the ruins of several once-flourishing farms and plantations, now transformed into expanses of lava and stone. Among others, Captain Brown's place was a perfect picture of desolation. I found this unfortunate man along with several Kanakas attempting to locate the grave of his daughter, who had died several years earlier and was buried near her home. He had scarcely been able to distinguish the site of his cottage. The flood of lava had poured down into the plain during the night. The youngest daughter had cried out to ask what that strange noise was that sounded so like the roar of a waterfall. She had gone out on the veranda in the dark night and there had seen the fiery, boiling river making its headlong descent to the sea. Without time to save anything, with no other clothing than what they were wearing, unable even to slip into their shoes, the Brown family—himself, wife, and children—fled from the house for refuge on a hill about 400 meters from the property. The lava was approaching like an inundation of liquid fire, covering the plain to a width of more than one kilometer. Surrounded by the flow, Captain Brown's house and farm buildings burst into flame like a handful of dry hay. Everything was destroyed instantly in the all-encompassing flood. The very moderate thickness of the lava caused it to cool rapidly, as the main route of the eruption forked off to the left. After entrusting his wife and children to the kindness of less unfortunate neighbors, Captain Brown was now trying to find the grave of the dead child.

I listened to his sad story and offered my help, which he accepted with gratitude. He made me responsible for placing his family aboard the steamer and for taking them with me back to Honolulu, while he would be building a new home and rounding up the few surviving cattle from his herd.

By five o'clock in the evening we reached Kahaulala. Our Kanakas had preceded us by several hours and had received from the king the necessary assistance. They were now readying themselves to return to Waiohinu. Their fears had been calmed; the king had been right in the matter. Reassured by his presence and council, they began to settle down to their tasks. Within a few days a schooner speeding from Honolulu should be bringing in the needed lumber and tools. Meanwhile, awaiting the boat's prospective arrival, a supply depot had been organized at Kahaulala and placed under the direction of a member of our native staff, whom we planned to leave in charge. He would report regularly in behalf of the natives what and how much was required.

I gave the king a full account of what I had seen. During the afternoon, when everything was finished at Kahaulala, we embarked on the steamer to sail round the tip of the island. We intended to return to Honolulu by way of short calls at Kealakekua and Kailua.

The extreme southern end of the island of Hawaii, known as Kalae Point, forms a steep headland or cape, which on its northern side geographically links two sets of cliffs separated by a narrow ravine and basin. It was at Kalae that the river of lava found its outlet and finally poured into the sea. Flowing between the high walls of the ravine, it fell from a height of 500 meters into the ocean, where it created a huge cone in the form of a pyramid. We could not approach it closely enough to note all its details, but with our field glasses we distinguished the general layout quite clearly. Evidently the volcanic torrent was weakening in intensity, but as twilight gathered the spectacle was still most impressive and awesome. The massive black stream with its flamelike iridescence dropped from the summit of the cliff upon the peak of the cone, pouring down in cascades along the pyramidal sides, where it vanished in the boiling water. As it disappeared, it gave off a low hiss that carried far enough for us to catch the sound.

We soon rounded Kalae and were again on the open sea. However, by describing a great sweeping curve, we were able to put in at the north end of the cape, from where, traveling at full steam, we quickly arrived at Kealakekua. There at daybreak we lowered anchor.

Kealakekua had unquestionably suffered from the earthquake. Fortunately, the village is situated on the lower slopes of Mauna Loa, its back to the mountain and fronting on the sea, while the erupting volcano was then most active on the opposite sides. A number of ruined dwellings, the undermined and crumbling cliffs, the general vegetation and subsequent plantings destroyed at their very roots, attested to the violence of the quakes. Luckily the disaster had spared the inhabitants, and one noticed only several injured Kanakas, victims of the collapse of their houses or of falling trees. Not a single human being had been killed. We rested for only a few hours to confer with the local authorities about measures for action, and then we left for Kailua.

This small village, historic place of residence of early kings of Hawaii, had suffered still less than Kealakekua. The villagers had only minor needs in the form of fresh provisions, and it did not require much time to supply them. We were in a hurry to return to Honolulu. We left Kailua at nightfall and immediately set out by the most direct route for the capital of the kingdom. Traveling at full steam, by the afternoon of the following day we were in sight of Oahu. The battery on Punchbowl Hill gave its signal upon our arrival, running up the royal ensign and firing twenty-one-cannon salutes. One hour later we entered the port.

The quays were swarming with the crowd, anxiously awaiting the king's return and the official news we were bringing. During our absence the wildest rumors had circulated, for according to report the steamer had sunk and the king was dead. Therefore his presence on the bridge was greeted by most joyous acclamations.

The legislative assembly was then in session. To that body I reported immediately after taking leave of the king. Upon my arrival, the agenda of the day was laid aside in order to enable me to present to the impatient legislators the news they had been awaiting. I delivered to the tribunal a terse account of our voyage and the measures we had taken.* I announced that I would submit to the legislature a bill of indemnity for the expenses incurred and a request for further credit to cover whatever new ones would be needed. Loud applause welcomed these statements, and the assembly sitting in formal session voted their approval of a resolution congratulating and thanking the king. A delegation was named to present the tribute to him in person.

On the following day the two bills I had introduced were unanimously adopted, and on the day after that the steamer left for Hawaii. Its mission was to bring whatever assistance was necessary to the unfortunate people of Kau and Puna.

With this action the task of the government was ended and that of private charity began. Meetings were held, house-to-house collections were organized, as were lotteries and sales, and in less than a week more than 200,000 francs had been raised to furnish aid to widows and orphans.

Thanks to the eager cooperation of all classes of the population, and also to the generosity of the legislature, the material damage of the eruption was promptly remedied. Few natives immigrated to other islands. That detached and almost cheerful fatalism which is one of the characteristic traits of the nonchalant Hawaiian race helped them promptly to forget past woes. Instead, they straightway settled down to the job of rebuilding their ruined cottages and huts and taking up again the interrupted routines of their normal occupations.

---

*In his report to the legislature, Varigny noted that at Hilo clothing was distributed to 110 persons; at Keauhou relief was given to 68 men, women, and children; at Punaluu clothing and lumber were distributed to 364; at Kaalualu, where "some were really famishing," 257 persons received aid. Hence, the total number of the afflicted was about 800 persons. [A. L. K.]

CHAPTER 19

MY LEAVE OF ABSENCE, 1868–1870

Legislative session of 1868.—Struggle with the opposition. —The steamship subsidy.—Departure for Europe.— Voyage to San Francisco.—The coast of Mexico.—Panama. —New York City.—Arrival in France.

Again the Hawaiian Legislature, after its temporary preoccupation with the disaster on the island of Hawaii, turned its attention to public affairs. The budget was approved without discussion, and the legal measures proposed by the government were adopted. Only one of these bills provoked warm argument. We had considered it a matter for the cabinet's decision, but the opposition was exercising its right to make it a question of party policy, as has been earlier indicated. We were requesting the legislature to grant us special funds sufficient to subsidize a steam navigation company operating between Honolulu and San Francisco. In doing so, we were infringing upon some vested interests with strong local ties. For years on end, the numerous sailing vessels providing this service had been owned by the leading merchants of Honolulu, and they understood perfectly well that the establishment of a steamship line would present them with some stiff competition that would take over, first of all, their passenger and small freight customers and then, in the very near future, deprive them of their business as carriers for the sugar planters.

These interests exerted all the influence they could muster among the members of the legislature, in an attempt to persuade them to reject the subsidy measure. In building their case, the proposal's critics emphasized important economic considerations of deepest concern to the native representatives, because the measure in question would particularly involve sending money outside the country. Some accused us of dangerous extravagance, of desiring to rush ahead too hastily along the path of progress, and furthermore of delivering our export trade over to a foreign flag, to the detriment of vessels flying the Hawaiian ensign.

We felt no embarrassment in replying to these puerile accusations, but it was more difficult to persuade the representatives to make the sacrifice we were soliciting. Discussion grew lively, even emotional; the most remarkable arguments were dragged in, as when the opposition, who actually were well aware of the benefits the proposal would bring, disputed it stubbornly in the hope of overturning the ministry.

But in this they did not succeed; public opinion, for a moment shaken, was restored in our favor and the appropriation was passed by a rather respectable majority. The rest of the session slipped by without incident.

In the midst of all this unremitting effort my health deteriorated. The king was aware of my condition and agreed to permit me, after the prorogation of the legislature, to take a leave of absence and visit Europe. Circumstances were such that I could take my leave without causing inconvenience. All the important policy questions were settled; only the revision of our commercial treaties required my attention. Kamehameha V told me of his wish to shift the scene of negotiations to Paris, and entrusted to me their direction. I should be leaving the kingdom in my capacity as minister of foreign affairs, charged with a special mission requiring me to consult with officials of several European governments. The length of my absence was limited to one year, and the king left it to my judgment to choose one of my cabinet colleagues as deputy minister for the interim.

The legislative session ended on July 15, 1868, and I immediately set about preparing for my departure. I designated Mr. Stephen H. Phillips, attorney general, as my replacement during my absence, and on July 22 I embarked with my family on board the steamer *Montana* for the voyage to San Francisco.

Though I felt great pleasure at the thought of seeing my native land again after an absence of eighteen years, still my heart was saddened when I left the islands. I was parting from some dear friends, along with other memories and tokens no less dear. I had spent fourteen years of my life in Hawaii, watching the country as it developed. Thanks to a happy set of circumstances, I had been successful in seeing some of my ideas adopted, and indeed in contributing to the progress of this emergent young civilization. True, I fully believed that my absence would be a short one and that later I would be able to carry out the task I had undertaken in Hawaii; but this would no longer be possible under quite the same conditions, for I should have to leave my son behind me in Europe, and the thought of this painful separation darkened the prospect of my eventual return.

The king came aboard ship to say goodbye. I was touched deeply by our farewells. Was it a premonition that our parting would be for good? I clasped his faithful hand for the last time; at four o'clock we lifted anchor and left Honolulu harbor behind us. While nightfall descended upon the hilltops of Oahu, and as the island faded on the horizon, the bold contours of Maui on our left arose in the hazy distance. I remained on deck to the last moment, watching with lingering eyes as, little by little, both coastlines alike were lost in the evening dusk.

By next morning we had reached the open sea and all land had vanished. Heading northeast, we were well set for the voyage to San Francisco.

On August 10 we reached the Golden Gate and lowered anchor. Fourteen years earlier I had left this embryonic city. But what a change—and what activity and commotion! I arrived at the Metropolitan Hotel, a veritable marble palace comprising everything one could imagine in the form of luxury and comfort. I spent eight busy days there. What had become of the canvas tents, the frame houses, the rude shops and primitive quays of that bygone San Francisco? Instead, large handsome buildings everywhere, splendid streets, chapels and churches, elegant private dwellings. Never has human energy produced a greater transformation in so brief a span of time.

I embarked on August 18 for New York City aboard the steamer *Ocean Queen*. In place of this long and dangerous journey by sea, I should have much preferred the marvelously shorter railway route from the Pacific to the Atlantic, but this had not yet been completed. The two opposite lengths of roadbed were still separated from one another by a distance of 250 miles, difficult to link together in the midst of a desert inhabited by Indians.

Traveling at full steam, we followed the coast of Mexico, pausing only at Acapulco. The temperature there was suffocating. The heat-laden skies, charged with electricity, flashed upon the evening horizon fantastic illuminations that wrapped the barren mountains in a garish spectacle of light. Though there was a steady rumble of thunder, no rain watered the desiccated earth nor revived the exhausted vegetation.

Next came Manzanillo, a woebegone village just barely habitable. Several long files of armed men, mounted on half-broken horses and bravely decked out in tattered military garb, lined the roads leading to the interior of the country. These were escorts protecting heavy carts loaded with certain dirty gray bricks: a mere token of the millions of their kind being shipped to Europe. For these bricks were silver ingots stacked for loading aboard our vessel, destined for New York and England; and the soldiers, resembling bandits more than honest men, were serving as guards during the perilous journey through the mountains. As usual, a civil war was on in Mexico, and the silver bricks did not invariably reach Manzanillo.

We entered the Gulf of Panama, gulf but in name, in reality a sea, the sea of a thousand islands, as the Mexicans call it. These rose up on all sides charming oases, calm and clear, like seeds scattered upon the blue ocean. A jungle growth of vegetation covered the ground and extended even down to the beaches. Nothing but the wildest of creatures, including snakes and monkeys, apparently inhabited these islands. All the animals of creation seemed to be maintained there as on a reservation, lest their species should perish elsewhere.

For thirty-six hours we navigated amidst these miniature archipelagoes. After nightfall they appeared as if submerged, indeed drowned, in the vaporous brilliance of a tropic moon. Not a ripple on the water, not a breath of air stirring the atmosphere, the ship gliding without effort on a glassy sea.

Just at daybreak Panama came into view, its old gray walls silhouetted against the green shore. We moved alongside a great wooden quay at the end of which appeared a closed barricade constructed of stout railings, similar in every respect to a cattle stockade. There all passengers disembarked, accompanied by the innumerable pieces of luggage with which our ship was loaded. We were absolutely forbidden to leave the cattle pen. Two peremptory reasons were given us: first, an epidemic of fever was just then raging in the town; second, the natives had recently massacred twenty travelers as a result of a brawl in one of the local cabarets. It is unfortunately only too true that if passengers are permitted to leave their ships freely, a substantial number of them will be dead drunk by sailing time.

Our huge steamer was unloaded in less than two hours; baggage and merchandise were stacked aboard the railroad train that was building up a head of steam on the other side of the stockade and making ready to carry us to Aspinwall, where another company vessel was awaiting to transport us thence to New York. We climbed aboard our coach and left Panama behind us.

The railroad linking the Pacific Ocean with the Atlantic was constructed with the help of American capital. Built upon marshy terrain, the roadbed runs through extensive virgin forests and dense jungles, obstacles surmounted only at an immense cost both in money and in lives. It is a common saying in Panama that every trip on the railway represents a human life. Tropical fevers have decimated whole armies of laborers, recruited among the Irish, the Germans, the South American Indians, and the coolies of India and China.

One of the railway engineers, personally acquainted with our traveling companion, Admiral [H. K.] Thatcher, passed along to us some interesting details on this subject, and confirmed the fact that construction work was frequently suspended because of the terrible mortality rate among the ditch diggers. In fact, the project depopulated the town and peopled the cemeteries. But American perseverance was justified in the face of these difficulties, and success has rewarded the persistence of the investors, who are today receiving a seventy-five percent return on their capital outlay. This should cause no surprise if one considers the fact that each six-hour trip across the isthmus brings in 125 francs per traveler.

The train route traverses thick forests abounding in monkeys and parrots. Flowers unknown in Europe, exotic perfumes, a wilderness of vegetation, formed a striking contrast to the locomotive engine that hauled us through a thousand twisting bends and, at every moment, seemed about to hurl us against an impenetrable wall of interlaced vines begrudging us our narrow passage. A humid heat hung round us; the electricity-charged air became oppressive; we instinctively felt that the white race was not meant to live here, and that the rank vegetation entwining and charming us also stifled our very breath.

About halfway through our journey we drew to a halt. The storm, threatening us from morning on, suddenly burst upon us with fury. Loud reverberations of ear-rending thunder continued without pause as a pelting rain of huge drops beat down upon us and transformed the porous earth into a lake. The storm ended in less than an hour, the sky cleared, birds and monkeys returned to their interrupted frolics, and continuing our journey we finally confronted the Atlantic Ocean.

All is relative in the world. As we beheld the same tides that wash the shores of France, it seemed to us that our journey was already ending even though 10,000 miles still separated us from our own country, for we had yet to stop at New York City before again taking ship en route to Europe.

At Aspinwall we once more encountered the cattle yards we had been introduced to at Panama. However, by special favor, only Admiral Thatcher and ourselves were permitted to make a tour of the town. We soon saw as much of it as we wanted. There was nothing whatsoever of interest: several large shops; the warehouses of the steamship company and the Panama railroad firm; some fifty dwellings of the American employees who with hangdog expressions stroll Aspinwall's two streets; a population chiefly made up of negroes, Indians, and ragged half-breeds; soldiers in uniform, without stockings or shoes, bandit style—such is the outward aspect and atmosphere of Aspinwall. No one ever stops there but simply passes through, with no wish to return; there is so little to see that it is scarcely worth mentioning. The cemetery is larger than the town and infinitely more inhabited.

We left this dismal spot without regret. At four o'clock we drew anchor and by nightfall were rounding the northeast cape and turning our backs on the coast of South America. A journey of eight days brought us to New York City. We had skirted the shores of Havana without stopping. Our eager impatience increased in proportion to our progress. Almost all our companions were approaching the end of their voyage. No one spoke of anything but the joy of arrival, of the relatives and friends about to be greeted.

So here we are, at Staten Island, in New York's noble harbor; there is Brooklyn, the city of churches; then the East River, furrowed by innumerable steamboats. Along the wharves stretches one after the other an endless file of oceangoing vessels decked out with flags of all nations.

New York City is too familiar to need description. We spent only three days there, and on September 8 embarked for Southampton. We had no other choice except to book passage aboard one of the steamers of the Hamburg Line. I had hoped to arrive in time for the departure of the *Pereire,* but it was leaving the harbor just at the moment we entered it. We did not have the patience to wait ten days more until the next French steamship was scheduled to arrive. We left New York on a day of dazzling sunshine and suffocating heat. Five days later we were freezing, while enormous icebergs loomed into view on the horizon. We entered the fogs of the Newfoundland Banks, fearful latitudes where ships have collided with each other amid weather conditions of total invisibility. At noontime, seated on the afterdeck of the vessel, we could not even make out the mainmast. Minute after minute the ship's bells clanged lugubriously. Both night and day the foghorn sounded its loud, hoarse blast through the oppressive vapor-laden atmosphere.

Finally, on September 20, we outran the fog and caught sight of the lights of Lizard Point, vanguard of the coast of England. Cowes appeared next, where the Isle of Wight presented to our eyes the broad royal park with its carpet of green velvet. Then Southampton. Only twelve hours of ocean separated us from France.

However long that last night of the voyage may have seemed, however uncomfortable had been (indeed dangerous at times) our fifty-five days at sea, all was nevertheless forgotten in the sudden burst of joy that quickened our hearts as we heard the cry "Land!" It was true: *la France,* the country we had sailed from eighteen years ago and now we greet with long and loving gaze. We can only gesture and point, so constrained we are, so hesitant to speak, as our throats catch and we suppress our feelings. Such tears as these are dear ones that leave, together with their counterpart of emotion, their unforgettable seal upon our lives.

EPILOGUE

My resignation.—Ministerial changes.—Death of the king.—Election of Prince William Lunalilo.—Negotiations for annexation.—Preservation of Hawaiian independence.

In November 1869 I wrote to the king requesting him to accept my resignation as minister of foreign affairs. The treaty negotiations with which I had been charged were far from being concluded; my absence, as it became prolonged, imposed added burdens of work and responsibility upon my colleagues in Hawaii; the Hawaiian Legislature was about to reconvene in March of 1870, and the cabinet membership could not remain incomplete any longer. Furthermore, family matters and concern for my health required a protracted European sojourn.

The king replied by offering me a more extended leave, by his own wish allowing me to determine the length of my stay. He added that he hoped I would decide to return to Hawaii, and assured me in the most friendly terms of his desire that I might keep my ministerial portfolio. His trust in me, his unfailing kindness, obliged me not to abuse it. I abided by my resignation, which he finally accepted, with the proviso that I would retain my functions as minister plenipotentiary assigned to various European governments. Mr. Harris was appointed minister of foreign affairs and was replaced as minister of finance by Mr. John Mott-Smith, one of our mutual friends, a member of the House of Representatives, and a gentleman much respected in Honolulu.

These choices were coldly welcomed by the American party. Despite all his energy and undeniable ability, Mr. Harris had been unpopular for years, and his summons to the leading post in the cabinet was not of a sort that would strengthen the ministry. He was unable to hold his office for more than eighteen months, and in 1871 the entire cabinet were obliged to hand over collectively their resignation to the king. Messrs. Harris and Mott-Smith left the ministry; their associates were maintained and Mr. Hutchison, minister of the interior, was called to foreign affairs with the mission of reconstituting the ministry. Mr. Stirling, an Englishman and a capable and much esteemed engineer, was assigned to finance; but, emboldened by success, the opposition did not consider this cabinet shift quite sufficient. While attacking certain individuals, these critics were seeking above all to overturn the constitutional policy inaugurated by the coup d'état of 1864. They were clamoring for the reestablishment of the constitution of 1852, the work of the American missionaries, an organic act that at the appointed time would facilitate the annexation of Hawaii to the United States.

As I earlier indicated, the essential difference between the constitution of 1852 and that of 1864 is this: the former placed no restriction on the right to vote while the latter, by imposing both a residence and a property or income requirement, completely prevented the floating foreign population of Hawaii along with the Chinese laborers recruited by the plantation owners from exercising political influence. The constitution of 1864 has been much criticized in the islands. At this moment, as I write, it is an object of sharp attack. Some of its authors are dead; others are no longer active in public life. Looking back now on the constitution of 1864, after an interval of nine years in which to observe its accomplished results, I remain convinced that we were in the right and that the act of 1864 fully satisfies the principle of legitimate rights. Above all I am certain that its abrogation will shortly lead to the annexation of the Hawaiian Islands to the United States.

I still believe, as I believed on that earlier occasion, that there are no rights without duties, and that for every duty there is a corresponding right. I consider that in political matters the privilege of the franchise depends on the fulfillment of certain social obligations, which are a duty required of those who want their voices to be counted; and that to accord everyone the right of the franchise is to subordinate intelligence to numbers, and to dethrone the first for the benefit of the second.

However that may be, the opposition never would have been able, on this point, to overcome the resistance of the king. They knew it, and yet went on expecting to do so, but without high hopes. An unexpected circumstance occurred which was to furnish them the occasion for attempting to recover power.

Kamehameha V died suddenly on November 11, 1872, the anniversary of his day of birth. He had reached his forty-third year. Strong and vigorous, he had seemed destined to reign for a long while. Like his brother, Kamehameha IV, he was snatched away within a very few hours, without the attention of physicians, who were called in too late to be of assistance. With the king's death the Kamehameha dynasty came to an end; and the danger which I had vainly tried to exorcize was revived at the moment I was least expecting it. The king had written to me several days before his death, but his letter revealed no serious preoccupation with the question of his health.

The throne was vacant. According to the terms of the constitution of

1864, the selection of the new sovereign rested with the two houses of the legislature. The choice was limited to one of the native chiefs, to a member of the *Alii*—in other words, the class of racial stock of the nobles. Four candidates were being singled out on account of their chiefly rank and popularity. Highest in lineage was Prince William Lunalilo, cousin of the late king, aged thirty-nine. A member of the House of Nobles, Prince William, with whom I was well acquainted, was an extraordinarily handsome man. Energetic, intelligent, ambitious, during his youth he had been markedly ungovernable and wild. As heir to a large estate, he was able to indulge in every form of dissipation his impulsive temperament found exhilarating. Because of his sound constitution he had been able to survive his pleasurable excesses, and his health at least did not appear to have been much affected. Very popular among the natives, and also extremely well liked by the foreigners, who found his natural grace and genial character charming, William Lunalilo had only two political hindrances: the record of his past folly and the fear of seeing him succumb to his old scandalous habits.

The sole figure who could rival Lunalilo among the chiefs was David Kalakaua, a young man of noble but lesser rank, worthy of everyone's respect, whose steady conduct and character differed markedly from Prince William's. Less intelligent, and without Lunalilo's vitality and high spirits, David Kalakaua had occupied with some success several political posts in the government, but none of prime importance. He was strongly backed by Mr. Harris, who despite the fall of the ministry nevertheless continued to be one of the most influential men in the islands.

As there is no law excluding women from the succession to the throne, it was possible for Queen Emma to be elected; her unfailing charity and good works, her exemplary life, would have rallied the voters in her favor, if only they had been unaware of her resolve never to marry again. To summon her to the throne would serve merely to postpone, not to settle, the succession question. The same reason ruled out another chieftainess of high rank, Bernice Pauahi, married to an American, Mr. Charles R. Bishop, but Mrs. Bishop was unfortunately childless.

The choice was thus restricted to Prince William and David Kalakaua. The majority of the natives supported the former, whom they considered to be the candidate of highest rank and the one most authorized by hereditary claim. The energetic assistance given David by Mr. Harris weakened his chances, for the unpopularity of the ex-minister was deflected upon the candidacy of Kalakaua.

The cabinet, gathering in session on the day after the death of the king, decided to call a meeting of the two legislative houses on January 8, 1873. On the same day, Prince William, benefiting from skillful followers and their advice, announced his candidacy and invited the voting population to go to the polls and cast their ballots after January 1. Lunalilo's proclamation, printed and circulated in thousands of copies, promised that if he were elected the constitution of 1864 would be annulled, that of 1852 reestablished, and the right to vote would be restored without restriction.

This campaign platform assured the prince the backing and votes of the missionary party; his distinguished rank and his popularity won the approval of the natives. Furthermore, the unorthodox ballot to which he had invited the voters, and which the cabinet sought in no way to impede, gained him so impressive a majority that the legislature, when summoned for its meeting on January 8, proclaimed Prince William Lunalilo as ruler of the Hawaiian Islands. The tally was nearly unanimous, lacking only three votes.

The cabinet again submitted its resignation to the new sovereign, which he accepted, and the ministers all relinquished their posts, with the exception of Mr. Stirling, who was retained as minister of finance.

Three Americans promptly assumed the reins of office: Mr. Charles R. Bishop, a wealthy banker, a member of the House of Nobles, and a cousin by marriage to the king, was appointed minister of foreign affairs; Mr. Edwin O. Hall, allied with the American missionary party, received the portfolio of the interior department; and one of the sons of Mr. G. P. Judd became attorney general. The opposition was restored to the place of power from which it had been excluded since 1854; but however significant the new king's selection of his cabinet members appeared to be, it nevertheless satisfied only half of the proponents of annexation. Messrs Bishop and Hall—prudent, even timid, men—were lacking in the necessary energy to bring about so radical a policy of change. The king himself was in no hurry to part with Hawaiian independence forever and preside over the dissolution of a kingdom of which he was the uncontested head. Consequently, just when communications from Honolulu suggested to the United States government that the moment had finally arrived to open systematic bargaining on the subject of annexation, official Hawaii turned hesitant—and this delaying tactic did not augur well for the success of the American plans.

In fact, a direct offer from the United States to negotiate an annexation treaty had definitely collapsed. This failure was not the fault of the cabinet then in power in Washington. The Hawaiian authorities had themselves proposed to let the negotiations proceed, but with the following understanding. Hawaii would cede to the United States the right to establish a naval base and wharves at the mouth of the Pearl River, sixteen kilometers distant from Honolulu. The United States would be free to erect buildings and necessary shipyards and to station there, in a permanent post, an administrative officer. The lands ceded by Hawaii would become the national property of the United States, be regulated accordingly by the United States, which would possess all sovereign rights of the concession, and also be free from interference by the local Hawaiian authorities. On its own side, the United States government would permit the admission, duty free, of agricultural and industrial products from the Hawaiian Islands into territory of the American union.

These proposals, announced publicly and disseminated by the very vocal press of the two countries, rallied the support of plantation interests and annexationists. These groups met with staunch opposition on the part of the native Hawaiians, however, who suffered no illusions concerning the consequences of such a cession of their heritage, and who fully realized that from the day when the United States would set foot upon the islands the absorption of the kingdom as a whole into the American union would become only a matter of time.

If today the majority of foreigners in Hawaii prove themselves to be self-interested advocates of this prospect, there still remain others who rise above egoistical motives and who, in public meetings and in newspapers and magazines, vigorously do battle with a treaty they denounce as synonymous with the downfall of the Hawaiian race and the destruction of Hawaii's independence.

Among the front rank of these last, I recall with pleasure the name of one of my old friends. A member of the Hawaiian Legislature, of English origin, but very sympathetic toward France, Mr. Godfrey Rhodes* is a wealthy Honolulu merchant and a devoted supporter of the independence of the country where he has resided for thirty years. He acknowledges his gratitude today by placing his influence and the authority of his word at the service of a just and honorable cause.

The question has been posed, but remains as yet unresolved. The indecisive ministry wobbles haphazardly this way and that, desiring and not daring, dragging out its deliberations, avoiding offense to some irreconcilable opinions, yet surely compelled before very long to surrender the Pearl River and estuary either to the proponents of cession or else to its enemies.

---

*From July 1 to November 1, 1884, the *Pacific Commercial Advertiser* published serially a partial translation and running summary of *Quatorze Ans Aux Iles Sandwich*. The anonymous contributor has not been identified, but in my opinion Godfrey Rhodes (1815–1897) comes closest to qualifying. Whether or not he read French is not certain, but several of his sisters are remembered as liking to do so. Furthermore, his dates, his role in Hawaiian politics as a member of the Hawaiian Legislature and the Privy Council from 1867 to 1891, and Varigny's own remarks above are all relevant. Like Varigny he was very distrustful of the probable political consequences of a reciprocity treaty with the United States. In a public address by Rhodes quoted in the *Pacific Commercial Advertiser* of July 5, 1873, he stated: "Reciprocity would benefit three parties, viz.: the owners of sugar plantations numbering from fifty to a hundred individuals; the proprietors of large tracts of land who would make fabulous sums from the enhanced value of real estate; and the United States Government, which, if it once got a footing here, would most assuredly in a short time become the sovereign power of the land, however honest its pretensions might be." [A. L. K.]

I do not need to add that I sympathize profoundly with these last, and that I offer most sincere wishes for their success. Nevertheless, however imminent the annexation of the Hawaiian Islands to the United States may appear to be, it has not occurred thus far, and it will triumph only by overcoming the intense repugnance of those who resist annexation. Annexation was considered a certainty in 1853; it was deemed assured in 1863, then again in 1872. No more do I believe in its promises in 1874; and my greatest regret for having left the islands is not being able to do battle with the annexation movement today, as I did on earlier occasions of the ongoing struggle.

When I returned to France in 1868, one of my friends, whose name is a synonym for searching insight and wit, M. Edmond About, told me one day in the midst of a conversation about my political life in the Hawaiian Islands: "You have fought against annexation of the islands to the United States, but is not annexation after all a matter of destiny? Your constitution of 1864 strikes me as a mere pebble in the path of a locomotive engine." He was correct. The constitution is exactly that; and so there are those who would seek to destroy it. Nevertheless, it still survives, and we have heard of pebbles that derailed locomotives.

P.S. At the moment of sending this manuscript off to the press, I find some dispatches from Honolulu announcing that the ministry are about to withdraw officially the Pearl Harbor treaty project, because of its drafted provision for ceding native Hawaiian lands. The cabinet ministers of the Hawaiian Kingdom, in notifying the United States government of this unanticipated decision, give as their reason the insurmountable obstacle they would face in any attempt to persuade a sufficient number of the legislature to ratify such an act. Following this announcement, the ministers resigned in a body. Annexation, by winding and roundabout roadways indeed, once more has been indefinitely postponed.

Paris, January 20, 1874　　　　　　　　　　　　　　　　　C. DE VARIGNY

A closing note: Within two weeks after Varigny signed and dated both his preface and epilogue, the Hawaiian Kingdom again underwent a succession crisis, when King Lunalilo died in Honolulu on February 3, 1874, after a reign of only thirteen months. That his rule would not be a long one is foreshadowed in Varigny's cautious remarks on the young king's uncertain health, undermined by pulmonary tuberculosis and dangerously aggravated during the last year of his life by his bouts with alcoholism. [A. L. K.]

APPENDIX A

A CHRONOLOGICAL RÉSUMÉ

1829	Charles-Victor Crosnier is born, November 25, at Versailles during the last months of the reign of Charles X, king of France (1824–1830). The boy will later add his mother's *nom à particule* (de Varigny) to that of his father, M. Crosnier, "an employee of the prefecture."
1842–1847[?]	Educated during the reign of Louis-Philippe, Orleanist "king of the French" (1830–1848), at Lycée Bourbon in Paris (later renamed Lycée Bonaparte, finally Condorcet). He is a schoolfellow of notable students and becomes an intimate friend especially of Hippolyte Taine (1828–1893) and Lucien Prévost-Paradol (1829–1870), both of whom (after Condorcet) proceeded to the École Normale Supérieure. Varigny's youthful association with Taine and Prévost-Paradol, along with other prominent *lycéen*s and *normalien*s of their generation, will be renewed after his return from Hawaii to France in 1868.
1848–1850	The July monarchy of Louis-Philippe ends with the February Revolution of 1848 and establishment of the Second Republic, with Louis Napoleon as president. Lack of biographical data concerning Varigny probably reflects his straitened circumstances and general uncertainties. According to family tradition, Varigny had originally hoped for a career in commerce.
1851	He is appointed one of three youthful "directeurs" in charge of escorting an emigrant party ("La Bretonne") to California in the wake of the Gold Rush, a party organized by the Compagnie des Lingots d'Or under sponsorship of the Second Republic. Varigny sails from Le Havre for San Francisco on the *Anna* (November 27, 1851, to June 13, 1852). Meanwhile, in Paris (December 2), Louis Napoleon dissolves the French legislative assembly and assumes plenary powers under the new constitution (January 1852), an act which leads to proclamation of the Second Empire and his confirmation as Napoleon III (November 1, 1852).

1852–1853   In San Francisco, after a shipboard courtship, Varigny marries (August 14) Louise Constantin (1827–1894), the only child of Jean-Isaac Constantin and the late Marie Henriette Pauline Picard (died April 13, 1850). M. Constantin, one-time madder manufacturer in Avignon and Vaucluse, also broker and trader in Naples, Algiers, and Paris, had suffered severe financial losses during the 1840s. He emigrated in hope of a fresh start among French settlers in California. In the autumn of 1852, after brief employment in a San Francisco lawyer's office, Varigny becomes editor and copywriter on the staff of *L'Echo du Pacifique,* owned and directed by Étienne Derbec (b. Dijon, 1817; d. San Francisco, 1897), formerly typesetter in Paris for the *Journal des Débats.* Varigny's connection with *L'Echo* was facilitated by his very cordial relations with Patrice Dillon, French consul in San Francisco. M. Constantin found employment on the business side of the same paper.

1854–1855   Birth of "a stillborn boy," December 4. Varigny resigns from *L'Echo* and decides to return to France with his wife by way of the Far East, leaving her father in San Francisco. The couple sails for the Hawaiian Islands on the clipper-bark *Restless,* January 21, 1855; they arrive at Honolulu on February 18. A son, Henry de Varigny (1855–1934) is born in Honolulu on November 13. Meanwhile, Varigny is employed pro tem at the French consulate to assist Émile Perrin, French commissioner. The Varignys move from Franconi's Globe Hotel to the household of Jules Dudoit (b. Mauritius, 1803; d. Honolulu, 1866), sea captain and earliest French commissioner in the Sandwich Islands.

1855–1868   For Varigny's career as an overseas consular secretary during the Second Empire and as a cabinet minister of the Hawaiian Kingdom, see *Fourteen Years in the Sandwich Islands,* passim. Significant dates, bearing on his public career, family affairs, or vocational identity, are listed below.

1856   He is officially recommended for post of *chancelier;* the appointment is approved in Paris by the minister of foreign affairs on April 5. The Varignys are very friendly with congenial officers of the French brig *Alcibiade* during its six-months' station in Hawaiian waters. Mme de Varigny makes her first appearance at official court festivities on November 28, an anniversary celebrating Hawaiian national independence.

1857   The Varignys move from the Dudoit cottage to a house on Judd Street, corner of Liliha, owned by Dr. T. C. B. Rooke, foster father of Queen Emma. After this move, the Varignys are called upon regularly by Captain Gisolme, commander of the 20-gun frigate *Embuscade.* They see less of the officers of the next naval vessel of the Honolulu station, the corvette *Eurydice,* commanded by the veteran M. Pichon, "a cousin of the Taines." Leading a busy life, Mme de Varigny acts as official hostess at French receptions given by the bachelor consul, M. Perrin. Private friendships flourish, particularly with their new neighbors, Elisha H. Allen (1804–1883) and his much younger second wife (m. 1857). Other households are cordial, especially that of Thomas Brown (1804–1856) and his wife, through whom they meet a large contingent of congenial British residents. Dr. G. P. Judd and family are very close neighbors but "never become intimate."

1858 Early in the year the *Alcibiade* pays a farewell visit en route back to France. The officers are popular, and parties and balls are numerous. The Varignys are able to indulge their fondness for dancing and even learn a new dance, the Lancers, the latest from Europe. Captain de Marigny and his junior, M. Briot, will be visited by the Varignys in France ten years hence. In early summer they receive sad news of the death at Versailles, March 11, of Mme Hélène Crosnier de Varigny, mother of Charles. M. Constantin pays a midsummer visit but is bored by Honolulu and a child-centered household, enjoying only chess and violin and piano duets with Louise. Birth on September 25 of a daughter, Hélène (later Mme André Michel).

1859 Word is received of the death, December 11, 1858, of Léopold Crosnier de Varigny, one of Charles' two living brothers. In mourning and tied down by small children, the Varignys accept no invitations even from officers of the *Eurydice*. Charles explores the Honolulu region on daily horseback rides with Hermann Von Holt (1830–1867), partner in a German import firm and later consul for the Kingdom of Hanover. In spring the entire family makes a first overnight island journey to Kailua, Oahu, staying for a week at the rustic parish house of the Abbé Maréchal.

1860 Birth in Honolulu, June 27, of second daughter, Pauline (later Mme Paul de Franquefort). Mme de Varigny becomes well known in musical circles in Honolulu, and soon becomes acquainted with numerous German residents.

1861 In early summer the Varigny family visits Hilo, accompanied by Hermann Von Holt. The three adults and Henry make an overnight excursion to Kilauea Crater.

1862 Varigny is appointed acting French commissioner after the death (March 29) of Émile Perrin from tetanus poisoning caused by a fracture resulting from a fall off his horse. After the ordeal of settling Perrin's affairs, Varigny decides on an early summer holiday in the northern districts of the island of Hawaii. The Varigny household is accompanied by Alice Brown (1840–1904), daughter of the Thomas Browns, and by Charles' favorite riding companion, Mr. Von Holt. Much of the French consular business is now with German importers of the products of France. The last French whaling vessel is seen in Hawaiian waters.

1863	The Varignys move from their Judd Street house to a larger dwelling built and owned originally by Joe Booth, tavern keeper, "on River Street in the lower [Nuuanu] valley near the bridge." They undertake a three-week family excursion to the island of Kauai. Maxime Desnoyers is appointed Perrin's successor (October 26); Charles de Varigny is praised officially by superiors in Paris for interim management of the consulate. The post of minister of finance of the Hawaiian Kingdom is offered Varigny by Kamehameha V (1830–1872); Varigny is authorized by Drouyn de Lhuys, French minister of foreign affairs, to accept the appointment without loss of French citizenship and rights.
1864	Varigny takes over the office of finance minister (February 18) and is named by Napoleon III Chevalier de la Légion d'Honneur. Before news of French approval reaches Hawaii, Varigny decides that his wife, who is having migraine headaches, should go to San Francisco, visit her aging father, restock her wardrobe, and buy household furnishings appropriate to their new status. She and the children sail on the *Young Hector*, February 14, reaching San Francisco on March 4. The visit achieves its purposes, but mother and children find the change of climate trying. Shortly before their scheduled return to Hawaii, April 25, Mme de Varigny comes down with pneumonia. Both she and Henry then contract measles, but their doctor permits sailing by the *Comet* as planned. Both patients suffer relapses and before the vessel reaches Honolulu, May 13, flying the quarantine flag, Hélène and Pauline and the captain's son contract measles ("Even a poor Kanaka sailor died").
1865	After the death on October 18 of Robert Crichton Wyllie, veteran minister of three Hawaiian reigns, Varigny is named Wyllie's successor as minister of foreign affairs and head of the cabinet.
1867	In early June the Varigny family makes a short stay with the Parkers at Manaiole. Soon afterward they receive word of the death (May 16) in San Francisco of Louise de Varigny's father, M. Constantin. On September 13, Charles de Varigny is commissioned Knight Commander of the Order of Kamehameha, by King Kamehameha V.
1868	Following a "national disaster," volcanic eruptions on Hawaii beginning in March, Varigny reminds Kamehameha V of a long-promised leave of absence. The king grants Varigny's request for permission to visit Europe, negotiate or renegotiate commercial treaties with various governments, rejoin remaining relatives in France, and restore his health. The family embarks (June 2) for San Francisco on the *Montana*, Holladay Line, and continues the voyage home by way of the isthmus and New York. They arrive on the *Germania* at Le Havre on September 22. Next day they journey to Paris. Their first weeks following their return to France are filled with a sequence of reunions in Avignon and Geneva with surviving relatives and girlhood friends of Louise de

Varigny. In November, on Henry de Varigny's thirteenth birthday, his family sadly take leave of him in Geneva, where he passes the school year in the household of a Swiss pastor. The others move on through Switzerland to Germany, where they encounter various Honolulu acquaintants, and visit the Hasslochers in Karlsruhe, who welcome them with warm hospitality. By year's end the family is back in Paris.

1869   Varigny meets with officials of several European governments to correct defects in standing trade treaties and negotiate new ones; little is accomplished in negotiations with major powers. He submits his resignation as minister of foreign affairs, and it is formally accepted by Kamehameha V in autumn of 1870. Meanwhile, Louise de Varigny has been introduced to a circle of Charles' French friends, both old and new. These include most notably, in addition to Taine and Prévost-Paradol, Edmond About and Françisque Sarcey. Varigny is formally presented to the Emperor and Empress on February 7, and to Prince Napoleon and Princess Clotilde on February 12. After Charles' appearance at court, both Varignys are twice invited to the imperial *"lundis"* —receptions at the Tuileries, where Mme de Varigny gets a close view of Louis Napoleon and Eugénie. During the season they are constant theater- and opera-goers. From Easter until autumn they pay visits in Provence, but end the year in Paris.

1870   Varigny leases Paris lodgings for his family (beginning January 3) at 82 Boulevard St. Germain, almost adjacent to Hachette et Cie. Henry de Varigny, after tutoring in Switzerland, is enrolled at the Collège St. Louis in the vicinity of the Panthéon and Sorbonne. After the beginning of the Franco-Prussian War, July 19, followed by military defeats leading to proclamation of the Third Republic, September 4, Varigny leaves Paris for Tours "to place himself at the disposal of the government." He is among the "escort" of Marshal Bazaine in the expedition to Normandy after Bazaine's ignominious defeat at Metz. His wife and daughters find safety in Switzerland and the south of France.

1871   The family is still dispersed; Louise de Varigny is near relatives and friends in Switzerland and Avignon. Varigny's activities are unclear during the period of the Paris Commune (March–May), but his earlier movements in sequence suggest that he accompanied leaders of the Third Republic to Paris during the closing struggles of France's bloody civil war. The family reassembles finally at 82 Boulevard St. Germain. Henry will eventually enroll at the École de Médecine nearby. Varigny becomes an early member of the administrative council of the newly organized École Libre des Sciences Politiques, established soon after France's crushing defeat by Germany. As a friend of Taine, he probably became acquainted with Émile Boutmy, the école's founder and first director, former writer for *La Presse,* intellectual disciple of Taine, and

	professor of his school's course in constitutional history. Varigny becomes active in several of France's proliferating geographical societies.
1872	Varigny publishes a signed article in *Le Temps*, February 12: "Variétés: L'Instruction Publique aux Iles Havai (Sandwich)"; he also publishes a short book, *Dépenses de Deux Guerres: Angleterre, 1793-1815; États-Unis, 1861-1865* (Paris: E. Dentu).
1873	He is launched as a travel writer and author of works of popular geography: *Voyage aux Iles Sandwich (Iles Havai), 1855-1869*, in the famous illustrated travel series *Le Tour du Monde* (Paris and London: Hachette). *Tour du Monde* was under the editorial direction of Édouard Charton (1807-1890), noted popularizer of "universal geography."
1874	*Quatorze Ans aux Iles Sandwich* (Paris: Hachette). Several chapters incorporate revised portions of *Voyage aux Iles Sandwich* in *Tour du Monde*.
1875	*Quattordici Anni alle Isole Sandwich (Isole Havai)* (Milano: Fratelli Treves). This Italian translation of the French edition of 1874 contained copious illustrations showing Hawaiian landscape and genre scenes. These illustrations originally accompanied the text in *Tour du Monde*.
1877	"Kiana: Un Roman de Havai," *Revue des Deux Mondes* (vol. 21, 9th series). Apparently the first of several attempts by Varigny to write adventure stories, drawing on his knowledge of the Hawaiian Islands and their history and recollections of romantic Hawaiian landscape.
1880s	He is listed among "collaborateurs" in the *Grande Encyclopédie* (Paris: H. Lamirault et Cie, 1886-1902); his name first appears in vol. 4, but it is dropped in vol. 26, in the year of his death. Henry de Varigny is also named among many distinguished contributors and is identified as "docteur en médecine et docteur ès sciences naturelles." Henry's marriage to Blanche Meyrue took place in 1880. Varigny publishes, most systematically and notably in *Revue des Deux Mondes*, a series of articles on Oceanic islands and Pacific peoples. A collection of such articles makes up his *L'Océan Pacifique*, listed below.
1888	*L'Océan Pacifique: Les Derniers Cannibales; Iles et Terres Océaniennes; La Race Polynésienne; San Francisco.* (Paris: Hachette).
1889	*L'Océan Pacifique* is selected by the Académie Française for one of several Monthyon awards honoring "works most conducive to the improvement of morals and manners."
1893	Becomes an overseas correspondent on the staff of *Le Temps*. His well sustained, but sometimes intermittent, series of signed contributions, headed mainly "La Vie d'Outremer" (beginning June 28), appears to have been written primarily from New York City and Washington, D.C., or from other centers along the Atlantic seaboard. He publishes

"La Crise Havaienne" in *Revue des Deux Mondes* (vol. 106), the first of several articles on the overthrow of the Hawaiian monarchy and the opening stages of the Hawaiian revolution. During his father's stay in the United States, Henry de Varigny is simultaneously engaged in scientific research at the Smithsonian Institution, Washington, D.C. Henry's monograph, "Air and Life," first published in *Revue des Deux Mondes* (in July 1893) and winner of the Smithsonian's Hodgkin's Prize, is translated and reprinted in the Smithsonian Institution annual report of 1893.

1894 Continuation of "La Vie d'Outremer" in *Le Temps*. He also publishes a second article on the Hawaiian revolution, "La Crise Havaiienne," *Revue des Deux Mondes* (vol. 125). The death at Montmorency, of Louise de Varigny may well explain the three-month gap in "La Vie d'Outremer" extending from April through June.

1895 "La Vie d'Outremer," *Le Temps*, February 27, signed, written aboard a "three-masted bark," the *Anna*, gives Varigny's impressions and reflections after visits ashore at Santiago and Valparaiso. "La Vie d'Outremer," *Le Temps*, May 19, signed, describes Varigny's arrival in Algiers: "Le Kasba d'El Djezaïr," first of a series of thoughtful articles continued after June 25 under the heading "Notes sur L'Algérie." (See especially "Notes sur L'Algérie, Conclusions," August 31.) *Le Temps*, September 23, publishes a special article, signed, "La Crise Hawaienne," on the establishment of the Republic of Hawaii.

1896 "La Vie d'Outremer," *Le Temps*, January 11, signed, discusses British-American nationalistic rivalry in Venezuela. Varigny endorses the interests of an emergent Venezuelan middle class "to whom the future of the country belongs"—neither to the economic power of the British Empire nor to the United States' doctrine of "manifest destiny."

1899 "La Vie d'Outremer," *Le Temps*, September 13, signed, repeats a favorite theme in Varigny's miscellaneous writings of the late 1880s and 1890s: "L'Influence de la femme américaine." Under "Nécrologie," *Le Temps*, November 11, prints a notice of the death of M. C. de Varigny, "notre collaborateur," age seventy. Three days later, on November 14, a brief account of the funeral also appears, as follows: "The funeral of our regretted friend C. de Varigny was conducted yesterday at Montmorency, attended by many people. After services at the funeral home, where the eulogy was delivered by Pastor Hollard, the cortège proceeded to the cemetery. Burial rites were performed by our colleague Henry de Varigny, son of the deceased, and by M. de Varigny's son-in-law, M. André Michel. At the grave side, a representative of the Geographical Society of Algiers bade a last, moving adieu to M. C. de Varigny, who was president of the society."

Louise de Varigny
(Paris, in the 1880s)

APPENDIX B

THE MEMOIRS OF MME CHARLES DE VARIGNY

The reader of *Fourteen Years in the Sandwich Islands* might never guess how much of a family man its author actually was. Undoubtedly his wife shared his views regarding what is suitable in public print and thoroughly *convenable*. Hence his wife's entirely private memoirs provide the only known evidence concerning a side of Varigny's Hawaiian experiences that otherwise would remain wrapped in obscurity. For that reason it has been judged desirable to include the following glimpses of their life in Hawaii as a family, and as viewed from the distaff side.

In the late 1880s, when Louise de Varigny began writing the private reminiscences she called *Mes Souvenirs,* the children for whom she wrote them were adults and she herself was over sixty and a grandmother. In turning to the Sandwich Islands period she hoped to revive and freshen whatever memories Henry, Hélène, and Pauline might still retain of Honolulu, their birthplace. She also desired to amplify their knowledge of persons and events which at the time had been beyond a childish comprehension. But above all she clearly wanted to foster pride in their father's achievements and to record some social and domestic successes of her own.

For the detailed record of their life in Hawaii Mme de Varigny could no longer draw upon the day-to-day style of journal she had begun in 1834, when her mother had literally guided her pen. Many pages of her early memoirs consist of straight transcriptions from this maternally inspired source, but she abandoned all systematic journal keeping on October 23, 1848, sixteen years after the first entry, although there is some evidence that she resumed the practice in 1869. For precise dating of the years in Hawaii her aids to memory were primarily those she mentions elsewhere, such as engagement books and old letters, but she also makes one intriguing reference to another irretrievable family resource: "As I move onwards to the time of our departure [from Honolulu] I realize that I have forgotten to mention many matters, and therefore I especially deplore the destruction of those twelve years of Charles' journals"—an unexplained disaster.

A reader today of Louise de Varigny's account of her girlhood is likely to feel that her true purpose in the entire project was to tell her grown children what it had meant to be Louise Constantin. She wanted to leave them with a frank and honest understanding of their ancestry. She wanted them to know about the scarcely remembered madder industry that founded the family fortune on the maternal side and finally caused great losses to the Picards of Avignon and Vaucluse. She also wanted to record the Huguenot connection of the paternal Constantins and to explain the effect of the Napoleonic wars and the British blockade on the fate of the old ship chandler and boat-owner, grandfather Constantin. Above all she wanted the three children to appreciate not only her own beloved and self-effacing mother, Marie, but to gain also a sympathetic insight into her charming but feckless father. Thus her narrative of the period between her seventh and fifteenth year is largely made up of continuous family journeys from town to town in the South of France and in Italy, followed by an overseas stay in Algeria, interspersed with extended sojourns in such Mediterranean mercantile centers as Marseille and Naples.

Wherever and however they journeyed (it was on foot for the length of the Grande Corniche and at times in the company of smugglers and bandits) her parents never neglected the education of their only child. From them she learned to take note of historic associations and to love especially the beauties of nature. However hard-pressed for funds, the trio never failed to visit most local art galleries, tour famous churches, and take in the important "sights." Along the way they also took care that Louise acquired the local language, and a special effort was made to maintain her musical education.

Not infrequently, in particular when Constantin was away in Algeria, his wife and child were dispatched to relatives in Avignon. As Louise grew older she understood her mother's discomfort in their frequent dependence on others, particularly her more provincial elders. Mme Constantin made new friends among Protestants in Avignon, with far-reaching consequences for her daughter. Having decided that Louise deserved further conventional and systematic schooling, Mme Constantin chose the Pensionnat Anglade In Paris, where both mother and daughter lodged for several years among congenial girls and women and where Louise shone as both a scholar and a performer on the piano.

Early in 1850, after the nearly simultaneous deaths of her mother, her dearest friend, and her favorite teacher, Louise had to make a fateful choice. She chose not to be parted from her father when, after his worst financial disaster, he announced his intention to emigrate to California and the scene of the Gold Rush. Father and daughter set sail from Le Havre for San Francisco aboard the *Anna* on November 27, 1851.

> It was a strange social setting for a girl of my age and education and often during the first doleful weeks I mulled over the arguments my uncles had used to dissuade me from emigrating. I admitted to myself (though I wouldn't for the world have allowed my father to draw this conclusion) that my uncles had not been wrong, and since that time I have never advised anyone to follow my example. However, Providence, which understands how to distill the good from the bad, was preparing the foundation for my life's happiness, even under conditions the least favorable apparently for it to emerge.

In this characteristic fashion Mme de Varigny first alludes to her courtship by the very correct fellow passenger M. de Varigny, who could share her reading on deck ("Michelet, André Chénier, and Lamartine") and gradually divert her from anxious thoughts and deep mourning. On the evening before the *Anna* reached Valparaiso (April 8, 1852), as they watched the phosphorescent sea, Charles de Varigny spoke "the first words that were to determine my future."

Fifteen minutes after their ship docked at San Francisco (June 13, 1852), letters seeking the approval of family and friends were dispatched to France. During the weeks of waiting, as well as later, Louise de Varigny showed great resourcefulness, self-reliance, and native skill in meeting family responsibilities. She demonstrated these attributes even on the day of her marriage (August 12, chosen because it was her parents' anniversary). She wore a wedding costume entirely of her own making and prepared the collation to be served their witnesses and friends. After a civil ceremony at the French Consulate, the religious service using the English Book of Common Prayer was performed in a nearby Methodist Church, and Louise de Varigny could add, "We did not have a Roman Catholic marriage, for Charles had adopted my faith and from that moment henceforth he accompanied me to my church."

EXCERPTS FROM THE MEMOIRS

The Sewing Society: 1855

It was the custom in Honolulu to call upon new arrivals. Curiosity, combined with the sheer emptiness of existence, played as great a part as did kindness in this seemingly gracious and hospitable practice. Everybody acquainted with Mme Dudoit (that is the whole of Honolulu) called on me in turn, and I found myself duly invited to attend the Sewing Society and the Musical Society. These two institutions were at that time the sole organized social gatherings or assemblies. The sewing circle was the largest and the better attended, meeting fortnightly at the house of one of the lady members of the group. It was supposed to do sewing for the poor, and under this pretext it met at two o'clock. Work was interrupted at five in order to partake of a substantial tea, in which sandwiches and cold salads supplied the place of dinner. After tea the feminine chatter began again. Some of the matrons returned home to put their children to bed (who meanwhile had been kept on exhibition in the garden), and the most faithful returned at about seven with their husbands, thus continuing the tea service for the benefit of the latter. At that hour a good many young people arrived, and innocent games were organized or some musical numbers were presented, without previous rehearsal—also without much merit. Because of the missionary preponderance, dancing was under a ban. . . .

The Musical Society: 1855 and 1860

The Musical Society followed the same procedures and had almost the same members as the Sewing Society, but it met only once a month. In it the puritan element was less dominant, which made it possible more often to prolong the party with a few waltzes. There was no lack of lovely voices, and I shall speak later about how much the society improved under really skillful direction. At the time of our arrival they hardly ever ventured any choral singing beyond English and American glees, with above all an abundance of parlor ballads. A duet between a tenor and a soprano was an event. . . .

When Pauline was finally weaned (at the age of three months) . . . I resumed my place in the Musical Society. When the King and Queen founded a public hospital, the Society gave a benefit concert at which I helped raise funds by playing in the Fort Street Church, before an audience that more than filled it for the occasion. . . . At the concert for the hospital, Mr. Barnard and I played the duet from *William Tell* (Osborne and Beriot) and needless to say we aroused warm enthusiasm. Also alone and by heart I played a piece by Goria on themes from Bellini—seventeen pages—and did not pause before the end. Mr. Reiners sang the famous *lied*, "Die Drei Liebschen."

The time was approaching when were to receive some help from important new members, who would greatly change the musical quality of the society. Messrs. Waldau and Hasslocher arrived sometime early in 1862. The first had a wife and child. He played the violin admirably, having been a pupil of Spohr. The second, an Alsatian, formerly in the German army, had a respectable talent at the piano and took over the functions of concert master. He was also assigned to the rank of major for directing the drill-exercises of the minuscule Hawaiian army. Each morning he would command the assault on Punchbowl Hill with a success all the more impressive as no enemy was involved. He quite transformed the Musical Society by organizing for it a regular subscription list and by providing for the remuneration of the musicians, so that since that time everybody took his duties seriously and systematic rehearsals followed a schedule. Everybody who had the faintest claim to any vocal ability was recruited, and the double chorus of men and women was split into three sections.

At a concert in the Fort Street Church the Society performed Haydn's beautiful oratorio "The Creation." . . . Mr. Hasslocher, preferring to act as conductor himself and thus to be of help to the singers, decided to turn over to me the function of rehearsal pianist. One of my most harrowing moments was when the sopranos missed their entrance for one of the choruses. More dead than alive, I exchanged a terrified glance with Mr. Hasslocher, but without a pause repeated my *ritornello* and the singers, with eyes fixed on the baton, managed this time not to miss their cue. The audience took in none of this, but the Society voted me their thanks for not having blundered. . . .

Visit of the Alcibiade: *March–September 1856*

The little garden house at the Dudoits' had become available at this time and turned out to be quite pleasant, although the comfort was relative. . . . The small verandah of the cottage draped with vines served as a living room, while in the rear were quarters for the Kanaka who did Baby's laundry. A bathroom completed our establishment. The verandah salon became useful because we had some fellow-countrymen to welcome. The French government had set up a permanent naval station for ships cruising [Pacific waters], but it lasted for only eighteen or twenty months because of the troubles stirred up by M. Perrin.

The first ship arrived while we were still living at the Dudoits', and a short while before the marriage of Kamehameha IV. It was the brig *Alcibiade* commanded by M. Arthur Marie de Marigny, a fine sailor and a charming gentleman who very quickly became our friend and continued so devotedly until his death in 1887. His first mate, M. Briot, an excellent man and a good companion, also remained our friend until his early death. Dr. Roland and the sub-lieutenants O'Neill, Blanc, Porge, and a little *midshipman,** a

---
*In English. [A. L. K.]

nephew of Baron MacGuckin de Slane, also called on us and little by little these gentlemen fell into the habit of congregating every evening on our verandah for the pure pleasure of conversation, because we had nothing else to offer. However, when we became settled in our own home we regularly served tea.

The King married Dr. Rooke's daughter, Emma, whom we often met at the musical society, and indeed at her own home. On the occasion of the wedding there were balls and parties, but I attended none of them—my small son served me as a reason and pretext for dodging the outlay for dress.

The appointment of Charles to the post of *Chancelier,* announced in Paris on April 5, 1856, finally enabled us to move into a house which Dr. Rooke rented to us . . . in the upper valley, on Judd Street at the corner of Liliha Street. . . . This island-style house included an immense room with windows opening on three sides, the fourth adjoining a smaller bedroom. A large verandah enclosed all three sides; the fourth was remodeled to accommodate a bathroom, a *dressing room,** and a butler's pantry. A kitchen (detached according to the local custom), a native hut, then beyond that a large open space, and cellar or store room beneath the verandah, completed this little *home*† when we settled there with an old lascar as cook and jack-of-all-trades. . . .

Visit of the Embuscade: *February 1857*

After the *Alcibiade,* the *Embuscade,* commanded by M. Ernest Gizolme, took over the Honolulu station. Because of our distance from town, intimate ties were not formed so promptly, but once established our friendship was all the warmer. However, the higher staff were not to be compared with those of the *Alcibiade.* Lieutenant Garnier was a rather unpolished sort, and the junior officers likewise. M. Lapersonne was the pick of the sub-lieutenants and favored by M. Gizolme (whose too early widowed niece he married). Dr. Gelineau, quite a man for the ladies, spent much of his time at Mrs. Henry Rhodes', where his commanding officer also went. The latter did not, however, care to mingle with his staff at the homes he visited. So it was not long before we had him to ourselves, and long evenings of talk from seven until ten or eleven o'clock became the regular thing. The Commander while still aboard ship would take up his telescope and assure himself when the household chores had been completed (we dined on the verandah), and soon thereafter he would join us up the valley.

*In English. [A. L. K.]
†In English. [A. L. K.]

First Island Excursion: Kailua, Oahu, 1859

The sole diversion this year [1859] was my first island journey beyond Honolulu. Charles himself had never passed twenty-four hours at any distance from Honolulu, and I had never even been on the daily horseback rides which had familiarized Charles with the Honolulu region. When Hélène was seven or eight months old, we allowed ourselves a trip to Kailua [Oahu], the part of the island separated from the Honolulu side by the *Pali* precipice. Alice Brown first lent me her horse for several rides so as to give me practice, and finally for this excursion. We were welcomed at the Catholic mission in Kailua by Father Maréchal. Our journey was made thus: Charles with Henry in front of him on a huge Mexican saddle, myself on Agamemnon, a small squat pony who hardly suggested the king of kings, and Hélène in a capacious round basket lined with cushions, slung by a pair of ropes from a pole carried by two Kanakas.

Abbé Maréchal, a very good man, received us in his rustic parish house, with the help of a lay assistant, Brother Paul, a native of Auvergne, who boasted of never having touched a drop of water since he took part in the campaign in Spain under the Duke of Angoulême. The beds were ships' bunks. I placed the baby in the lower berth and myself in the upper. Charles did the same in his cabin with Henry. The fare was plentiful but primitive—no bread, a bit of fried taro or some poi, roasted meat, and bananas. However, this stay of eight days in the country did us much good, for Charles was afflicted with a plague of boils: he had suffered from fifty-six in a period of three months.

I soon became very fond of riding but never had a horse of my own until 1863. Alice was so obliging that I borrowed hers without hesitation. However, about the beginning of 1860, I found it necessary to give up dancing and horseback riding, after feeling the first stirrings of Pauline.

Children's Name-day Celebration

On November 13, 1860, we had our first children's name-day fête. Henry was five, Hélène two years and six months, Pauline a little over four months. We chose this day for her baptism and I prevailed on Mr. Damon, chaplain at the Seamen's Bethel, to perform it. Our first two children had been baptized earlier by Monsignor Maigret, Roman Catholic Bishop of Arathia, with the proviso, however, only that we promise to bring them up as Christians. The excellent bishop was not unpleasant about it, and did not insist upon the oath requiring them to become communicants of the Roman Catholic Church. In any event, I now preferred that Pauline should be consecrated by

Mr. Damon, though it was not a common custom to baptize a child when so young. Indeed, the American sectarian churches let their children become fully grown before imposing baptism on them. It is a fact that they make the children desire baptism by providing them with religious instruction, which begins at a very early age. Mr. Damon nevertheless agreed to baptize Pauline at our house. Henry was deeply fascinated by the short ceremony. The doctor had vaccinated his sister only a little while before, and I believe that this coincidence established in the boy's mind a rather curious connection between the two operations.

Second Island Excursion: Hilo and the Volcano, 1861

To the best of my recollection, it was in 1861* that we made our first extensive trip to the island of Hawaii. We left on the *Kilauea* with our children and the servant Luika, and accompanied by Mr. Von Holt. At Hilo we were kindly received by the Coans, but had a separate cottage where we were able to leave my daughters in the care of Alexandre. Henry, who already had had a little practice at riding, rode along with us on a mule, and managed admirably his thirteen hours in the saddle while on the trip to the volcano. It must be admitted that on the journey home he became so weary that he fell asleep, and for fear of an accident we shifted to riding pillion. The route to the volcano was not an easy one, and there was nothing comfortable about sleeping on dry leaves covered with flea-infested mats.

We ate our provisions and then under our campers' bedding spent a wide-awake night, despite the aid of the regulation *lomi lomi* style of native massage. At dawn we descended into the volcano by a road that was something less than a road—a sort of makeshift ladder fabricated out of the roots of the brushwood, which prevented the ground underfoot from crumbling away. Thus far everything went well, but once arrived in the crater we were confronted by obstacles difficult for Henry and me to surmount. While I was crossing a fissure in the lava, the spot where I placed my foot gave way underneath, and if Charles had not managed to throw his arm around my waist, I should have fallen a good forty or fifty feet into a chaotic heap of lava rock, probably not far from the blazing fire. In any event, I had risked a pair of broken legs.

This fall, avoided so miraculously, unnerved me a bit. I wondered whether the pleasure of viewing the lake of fire, and of taking refuge from the small wave of lava that arose at regular intervals, was really worth endangering the life of a mother of three children and that of the eldest among

---

*Newspaper passenger lists confirm their presence aboard steamer *Kilauea* bound for Hilo, May 13; return to Honolulu from Kona, June 13, 1861. [A. L. K.]

them. I gave up the opportunity to boast that I had reached the edge of the active crater, and left it to the gentlemen alone to explore the antechamber of Pluto—or rather of Pele, some of whose "hair" (fine-spun threads of lava) they brought back with them.

An attractive small red fruit called *ohelo,* the size of a wild cherry, was our delight while returning from the volcano to the shelter-house. The trip back to Hilo went off without a hitch, although mules are decidedly disagreeable animals for riding.

Mr. Von Holt sprained his ankle at Laupahoehoe and was obliged to spend several days off his feet, resting in our cottage at Hilo. Pauline took her first step at ten months in this Hilo garden, and while serving to keep Mr. Von Holt amused she won the surname of Kaupukaea, a native bird with a comical running gait. Hélène was afraid of Mr. Von Holt, however, and very shy in his presence. The poor man did not have a very pleasing countenance. Hélène said, *"He is too big for a darling!"**

On our return to Honolulu from Hawaii, we were disappointed to find that meanwhile our poor cat had died. Henry wept over the loss—his first encounter with death.

Third Island Excursion: Northern Districts of Hawaii, May–June 1862

We left for Hawaii by the *Kilauea* on May 13 [1862], traveling as a family, accompanied by Mr. Von Holt and Alice Brown, whose mother had entrusted Alice to us. Our first stop was at Kawaihae, where a son of Judge Allen, Willie, who has since married a niece of Mr. Bishop, was operating a store and received us at his tourist lodge down on the beach. We had a brief stopover, enjoying the restful *dolce far niente* atmosphere, the magnificent view of Mauna Kea, the glorious climate, the translucent sea which one could enter easily at any moment for bathing or fishing. Once Henry was actually capsized during an ocean canoe race with Mr. Low as his rival, who accompanied us on our later excursion.

For the upland journey to Manaiole, the site of the Parker Ranch, we loaded the baggage and the children into an ox-cart, a most tedious mode of transportation. We completed the first stage of our journey by staying at the home of Frank Spencer, situated in the midst of a great plain which furnishes the islands with beef cattle. It was an extremely primitive spot, and one felt that the owners of the area were not *gentlemanly,*† as were Mr. Allen and Mr. Low, decidedly. A particular stew we had at the Spencer

---

*In English. [A. L. K.]
†In English. [A. L. K.]

establishment was so liberally flavored with pepper that Pauline, to whom meat was not yet permitted, began to cry because of not having her customary dear potatoes to gobble down.

At Manaiole they did very well by us. We had the travelers' lodge entirely to ourselves, and a well-trained steward served us abundant and appetizing meals, from which not a thing was missing except the wine. In fact, we drank milk whenever we felt like doing so, milk so rich in cream that all of us benefited from it. The weather was not hot and consequently the butter did not melt on the table, as it had done at Kawaihae. A kind of cold mist hung over everything throughout the morning, and did not dissipate until the afternoon hours, meanwhile depriving this elevated region of much of its charm by concealing the sweeping scenic views. The woods were nevertheless amazingly beautiful. Henry and his sisters comported themselves like conquerors of an invaded country, lighting fires while we rushed behind to extinguish them.

Charles and Mr. Von Holt, having engaged a famous local guide, Jack Purdy, left us for several days in order to climb Mauna Kea, the main mountain. It was a rugged expedition that took them seventy hours, with several very disagreeable stops, and certainly not without certain physical hazards. But they returned home so enthusiastic that Alice and I conceived the crazy desire to make the ascent ourselves, but by an easier route which from our direction alone was feasible, although we would be the first women to make it. Mr. Low, son-in-law of Mr. Parker our host, offered to escort us. He knew the mountain fully as well as Purdy did, and better still he understood the capacities and needs of our sex. Thanks to him, all situations were anticipated, and we had nothing more dreadful to contend with than the fleas infesting one of the caves. Alas, this grotto of ours had little in common with that of Calypso!

Still one was happy to bed down on the heap of dry leaves with which the hungry traveler had to be contented, near a huge bon-fire for which four trees provided the logs. The care lavished on this blaze, where hot coffee was kept brewing throughout the night, entertained us enormously. At some distance one could hear the howling of Mr. Low's hounds, and an old American—"*Anyways* . . ."—recounted for our benefit some local legends which caused Henry's big eyes to grow even bigger. The boy had all but suffered the fate of Absalom because of a tree-branch projecting dangerously over the road, a barrier he had missed noticing because of his rapture upon riding so fine a horse.

At three o'clock in the morning we made ready to leave at sunrise for the climb to the summit. Despite the difficulty of the route, which became gravelly and precarious after we left the forest, and notwithstanding the altitude when it began to interfere with our breathing, we arrived quite soon at the summit of Mauna Kea. It was an awesome panoramic spectacle, bringing to mind the temptation of Our Lord in the wilderness. We arrived none too soon. After ten o'clock veils of mist creeping along the floor of the valleys gradually began to rise, and we were not in our saddles for an hour before we found ourselves utterly surrounded by cloud banks. Before leaving the summit we had a delicious refreshment, an ice made of currant jelly granulated by the freezing snow. This we washed down with bottles of champagne, accompanied by a toast to our representative countries. We were at an elevation higher than that of Mont Blanc.

Thanks to Mr. Low, who retraced his route downward according to a principle I failed to comprehend, we did not lose our way on our descent but arrived at Manaiole at five o'clock in the evening, without any other mishap than that of being fiercely stared at by a wild bull who was accustomed to staging a fight at this point. Or so we were told. I triumphantly brought back a handkerchief full of snow for my daughters.

This expedition served to put Alice and me in good condition. We also made an excursion to Waipio Valley, a fascinating adventure, and one that did not require us to stay the night, although a thick fog caused us to stray from the route a bit and to return home late. Mrs. John Parker, an excellent lady and wife of the son of our host and the sister-in-law of Mr. Low, looked after Hélène and Pauline during our absence. In addition, we had our own assigned servants. The incident of the little roebuck that trampled Pauline, beating his hooves upon her back as if he were a drummer boy, took place at Manaiole.

Fourth Island Excursion: Kauai, 1863

We moved on April 16, 1863, to this charming residence—Joe Booth's—with a huge garden, bordered by the river, in the lower valley near the bridge. On the ground floor, reached by ten steps, we had a handsome drawing-room with a dining room in a recess, and a German kitchen (an exceptional feature), and on the other side two rooms adjoining with an arch between, which we turned into a garden room and library on occasion, and formal dining room. The large hall which separated these two portions of the house contained the staircase leading to an immense room exposed to the trade wind (where we slept near our daughters in an adjacent room), and also to a second spare bedroom with a small one adjoining, in which Henry slept. The numerous outbuildings, the garden full of magnificent rose bushes, the expanse of lawn, the bank of the stream planted with willows, the large cellars and bathrooms under the spacious veranda, completed the comforts of this *home** where we settled ourselves with pleasure, at first with only one servant, Joe the Portuguese, who replaced the Alexandre couple. Later we had two Chinese. . . .

For me the first months were exhausting, the stairway to climb, and especially the details of managing this very well equipped house, wore me out and increased my migraine headaches to the point when a visit to San Francisco became necessary. However, before making the journey to California we first enjoyed a vacation on Kauai. A French couple, M. and Mme Bourgoing, had arrived in Hawaii from the Isle of Pines (New Caledonia), where they had operated a plantation which had brought them troubles. Charles had been helpful to them, putting them in touch with a Mr. Stapenhorst, a German who owned a sugar plantation on Kauai. M. Bourgoing was now manager of this property and had urged us to spend our vacation with him. In July, after having experienced in June a flood which demolished the bridge near our place in Honolulu, we paid him a visit lasting several weeks. We did not make any large-scale excursions on Kauai, whose picturesque beauty consists chiefly in the vegetation and has generally none of the grandeur characteristic of the scenery of the island of Hawaii. The river, the bathing, the boat rides for gathering lemons, were our distractions. . . . The naughty children set free Mme Bourgoing's rabbits, who was not very sorry, I think, to see us leave. . . .

The absence of schooners between Kauai and Honolulu prevented our returning to Honolulu in time for August 15. This relieved us of the expense of a ball at the time of the Fête Napoléon. It was a good thing, considering the mood we were in for dancing. . . . The Bishop conducted a solemn mass and that was the extent of the celebration.

Fifth Island Excursion: Maui and Haleakala, 1865

On May 29 we left for Lahaina, where the Masons wished to repay us for the hospitality they had enjoyed at our house during the preceding winter. . . . We stayed only a few days in Lahaina with the Masons, whose household arrangements were exceedingly primitive and where we felt we were giving trouble. . . . We set off with Mr. Mason and his sister, a very nice English spinster beneath her starchy English exterior . . . while Henry and the little girls remained behind with a kanaka woman under the protection of Mrs. Mason. The governor of Maui lent me an excellent black horse who had the single fault of being more ambitious than I was. I had not the least inclination to take the lead of the procession but only to avoid a tumble. Luckily everything worked out well. When one travels, one becomes inured and ac-

*In English. [A. L. K.]

customed to danger. I had no falls and I even left behind me a reputation as a woman who *"sticks pretty well to her horse."**

We were welcomed at Makawao by an American, Mr. Armstrong, and by Father Léonor, a Roman Catholic missionary, who had turned priest after a romantic disappointment in his youth. From there we visited several other plantations, and at one house, in the absence of Judge Jones, we were welcomed by the Chinese steward, quite in accord with the hospitable customs of the country. This was by no means the establishment where we were least entertained. The Masons were charming and our conversations left me a delightful memory of this little journey. The climax of our sight-seeing was the ascent of Haleakala—the House of the Sun—the extinct volcano of the island of Maui.

There we found no cave for our protection—hardly any rocks to which we could fasten our blankets and shawls for shelter, and worst of all no trees, but only poor clumps of scrub that provided only some blazes but never an honest fire. In fact we had pushed on to the summit before evening in order not to miss the beauty of the view before it was invaded by clouds, as happened to us on Mauna Kea. Consequently we felt the cold more, even though there was no surrounding snow, and we hardly did anything except to wander about all night gathering anything we could find to keep up our fire. The efficient foresight of Mr. Low was missed. The Masons did not replace him in this respect, although they were so much his social betters. In any event the night passed. . . .

After daybreak, having filled ourselves with coffee, we were able to enjoy the marvelous panorama, perhaps more impressive than the view from the top of Mauna Kea, because Maui, being a smaller island, appeared as a whole at our feet, while Hawaii at a distance was taking on an indescribable grandeur, looking as if it were suspended from the sky. The other islands led the voyaging gaze in the same way, perched as these were well above the familiar horizon. The weather was superb. Our journey as a whole ended exquisitely. After our return to Lahaina, we took several other day-long junkets, on which we were accompanied by the Masons. On one of these expeditions we crossed a single stream seventeen times and I drank of its water every time.

Official Entertaining

At the sale of M. Perrin's effects, Charles bought his piano, a good one, and replaced the spinet on which I had hitherto been playing. We also made a few alterations in the house. The primitive bedroom was joined to the salon

---

*In English. [A. L. K.]

by an archway as entrance, in the American style. This change took place in time for August 15 [1862], when we were obliged to give an evening party.* This was a major social enterprise, especially when one considers the servants I had or rather the servants I lacked. I was on my feet from four o'clock in the morning of the appointed day. My neighbor, Lizzie Richardson, a splendid woman and superb housekeeper, helped me to bake the cakes by working the entire morning, and likewise to prepare the chicken and lobster salads. It was not until later that a German named Horn established the first bakery-confectionery-ice cream shop in Honolulu.

From Miss Montgomery and Mrs. Hillebrand I received tremendous masses of flowers with which I embellished the drawing room. The new entry resembled an *arc de triomphe,* hung with lilies and the red tendrils of Virginia creeper, while flags everywhere completed the decoration. It was a tour de force to give such a party well up Nuuanu Valley, at a spot so difficult of access by carriage, and in a house so very small. In 1861 our predecessor, M. Perrin, had invited seventy persons and sixteen had appeared. We invited seventy and sixty-four accepted and amused themselves until two in the morning. I kept myself on my feet by drinking tea throughout the day, thus bringing on a fierce headache caused by fatigue, and by the sheer worry of making the affair a success.

I realize I have never mentioned an objection I had to Mr. Damon's church, and indeed to all the American sects not Anglo-Catholic. I did not approve of those occasions when Christmas Day fell during the week but was not celebrated until the following Sunday. In their desire to protest against the multiple days of special services with which they reproached the Roman Catholics, the Puritans had uniquely settled on establishing the cult of the Sabbath. I was pained each year to watch Christmas Day pass by in silence, or be observed merely with setting up and decorating the Christmas tree.

By way of recompense, the First of January was a universal festival. In Honolulu, however, particularly after Charles became minister of foreign affairs, I was obliged to follow local custom. From the crack of dawn we kept open house, presenting arms on parade. A table was all laid out with additional decorations in the dining room: galantines, turkeys, fish and mayonnaise, chicken and lobster salads, custard creams, cakes, and fruits. Various wines of course, along with tea and coffee for the teetotalers. From nine in the morning the line of visitors began to form and did not finish until five or

---

*During the Second Empire, August 15 (already identified in the Church calendar with the Feast of the Assumption) became a French national holiday with political and dynastic significance. Known as the Fête Napoléon and honoring the Emperor Napoleon III (Louis-Napoleon), the celebration simultaneously commemorated the birthday of his uncle, Napoleon Bonaparte, and the anniversary of the latter's signing of the Concordat (1801) with the Papacy. [A.L.K.]

six in the afternoon. Gentlemen arrived one by one or in groups of three (in order to take advantage of a single carriage) Various formulas were recited unfailingly. *"Happy New Year!"** or, better still, *"Many happy returns of the day!"** remarked the great number (or the small) of the successive troops of visitors, whether they accepted or refused refreshment, before vanishing after some original observations on the weather, only to reappear in the same fashion in a hundred other houses.

So I met some wives I had never called upon. It was excruciatingly boring, at times worse than boring—particularly the Americans, together with the English who chose to imitate them, by imbibing far too many glasses of sherry. However, our true friends managed to share with us afterward, in our own home, the kind of repast needed by a man who has been paying visits from nine in the morning until seven in the evening.

As a matter of fact I was the innovator at Honolulu who created a taste for filet mignon steak, unknown before our time. We also had preserved foods shipped by order from San Francisco. But one was informed very quickly that such things were too delicious—the potted meats and pâtés were *"too rich."*† Obviously, one could not deviate too far from certain culinary customs. Most of our diplomatic colleagues constituted their menus thus: a fish course; a boiled leg of mutton, with white sauce; a roasted turkey; a roast of beef; a pudding; some cream custards. It was deadly monotonous. . . .

*In English. [A. L. K.]
†In English. [A. L. K,]

INDEX

About, Edmond, 253
Acapulco, 7, 244
Agricultural Society, [Royal] Hawaiian, 192
Agriculture, 100, 105–106, 113, 116–118, 133–134, 171, 198–199, 203–205; as means of regenerating Hawaiian people, 146–147. *See also* Sugar industry
Ahuimanu (Roman Catholic school), 51
Albert Edward Kauikeaouli (Prince of Hawaii), 97, 102
Alcibiade (French naval vessel), junior officers of, 267, 268
Allen, Elisha H. (chief justice), 29, 58, 59, 144, 271
Allen, William F., 132, 209, 271
America, Central, 69
America, North, 5, 6, 7, 8, 46, 54, 67, 147. *See also* United States
America, South, 7, 8
American party, 61, 62, 98, 99, 102, 128, 129, 131, 135, 138, 158, 161, 162–163, 166–167, 195, 196, 203, 248–249. *See also* Annexation party; Missionary party
Americans, 129, 130, 131, 143, 198; as traders, 22–23; rivalry with British, 33; national character of, 34, 45–46, 54, 58, 136, 137, 138, 202–203, 245–246; Americans overseas, 110. *See also* American party
Anglican Church. *See* Missionaries, Anglican
Anna (ship), 265
Annexation of Hawaii by U.S., 49, 53, 59, 65–66, 96, 104; as issue under Kamehameha III, 55–56, 122; under Kamehameha IV, 118, 143; under Kamehameha V, 174, 175, 176, 196, 205, 206–207; under Lunalilo, 249–253.

See also Independence (of Hawaiian Islands)
Annexation party, 104, 143, 200–201, 206–207, 251–253. *See also* American party; Missionary party
Annie Laurie (ship), 107, 108, 109, 112, 121
Anson's map, 14
Armstrong, Goodale, 275
Arrowroot, 7
Artémise (French naval vessel), 52
Asia, 8, 67, 69; as source of labor, 7, 54, 148, 150
Aspinwall (Isthmus of Panama), 245, 246
Assimilation, racial and cultural, 96, 148, 228
Atlantic states, 6, 150, 204
Attorney general, 144, 146, 151, 186. *See also* Harris, C. C.
Au Koa, Ke (Hawaiian language newspaper), 153
Australia, 111

Bachelot, Rev. Alexis, 47, 48, 52
Baja California, 51
Bananas, 9, 16, 86, 112, 269
Barbarism, xxvii, 5, 19, 22, 28, 31, 33, 34, 45, 54, 95–96, 228–229. *See also* Paganism; Society, traditional Hawaiian; Superstition
Barnard, John E., 266
Bass Islands, 227
Bennet, George, 37
Bérenger, Paul (French Consul), 212–213
Bering Straits, 33, 105, 146
Bingham, Rev. Hiram, 39, 44, 45, 46, 47, 48, 50, 51
Bishop, Charles R., 175, 250, 251, 271

Bishop, Mrs. Charles R. (Bernice Pauahi), 250
Blonde (ship), 42, 43
Board of Health, 132
Board of immigration, 150–151, 229. See also Immigration
Board of public instruction, 151, 154, 191. See also Education
Boki (early governor of Oahu), 37, 47, 49, 50, 51
Booth, Joe, 273
Borden, James W., 97
Borneo, 227
Boston, 33, 204, 206
Bourgoing, M. and Mme, 106, 109–112, 122, 274
Bowring, Sir John, 102, 103
Brazil, Emperor of, 42
Brenchley, Julius L., 88–90
Briot, M. (first mate of *Alcibiade*), 267
British Columbia, 88
Brooklyn, 247
Brown, Alice, 269, 271, 272, 273
Brown, Captain J., 239
Bullocks, 23, 82, 86, 89–90, 91, 117, 238, 273
Bureaucracy, 68–69, 172–173
Byng, Hon. Frederick, 42
Byron (George Anson), Lord, 43

Cabinet, Hawaiian, 118, 127, 129, 131, 135, 142–143, 188–189, 194, 195–196, 209, 212, 242–243, 248–249, 250–251, 253; role in constitutional convention of 1864, 168, 169, 174, 177, 178–179, 180–181, 182
Calabashes, 225, 233
California, 6, 7, 105, 147, 150, 200, 204
Canoes, 5, 9, 11, 12, 14, 15, 16, 17, 18, 19, 23, 24, 25, 73, 122, 218, 271
Cape Horn, 7
Capital, problem of, 105, 114–115, 147
Catholics and Catholicism. See Missionaries, Roman Catholic; Roman Catholics
Cattle raising, 7, 9, 23, 94, 105, 214, 216, 226
Ceded lands, 251, 252, 253
Celebes, 227
Ceram, 227
Chants, songs, stories. See Hawaiian language
Charity, 220, 250. See also Hospitality
Charlton, Richard (British Consul), 47, 48, 51, 52
Chiefs, 36, 39, 44, 55, 116, 217, 222. See also Council of chiefs

Children, Hawaiian, 219, 225, 226, 231, 236, 241. See also Education
Chile, 6, 7
China, 7, 23, 28, 147, 156, 227, 245
Chinchas Islands, 150
Christmas Day, 276
Circuit Court, 144–145
Citrons, 113
Civil rights. See Liberty
Civil servants. See Bureaucracy
Civil war (France), x, xii
Civil War (United States), 103, 147, 180–181, 204, 206
Civilization, xvi, xvii, xviii, xxvii–xxviii, 53. 54, 111, 243; as inaugurated by Vancouver's visits, 22; ambiguities of, 45–46, 86, 148, 220; relation to national identity, 57, 65–66, 96; prospective spread through Oceania, 150, 228–229. See also Barbarism; Progress
Climate, Hawaiian, 6, 33, 55, 63, 156
Coan, Rev. Titus, 270
Cochin China, 149
Coconuts (tree and fruit), 4, 6, 9, 16, 18, 71, 219
Coeducation, Hawaii and France compared, 189–190
Coffee growing, 105, 112, 118, 146, 147, 204
Colonialism, 53, 203, 227. See also Assimilation
Common people, Hawaiian, 5–6, 65, 74, 96, 99, 105, 115–116, 118, 133, 139, 149, 187, 199; their obscure preliterate history, 10; their tradition of hospitality, 12, 65, 220, 225; reactions to new laws, 41, 45; foreign influences on, 54; as viewed by annexationists, 56; indigence among, 63, 170; paradoxical vigor of, 86; opposition to Pearl Harbor treaty, 152; attitude toward constitution of 1864, 159; effectiveness as speakers, 169–172; talent for government, 172; instinctive monarchists, 174; attitude toward chiefs, 217; back-country people, 220; elders as spokesmen, 218; imaginative faculties of, 221; tendency to exaggerate, 234; fatalistic attitude of, 235, 241. See also Kanakas
Constitutions, Hawaiian: of 1840, 53; of 1852, 62, 137–138, 157–158, 161–163, 164, 169, 170, 173, 174, 177, 178, 180, 183, 186, 249; of 1864, 131, 133, 134, 137–138, 183, 184, 188–189, 207, 249, 253; constitutional convention (1864), 161–182; Kamehameha V and constitu-

tional reform, 131. *See also* Estates, the three
Cook, Captain James, 3, 8, 10, 11, 14-18, 19, 22
Corsica, 210
Cotton growing, 147, 204
Council of chiefs, 34, 37, 43, 44, 46, 48, 49, 51-52, 54, 55, 57, 116
Cowes, 247
Crab catching, 15
Cuba, 204

Damon, Rev. Samuel C., 269-270, 276
Dancing, 202-203, 266, 269, 274. *See also* *Hula* dancing
Davis, Isaac, 21-22
Davis, Robert G., 165
Diamond Head, 4
Dibble, Rev. Sheldon, xv-xvi
Dillon, Guillaume Patrice (French Consul, San Francisco), 60
Discovery (ship), 14, 15
Discovery of the islands, history of, 8, 10-11
Diseases. *See* Population
District court, 144
Dolphin (U.S. naval vessel), 46
Dowsett, James I., Sr., 162
Du Petit-Thouars, Captain (later Admiral) A., 52
Dudoit, Mme Jules (wife of earliest French consul), 266

Eagle (ship), 37, 38, 42
Earthquakes, 209, 210, 211, 212, 213, 215, 216, 219, 235. *See also* Volcanic eruptions and earthquakes
East Indies, 55, 61, 156
Eastern states, 207. *See also* Atlantic states
Eating tabu, 32
Economic growth, 6, 100, 104-106, 116-117, 133, 146-147, 192-193, 198-199, 203-205, 242-243; early trade under Kamehameha I, 22-23; under Kamehameha III, 55, 62-63; under Kamehameha IV, 65. *See also* Agriculture; Market economy; Sugar industry
Education: aims of first missionaries concerning, xix, 34-36; progress under Kamehameha V, 151-154, 191; responsibilities of parents for, 151, 152, 153; role of local communities in, 151-152; financial management of, 151, 152, 153; separation of church and state, 152-153; private schools, 153, 189-192; preoccupation with religious issues, 154; American compared with French, 190-191. *See also* Public instruction, board of; Punahou School; Schools and schoolhouses; Teachers
Eleanora (ship), 22
Elections and campaigns, 134, 136-137, 159-160, 171-172, 183-184, 198-199
Ellis, Rev. William, xv, 37
Elmira (ship), 42
Embuscade (ship), 268
Emma, Queen (consort of Kamehameha IV): ancestry and upbringing, 22, 64, 102; character, 22, 64, 150; marriage, 22, 64, 102, 268; birth of son, 97; role in Neilson affair, 101; widowhood, 123, 127, 139; travels abroad, 22, 194-195, 202; possible successor to throne, 250
England, 7, 24, 36-37, 42-43, 58, 60, 62, 68, 123, 187, 204, 244, 247; Hawaiian independence recognized by, 23-24; and economic rivalry with U.S., 33; as major exporting country, 136; and "great power," 96, 102-103. *See also* Missionaries, Anglican; Treaties and conventions
English language, 5, 66-67. *See also* Literacy
English residents overseas, 110
Estates, the three (relation between throne, nobles, and commoners), 157, 159, 170, 177, 180, 182, 183, 184; rights of the people, 173. *See also* Monarchy; Republicanism
Europe and Europeans, 5, 7, 11, 22-23, 28, 37, 45, 46, 67, 68, 148, 150, 243, 244, 246

Fair American (ship), 22
Famine in South Pacific, 148, 229
Fête Napoléon, 274, 276
Feudalism, 131, 137
Fiji Islands, 228
Fishing, 9, 15, 19, 27, 105. *See also* Whalers and whaling industry
Flax growing, 204
Foreigners, 21, 22, 23, 28, 31, 33, 41, 47, 49, 66, 118, 133, 187, 188, 189, 202; antagonism toward early missionaries, 34-35
Forestry, 27, 171. *See also* Sandalwood
Fornication, 116
Fort Street Church, 266, 267
France, 58, 59-60, 62, 63, 65, 96, 97-100, 103-104, 130-131, 137, 181, 187, 192, 200, 203, 246, 247; under First Empire, 24; under Second Republic, 58; gun-boat

diplomacy in Oceania, 52-53, 56, 68-69; qualifications of French consular officials, 67-69; political parties in, 159; bureacracy in, 172-173. *See also* Treaties and conventions
Franchise, 131, 133, 134, 137-138, 249; as issue in constitutional convention (1864), 169-171, 173-179
Franco-Prussian War, x, xi, xii, xiii
French language, 66-67
French naval station at Honolulu, 267
French residents overseas, 66, 68, 110-112

Gaetano, Don Juan, 8, 10
Garnier, Lieutenant, 268
Gelineau, Dr., 268
Geological origins of Hawaiian Islands, 8-9
George III (King of England), 24
George IV (King of England), 37, 43, 44
German kitchen, 273
German language, 67
Germans overseas, 66, 111, 245, 267, 274, 276
Germany, 66, 68, 111, 194, 204, 214, 245
Gizolme, Commander Ernest, 268
Goats, wild, 9, 214
Gold Rush, 6, 100, 265
Golden Gate, 244
Government, Hawaiian. *See* Legislature, Hawaiian; Cabinet, Hawaiian; etc.
Grass houses, 5, 9, 16, 71, 72, 76, 218, 220, 225, 236
Greeley, Horace, 181
Green, J. P., 163
Gregg, David L., 97, 98, 102
Gulick, Rev. Orramel H., 163, 165

Hachette and Company, ix, xi, xiii, xx-xxi
Haena caves (Kauai), 120-121
Haleakala (Maui), 9, 92-93, 275
Halemakule (a guide), 81-82, 83, 85, 86, 87
Hall, E. O., 251
Hamakua (island of Hawaii), 82
Hamburg Line, 247
Hanalei River and Falls (Kauai), 113, 119-120
Hanalei Valley (Kauai), 106, 113, 115, 116-121
Haole, 105. *See also* Foreigners
Harris, C. C., 129, 130, 137-138, 146, 164, 165, 166, 168, 169, 173, 175, 176, 178, 179, 186, 197, 204, 205, 248
Hasslocher, Eugene, 266-267
Hau tree, 9, 17, 71, 115
Havana, 246

Hawaii, island of, 8, 9, 13, 14, 19, 20, 21; governor of, 22, 213, 217; excursions of Varignys to, 69, 70-96, 270-273; earthquakes and volcanic eruption on, 209-240
Hawaiian Gazette, xii, 141
Hawaiian language: in traditional song and narrative, 10-11, 13-18, 38, 86, 87; primitive affiliations of, 35-36; as written system, 36; newspapers, 153-154; in political discourse, 169-172; tendency to exaggeration, 234. *See also* Literacy
Hawaiian Reformed Catholic Church, 159. *See also* Missionaries, Anglican
Heiau (ancient place of worship), 94, 95-96
Heilbroner, Robert L., *The Great Ascent: The Struggle for Economic Development in Our Time,* quoted, xx
Hervey Islands, 228
Hillebrand, Dr. William, 192
Hillebrand, Mrs. William, 276
Hilo, 20, 21, 24, 74, 77, 78, 80-81, 184, 209, 210, 211, 212, 213, 219-221, 222, 270, 271
Honaunau (island of Hawaii), 15
Hong Kong, 28
Honoipo (island of Hawaii), 73, 94
Honolulu, 4-6, 38, 54, 72, 107, 109, 184, 212, 213, 214, 239, 240-241, 242, 243; harbor and maritime facilities, 4-5, 6, 7, 10, 27, 66, 193; and "free city," 45, 92; popular demonstrations in, 99; customs receipts (1863), 146; stronghold of missionary party, 198; popular naval station, 202; a colonial-style society, 202-203
Hopkins, Charles G., 132, 146, 154, 165-166, 169, 174, 175, 176, 178, 194, 195
Hopkins, Manley, xv, 132
Horn's confectionary, 276
Horses, 5, 82, 83, 114, 230-231, 238, 269, 270, 274, 275
Hospitality, 12, 65, 202, 220-221
Hualalai. *See* Mauna Hualalai
Hula dancing, 116
Humanitarianism, xxviii, 36
Humehume, 38, 39
Hutchison, F. W., 195, 212, 248

Iao (stream on Maui), 20
Immigration, 148, 150-151, 155, 184; advantages and disadvantages of, 174-175, 227; board of, 192. *See also* Labor supply
Independence (of Hawaiian Islands), 143, 148-149, 184-185, 198, 199, 200, 205, 249, 251-253; recognized by France and

Great Britain, 24; object of tripartite treaty, 59–60, 102–103; anniversary celebration, 123; reciprocity with U.S. as threat to, 205, 206; and Pearl Harbor treaty, 251–253. *See also* Annexation of Hawaii to U.S.
India, 7, 150, 192, 204, 245
Indians, American, 13
Indians, South American, 245
Indigo, wild, 94
International treaty. *See* Treaties and conventions
Irish overseas, 111, 245
Iron, 16, 21, 23
Isle of Wight, 247
Italian language, 67
Italy, 4, 194

Japan, 6, 117, 134, 168, 169, 192, 227
Jarves, James Jackson, xv, xvi, xvii; his *Kiana* cited, 10
Jones, William Ap, Judge (police magistrate), 275
Judd, Albert F., 251
Judd, Dr. Gerrit P.: resigns from mission to serve government, 53; character, 54, 55, 58; relations with Wyllie and fall from power, 59; role in constitutional convention (1864), 163, 165, 168; death, 53
Judicial system, 144, 164–165
Justices of the peace (police magistrates), 151

Kaahumanu, Queen and Regent: regency of, 29, 30–32, 34–35, 37, 38–42, 43, 44, 46, 48–50; appearance and character, 30, 39–40, 41; urges breaking the tabu, 31–32; puts down rebellions, 32–33, 38–39; welcomes American missionaries, 34–35; "Semiramis of the Pacific," 39; her conversion, 40–41; her coercive edicts, 44–45, 116; opposes Roman Catholic missionaries, 48–50; death, 51
Kaalualu (island of Hawaii), 231
Kaeo (last ruling chief of Kauai), 24, 25
Kaeo, Albert, 121–122
Kaeo, Jane Lahilahi Young, 121
Kahaulala (island of Hawaii), 235, 236, 237, 239, 240
Kahekili (last ruling chief of Maui), 20
Kaiana, 20
Kaikilani (legendary chiefess), 13–14
Kailii [Kūkāilimoku], 15, 16
Kailua (island of Hawaii), 19, 27, 34, 240
Kailua (Oahu), 269, 271–272
Kalae Point (island of Hawaii), 240

Kalaieha (island of Hawaii), 90–91
Kalaimano (chief of Kealakekua), 15–18
Kalaimoku, 31, 38, 39, 40–41
Kalakaua, David (later King Kalakaua), 250
Kalama, Queen, 121
Kalaniopuu, 19
Kalepolepo (Maui), 71–72
Kamamalu, Queen, 37–38, 42–43
Kamehameha I, 14, 34, 57, 64, 87, 210; as "Napoleon of the islands," 7; a "new Alexander," 28; a "new Attila," 31; his hereditary lands, 19–21; military skill, 19–21, 24–25, 122; naval forces, 25; battle of Nuuanu Valley, 24–25; and relations with Vancouver, 22–24; relations with Kaumualii, 25–27, 38; consolidates archipelago, 27; character and leadership of, 23, 27–28, 122; kindness to foreigners, 21–22, 23; interest in Christianity, 24, 28, 34, 102; vision of hegemony over Oceanic peoples, 28–29, 148; death and dynastic succession of, 29
Kamehameha II (Liholiho), 34, 35, 37, 38, 44; succession as king, 29; character of, 30, 31, 32, 35; wives of, 36; breaks the tabu, 63–64; temperate with rebels, 33; mission to England with Queen Kamamalu, 37–38, 42; death in London, 42–43
Kamehameha III (Kauikeaouli), 7, 37, 43, 44, 49, 51, 52, 56, 57, 58, 59, 121, 159–160, 178, 189; character of, 49, 51, 55, 56; approves constitutions (1840, 1852), 53, 54, 137, 158, 173, 177, 180; attitude toward annexation by U.S., 55–56; death, 56
Kamehameha IV (Alexander Liholiho), 22, 59, 60, 61–62, 97–98, 99, 118, 129, 132, 138, 142, 178, 194, 195, 200; appearance and character, 57–58, 61–62, 63, 64, 100–102; travels in United States, England, France, 58; succession as king, 57, 59; marriage and family life, 64, 65, 101; birth of heir, 97; dissatisfaction with constitution of 1852, 62; advocates tripartite treaty, 59; the scandalous Neilson affair, 100–102; his Anglicanism, 102; chronic ill health, 64, 101, 102; death and funeral, 123, 127, 139, 249
Kamehameha V (Lot Kamehameha), ix, x, xi, xix, xxii, xxiii, 8, 64, 65, 98, 143, 151, 159, 160, 162, 170, 178, 188, 195–196, 199, 203, 205, 207, 217, 226–227, 230, 234, 235, 236, 239–240, 241; a youthful swimming exploit, 222; travels in United States, England, France, 58; character, 58, 139–140, 175–176,

184; compared with Kamehameha III and Kamehameha IV, 178; identifies with Kamehameha I, 29; his "liberal" conservatism, 128, 131; and Anglicanism, 159; advised by Varigny to marry, 199–200; appoints cabinet (1863), 128–129, 131; ideas and policies, 128, 137–138, 148–151, 164, 177–178, 184–185, 187, 205; vision of union of Oceanic peoples, 148–151, 227–229; concern with constitutional reform (1864), 131, 133, 134, 136, 137–138; views on education, 151, 154, 192; role in constitutional convention (1864), 157, 161–182 *passim;* views on franchise, 131, 137, 173–174, 175; abrogates constitution of 1852, 177; proclaims constitution of 1864, 182; mission to volcanic disaster, 209–218 *passim;* sudden death, 249. See also Constitutions, Hawaiian
Kamehameha dynasty, 7, 21–22, 24, 25, 26, 29, 59, 97, 102–103, 184–185; beginning of, 27; end of, 249
Kamohoalii (a god), 13
Kanakas, 7, 12–13, 17, 18, 21, 22, 31, 35, 41, 44–45, 73, 84–85, 88, 95, 110, 118, 119, 149, 153, 169–170, 214, 222, 224, 225, 226, 230, 234, 236, 237, 239, 240, 267, 269, 274; meaning of, 11; as guides, 74, 77, 78, 79–80, 81–82, 83, 84–85, 120, 221, 232, 234, 235, 236–238, 239. See also Common people, Hawaiian
Kanana (volcano guide), 80
Kanea, 122
Kanehekili (a god), 13
Kapapala (island of Hawaii), 214
Kapoho (island of Hawaii), 224
Kapu system. See Society, traditional Hawaiian
Kapupua, 15
Kau (island of Hawaii), 19, 20, 21, 211, 214, 215, 216, 220, 241
Kauai Island, 10, 14, 25–27, 38–39, 106, 107–123, 160
Kauikeaouli. See Kamehameha III
Kaumualii, 25–27, 38, 122
Kaupukaea (native bird), 271
Kauwahi, J. W. H., 169–172
Kawaihae (island of Hawaii), 31, 35, 72, 73, 81, 82, 94, 95, 209, 210–211
Kealakekua (island of Hawaii), 13, 14, 18, 240
Keauhou (island of Hawaii), 224, 227, 229, 230
Keeaumoku, 21

Keei (island of Hawaii), 19
Keelikolani, Princess Ruth (governor of island of Hawaii), 22
Kekuanaoa, 32–33, 37, 43, 49, 57, 64, 123, 127, 138, 151, 154, 176
Kenway, George, 85–86
Keoua, 20, 21
Kepaniwai (Maui), 20
Keuakepo (a god), 13
Kilauea (volcano and crater), 8, 69, 70, 71, 74, 75–80, 209–210, 270–271
Kilauea (interisland steamer), 212, 213, 227, 240, 241, 270, 271
Kinau, 52, 57
Kiwalao, 19–20
Koa (tree and wood), 87, 91, 139, 150
Kohala (island of Hawaii), 73, 93, 220
Koloa (Kauai), 107, 109, 110
Kona (island of Hawaii), 19, 20, 21, 211
Kuakini, 50
Kuamoo (island of Hawaii), battle of, 32, 87
Kuhina Nui (chiefly office), 29, 138, 168
Kūkāilimoku (god of war), 15n
Kukui (tree and nut), 71, 91, 115, 120
Kuokoa ("The Independent," newspaper), 153
Kupa and his attributed account of death of Captain Cook, 15–18

Labor supply, 105, 147, 169, 171, 184, 192, 199, 201, 203; and need for field labor, 134; China as source of, 134, 169, 184; Japan, 134; Asia, 148, 150; Oceania, 148; immigration bill to provide, 184. See also Immigration
Lackawanna (U.S. naval vessel), 205–207
Lahaina (Maui), 43, 45, 71, 171, 184, 189, 213, 274–275
Lahainaluna Seminary, 153, 189
Lapersonne, M. (sublieutenant on *Embuscade*), 268
Laplace, Captain C. P. T., 52
Laumaia (island of Hawaii), 85–86
Laupahoehoe (island of Hawaii), 85, 271
La Valette, Charles-Jean, Marquis de, 103
Lava, 113, 237–238
Ledyard, John, 14
Lee, William L., 59, 62, 63, 65
Legion of Honor, ix, xxiii, 145
Legislature, Hawaiian, 61–62, 151, 163, 227, 241, 248, 252; powers and procedures of, 162–163, 243. See also Nobles, House of; Representatives, House of

Lemons, 112, 113, 274
Leo XII (Pope), 47, 51
Léonor, Father, 275
Lhuys, Drouyn de, 145
Liberty, 137, 151, 152–154, 158–160, 170–174, 177, 187–188, 197, 202
Liholiho. *See* Kamehameha II
Liliha, 37, 50
Liquor law, 187–188
Literacy, xxvii–xxviii, 151, 153–154; requirement for voting privilege, 170
Liverpool, 88
Lizard Point, 247
Local color, 5, 11
London Missionary Society, 37
Lono (a god), 13–18
Lot Kamehameha (Prince). *See* Kamehameha V
Louis-Napoleon. *See* Napoleon III
Louis-Philippe, 149
Louisiana, 204
Low, John S., 271, 272, 273, 275
Lunalilo, William Charles (Prince and King), 250, 253
Lyon, 4

Macassar, 227
Machinery, sugar mill, steam operated, 147; burdensome tarrifs on, 203
Mackau, Ange-Réné Armand, Baron de, 61
McCook, General Edward M., 204, 205
Maigret, Rev. (later Bishop), Louis Désiré, 52, 212, 269, 274
Makawao (Maui), 170, 171, 275
Malaysia, 36–37, 227
Malo, David, xv
Manaiole (island of Hawaii), 85, 86, 91, 93, 271, 272, 273
Manienie grass, 214
Manila, 192
Manuala (island of Hawaii), 217
Manzanillo, 7, 244
Marai (sacred place), 17
Marcy, William L., 63
Maréchal, Father Joachim, 269
Marigny, Arthur Marie de (Commander of the *Alcibiade*), 267
Market economy, 6–7, 145, 146–147, 171, 193, 199, 200–201, 203–204, 220–221
Marquesas, 228
Marseille, 4
Mason, Rev. George, and family, 274–275
Massachusetts, 54
Maui Island, 9, 20, 21, 24, 25, 39, 71–72, 93, 113, 160, 213, 243–244, 274, 275

Mauna Hualalai (island of Hawaii), 9, 72, 73, 90, 210
Mauna Kea (island of Hawaii), 9, 72, 73, 89, 90, 94, 210, 232, 271, 272, 273, 275
Mauna Loa (island of Hawaii), 70–71, 72, 73, 75, 77, 89, 90, 93, 94, 209, 210, 219, 232, 240
Metcalfe, Captain Simon, 21
Methodism, 102
Metropolitan Hotel (San Francisco), 244
Mexican saddle, 83, 269
Mexican War, 69
Mexico, 55, 244
Micronesia, 149
Minister of the Interior, 148, 151, 195, 212, 219. *See also* Harris, C. C.
Missionaries, American Protestant, xx, xxi, xxiii, 24, 43, 44, 57, 115–116, 118, 154, 189, 266, 270, 276; aims and achievements, 33–36, 37, 47; move into government, 53, 115; relations with Kaahumanu, 41, 44–45; influence on government, 45, 47, 55–56, 136–137, 183; rivalry with Roman Catholic missionaries, 47–51, 56; engaged in theological controversy, 154, 160
Missionaries, Anglican: requested by Kamehameha I from England, 23–24, 28, 37; branch of Church of England proposed by Kamehameha IV, 24, 102, 159; engaged in theological controversy, 154
Missionaries, Roman Catholic, 47–50, 149; expulsion from kingdom and return, 51–53; engaged in theological controversy, 154. *See also* Bachelot, Rev. Alexis; Maigret, Louis Désiré, Bishop; Walsh, Rev. Robert A.
Missionary party, 59, 118, 129, 136, 160, 183–184, 186–187, 188–189, 197, 198, 203, 206, 251; denies legal authority of constitutional convention (1864), 157–159, 162–163, 164–165, 170, 173–174, 175–178, 180–182; incapable of using force, 178–179, 180–181. *See also* American party; Annexation party
Missouri, 88
Mokualii, 16
Mokuaweoweo (island of Hawaii), 209
Molokai, 25
Monarchy, Kamehameha V's concept of, 128, 173–174, 176. *See also* Republicanism
Monsarrat, Marcus, 64
Mont Blanc, 72, 273
Montana (ship), 243

Monterey, 15
Montgomery, Miss, 276
Mookini Heiau (island of Hawaii), 95n
Mott-Smith, John, 248
Mulberry groves, 117–118
Mules, 74, 75, 76, 270
Mumuku (a strong wind), 94–95
Musical Society, The, 266–267, 268
Musset, Alfred de, 71

Napoleon III, ix, x, xi, xxiii, 58, 61, 276
Nation, concept of Hawaiian, xvi, xviii–xix, 53, 54–55, 65–66, 102–103, 117, 159, 171, 173–174, 180–181, 203
Naturalization laws, 134, 137. *See also* Franchise
Navigator Islands, 227
Negroes, 58
Neilson, Henry A., 100–101
New Bedford, 33
New Caledonia, 111, 274
New Guinea, 227
New England, 33, 34
New Haven, 33
New Hebrides, 149, 227
New Year's Day, 276–277
New York, 150
New York City, 33, 204, 244, 246, 247
New York Tribune, 181
Newfoundland Banks, 247
Newspapers, xii, xxi–xxiii, 140–141, 153–154, 186–187, 197, 252; and freedom of the press, 137, 154, 181–182. *See also* Literacy
Nobles, House of, 61–62, 134, 160, 161, 162, 164, 165, 183, 229, 251. *See also* Legislature, Hawaiian
Normal School, 189
North Carolina, 147
North German Confederation, x
Northwest Passage, 33
Nuuanu Valley (Oahu), 24–25, 268, 276

Oahu, 3, 4, 10, 20, 39, 70, 107, 108, 160, 189, 213, 243–244, 269
Ocean Queen (ship), 244
Oceania, xxvii, xxviii, 24, 37, 67, 69, 72, 112, 227
Ohelo (berry), 86, 90, 271
Okhotsk, Sea of, 33, 105, 146
Oral tradition, Hawaiian, 10–11, 13–14, 15–18, 21
Oranges and orange trees, 9, 16, 71, 112, 113, 115, 204
Order of Kamehameha, ix, xxiii, 29

Oregon, 200, 204
Osborne Hotel (London), 42
Oxen and oxcarts, 5, 271

Pacific Basin, 156
Pacific Coast, 204, 207
Pacific Commercial Advertiser, xxi–xxii, xxiii, 180–182, 183, 186
Pacific Ocean, 7, 8, 46, 193
Pacific railway, 150, 244
Paganism, xxvii, 12–13, 31, 40, 41, 42, 52–53, 71, 78, 116. *See also* Society, traditional Hawaiian
Panama, 7, 150, 244–246
Pandanus tree, 90, 91, 110
Paper money bill, 201
Paris, ix, xi, xii, xvii, xxi, 61, 68–69, 97, 99, 104, 122, 132, 243, 264
Parker, John Palmer, 35, 86–87
Parker, Mrs. John Palmer (2d), 273
Parker Ranch, 271
Paul, Brother, 269
Paulet, Lord George, xvi
Pearl Harbor, 251–253
Pele (volcano goddess), 13, 16, 17, 42, 48, 71, 78, 79, 80, 216–217, 230, 235, 236
Pennsylvania, 146
Percival, Lieutenant John, 46
Pereire (ship), 247
Perrin, Émile (French Consul), 59–61, 97, 98, 99, 100, 103, 104, 130, 267, 275, 276
Peru, 6, 7
Philippine Islands, 8
Phillips, Stephen H., 243
Pili grass, 113–114
Plantations. *See* Agriculture; Sugar industry
Police magistrates, 144, 151
Political parties, 136–137, 143, 159–160. *See also* Elections and campaigns; American party; Annexation party; Missionary party
Pololu (island of Hawaii), 95
Polynesia, 149
Polynesian (government newspaper), 132, 135, 140–141
Pomare, Queen, 36
Population, xvi–xvii; Cook's estimate of, 11; decrease of, 65, 86, 214, 227, 228; effects of venereal desease on, 30–31; and whaling hardships, 83–84; and small pox, 58–59; and liquor consumption, 187–188. *See also* Immigration
Portsmouth (England), 42, 43
Portuguese sailors, 48

Potatoes, 6
Pouzot, Father, 219–220
Primitive peoples, 148
Prince of Hawaii. *See* Albert Edward Kauikeaouli
Prince Regent (ship), 37
Princeville plantation, 119. *See also* Wyllie, Robert Crichton
Printing press, 36
Privy council, 98, 130, 142, 143, 151, 182
Progress, xxvii–xxviii, 65, 115–116, 128, 146, 148, 157–158. *See also* Civilization; Economic growth
Prophets, Hawaiian, 216, 230, 234–235, 236
Protectorate status, 24, 56, 149
Providence, xvi–xvii, 64, 180
Public instruction, board of, 151, 184, 185, 189, 191, 201; duties of superintendent, 151–152. *See also* Education
Pulu (fiber of tree fern), 82
Puna (island of Hawaii), 170, 241
Punahou School, 189–192
Punaluu (island of Hawaii), 227, 229, 230, 231, 234, 235, 236
Punchbowl Hill (Oahu), 241, 267
Purdy, Jack, 88–94, 272
Puuapa (island of Hawaii), 95, 96. *See* Pu'u Apa'apa'a
Pu'u Apa'apa'a (island of Hawaii), 95n
Pu'u Kohola (island of Hawaii), 95

Queen's Hospital, 64, 266

Raiatea, 149
Rainbow Falls (island of Hawaii), 221–222
Ranunculi (a plant), 92
Raratonga, 228
Reiners, Gustav, 266
Representatives, House of, 61–62, 134, 160, 161, 162, 183, 198, 229. *See also* Legislature, Hawaiian
Republicanism, 54, 58, 131, 134, 137–138, 174–175. *See also* Monarchy
Resolution (ship), 14–18
Restless (ship), 3, 4, 5
Revolution, political (in Hawaii), 180–181
Reynolds, Captain William, 205–207
Rhodes, Godfrey, xxi, 252
Rhodes, Mrs. Henry, 268
Rice growing, 147, 203–204
Rio de Janeiro, 42, 43
Roads and transport, 106, 132, 172, 192–193. *See also* Honolulu, harbor and maritime facilities

Robertson, George M., 98, 129, 130, 131, 136, 143–144, 145, 176
Roman Catholics, 213, 220, 265, 269–270, 275, 276. *See also* Missionaries, Roman Catholic
Rooke, Emma. *See* Emma, Queen
Rooke, Dr. T. C. B., 64, 268
[Royal] Hawaiian Agricultural Society, 192
Royal Mausoleum, 139, 195
Russia, 67, 68

Sacramento Valley, 6
Sailors, 21, 27 and *passim;* versus missionaries, 45–46
Saint Louis (Missouri), 88
San Francisco, 3, 5, 6, 134, 147, 207, 215, 242, 243, 244, 265, 274, 277
San Francisco, island of, 14
Sandalwood, 22–23, 27, 28, 33, 50, 233
San Joaquin Valley, 6
San Pedro, 51
Schools and schoolhouses: construction of, 151; primary and secondary, 153, 189; inspection by local committees, 151–152. *See also* Ahuimanu; Lahaina Seminary; Punahou School
Schooners, 3, 21, 25, 38, 101, 106–107
Seamen's Bethel, 269
Sebastapol, 76
Separation of church and state, 152, 183
Sewing Society, The, 265–266
Shark-gods, 13
Sheep, 87, 226
Shipping activities, 193, 242–243. *See also* Honolulu, harbor and maritime facilities; Roads and transport
Sierra Nevada, 6
Silkworm culture, 117–118
Silversword, 92
Slaves and slavery, 11, 134, 180
Society, traditional Hawaiian (pre-contact period and transition), 11–13; belief in many gods, 13, 221–222; the kapu system, 11, 31–32; rival chiefdoms and endemic warfare, 11–12, 20–21, 24–27, 38–39, 148; human sacrifice, 11, 13, 39, 95–96; hula cult, 116; Oceanic societies compared, 148, 228–229. *See also* Barbarism; Paganism; Superstition
Society Islands, 228. *See also* Tahiti
South Carolina, 147
South Pacific, 148
South Seas, 229
Southampton, 247
Southeast Asia, 35–36

Southern states, 147, 207
Spain, early Spanish navigators, 7, 8, 10
Spanish language, 60, 67
Spanish sailors, 48
Spencer, Frank (rancher), 94, 271
Spencer, Thomas (merchant), 213, 216
Stackpole, Charles, 215
Stapenhorst, Florens, 274
Staten Island, 247
Steam navigation company, 242–243
Stirling, Robert, 248–249
Strawberries, 92
Sugarcane, 7, 193
Sugar industry, 106, 133, 134, 147–148, 193, 198–199, 200, 203, 204–205, 252; need for irrigation, 106; need for transport and markets, 106, 193, 242; future on Kauai, 114–115, 119; sugar interests and constitutional convention (1864), 169. *See also* Agriculture; Economic growth; Immigration
Sumatra, 228
Sumner, William, 207
Superstition, 10–11, 12–13, 20, 121, 216–217, 221–222, 230, 234–235, 236. *See also* Paganism; Society, traditional Hawaiian
Supreme court, 144, 164, 165. *See also* Judicial system
Sweet potatoes, 91
Swimming and diving, 15, 77, 222, 224, 271
Synge, W. W. Follett, 135

Tahiti, 28, 36, 111, 114, 149, 228; as symbol of French power in Oceania, 37, 53–56
Taine, Hippolyte, 87
Taro and poi, 7, 15, 81, 86, 105, 220, 269
Teachers, training and selection of, 151, 153, 189
Temps, Le, xiii, xxi
Thaddeus (American ship), brings first Christian missionaries, 33, 34
Thatcher, Rear Admiral H. K., 202, 203, 245, 246
Thomas, Rear Admiral Richard, xvi
Ti root, 91
Titcomb, Charles, 117–118
Tour du Monde, Le, xiii, xxi
Tourists and tourist sights, 69, 70, 80, 121, 139, 210–211, 212, 271, 272
Traders, 27, 33–34
Treaties and conventions: general treaty (tripartite), 59, 102–103; treaty relations with France, 59–63, 65, 66–69, 97, 98–100, 200, 248; with England, 59–60, 200; with United States, 59–63, 65, 200; project to renegotiate treaties, 200–201, 243, 248; reciprocity treaty with U.S., 204–207; Pearl Harbor treaty, 251–253
Tree ferns, 89–90
Tyerman, Daniel, 37

Ulupalakua (Maui), 72
United States, 4, 33–34, 47, 48, 55, 58, 59, 60, 63, 68, 97, 99, 133–134, 135, 148, 172, 174–175, 187, 200–201, 202, 203, 227; Kamehameha III apprehends danger from, 55–56; missionaries as tool of, 55–56; as major exporting country, 66; as a "great power," 96, 103, 149, 150; political parties in, 99; actions of U.S. Congress, 200, 204, 205, 207; and U.S. State Department, 204. *See also* Americans; Annexation; Treaties and conventions
Uranie (French naval vessel), 31

Valparaiso, 43, 265
Vancouver, Capt. George, xviii, 9, 22–24, 34
Varigny, Charles de: secretary *(chancelier),* Consulate of France, Honolulu, 61, 62, 65–66, 98, 99–100; acting French commissioner, 103–104, 122–123; minister of finance, Hawaiian Kingdom, 128–132, 146–149, 179, 183–184, 185–187, 188, 196–197, 198–199; role in constitutional convention (1864), 137–138, 157–158, 161–162, 163–165, 166–167, 169, 173, 174–175, 176–177, 178–179; member of board of immigration, 150–151, 155; member of board of public instruction, 154, 155; a typical day as minister, 155–156; minister of foreign affairs, 196–197, 198, 199–201, 203–208, 212, 241, 242–243, 248; requests leave of absence, x–xi, 122, 196–197, 207, 243; resignation as foreign minister, x, xi, 248–249, 269; beliefs and attitudes of, 5–6, 35–36, 63, 65–66, 96, 104–105, 129–132, 139–140, 145, 148–150, 164, 174–175, 185–186, 198–199, 204–206, 228–229, 243, 249, 252–253; his Protestantism, 265; relations with Émile Perrin, 60–61, 98–100; with Robert C. Wyllie, 53–54, 55, 116–119, 128–130, 135, 136, 145–146, 160–161, 175, 195, 198, 200; with Kamehameha V, 8, 65,

INDEX 289

130–132, 162, 163–164, 176–177, 192, 196–197, 199, 200, 205, 212, 219, 222, 227–228, 243, 248, 249; his Hawaiian studies, 65, 96, 100, 104–105, 106, 121–122, 129–130, 133, 145, 227–228; as traveler and travel writer, xii–xiv, 4, 7, 70–96, 107–123, 242–247, 263–264, 269
Varigny, Mme Charles (Louise) de, xi, xii, 212, 225, 226, 230, 231, 235, 236, 237, 264–265, 266–267, 269, 274–276; homes of, in Honolulu, 267, 268, 273–274, 276; servants of, 267, 268, 270, 274
Varigny, Hélène de, 263, 269, 270, 271, 272, 273
Varigny, Henry de, xi, 212, 225, 230, 234, 235, 237, 243, 263, 267, 268, 269, 270, 271, 272, 273, 274
Varigny, Pauline de, 263, 266, 269, 270, 271, 272, 273
Vénus (French naval vessel), 52
Victoria, Queen, 194
Victoria Kamamalu (Princess), 64, 138, 199
Volcanic eruption (1868) and earthquakes (island of Hawaii), 20, 209–244; deaths resulting from, 214, 223. *See also Earthquakes; Kilauea* (volcano and crater)
Volcano House, 211, 215
Von Holt, Hermann, 70, 76, 77, 81, 84, 87, 270, 271, 272
Voting rights. *See* Franchise

Wai-a-kana-loa (Kauai), 121
Wai-a-kapa-lae (Kauai), 121
Waialua (Oahu), 108
Waianae Range (Oahu), 4
Waihee (Maui), 171
Waikiki, 25, 29
Wailua River and Falls (Kauai), 110, 112, 121
Wailuku (Maui), 14, 20, 171
Waimea (island of Hawaii), 82, 94
Waimea (Kauai), fort at, 38–39
Waiohinu (island of Hawaii), 216, 217, 223, 230–231

Waipio Valley (island of Hawaii), 82–84, 85, 273
Waldau, Mr., 266–267
Walsh, Rev. Robert A. (Roman Catholic missionary), 51
War of 1812, 33–34
Warembe (a New Caledonian), 111
Washington, D.C., 59, 62, 103, 203, 204, 205, 206, 207
Wenga (a New Caledonian), 111
Whalers and whaling industry, 6, 7, 33, 54, 66, 104–105; as menace to Hawaiian population, 133–134; decline of fleet and trade, 146–147
Whitney, Samuel, 39
Windsor Castle, 43
Women, foreign (*haole*, white), 35, 202–203, 266
Women, Hawaiian, 10, 12, 226, 231; love of horseback riding, 5–6; chiefesses break tabu, 31–32; visiting aboard foreign vessels, 44–47; law forbidding concubinage, 49–50; desire for foreign clothing, 105; as farm laborers, 118; troubled family life, 133–134
Wood Valley mudslide (island of Hawaii), 214–215
Wyllie, Robert Crichton, 60, 61, 62, 98, 132, 135, 136, 162, 165, 178, 188; character of, 53, 55, 117, 118–119, 127, 128, 145–146, 160–161, 175; as minister of foreign affairs, 53, 58, 59, 63, 128–129, 130; ideas and policies of, 102–103, 117, 118, 195, 198; advocates tripartite treaty, 102–103; his plantation at Princeville, Kauai, 106, 116–117, 119, 120, 160, 175, 180; role in constitutional convention (1864), 175, 176, 178; names Varigny executor of estate, 119; death and Scottish heir, 119, 195

Yang-tse-Kiang, 150
Young, John, 21–22, 27, 59, 64
Young, John (2d), 59, 65

Production Notes

This book was designed by Roger Eggers and
typeset on the Unified Composing System by
The University Press of Hawaii.

The text and display typefaces are
Garamond No. 49

Offset presswork and binding were
done by Halliday Lithograph. Text paper is
Glatfelter Offset, basis 55.